A Palm Beach Picture Book

LESLIE D. WEINBERG

AKER PRESS
PALM BEACH, FLORIDA

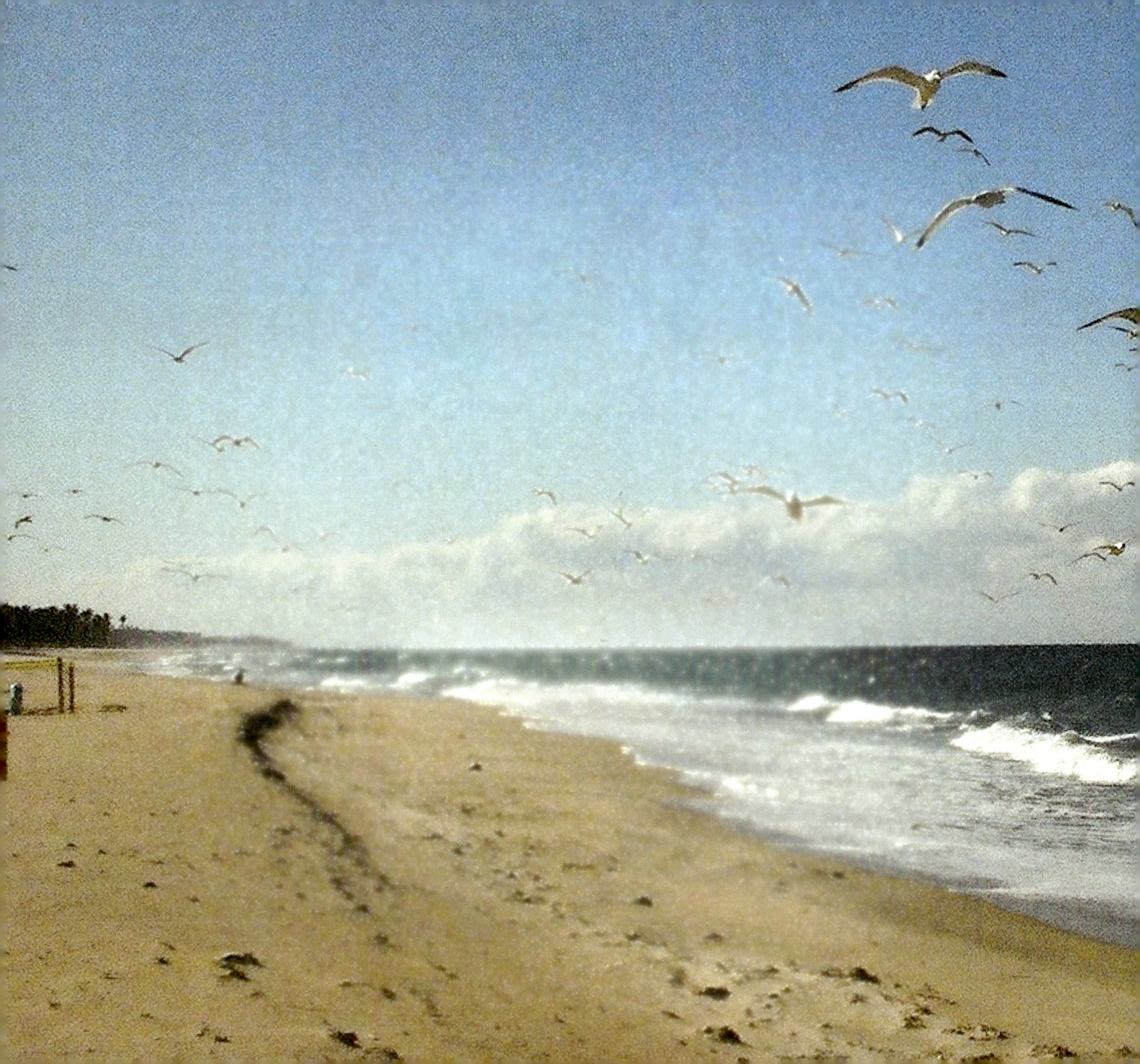

Dedicated to
my mother and father Joan and Sylvan Weinberg

With infinite love

My father, Sylvan L. Weinberg, a doctor and avid writer, was the impetus behind my first book in 1988, when he suggested I do a picture book about the island where I live. He urged me to do the second book in 2011. I still feel his gentle promptings to continue taking photos and write every single day.

My mother Joan, a gifted painter and visual artist, gave me the gift of seeing lines and colors and how they dance in the light. She is always with me when I see a butterfly or observe the outline of a tree.

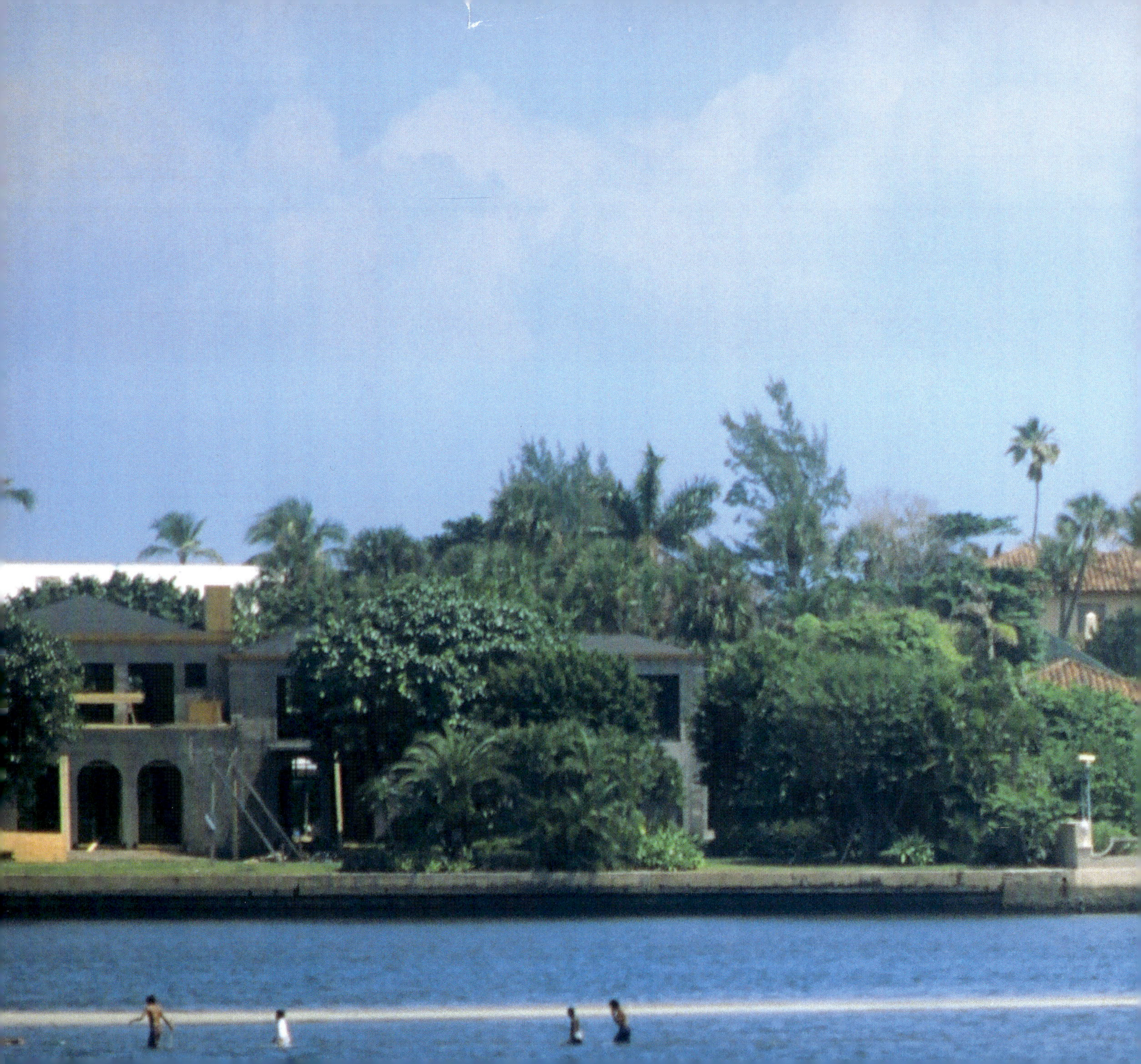

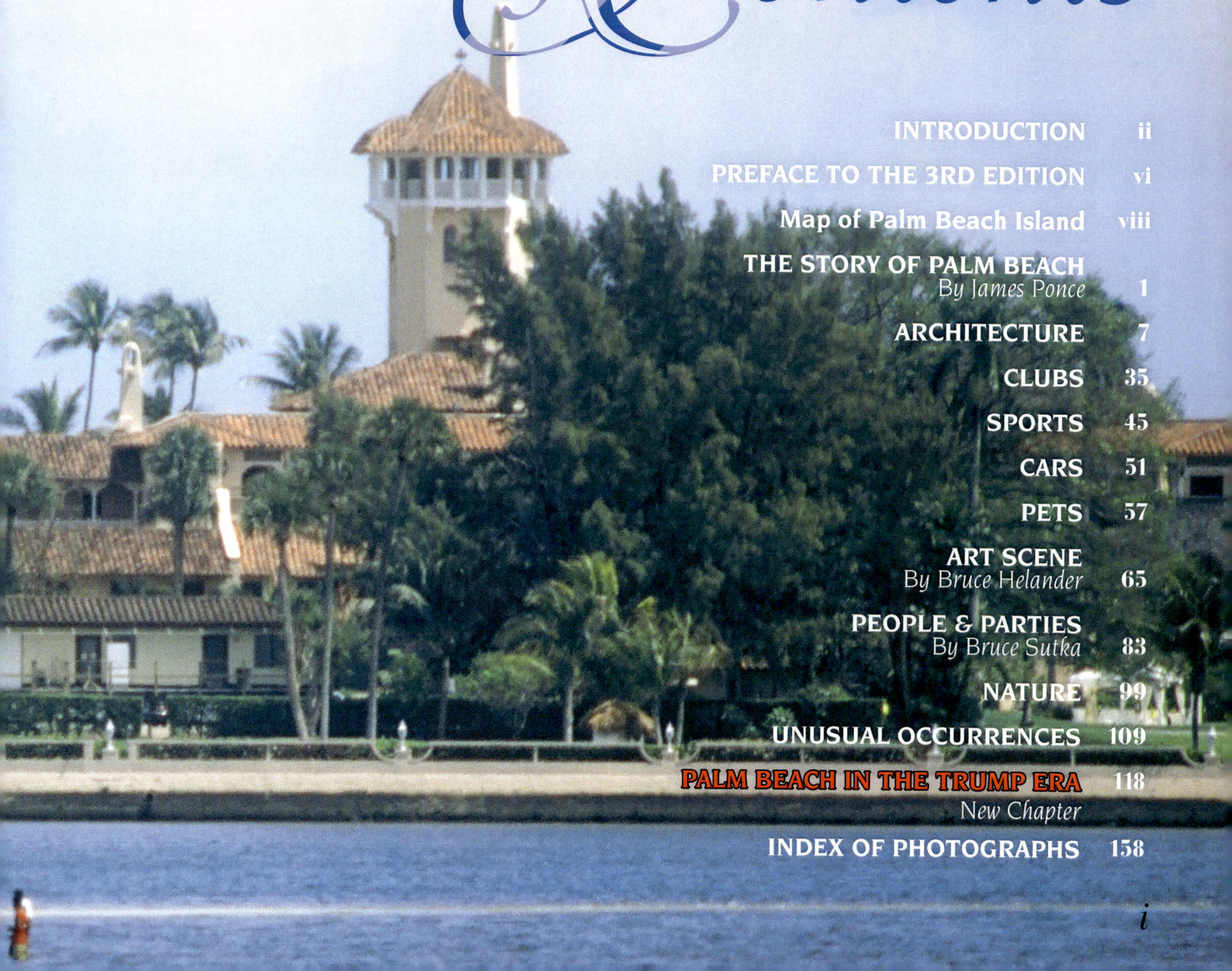

Contents

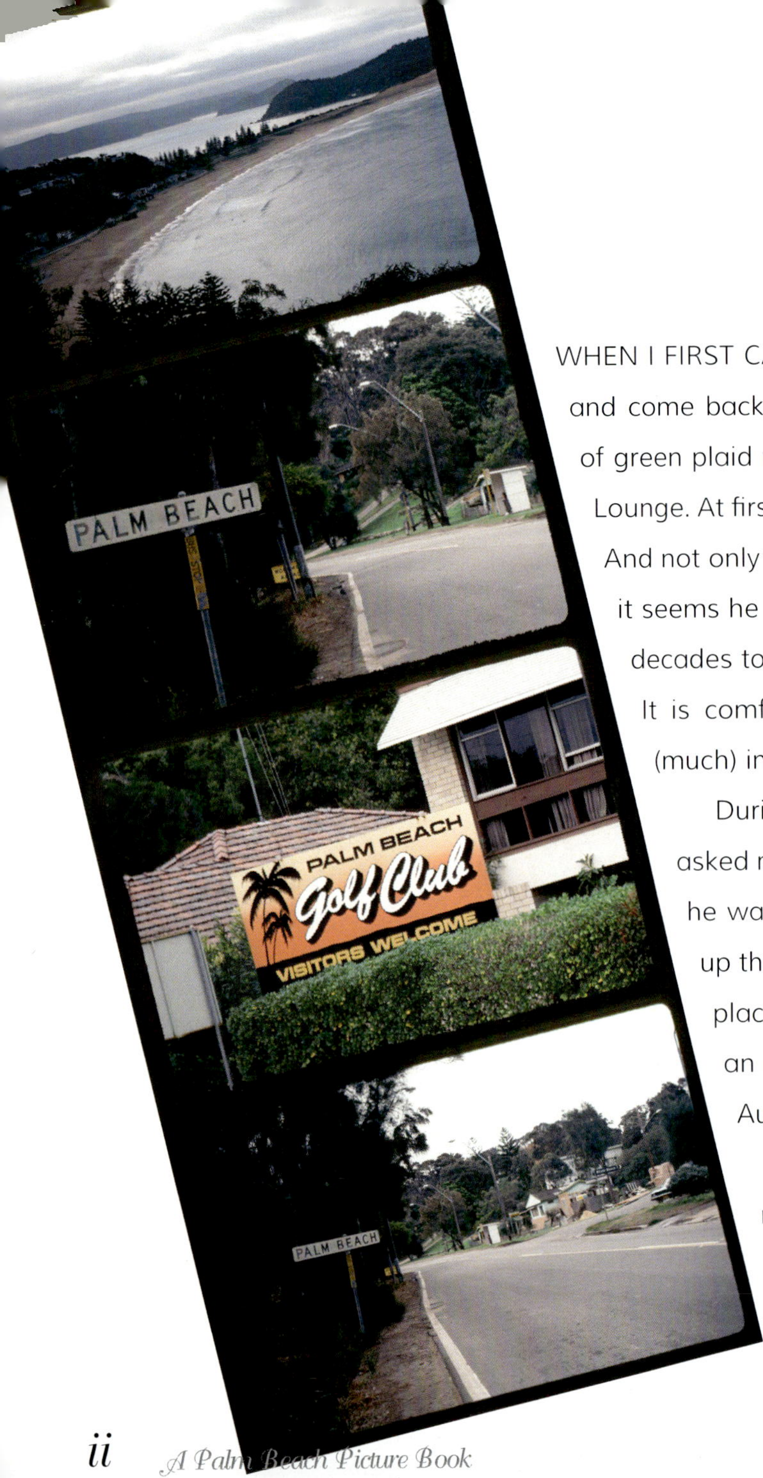

Introduction

By Leslie D. Weinberg

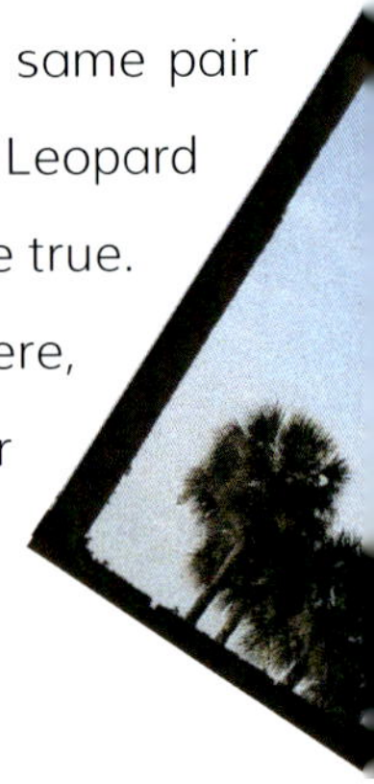

WHEN I FIRST CAME TO PALM BEACH, FLORIDA, I was told you can go away and come back ten years later to find the same guy wearing the same pair of green plaid pants sitting at the same bar stool at Taboo or the Leopard Lounge. At first I thought it was a joke, but have since found it to be true. And not only is that guy with the green plaid pants still sitting there, it seems he hasn't aged a bit. One can return to the island after decades to find it almost exactly as you left it.

It is comforting to find such a place that doesn't change (much) in the chaotic modern world in which most of us live.

During the early eighties on a trip to Australia, I met a pilot who asked me where I live. When I said Palm Beach, he lit up and said that he was from there too. He told me that it was not far from Sydney, up the coast. Eventually realizing we weren't talking about the same place, I had to find out more. Although Palm Beach, Australia is not an island, it's a prime piece of coastal real estate where many rich Australians have summer homes.

Could there be a parallel universe 'Down Under' where the nation's elite spend vacations? The Palm Beach down under was not quite as easy to stumble upon as the American version. I contacted the local newspaper, The Manly Daily News, and told them I was from Palm Beach, Florida, and having traveled so

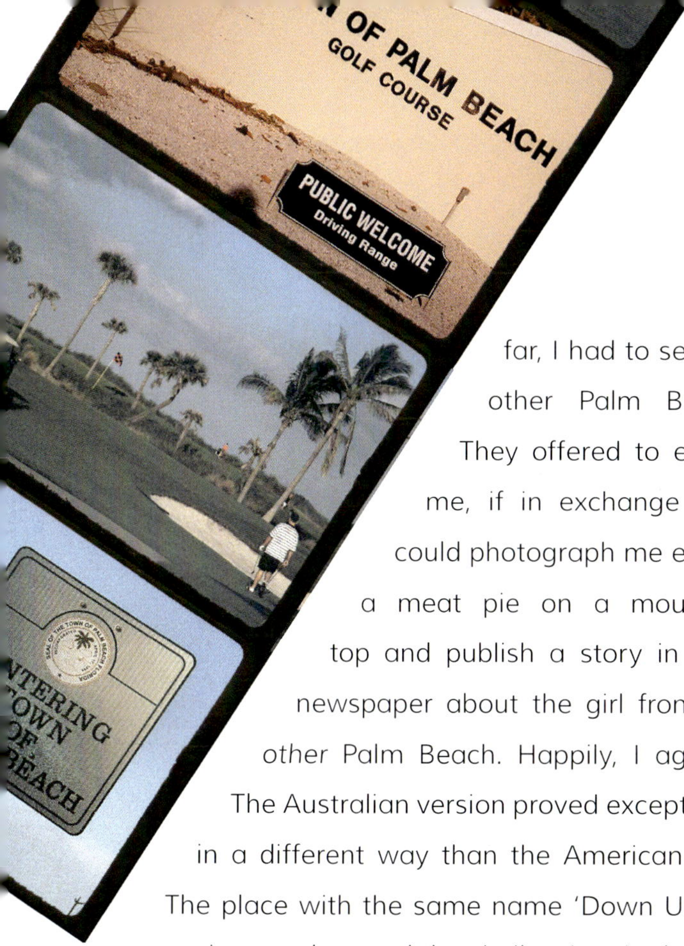

far, I had to see the other Palm Beach. They offered to escort me, if in exchange they could photograph me eating a meat pie on a mountain top and publish a story in their newspaper about the girl from the other Palm Beach. Happily, I agreed. The Australian version proved exceptional in a different way than the American one. The place with the same name 'Down Under' was pioneered around the similar time in the late 1800s and came to life in the early 1900s just like the one here. It had a wild natural beauty, only a little less manicured than in Florida. Both are a magnet to society and to nature lovers.

The thing about *our* Palm Beach is that it possesses a fixed quality of grace. The air is sweet and balmy with the ocean breeze, and feels insulated from the rest of the world. The light is soft and magical, especially at twilight when the sky appears airbrushed by Matisse.

Will the isle of Palm Beach retain its beauty and charm during and after the Trump Era? A question only time will tell. But If the guy in the green plaid pants is right, the more things change the more they stay the same.

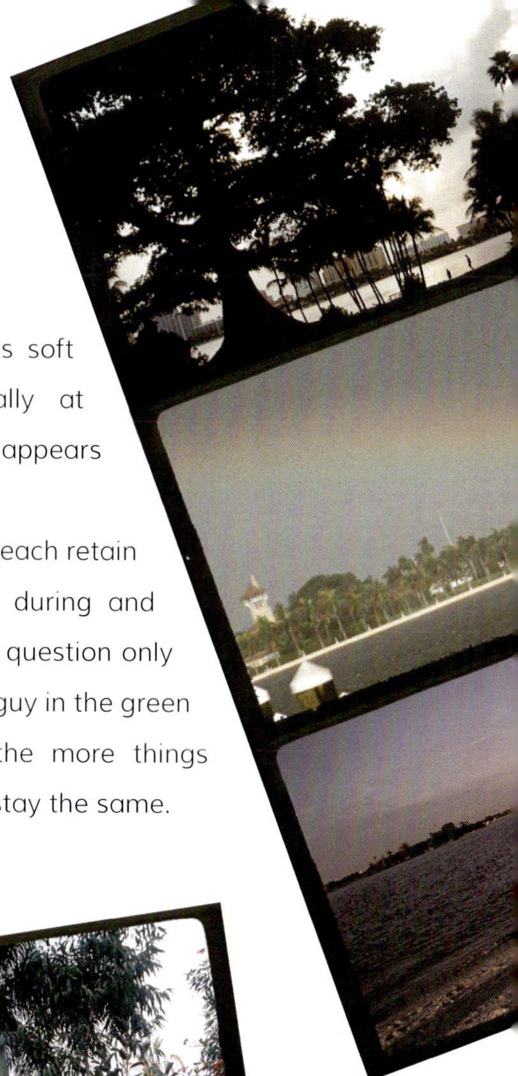

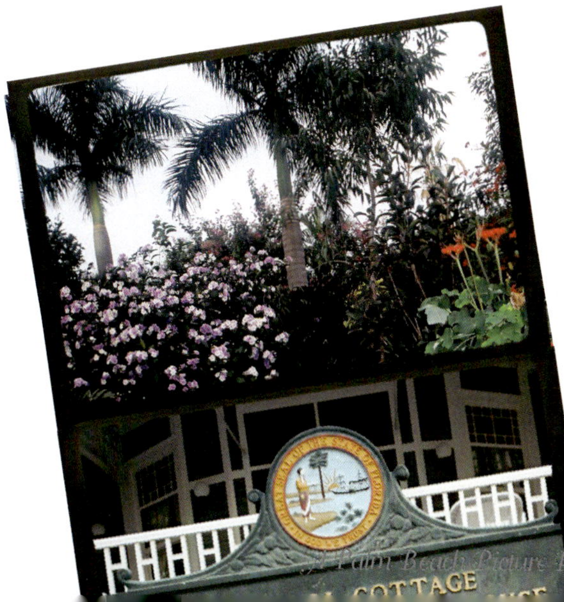

Contributors

I WAS LUCKY to find three divergent voices to accompany my picture book. Each voice is strong alone, and woven together they create a balance of the Old Guard, the New Guard, and the Avant-Garde, which appear to co-exist peacefully in Palm Beach.

FOR THE OLD GUARD, the late Jim Ponce, who has been around since the early days of high society as an historian and educator, helped to shape the island. He not only is an historical authority, but a delightful raconteur, and a southern Gentleman. He is also a social authority, having been invited to Mrs. Post's estate as one of the island's most eligible bachelors.

Bruce Helander,

THE AVANT-GARDE, is a Tour-de-force in the art world. He is a gallerist, a celebrated collage artist, and magazine publisher operating within the cultural microcosm of Palm Beach.

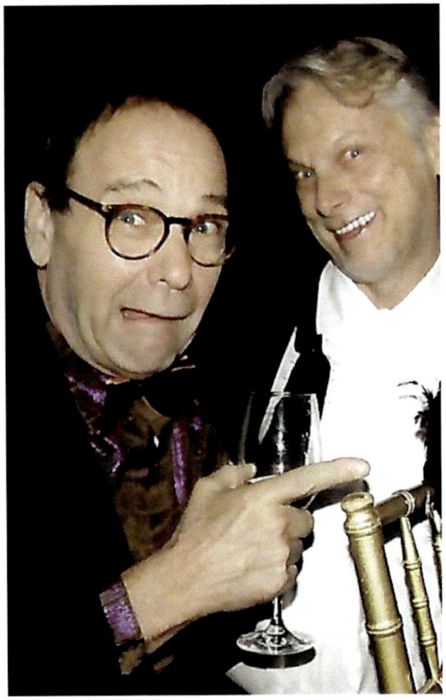

Bruce Sutka,

THE NEW GUARD, is a wizard of style and fantasy creating splendid escapes for the rich within this insular bubble. He has been a pioneer in his field for at least two decades. His parties are legendary.

James Ponce,

WAS BORN IN ST. AUGUSTINE, FL. Descended from the oldest documented family in the United States, his father was a funeral director who conducted Henry Flagler's funeral service. He grew up with the Flagler story and went to Palm Beach after serving in the Korean War in 1949.

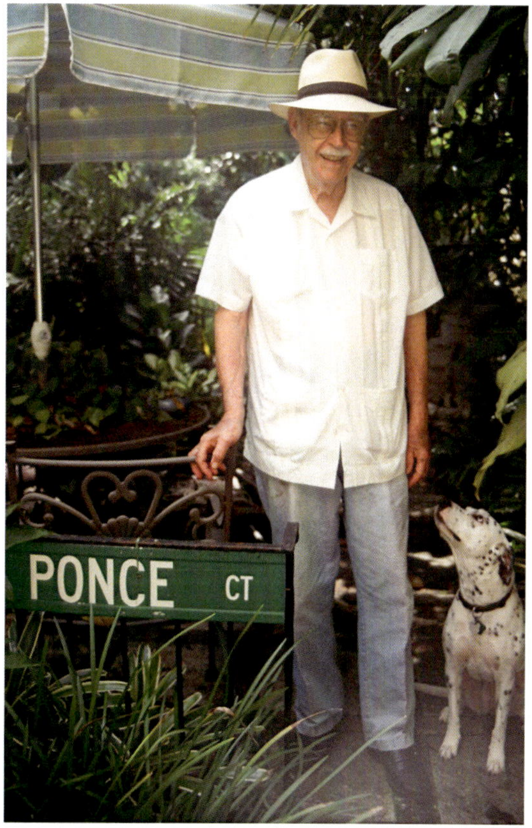

He worked for The Breakers, The Brazilian Court, and the Colony Hotel, where he served as executive manager for many years. Mr. Ponce has been associated with The Breakers for over 60 years, and was named the 'Official Historian' of the hotel. He continues to entertain and educate with his captivating tours showing off the architectural details of The Breakers, whilst telling stories of the island's past.

Receiving countless awards from the Historical Society and Preservation Foundation of Palm Beach, he was honored with a Florida Trust award and a Golden Mango award, and recently received the prestigious Providencia Award. With Proclamations from the Florida State Governor and the City of West Palm Beach, he was declared by the mayor of Palm Beach to be the town's only 'official two-legged Historic Landmark,' and got a bronze placard, normally reserved for noteworthy buildings.

We will always fondly remember Jim Ponce as a wonderful ambassador of the island of Palm Beach he loved so dearly.

Preface to the 3rd Edition

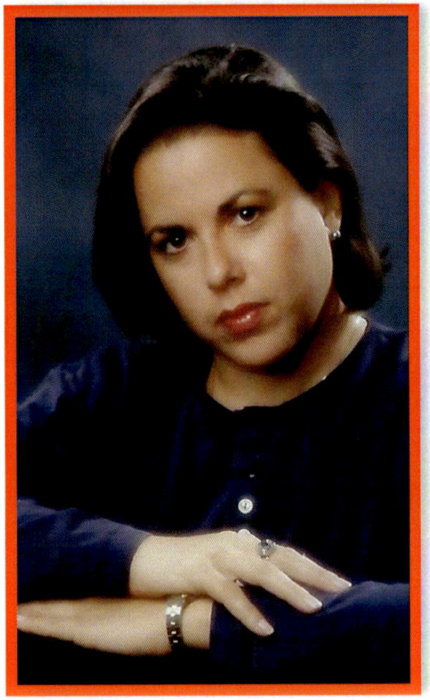

While beginning my career as a reporter in Palm Beach during the mid-1980's, a businessman named Donald Trump burst onto the scene when he scooped up the extravagant Mar-a-Lago estate for the ridiculously low price of seven million dollars in 1985. At that time the property had stood vacant for twelve years. The late cereal heiress Marjorie Merriweather Post had bequeathed the property to the U.S. government as a Presidential retreat, but both Presidents Kennedy and Nixon refused it due to the exorbitant taxes and the monumental expense to secure the property from land, sea and air as it was under a flight path. I was curious about this flamboyant character from New York buying up the most fabled property on the island, who would also become my neighbor. I resided across the pond from the pink palace, on the opposite side of the intracoastal waterway in West Palm Beach, now known as Zone One.

Within a few months of the Trumps arrival, I got an invite to a meet-and-greet party at Mar-a-Lago where 'the Donald' could show off his new digs while schmoozing with the locals. He was, at that time, quite jovial and charming introducing his first wife Ivana, a stunningly gorgeous European model, and their three beautiful children. The Trumps had taken on regal airs, as if the king and his queen had finally arrived to claim the castle in a storybook fantasy. Trump had grand parties, and like F. Scott Fitzgerald's Great Gatsby, all the rich and beautiful people gravitated there. This led to the idea of turning the estate into a private club and charging members enough to pay his taxes and keep the place well maintained. The people of Palm Beach welcomed and embraced Donald Trump wanting to be part of this symbol of grace and elegance of a bygone era, as they ponied up to join his club.

There have been numerous changes to Palm Beach since Donald Trump became President. Small businesses on the island endure losses with gridlock and road closures along A1A and other main streets on the island whenever POTUS rolls into town. The island is crawling with police patrol cars, secret service, bomb sniffing dogs and armed teams patrolling all the land, sea and air surrounding his club.

When this chapter of Palm Beach in Trump Era comes to a close, be it months or years, I believe that Donald will be welcomed back to the island and his club of supporters. Mr. Trump will always be a presence, a polarizing yet beloved character in Palm Beach, credited among other things for saving the Mar-a-Lago estate in the nineteen-eighties. Against all odds that Mrs. Post's estate would ever become a presidential retreat, Trump made it happen. He seized the opportunity to buy this property at a bargain, and had the vision to allow the property to pay for itself, sharing the tax burden with patrons, socialites and friends. Whatever you may think of Donald Trump, he does have a talent and a genius for real estate deals.

Democracy, he's still learning.

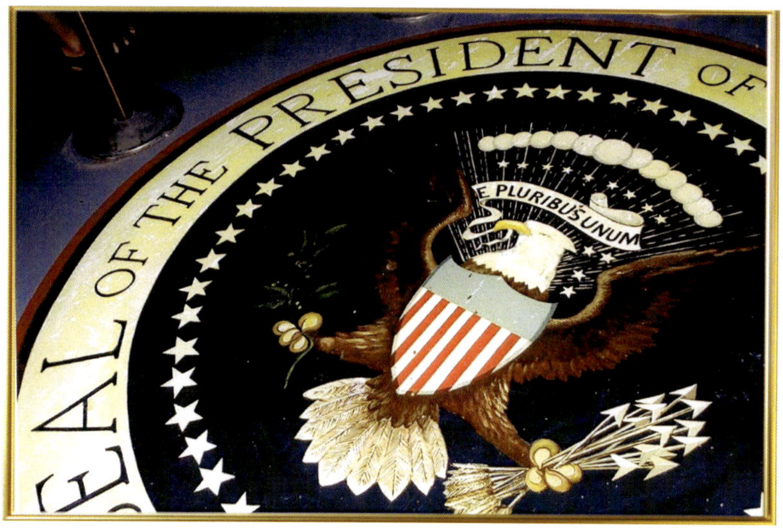

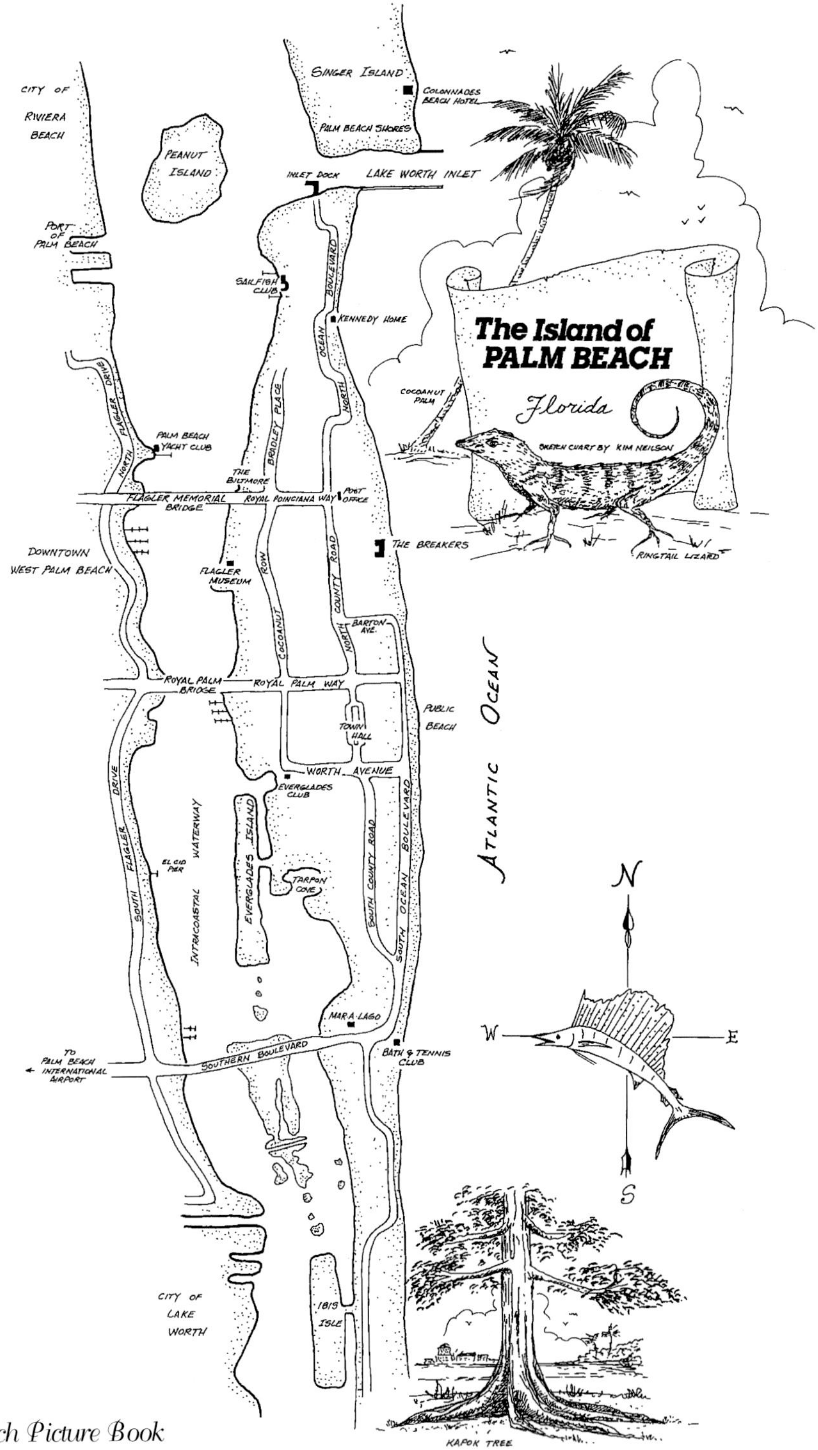
The Island of PALM BEACH
Florida
SKETCH CHART BY KIM NEILSON
SINGER ISLAND
COLONNADES BEACH HOTEL
PALM BEACH SHORES
LAKE WORTH INLET
INLET DOCK
PEANUT ISLAND
CITY OF RIVIERA BEACH
PORT OF PALM BEACH
SAILFISH CLUB
KENNEDY HOME
NORTH OCEAN BOULEVARD
BRADLEY PLACE
NORTH FLAGLER DRIVE
PALM BEACH YACHT CLUB
THE BILTMORE
FLAGLER MEMORIAL BRIDGE
ROYAL POINCIANA WAY
POST OFFICE
THE BREAKERS
DOWNTOWN WEST PALM BEACH
FLAGLER MUSEUM
COCOANUT ROW
NORTH COUNTY ROAD
BARTON AVE.
ROYAL PALM BRIDGE
ROYAL PALM WAY
TOWN HALL
PUBLIC BEACH
WORTH AVENUE
EVERGLADES CLUB
EVERGLADES ISLAND
TARPON COVE
SOUTH FLAGLER DRIVE
EL CID PIER
INTRACOASTAL WATERWAY
SOUTH COUNTY ROAD
SOUTH OCEAN BOULEVARD
ATLANTIC OCEAN
MAR-A-LAGO
BATH & TENNIS CLUB
SOUTHERN BOULEVARD
TO PALM BEACH INTERNATIONAL AIRPORT
CITY OF LAKE WORTH
1819 ISLE
COCOANUT PALM
RINGTAIL LIZARD
N
W
E
S
KAPOK TREE

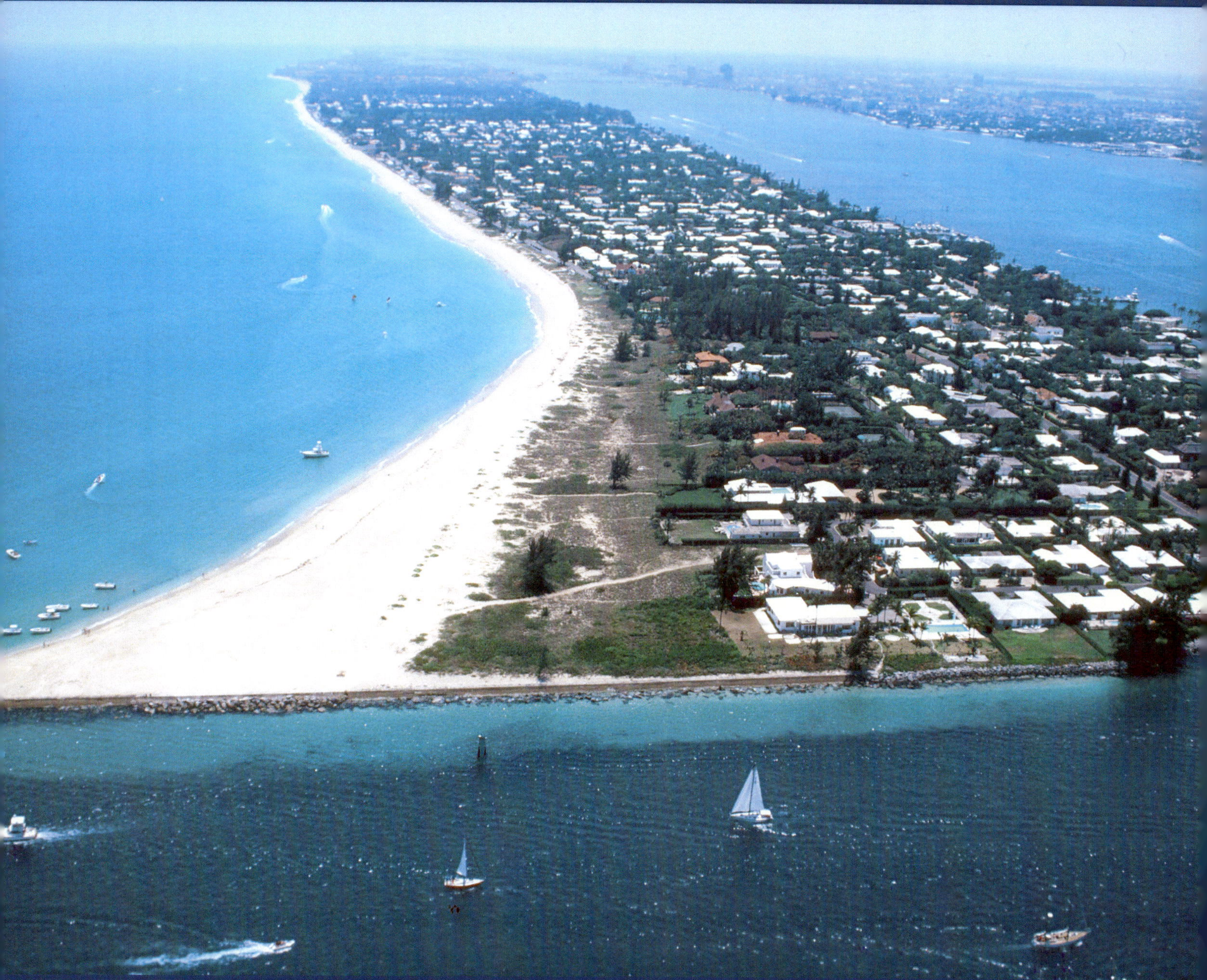

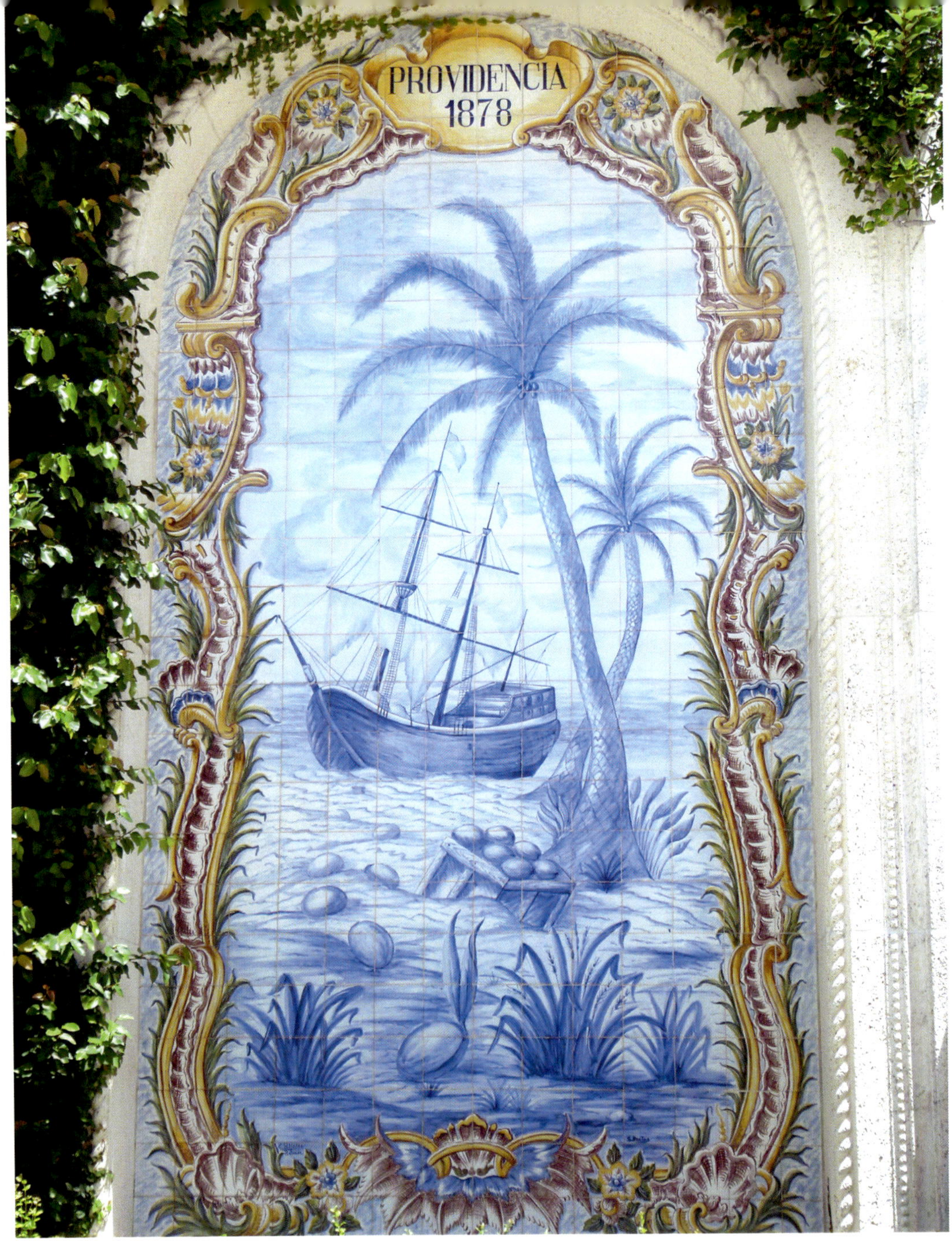
PROVIDENCIA
1878

The Story of

Palm Beach

As told by James Ponce

TO ME, ONE OF THE MOST INTERESTING THINGS about the story of Palm Beach is the fact that it's so short. As far as we know, the first non-native Indian to live in Palm Beach was Augustas Lang, who was a Confederate draft dodger. It was very late for the land to be developed. The Demick's came. There were three couples in 1876. And when the three Demick women arrived, that brought the number of ladies living on the shores of Lake Worth all the way up to six. That's why I say, the history is very short.

In earlier days, one of the most important things was beachcombing because wooden ships were so often damaged in heavy seas and pioneers could get every thing from wood to furniture from the beach. The most important wreck was the Providencia, loaded with coconuts on the way from Jamica. They had Rum and coconuts going back to Spain. That was 1878 when the Providencia wrecked. There were no Coconut Palms growing in the area. In those days, all the people were living along the lake. It was a very small colony of pioneers, and they all had little gardens to grow food. There was an abundance of things to live off of you know, like deer and fish.

Before the Providencia, there might have been a small number of coconut palms in Florida. Most of those were on the Keys. After the Providencia wreck, the local farmers decided, 'Why don't we plant them and have a good cash crop in a few years?' A couple of the fellows, Mr. Lainhart and Mr. Potter and Mr. Hammond, I think, they claimed the ship and paid a penny and a half per coconut. They planted them by the thousands along the lake trail. (James Ponce narration continues through p. 40.)

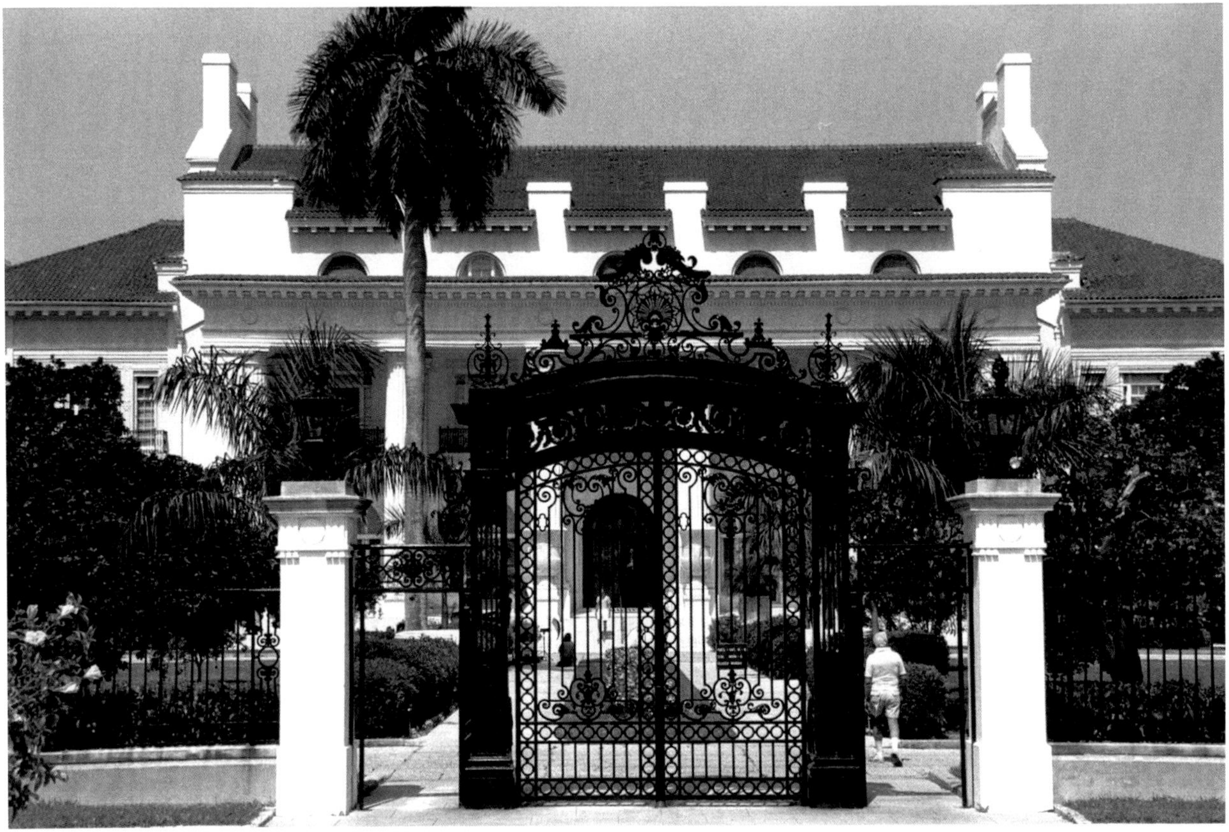

Henry Flagler

HE WAS BORN IN HOPEVILLE, NY, which is up in the Finger Lakes. He only had an eighth grade education. He actually left home at the age of fourteen to make his way in the world. And I'll say he did pretty good, as we know down the line. He first set foot in Florida in 1878. That was to bring a sickly wife, Mary Harkness. His first wife died shortly after his first visit to Florida. He later married her nurse companion, Ida Alice Shourds. She liked it so much when she was in Palm Beach, that she asked to go back there on her honeymoon.

In 1893, he came back to Palm Beach looking for a site to build a resort. And then he built the Royal Poinciana

Hotel. The original building had 540 rooms. It was so successful, that after two additions, it was the largest wooden structure and hotel standing in the world.

The Breakers started out as a smaller nearby hotel, but of course people liked it, so it was enlarged several times. In 1903, the original Breakers burned down, and he replaced it with a much finer building. When that building burned down in 1925, Flagler had already been dead 12 years. The heirs decided they would replace it with something a bit more permanent.

The Flagler Museum, Whitehall as it was known, was completed and opened in 1902 as a wedding gift to his third wife, Mary Lily Kenan. The nurse companion was wife number two. She was put into an asylum after she lost her mind. Flagler got a divorce, which wasn't easy.

Mizner got here in 1917, so the Mediterranean style hadn't yet arrived. I think Mr. Flagler dreamed of Palm Beach becoming the Newport of the South, which is why he wanted to make it look like the mansions up there. It's like a big southern mansion. When he built his Newport style mansion, he was hoping other people would follow suit. It wasn't until Mizner came along that the style changed to more Mediterranean. In those days, Flagler's hotels were so far ahead of anything else being built in the country, people were perfectly happy living in the hotels.

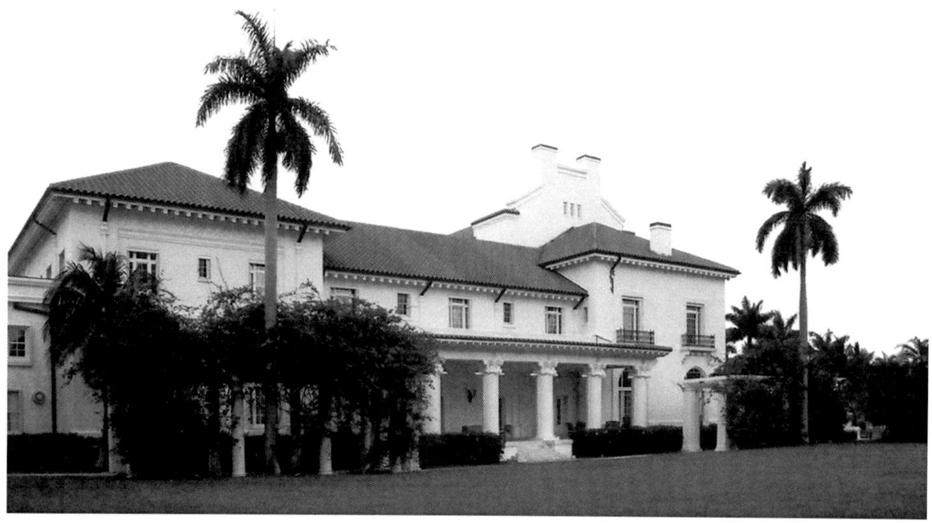

Flagler Railroad Car

BESIDE THE ROYAL POINCIANA HOTEL, they had side tracks that would accommodate twenty-two private railroad cars. In the late 1800s and early 1900s, having your own private railroad car was having your own private Learjet. They said at the height of the season, the latecomers couldn't even get their car into Palm Beach. The Historical Society recently found an account of the fact that John D. Rockefeller came to Palm Beach. It said he spent the night in his railroad car parked behind the Royal Poinciana. It was very commodious. Flagler had two of them. They were his rolling house when he went north and south. Ninety-one is at the Flagler Museum and Ninety is up at the railroad museum in Indianapolis.

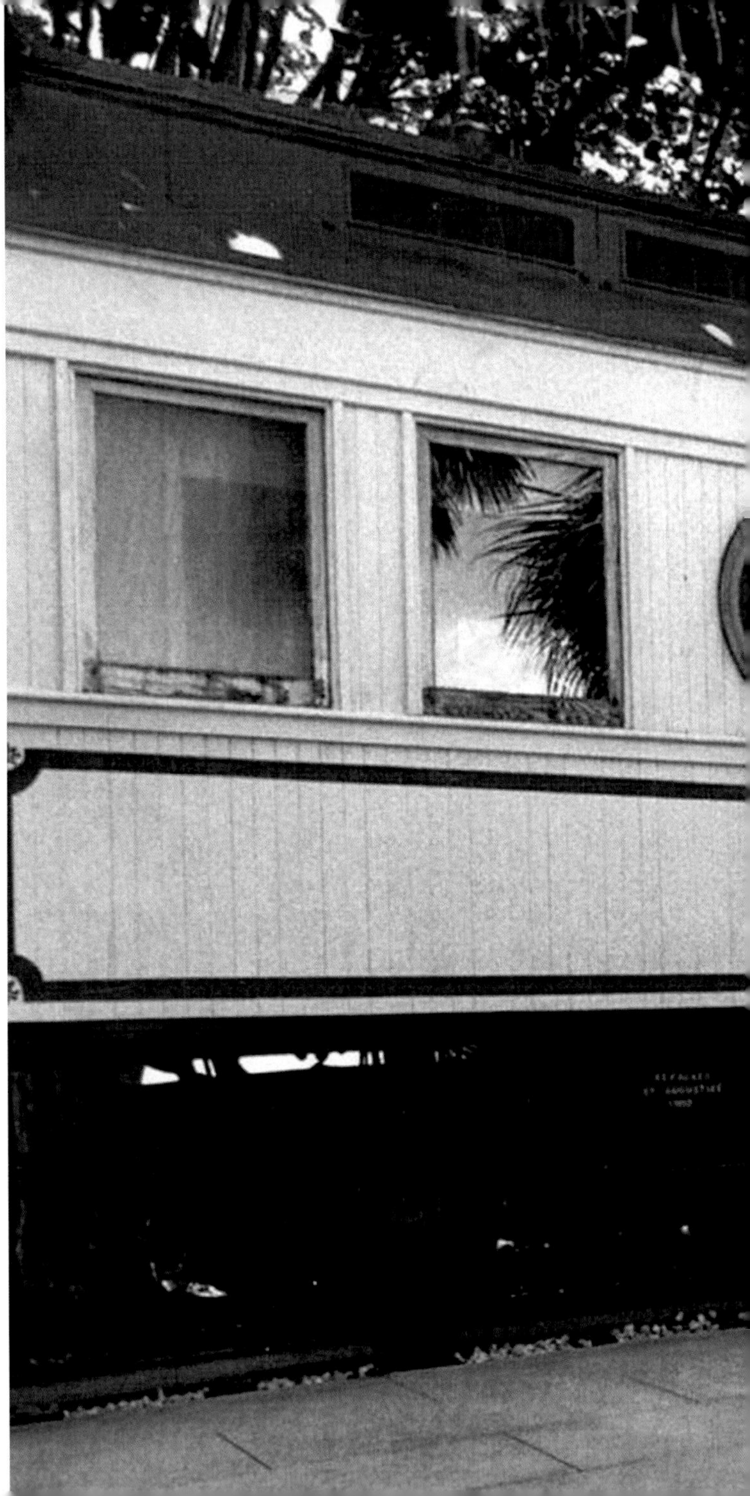

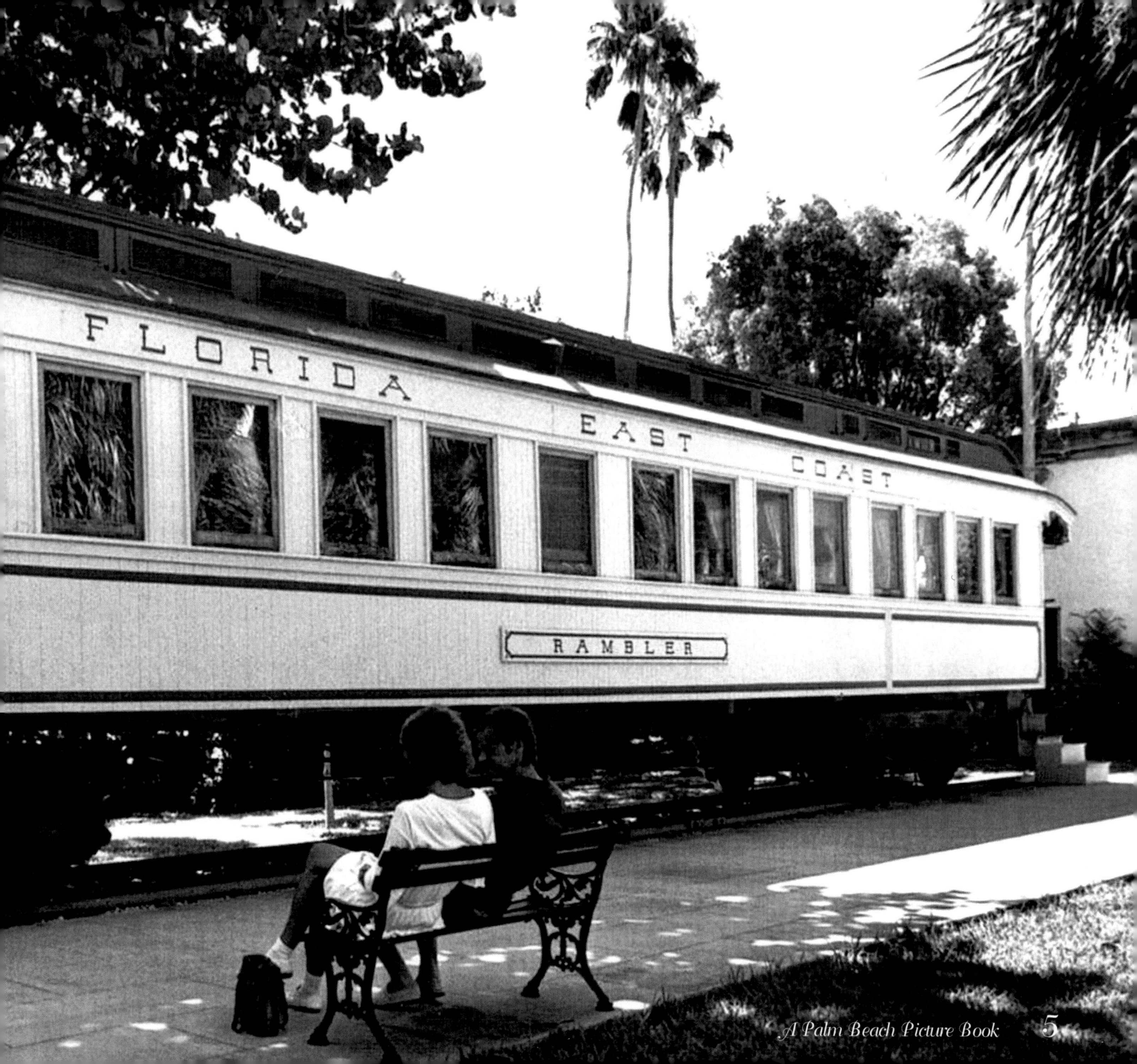
FLORIDA EAST COAST
RAMBLER

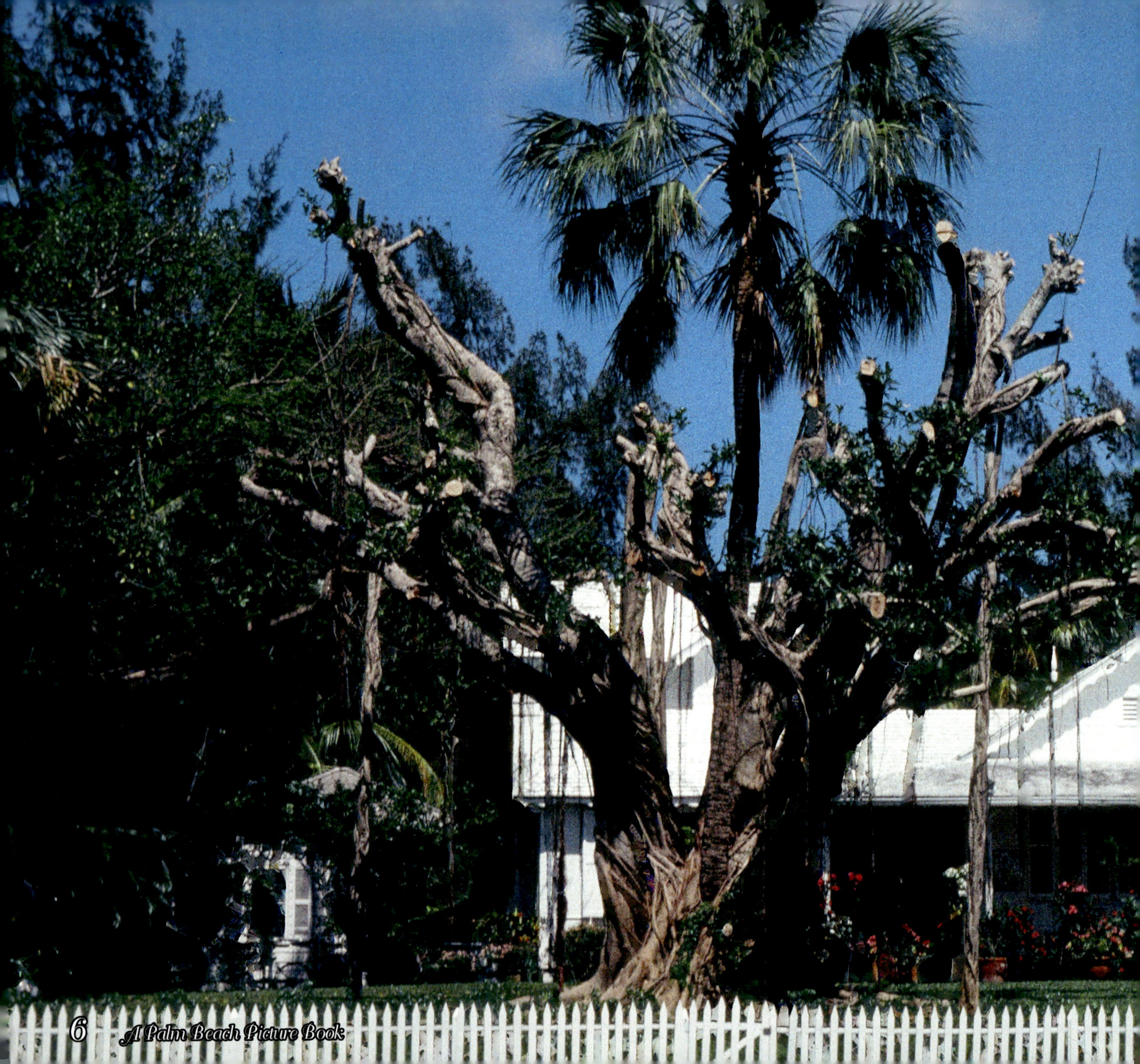

Architecture

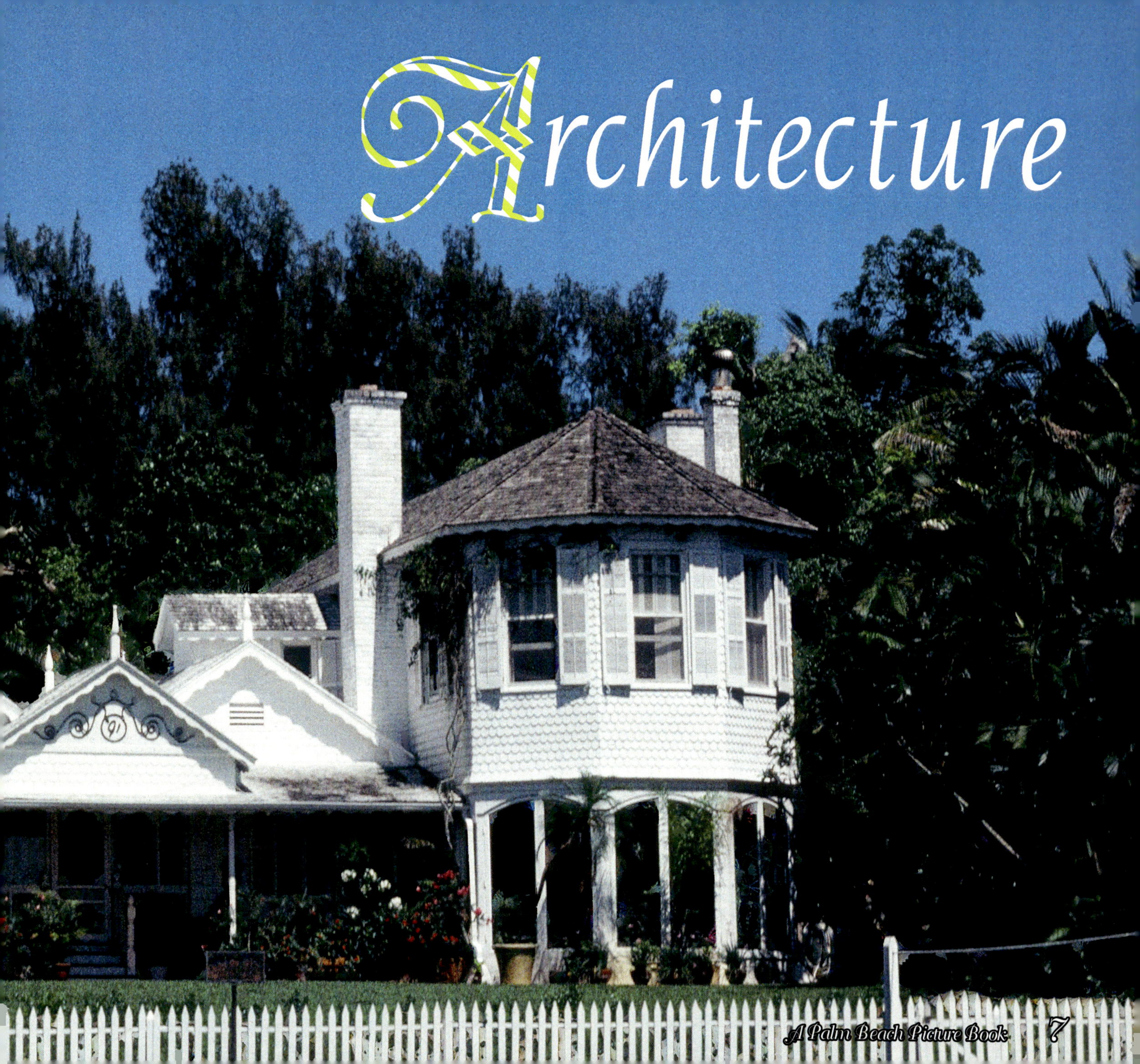

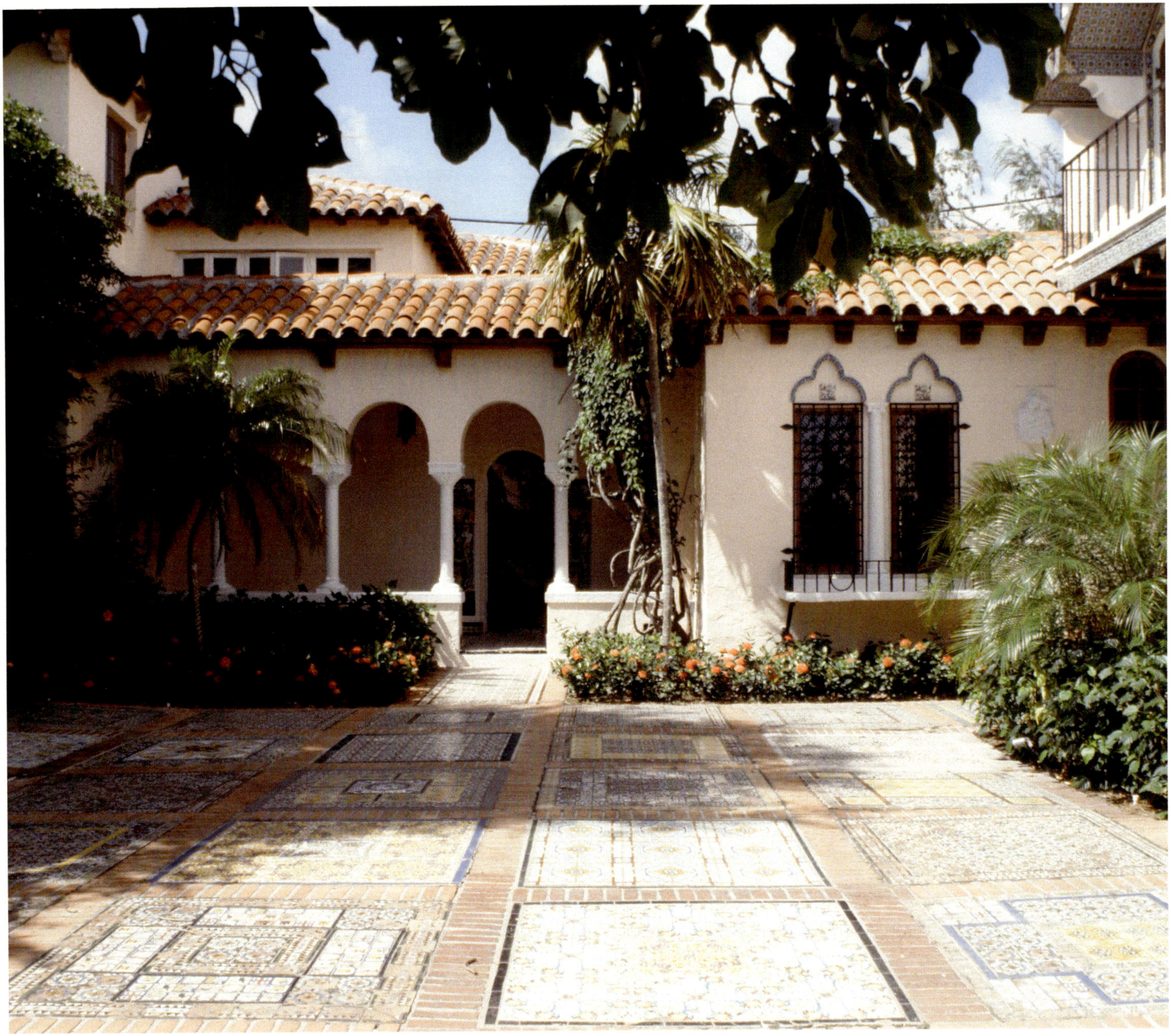

The Mizner Era

AFTER THE WAR, some of the wealthy people who were tired of staying in the big hotels decided to build their own homes when they saw the beautiful buildings that Mizner had designed. With his first two Vias on Worth Avenue, Via Mizner and Via Parigi, he immediately got commissions for similar styled villas, starting with Mrs. Stotesbury. Mizner would establish the Mediterranean look in Florida buildings while the rest of the nation was going more into Art Deco. Palm Beach introduced Mizner's distinctive Mediterranean style which spread quickly throughout Florida, and then California.

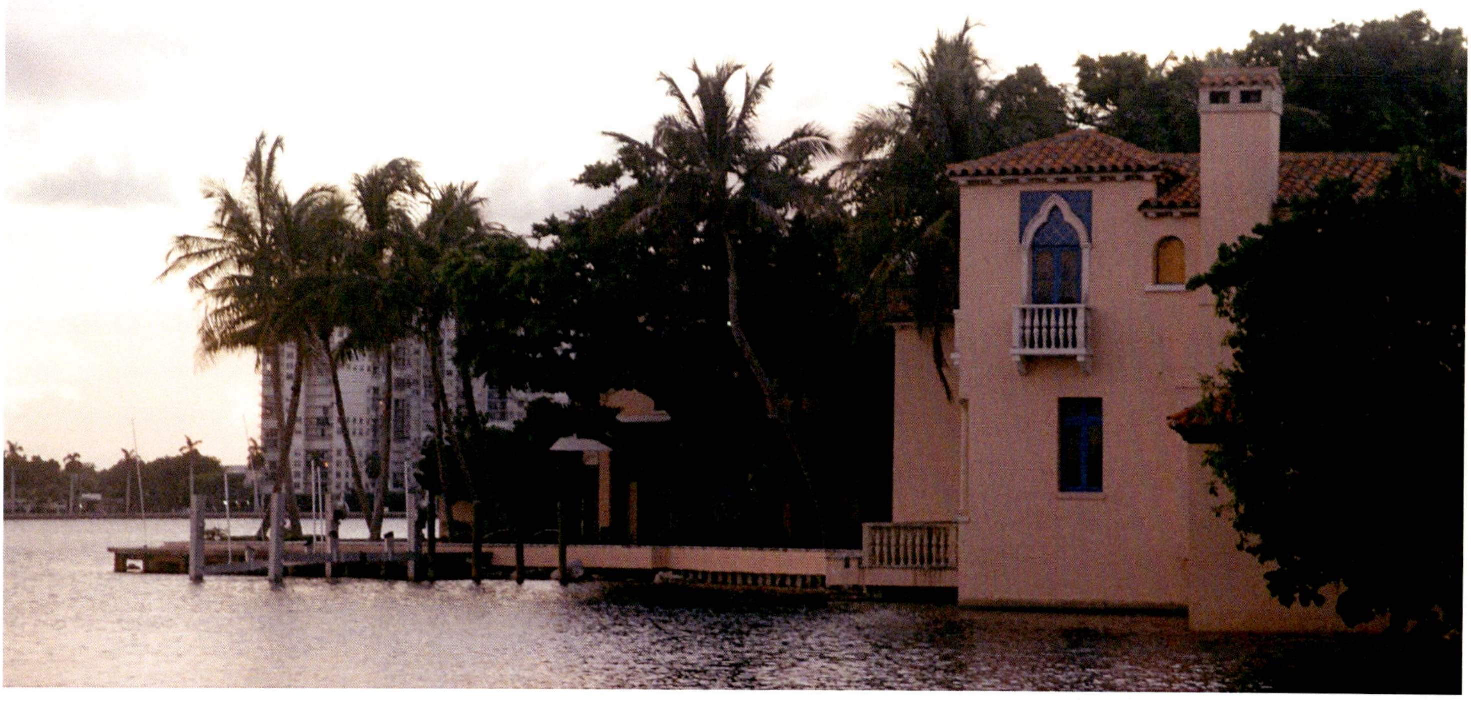

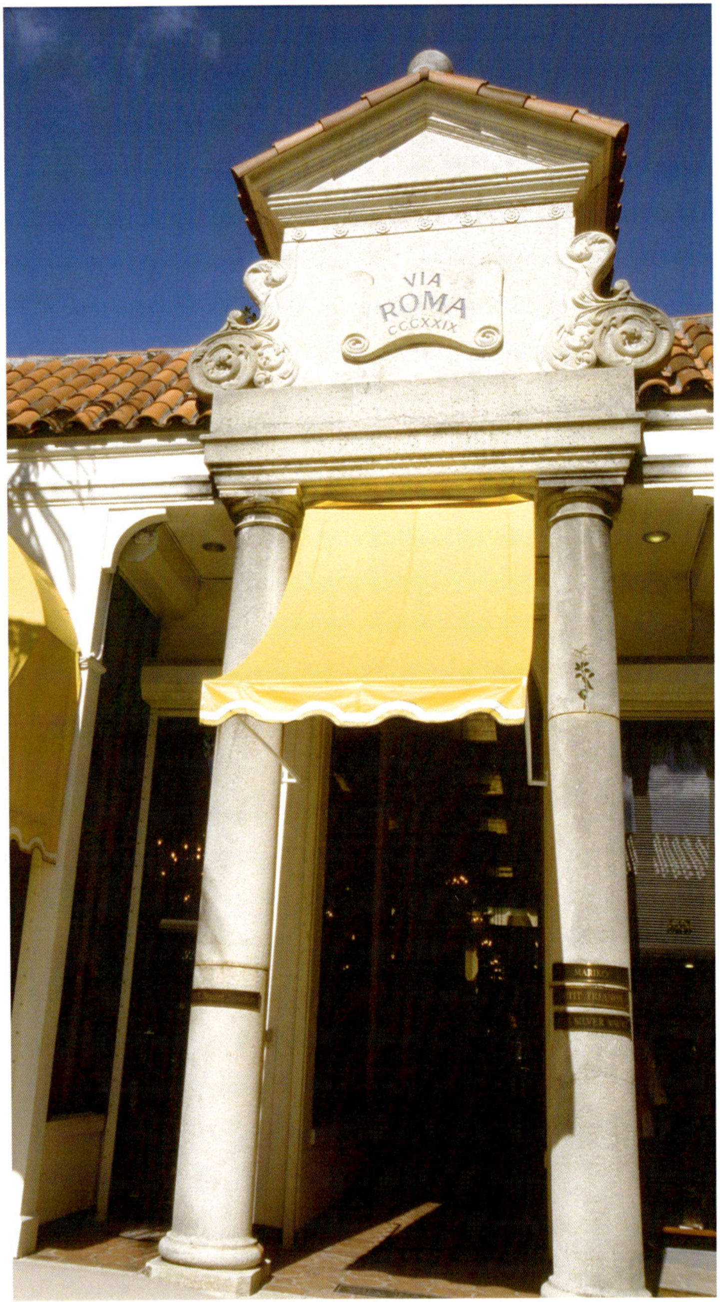
VIA
ROMA
CCCXXIX

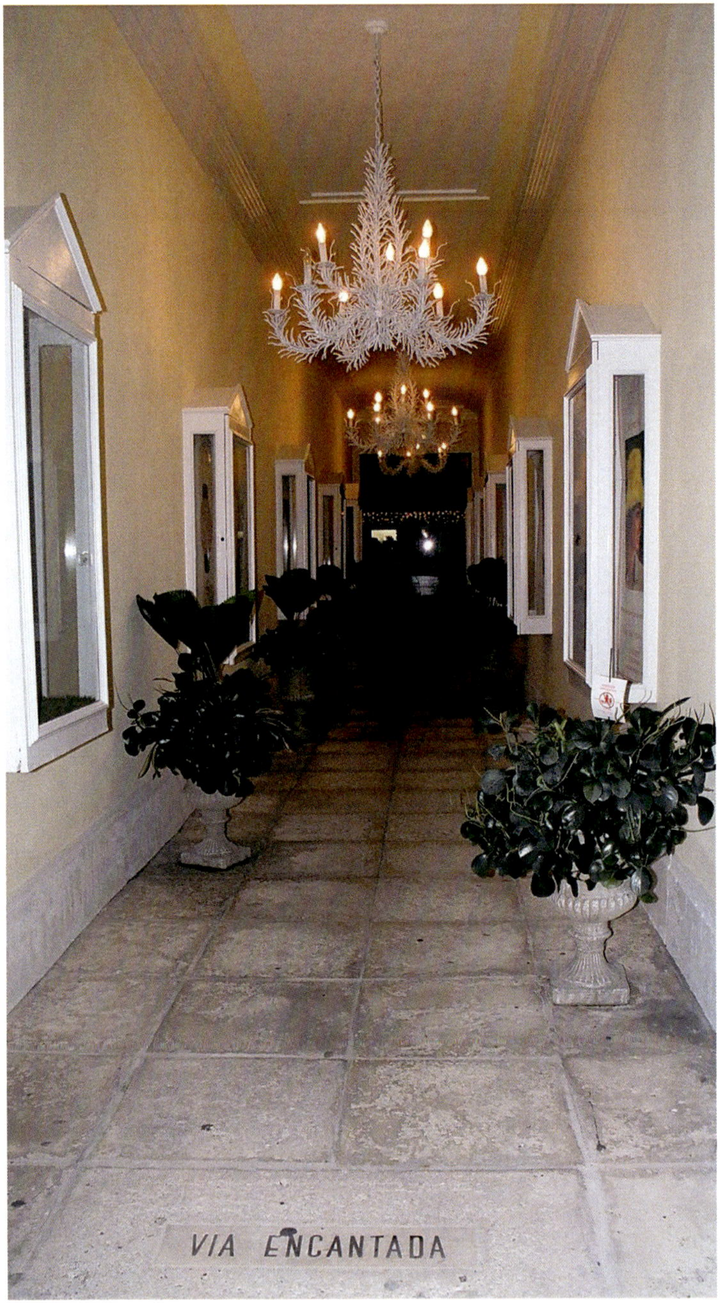
VIA ENCANTADA

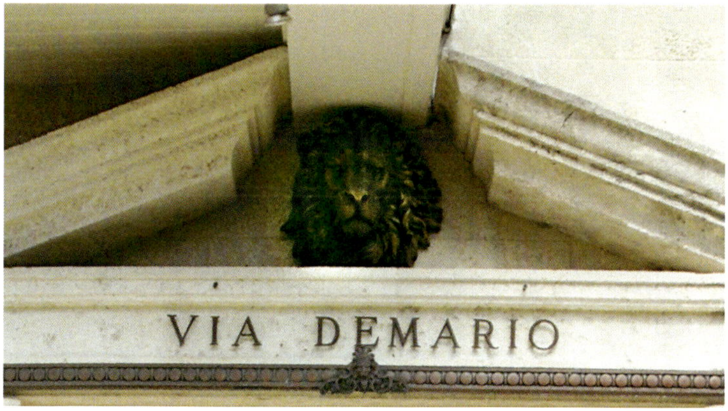
VIA DEMARIO

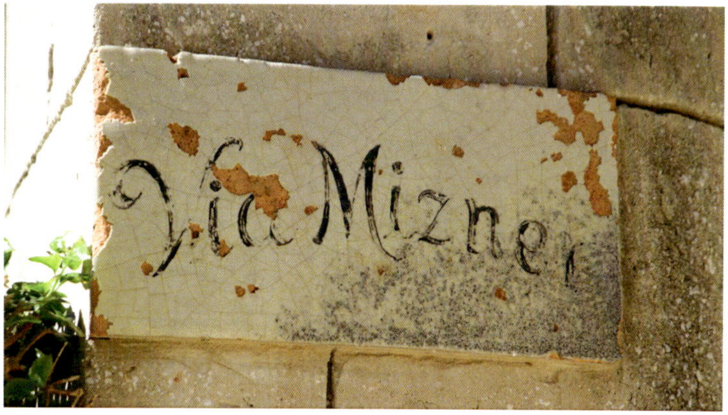
Via Mizner

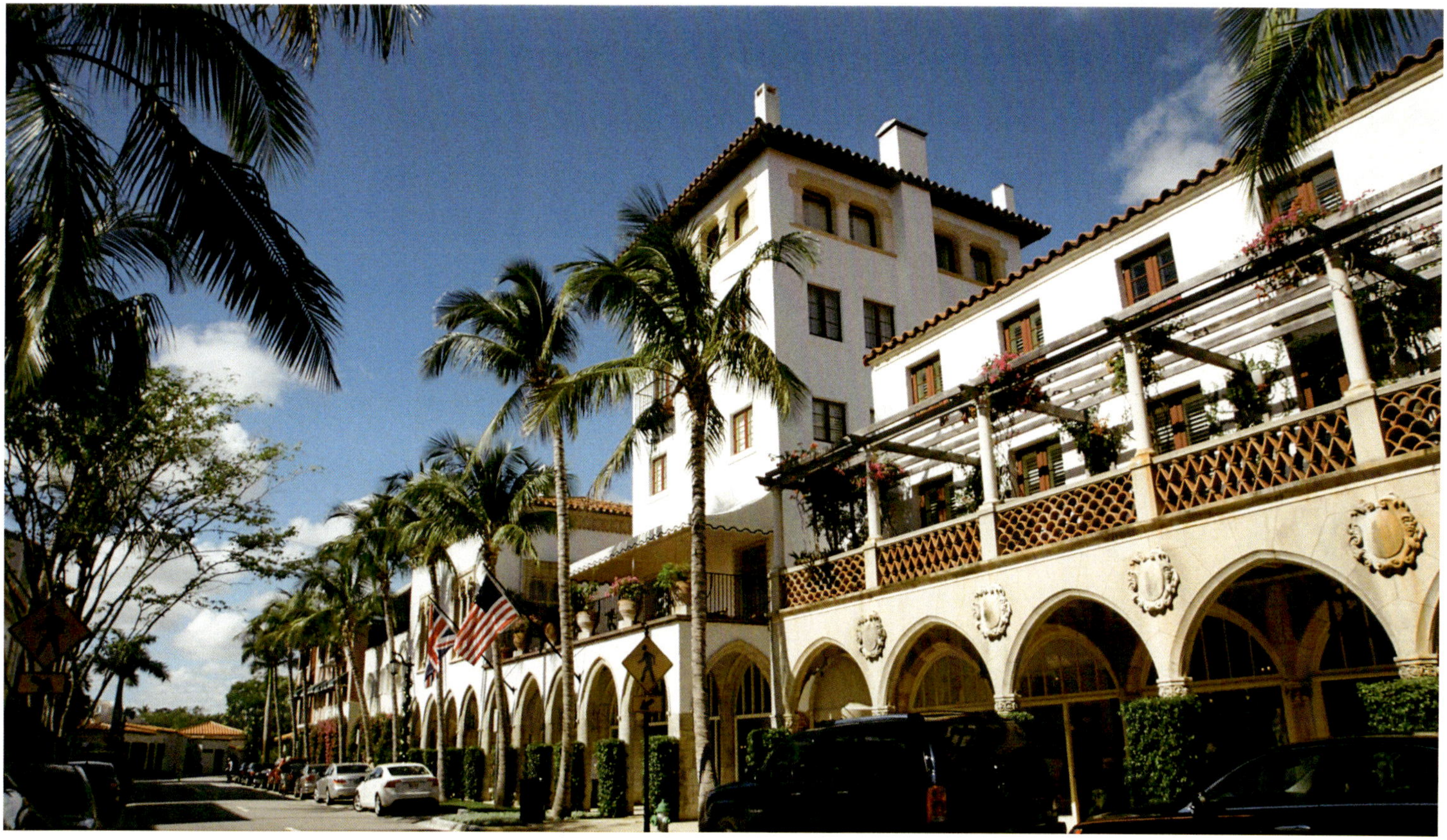

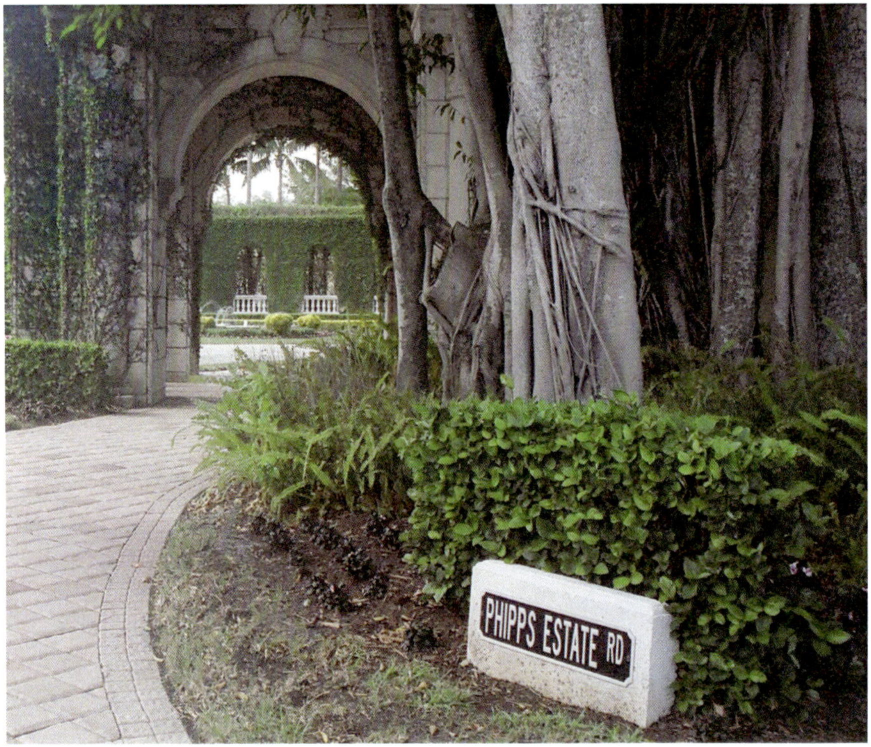

IN THE SIXTIES, people thought that they weren't going to be living in grand homes any more, and the whole north end of Palm Beach was developed after WWII. They built little two and three bedroom houses. They're very charming. But today, people will buy two lots and tear the houses down and put up a bigger one. Sometimes they even separated

the houses. The Donahue house had a 'great room' that was so big it had a music conservatory on the upper floor. They actually ripped that great room in half and put a street right through it! There are two big mansions, what's left of the houses now. Even the Mizner house at the end of Worth

Avenue is now two houses. Casa de Leoni and the villa next door were originally a single house. They just took out a small portion. When they split a house, they always leave one original section as an archway that connects both houses.

It's really a shame they tore down so many of those Mizner houses. If they were still standing, they'd be worth millions. They were on twenty to thirty acres of land stretching from the ocean to the lake with a yacht pier on the lake front. They'd have an orange grove or a citrus grove, a garden and guest homes. Like the Stotesbury property; when they tore down the estate, they got two streets out of that property. They only thing left there now is the gate. It's a beautiful Moorish gate on County Rd., previously the entrance to the estate. That house was rather unique. The outside was Mediterranean looking, but the inside was very Gothic.

MIZNER LOVED TO USE DIFFERENT KINDS OF ARCHITECTURE. While growing up, his father was in the diplomatic service, and he spent time in South American towns in beautiful homes and government buildings. I guess that's where he got a lot of his appreciation for the Mediterranean style with barrel tile roofs. Everything he built had a barrel tile roof on it.

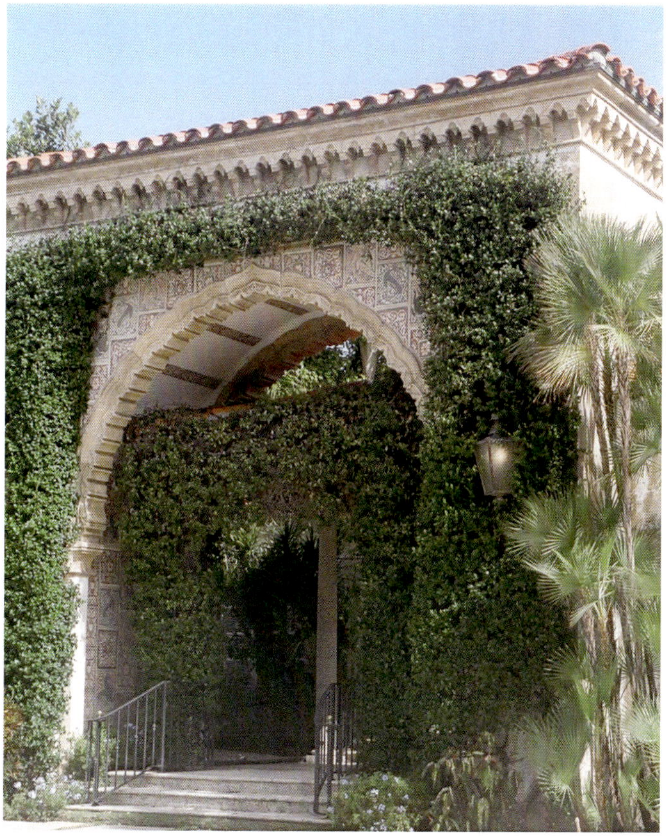

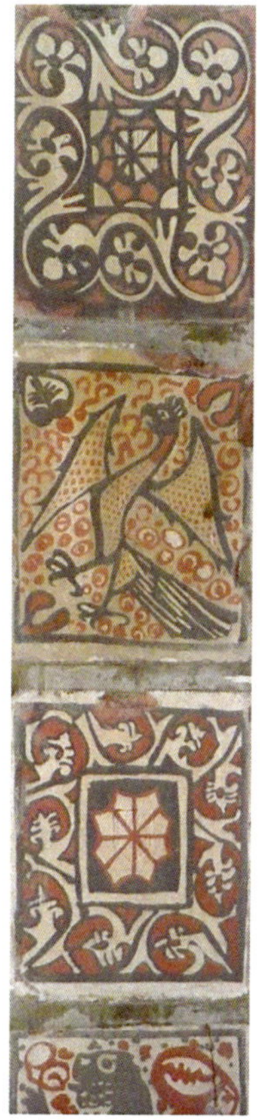

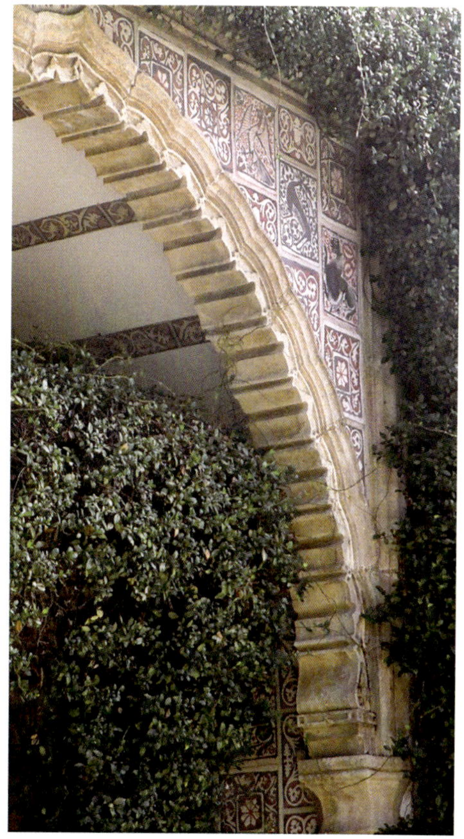

Worth Avenue

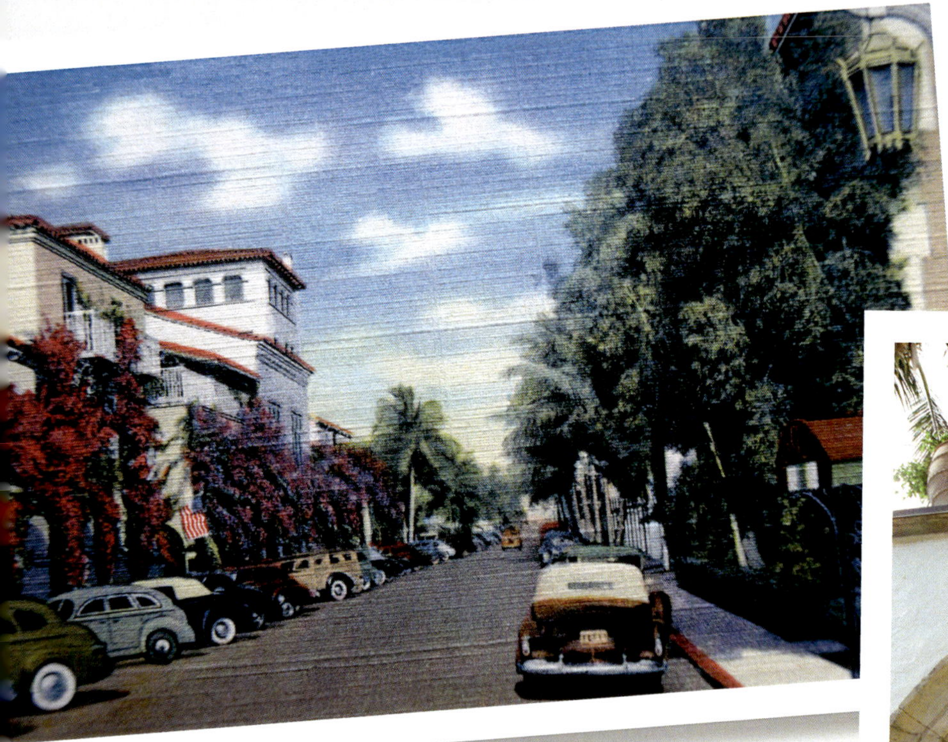

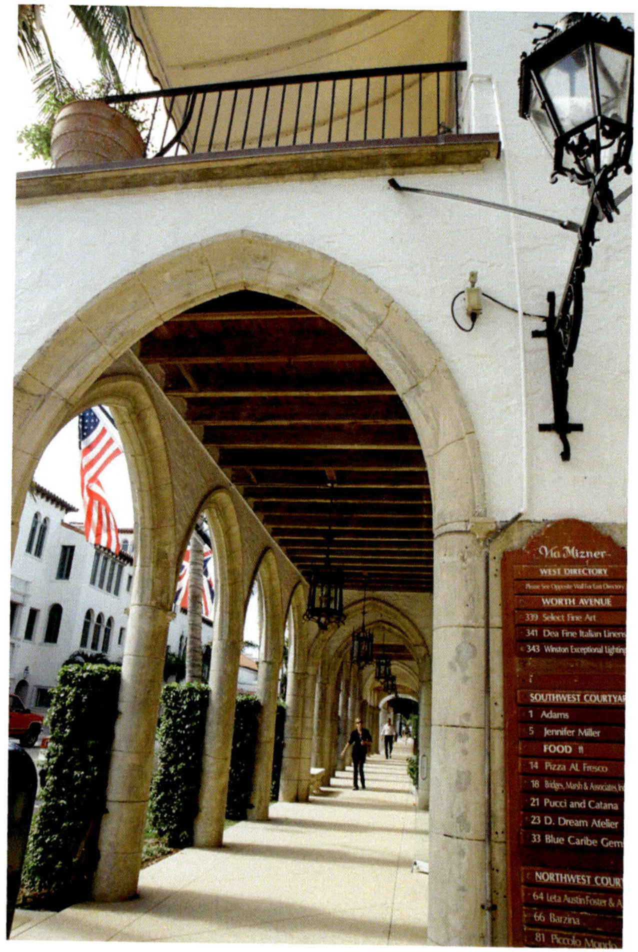

YOU HAVE TO REALIZE that where Worth Ave. is today, it was very low. It was a veritable jungle. Flagler had the brilliant idea of cutting a path right through it which became Jungle Trail. You actually had to pay to get on the trail. It wound around through the jungle and just about where the Everglades Club is now.

Alligator Joe, as he was known, set up a wild animal farm. It was mostly bears and other animals running wild that would have been here then. But the big attraction to the northern folks was the alligators. Of course, he would wrestle them because he was a big hefty guy.

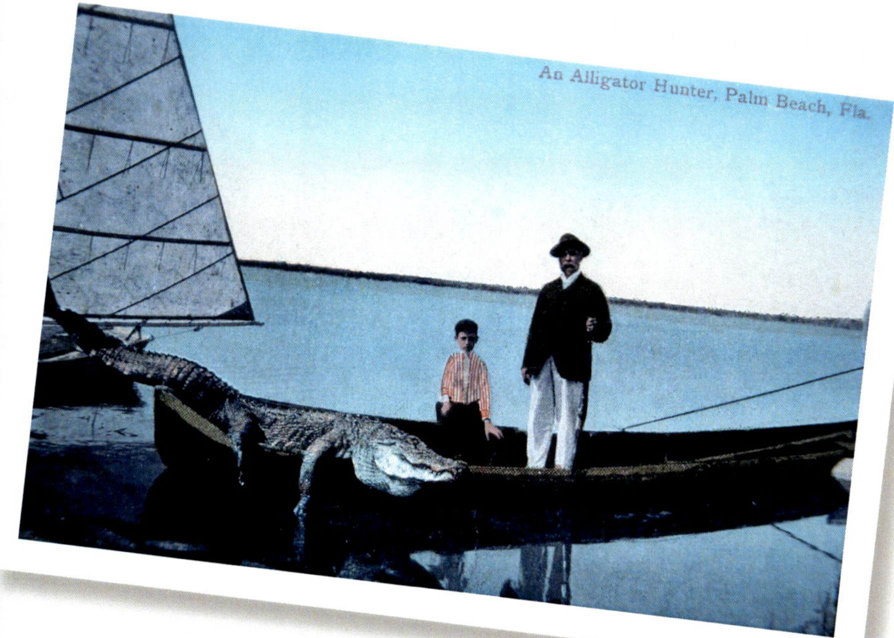

IT COST YOU A QUARTER to get on the trail and another quarter to get into Alligator Joe's. The lunch was further back down the line on Jungle Trail under the Banyan tree. They had a place set up where you could buy refreshments, cool drinks and what not. That was around the end of the 1800s when the trail was put in. It was something to entertain the tourists. Eventually, Alligator Joe sold his property to Paris Singer in 1917.

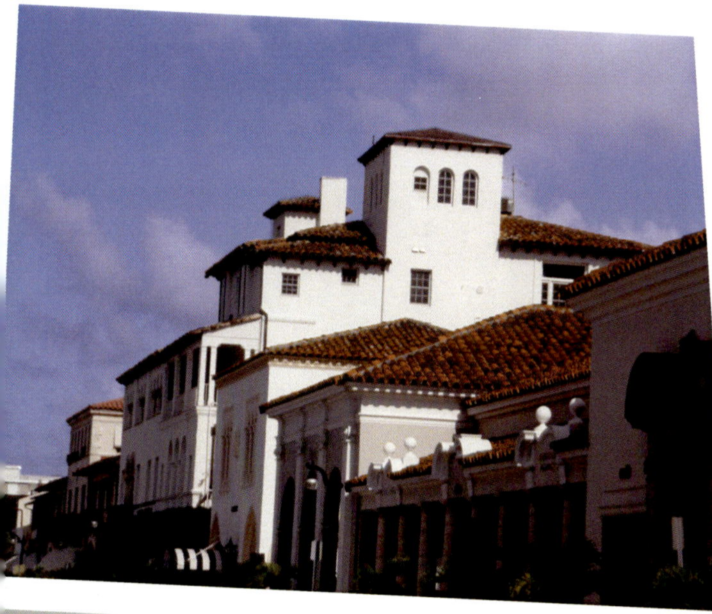

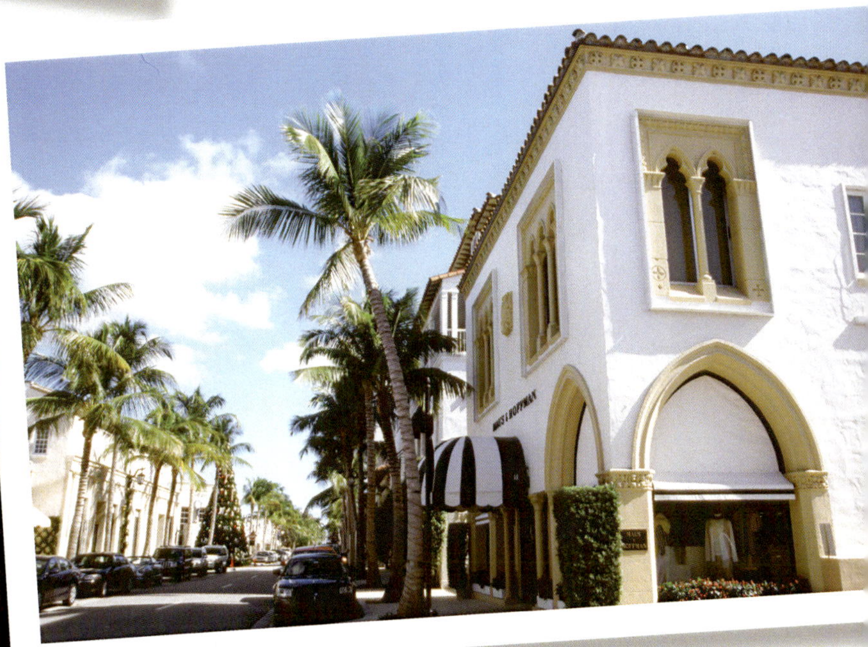

MIZNER FIGURED OUT A WAY TO USE ROTTEN CORAL. He would grind it up and put it together with cement. They could cast a column or a half a column or whatever they needed. It would come out looking very old, when they were brand new.

They still use original molds that Mizner used today for window sills and pylons. If you want to add columns to your house in the original Mizner style, you can use his molds. They used other natural material down here like agate, which came from under the ocean from old coral beds back when all of Florida was under water. Depending on the condition of the coral beds, in some places they can cut it and use it as building blocks, which they call coquina. Everyday there are trainloads of it going up country to pave streets. Mizner didn't use coquina in his buildings, except for his stone castings.

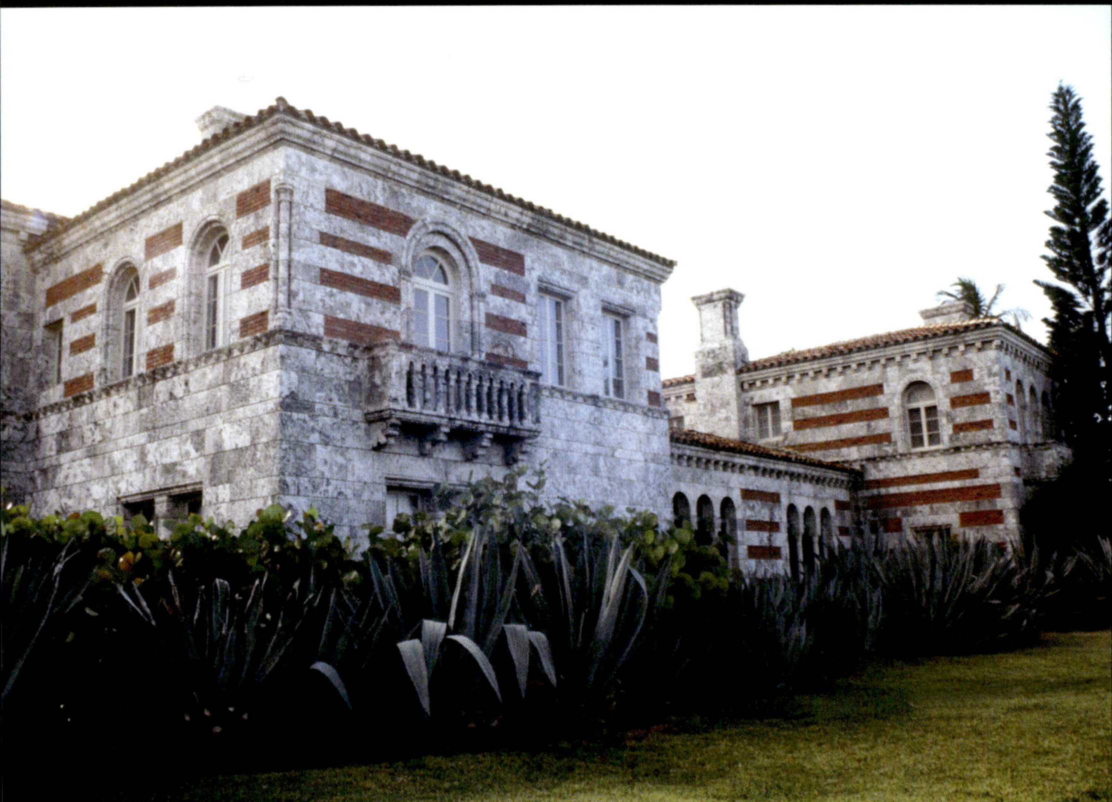

Famed Swiss architect, Maurice Fatio used coquina in nearly all of this buildings. One of his most famous homes, known as the ham-and-cheese house, used coquina and red brick. This house, on left, was built in 1928, as well as the gate of the Stotesbury residence (pictured on page 13.)

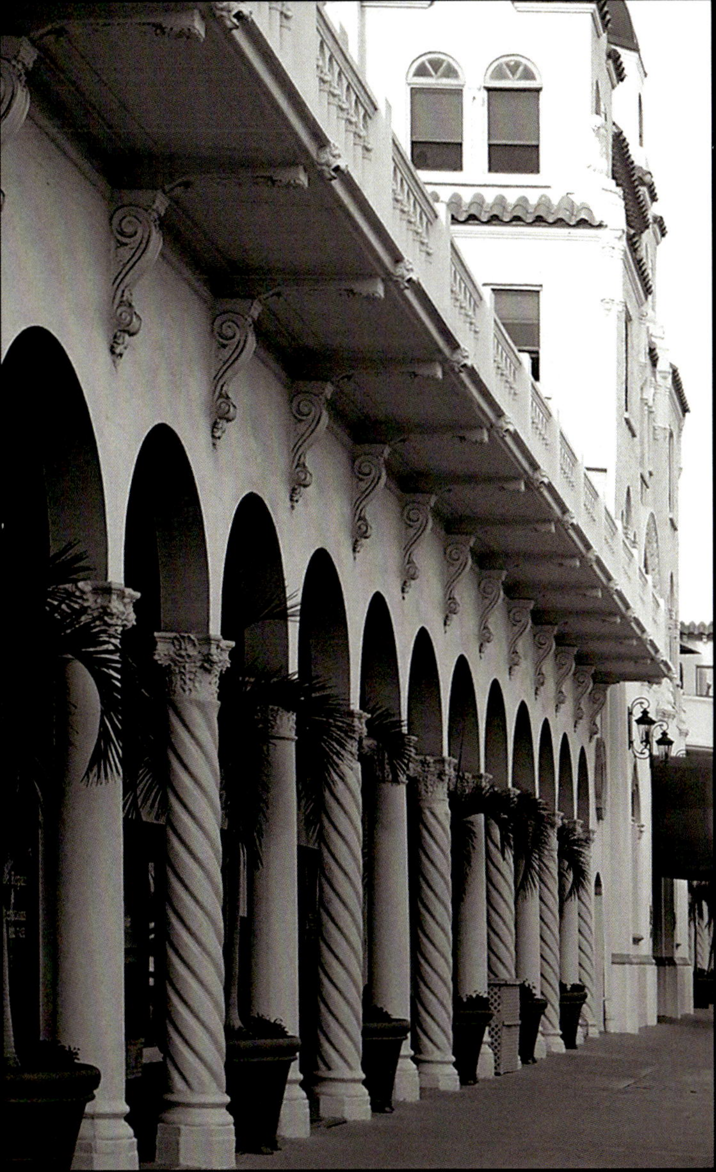

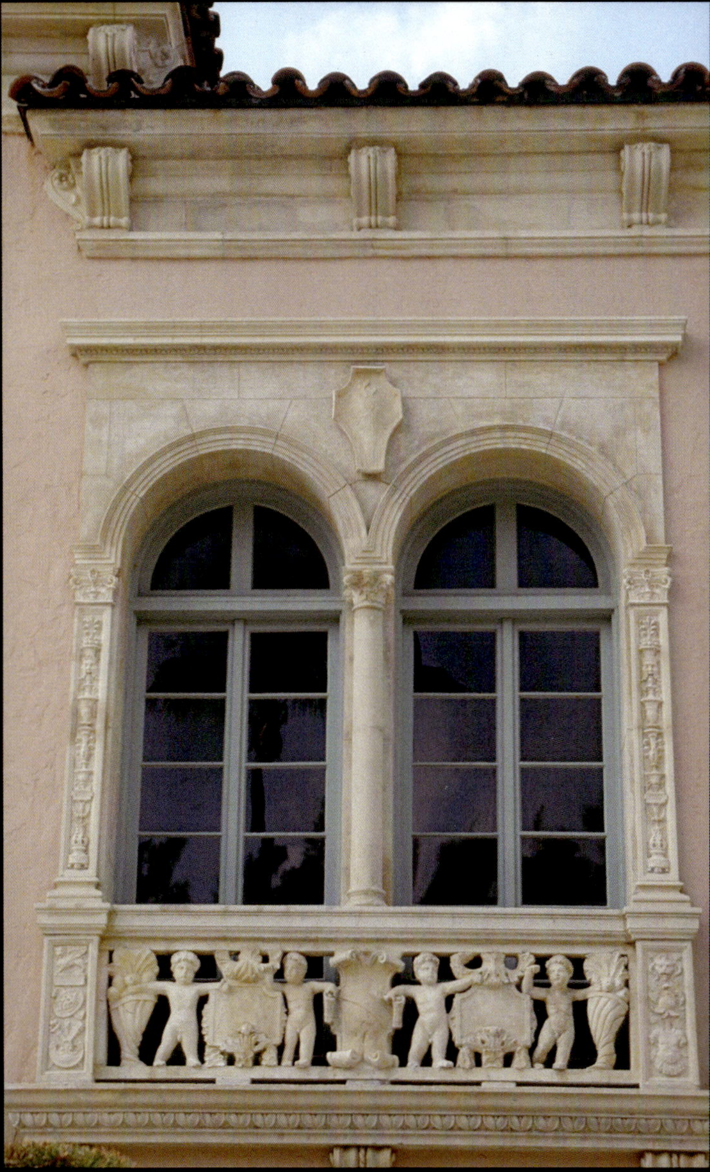

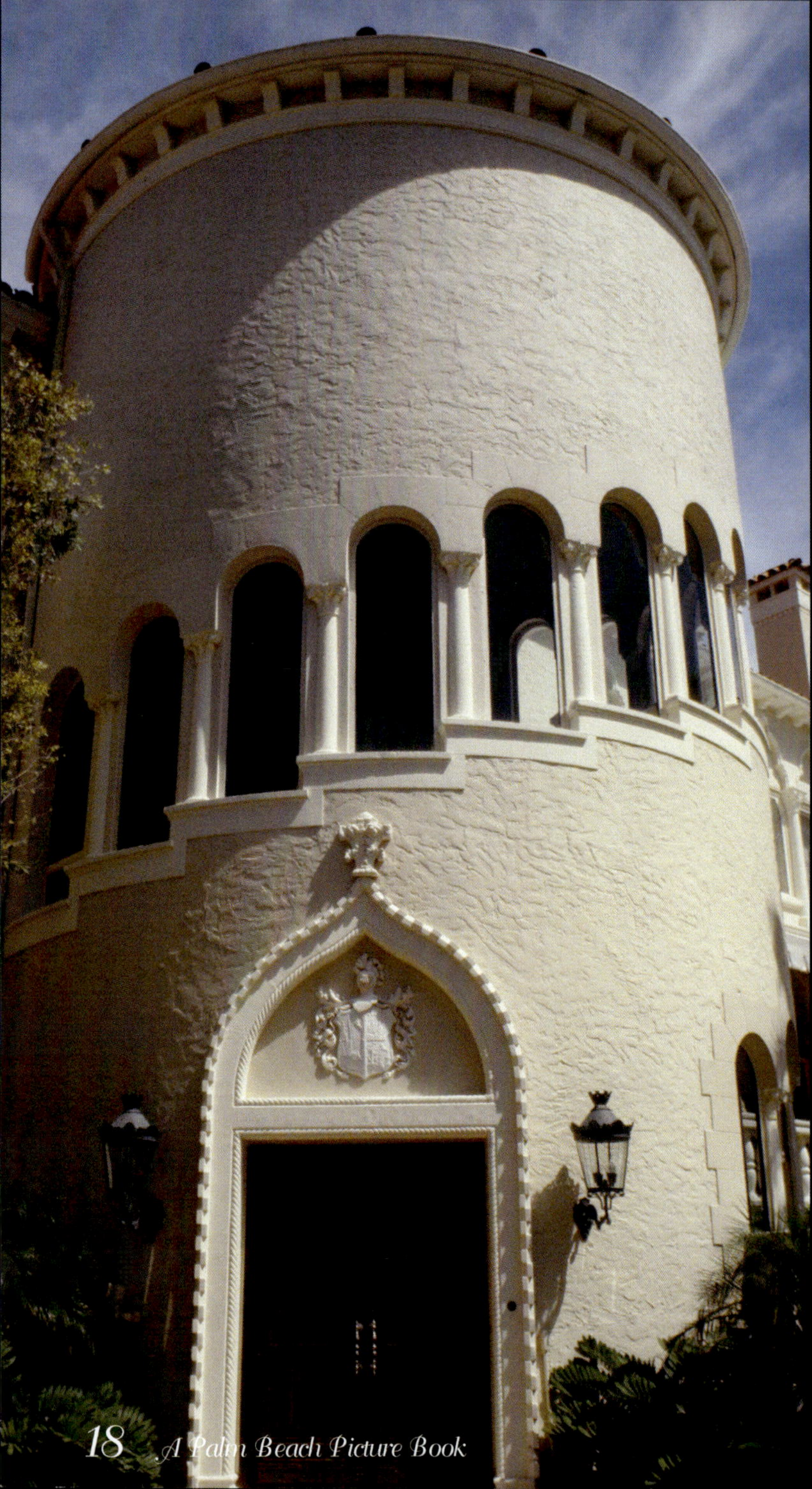

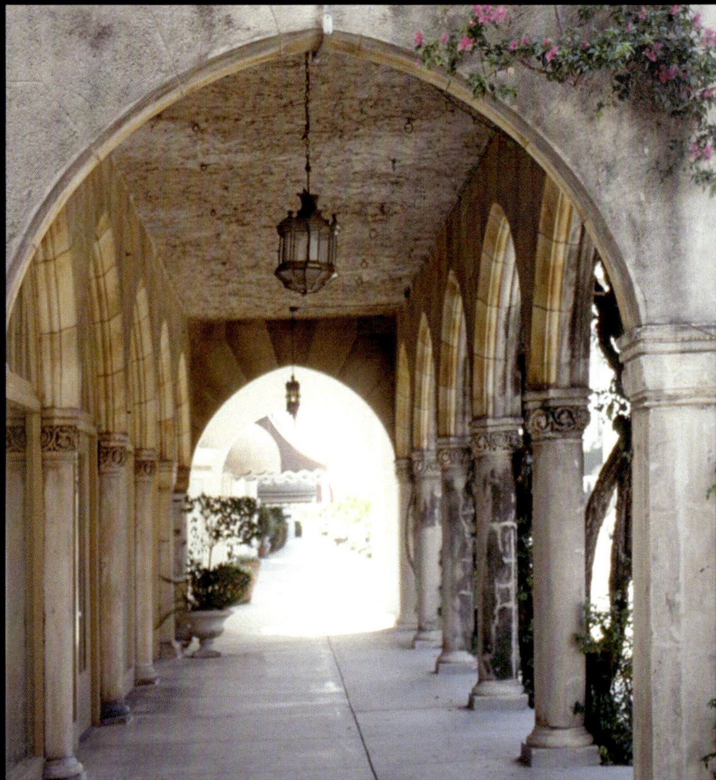

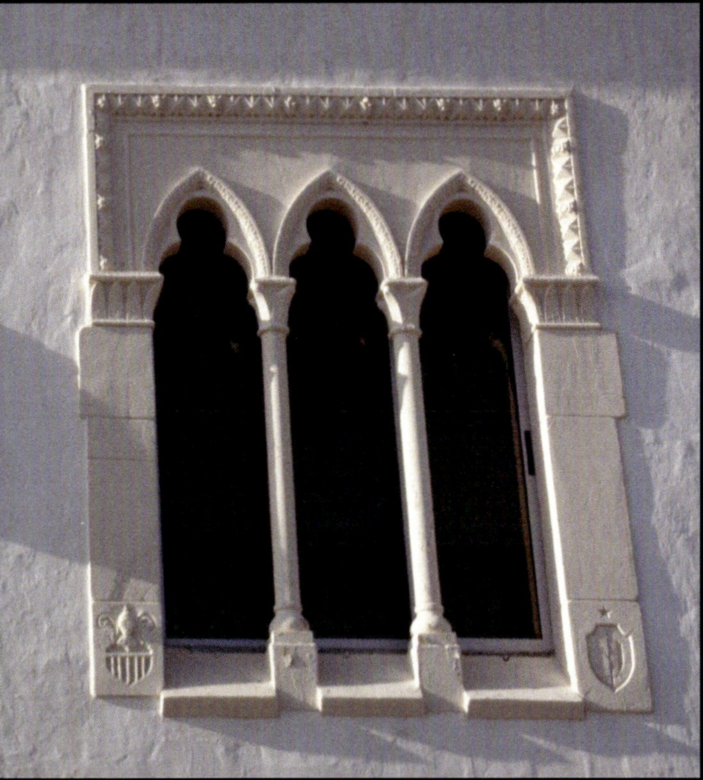

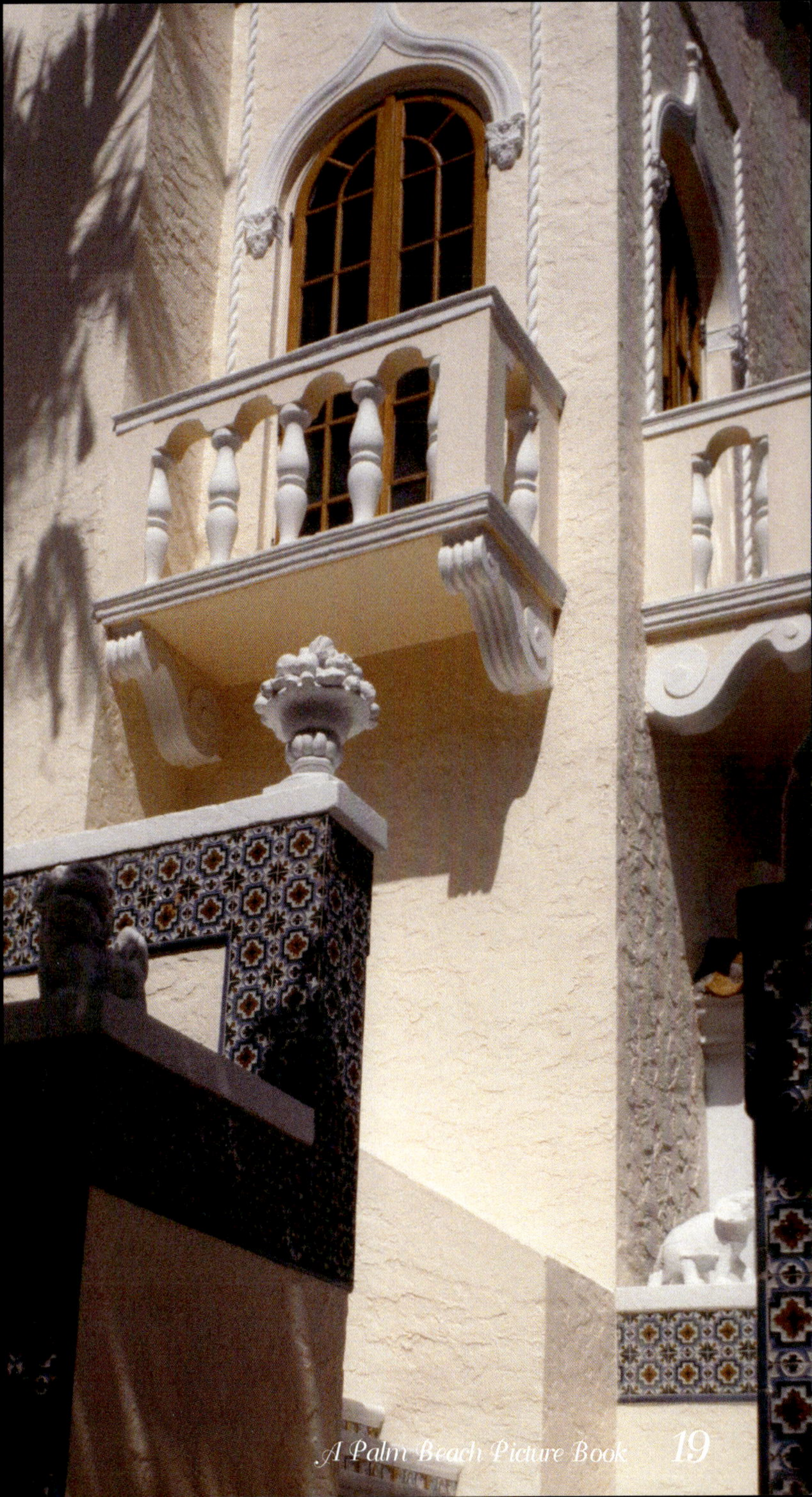

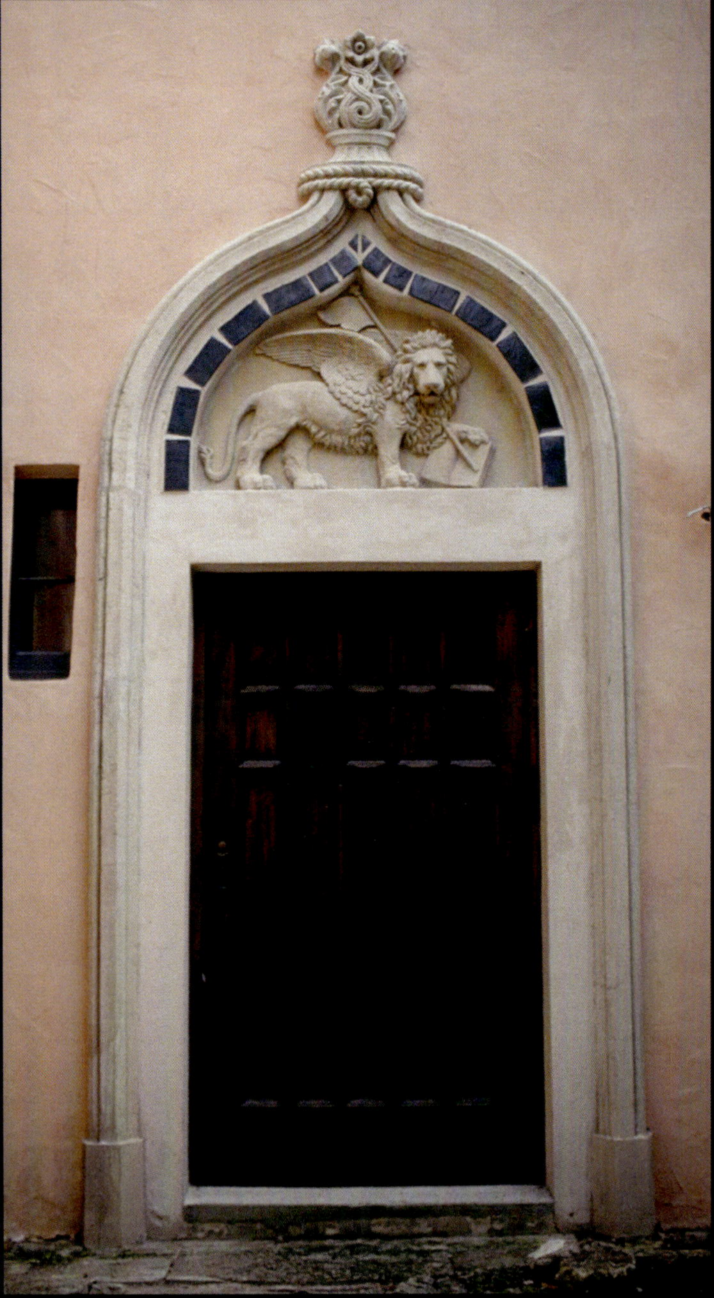

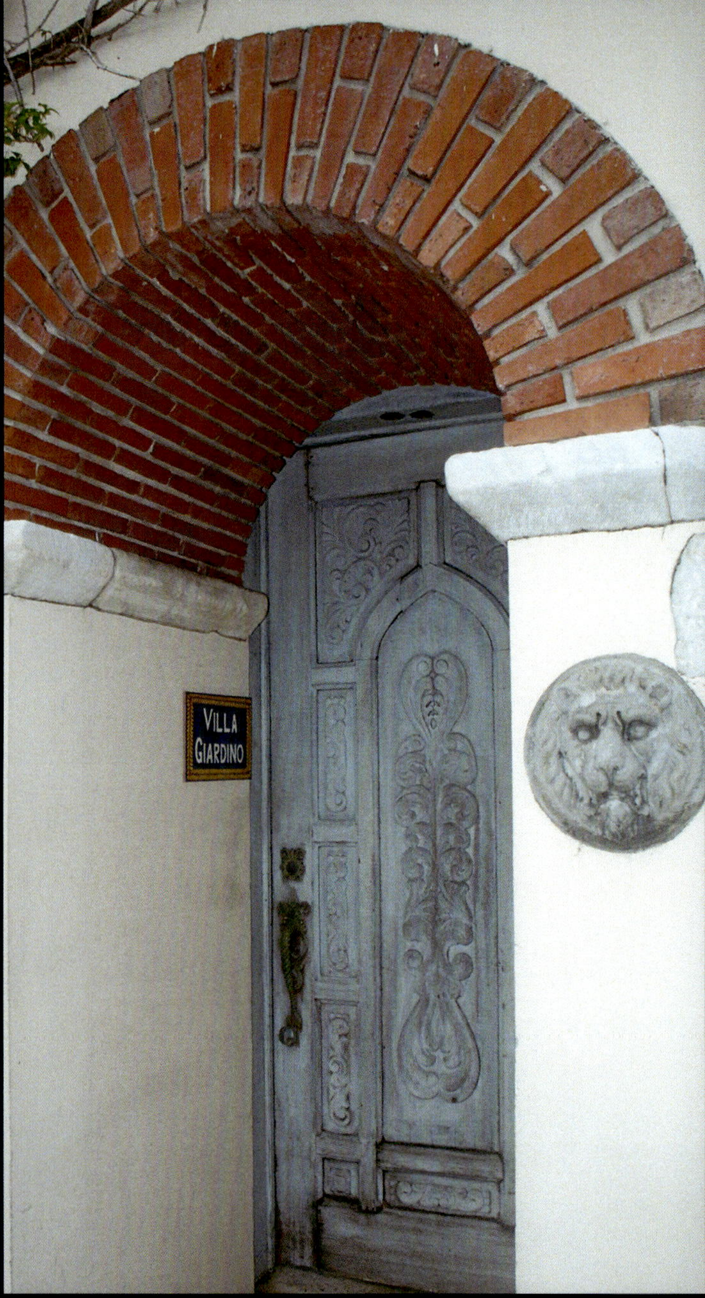
VILLA
GIARDINO

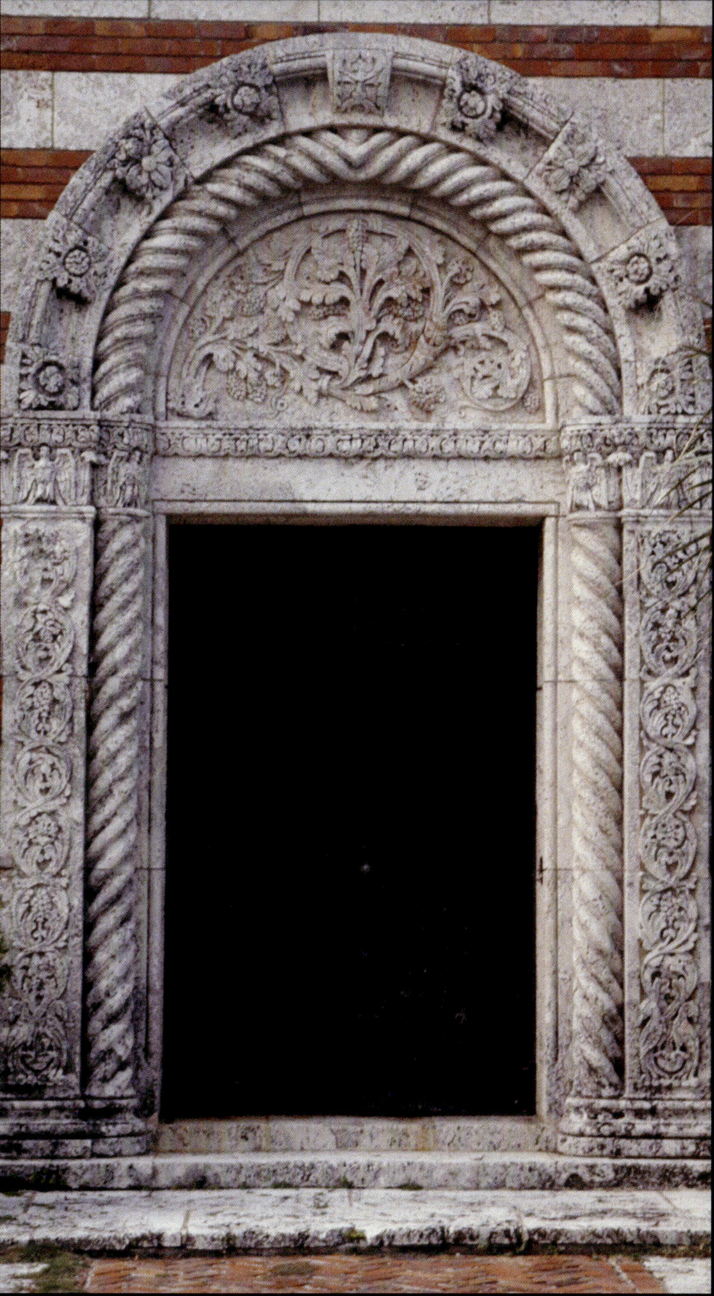

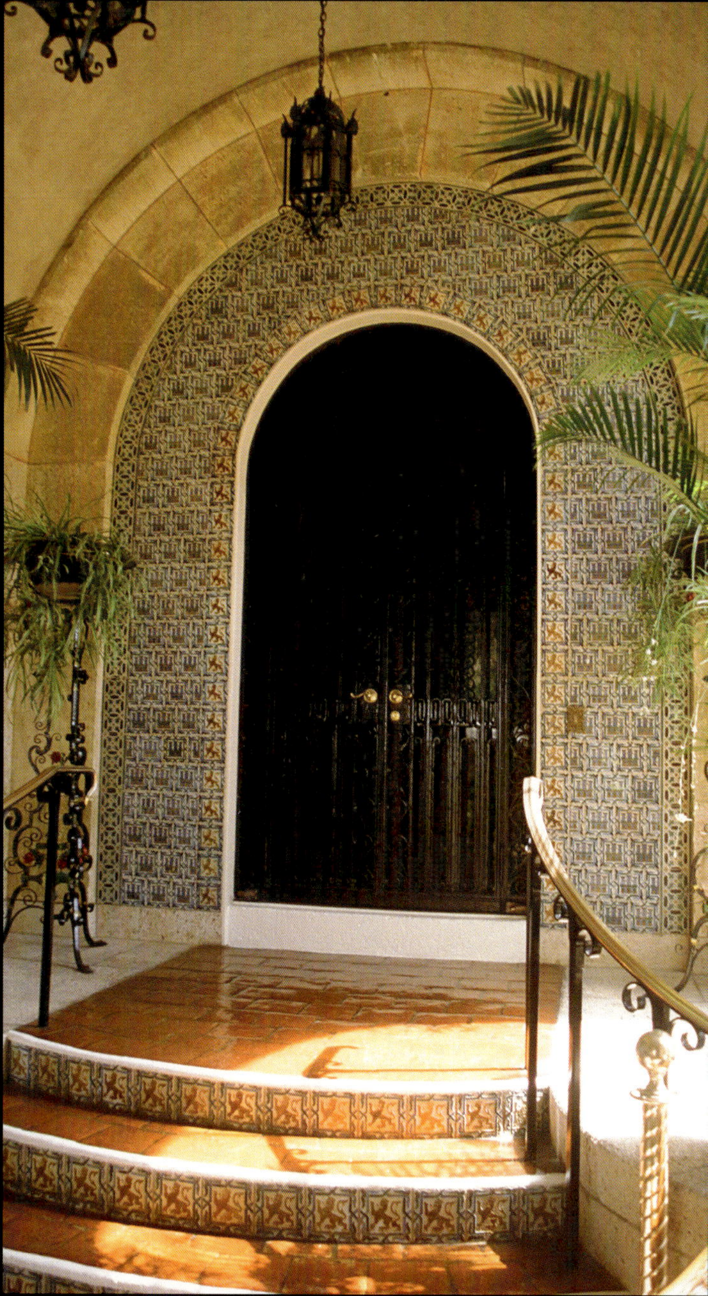

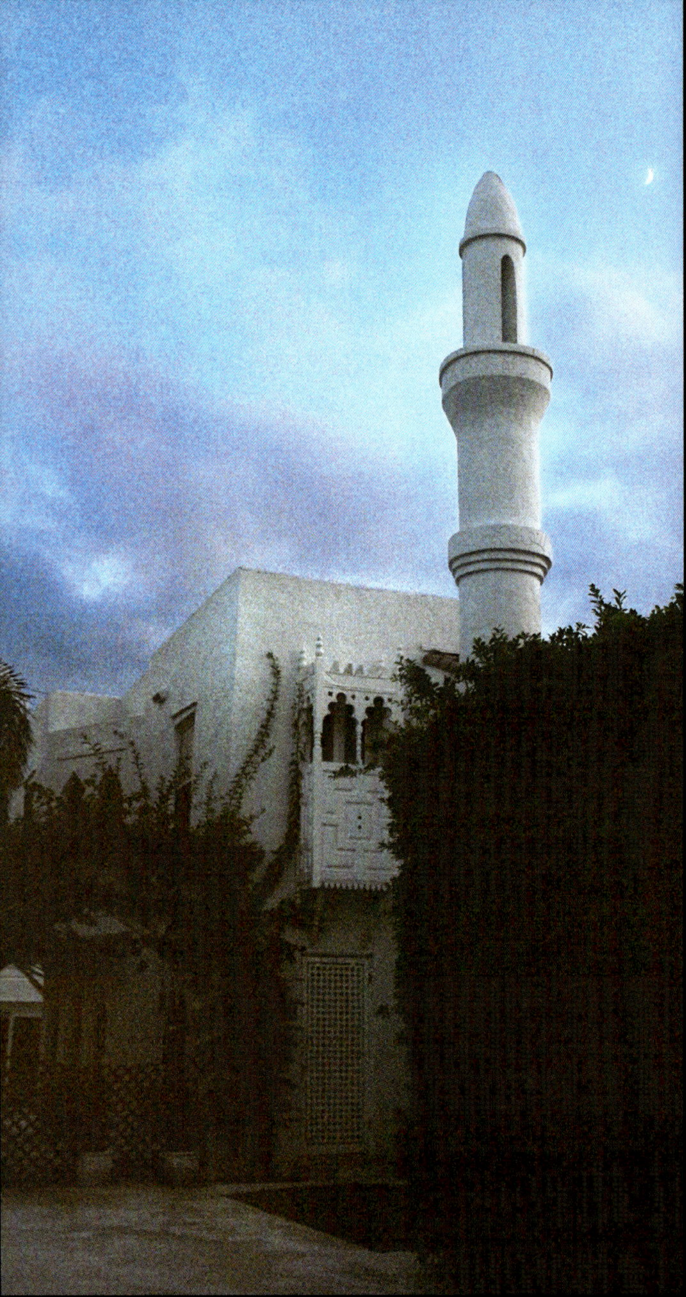

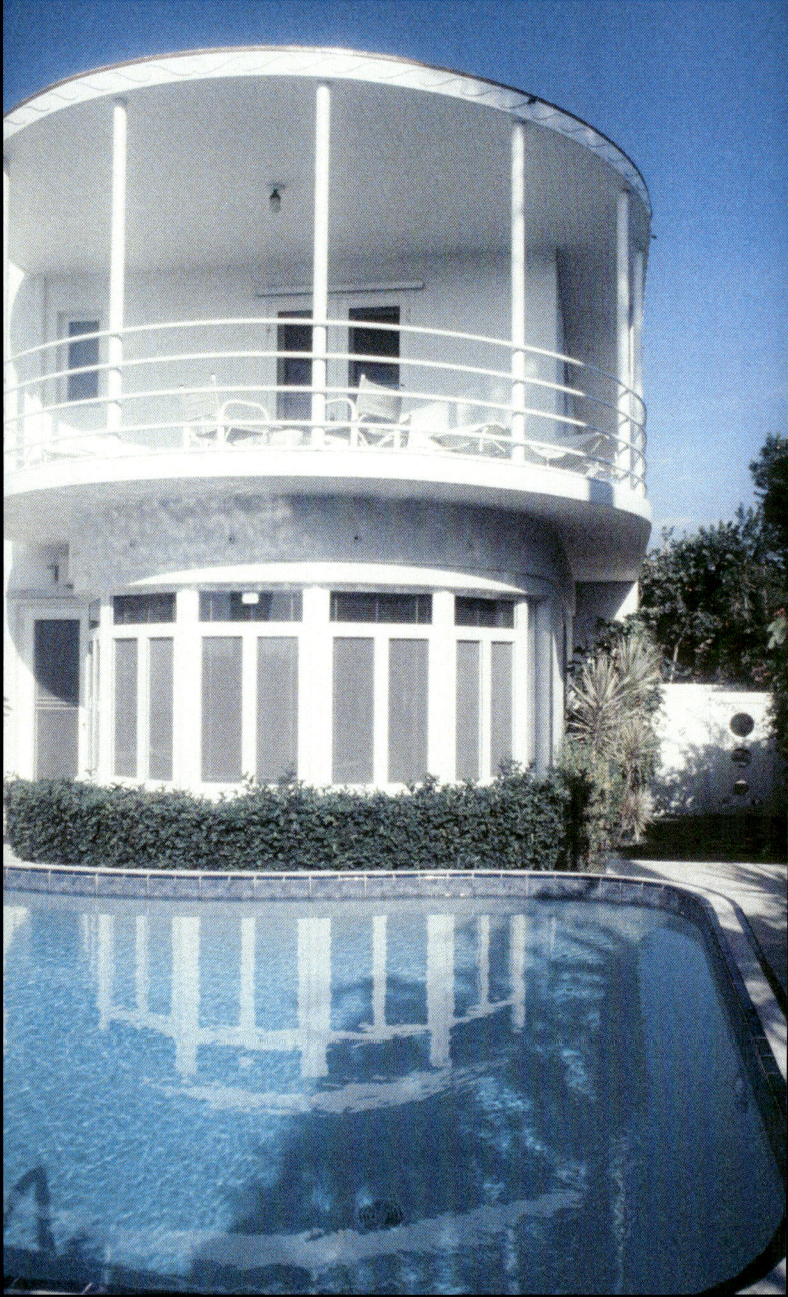

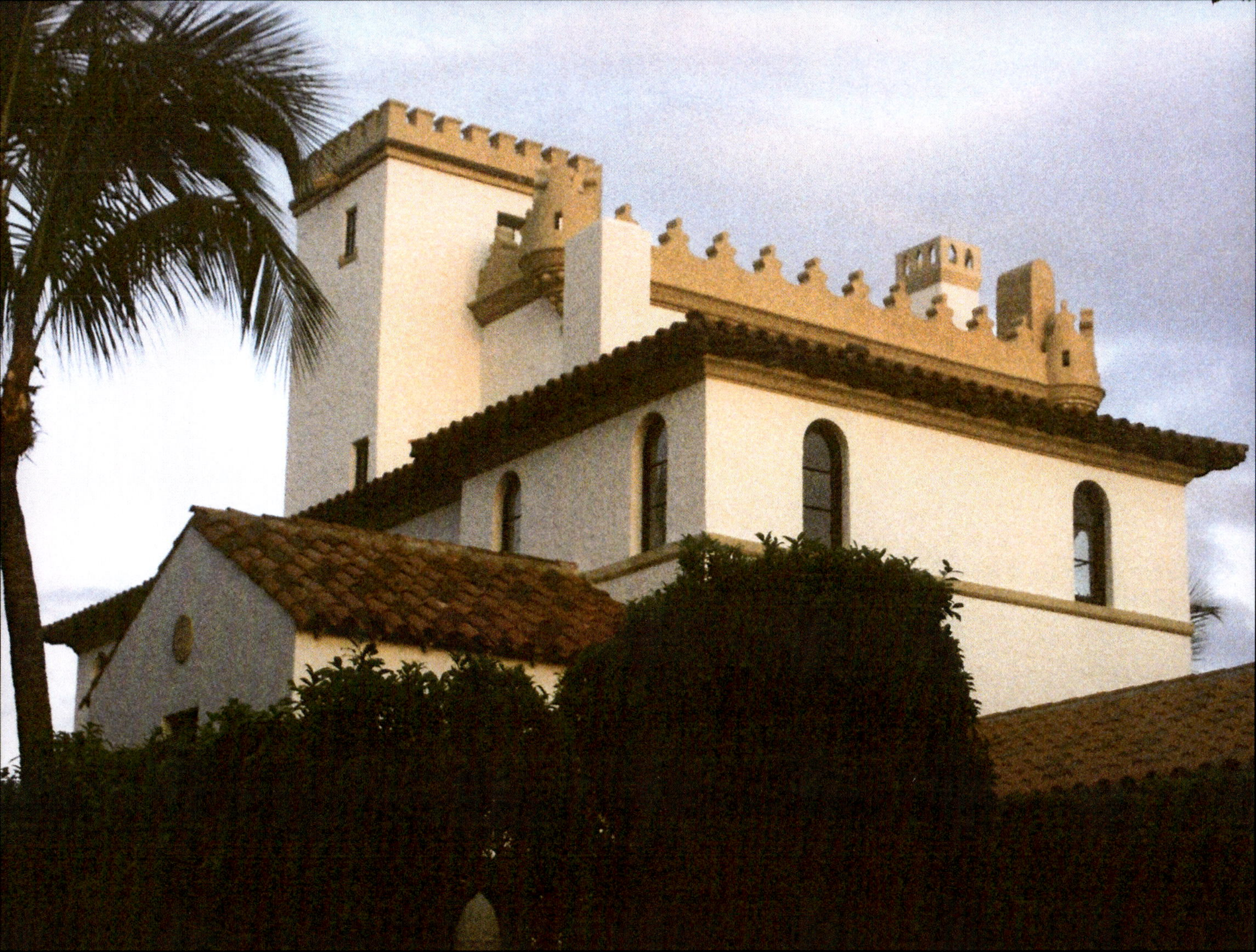

THE ECLECTIC STYLE OF PALM BEACH includes everything from Moroccan to Art Deco and Beaux Art Nouveau, Venetian Gothic, to Spanish tiled Bungalow. You'll find Swiss Chalet as well as ultra modern glass houses. Many houses have names in Palm Beach.

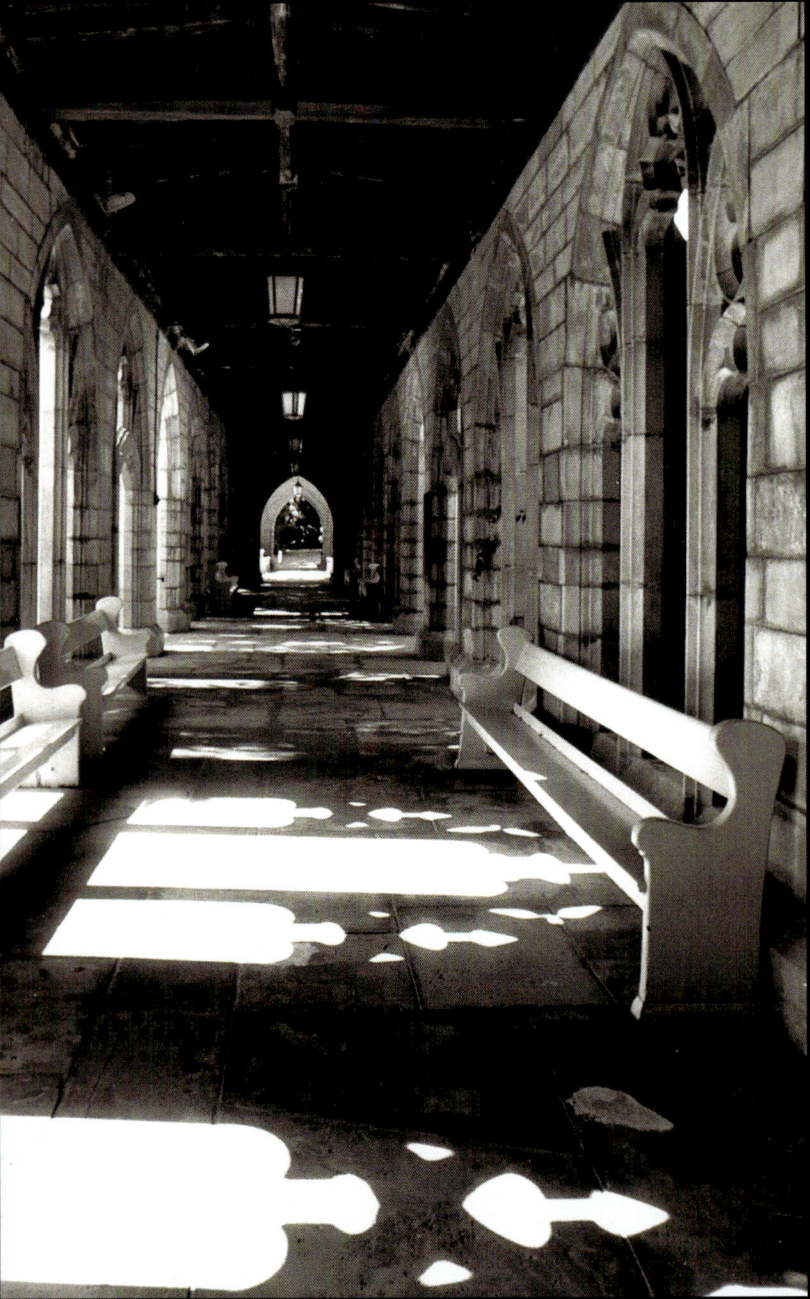

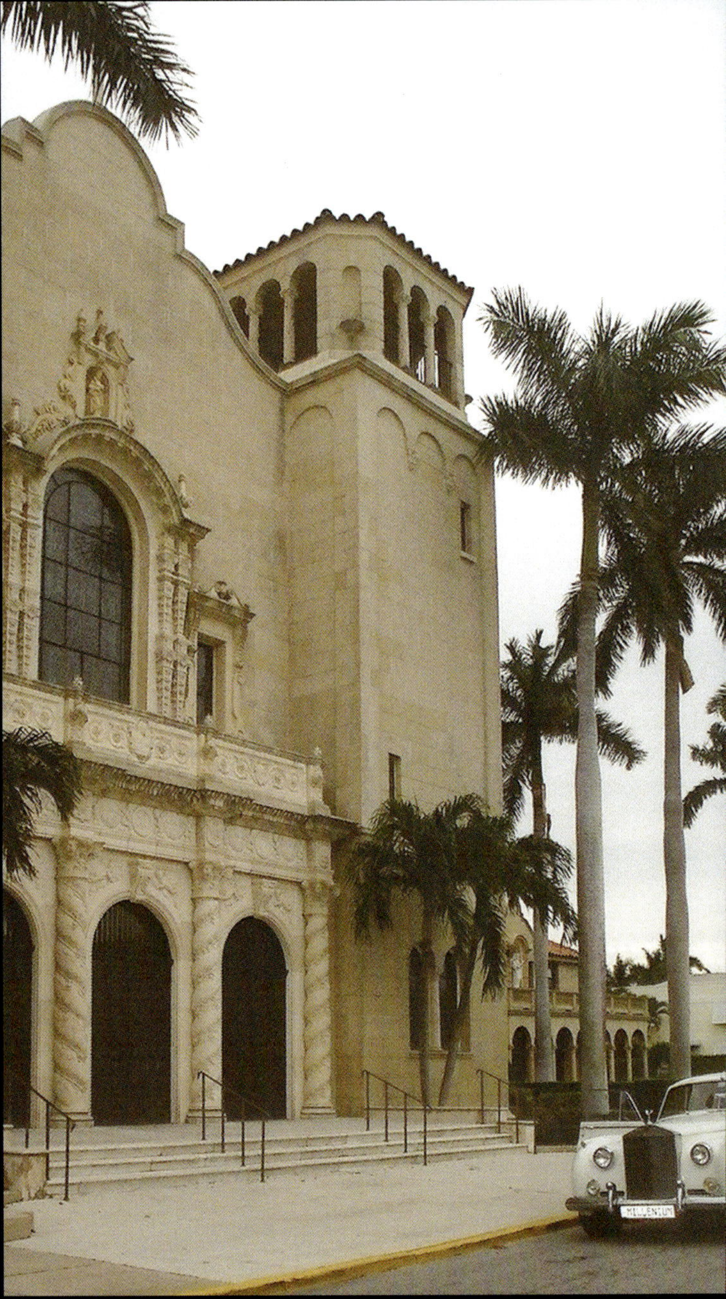

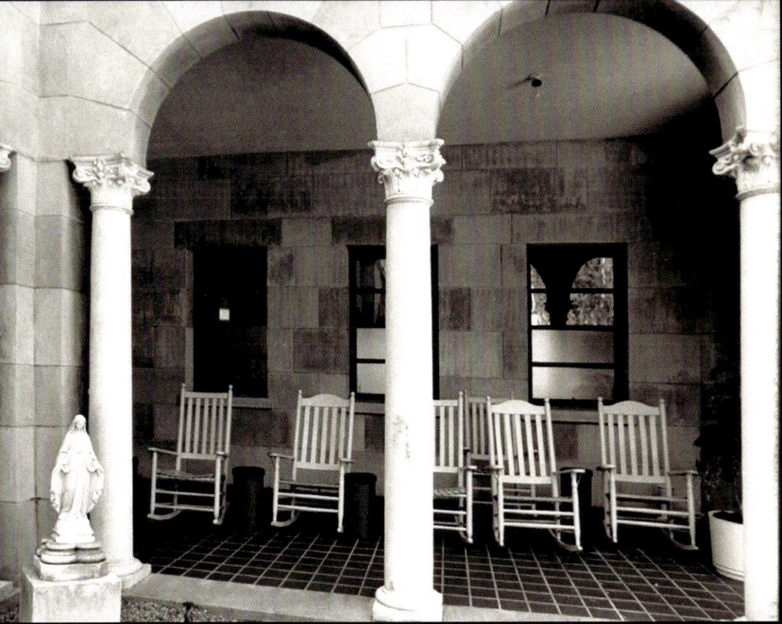

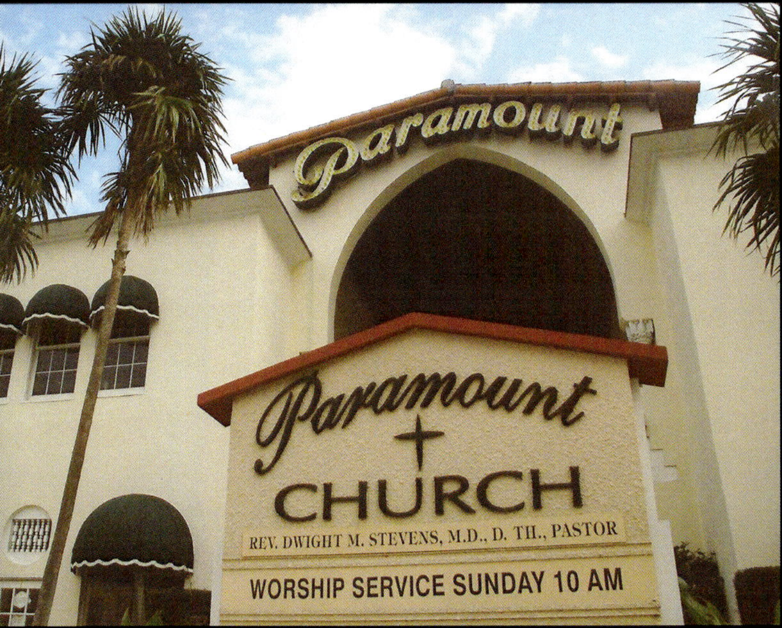
Paramount
Paramount
CHURCH
REV. DWIGHT M. STEVENS, M.D., D. TH., PASTOR
WORSHIP SERVICE SUNDAY 10 AM

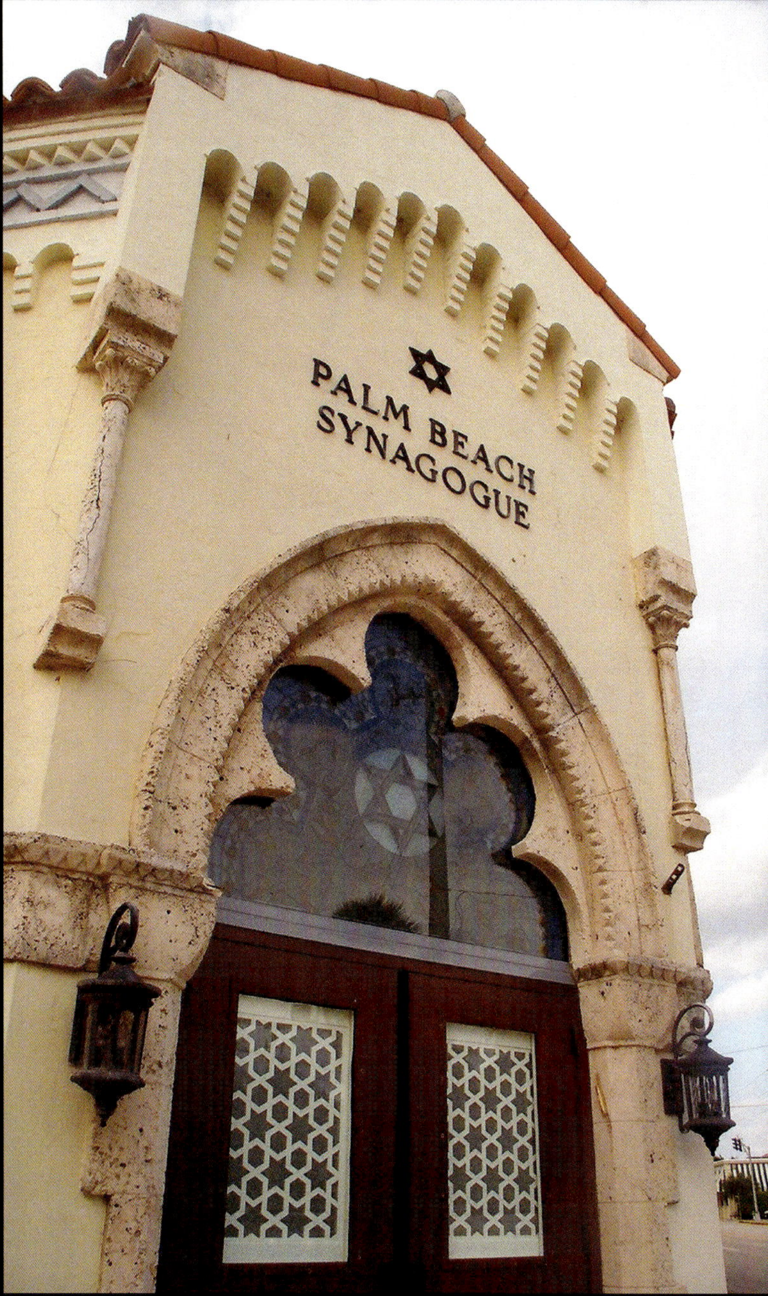
PALM BEACH
SYNAGOGUE

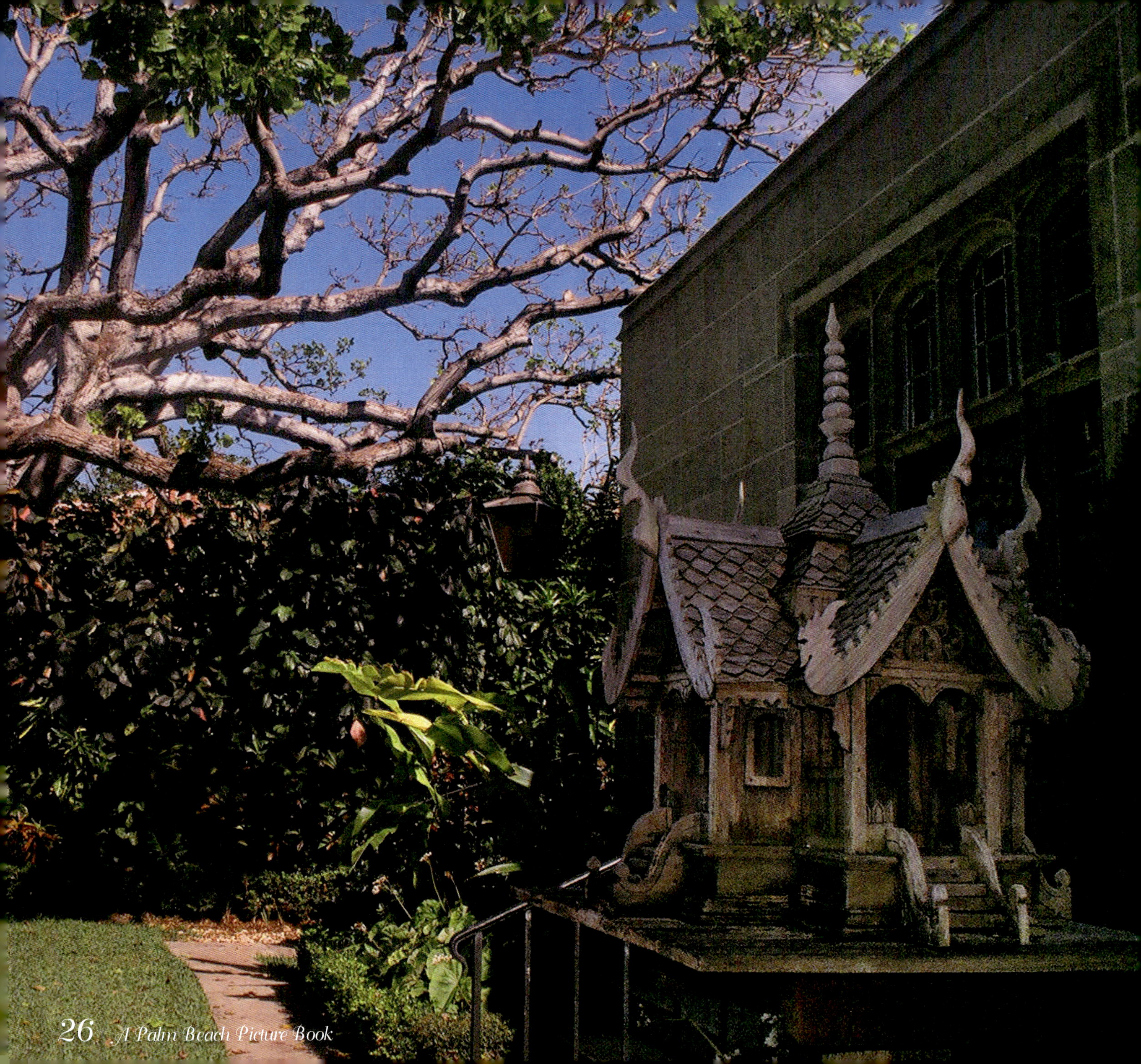

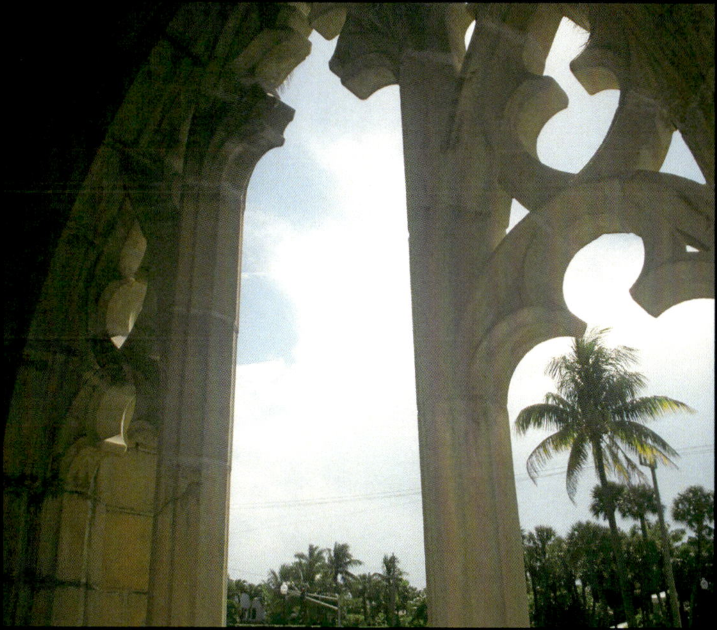

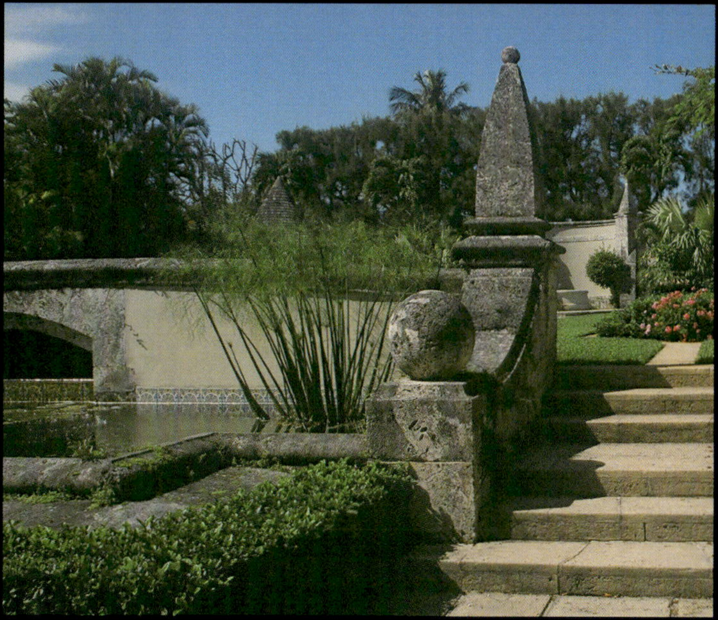

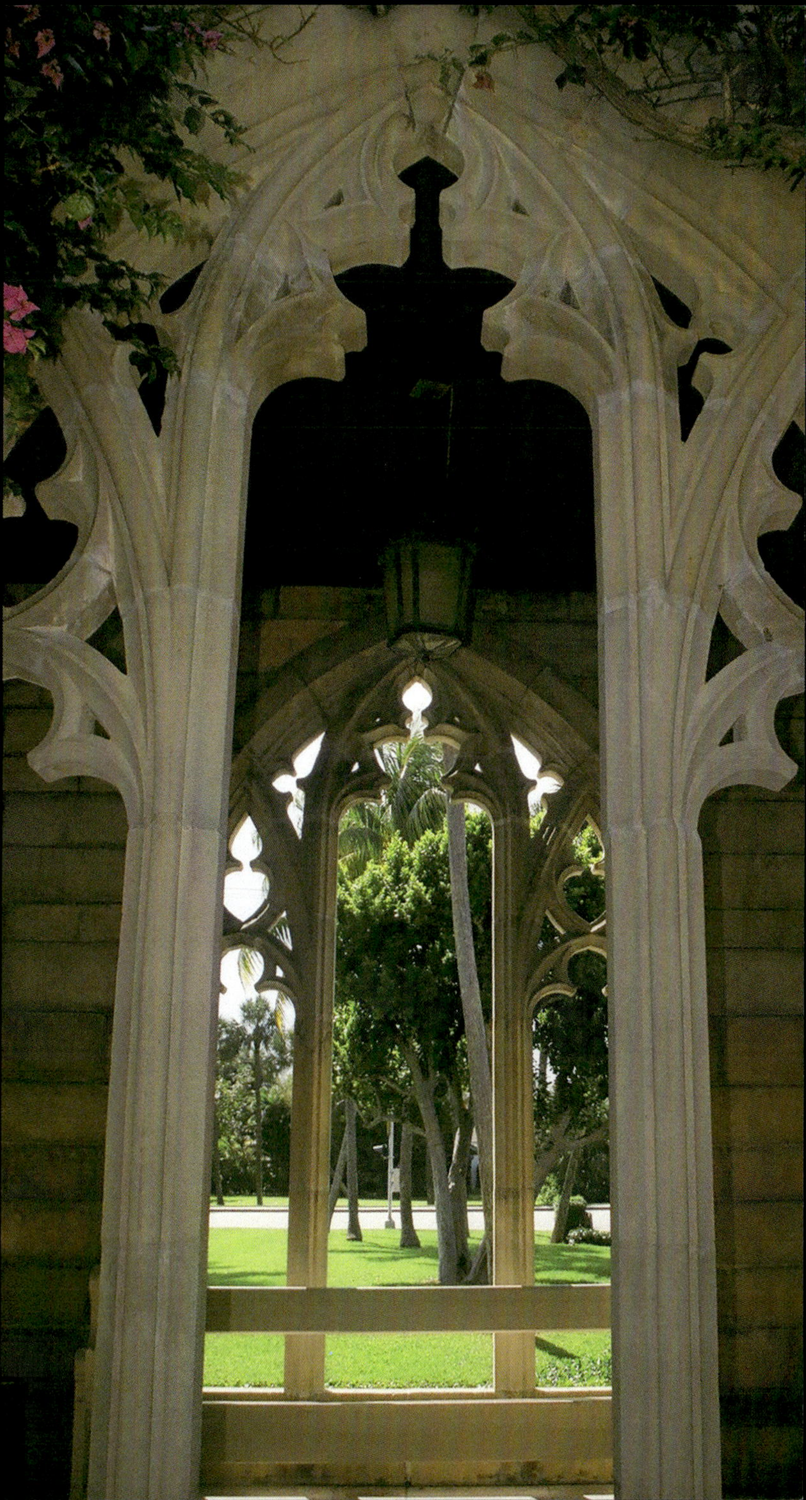

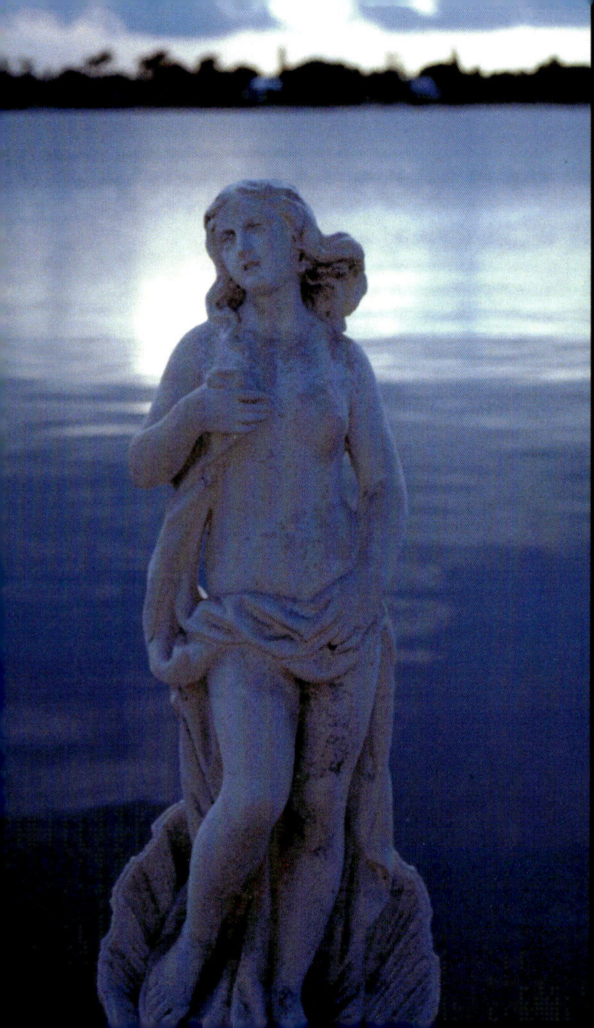

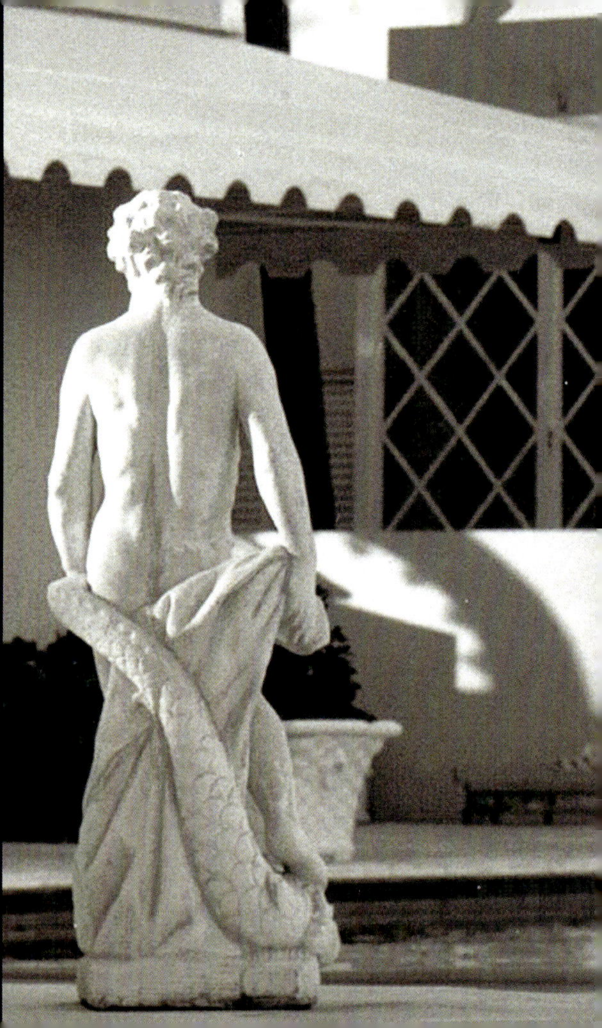

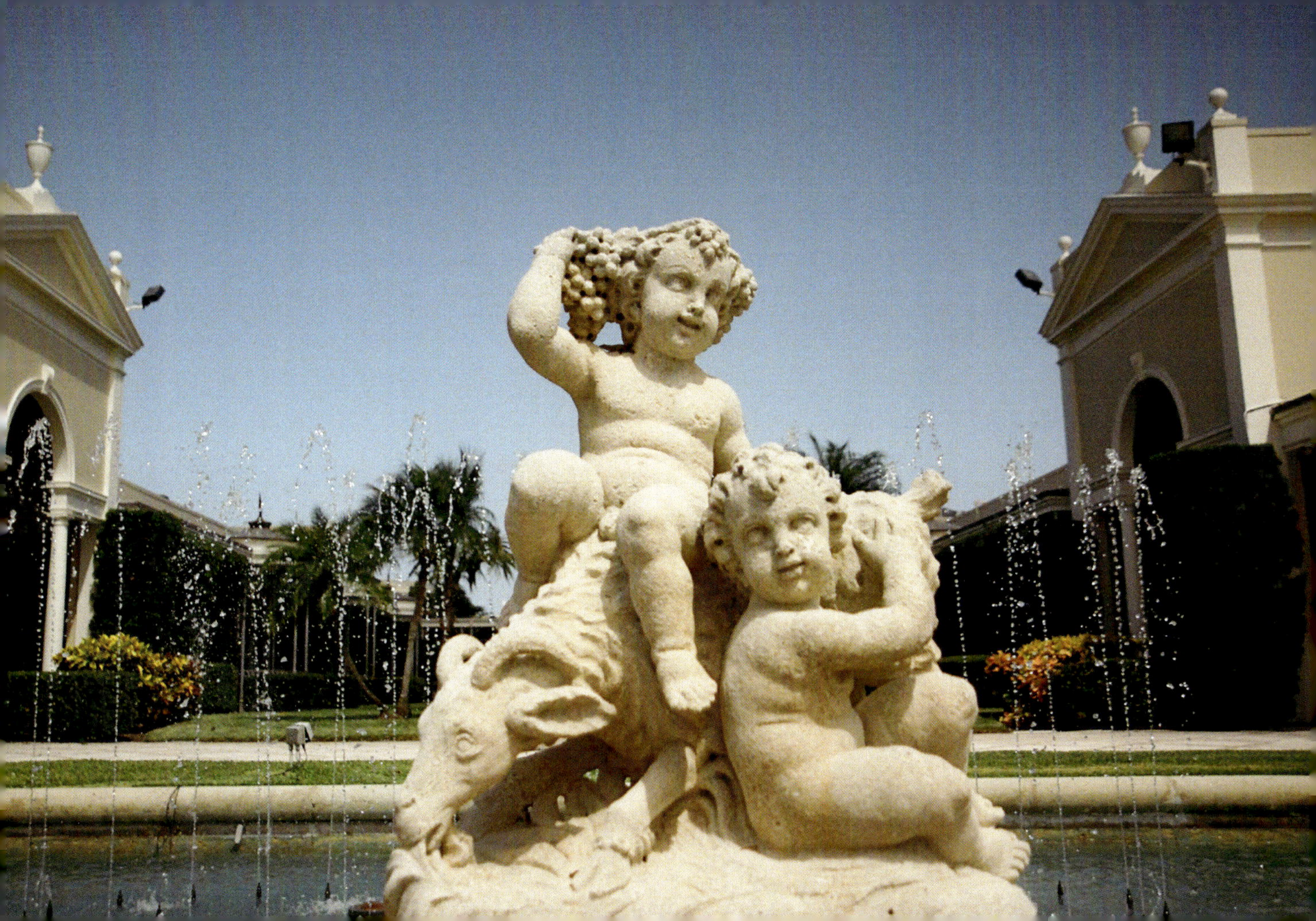

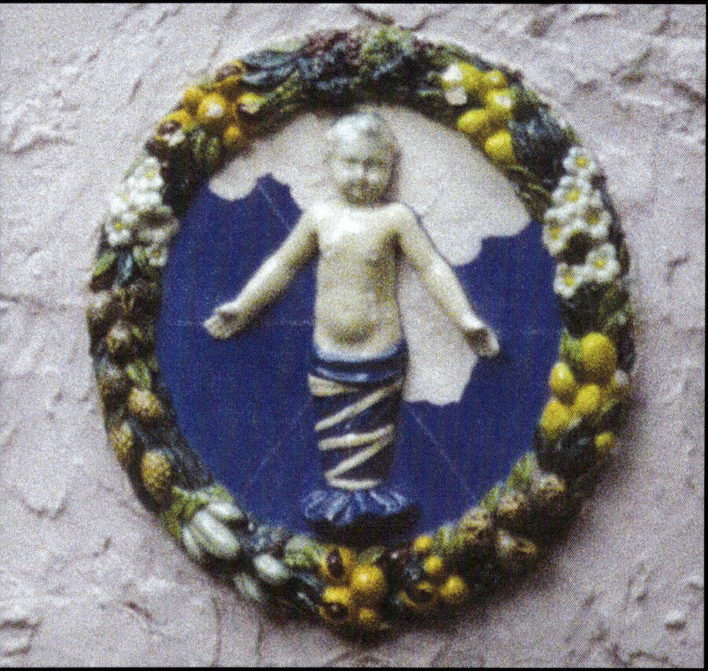

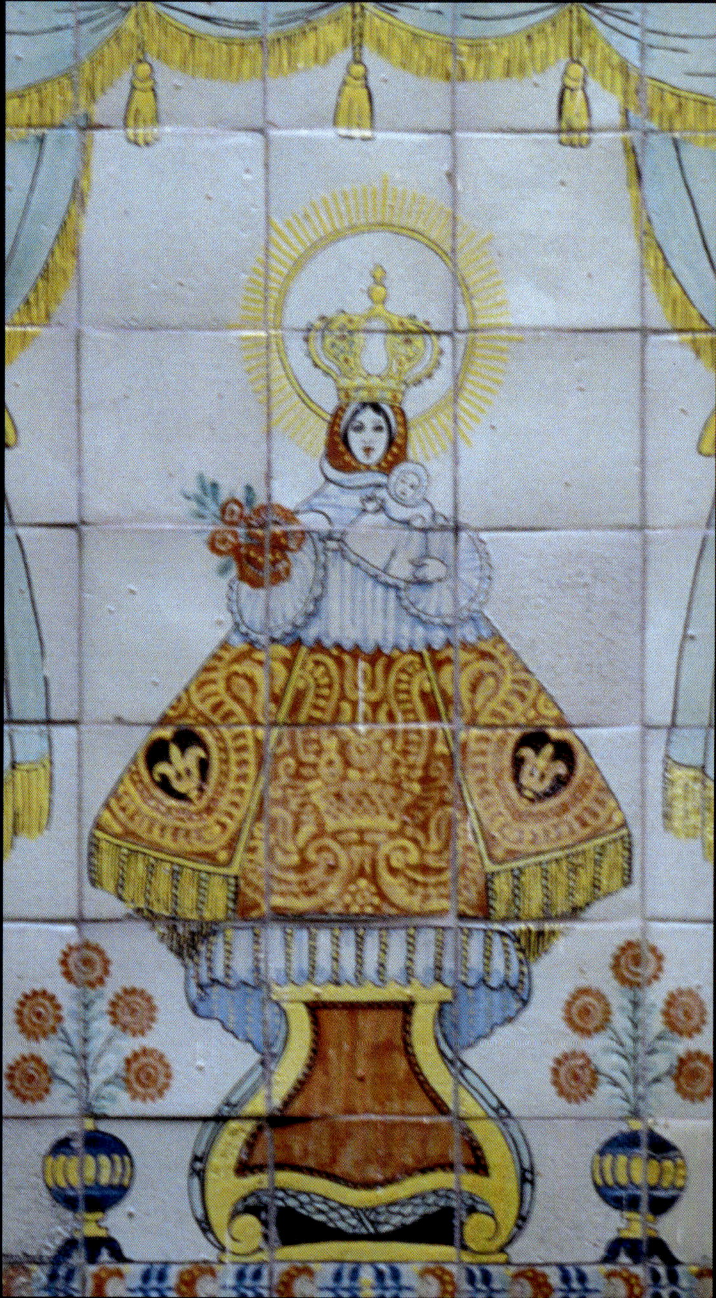

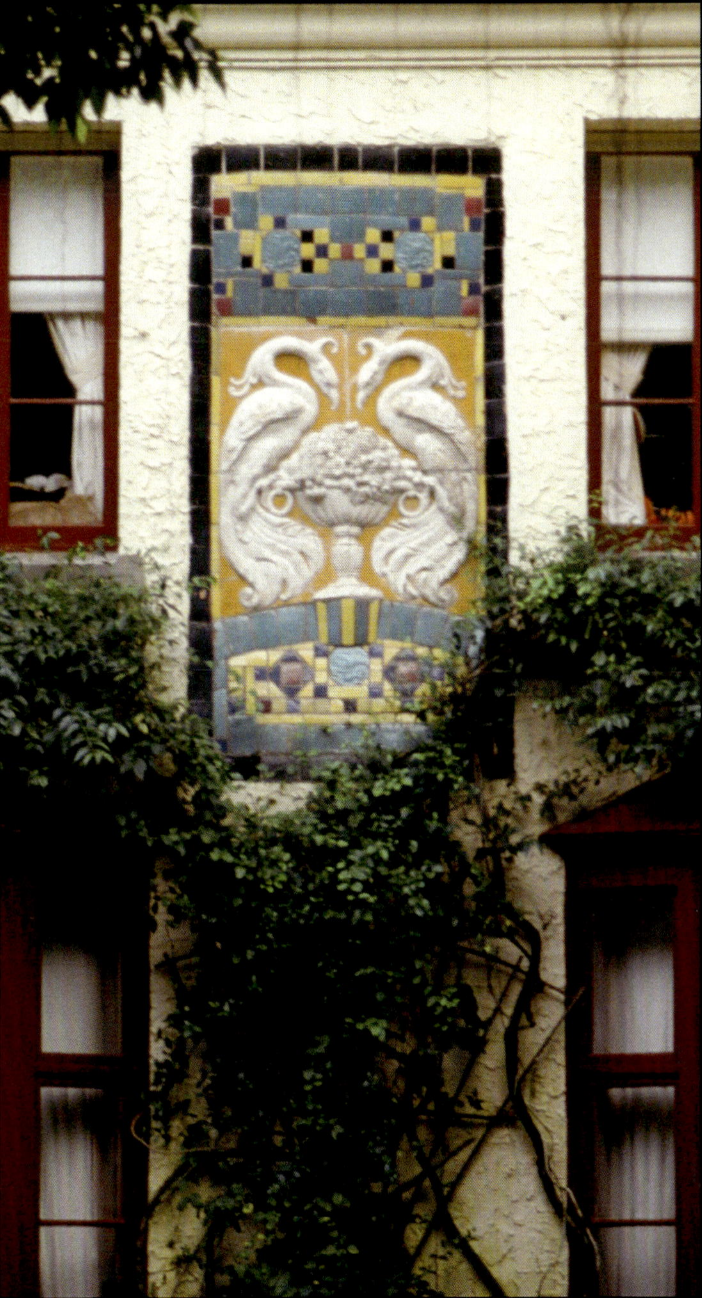

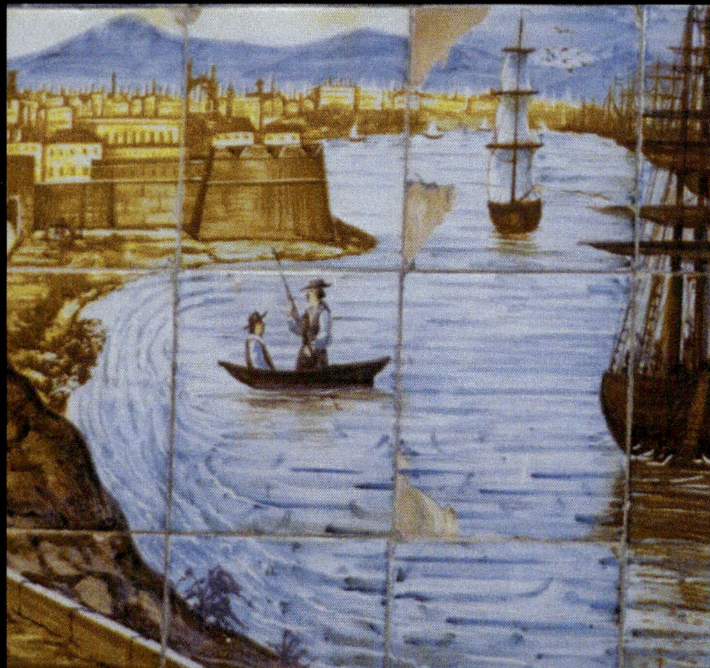

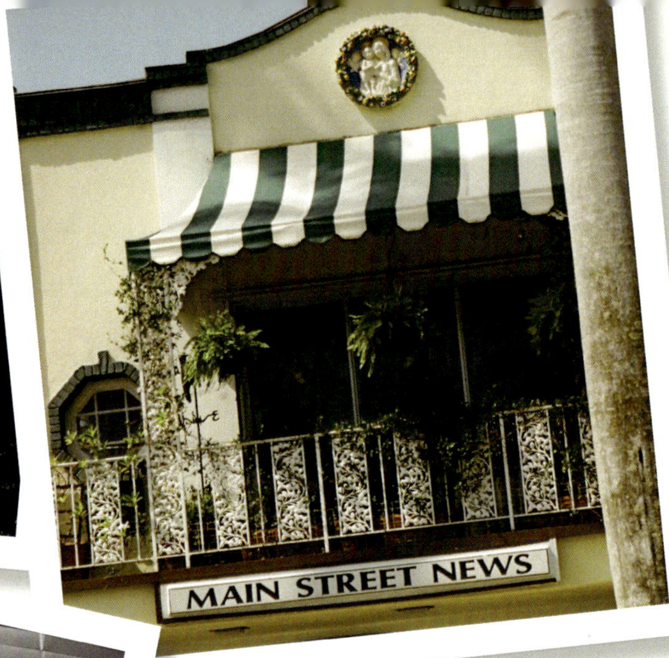
MAIN STREET NEWS

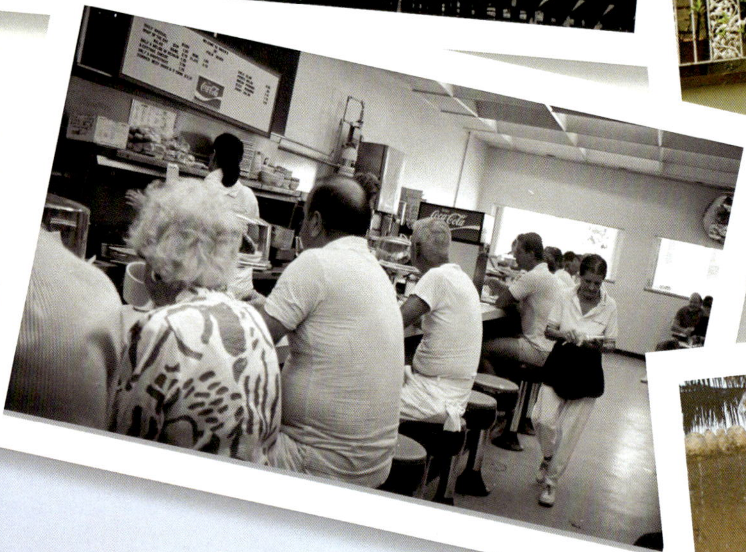

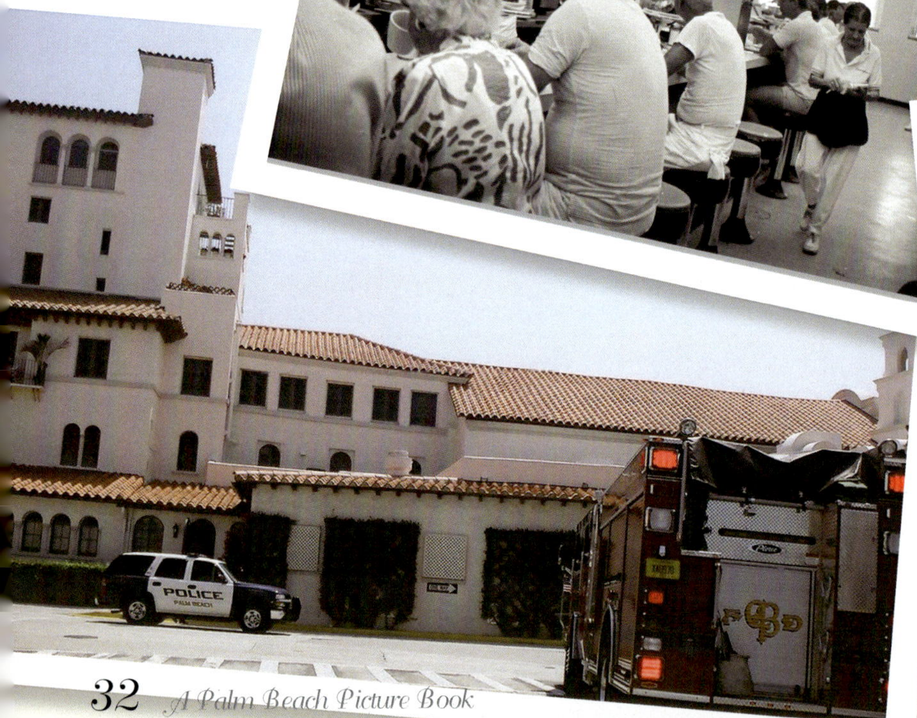
POLICE

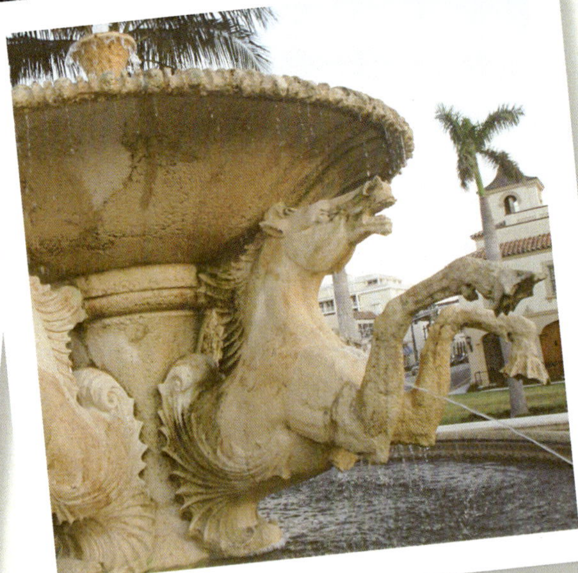

Old Familiar Places

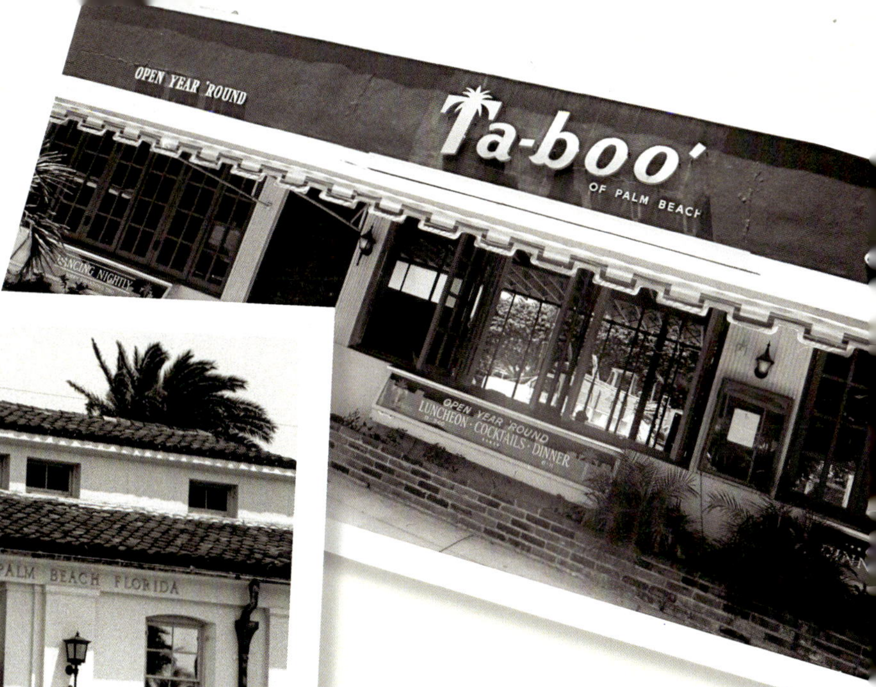

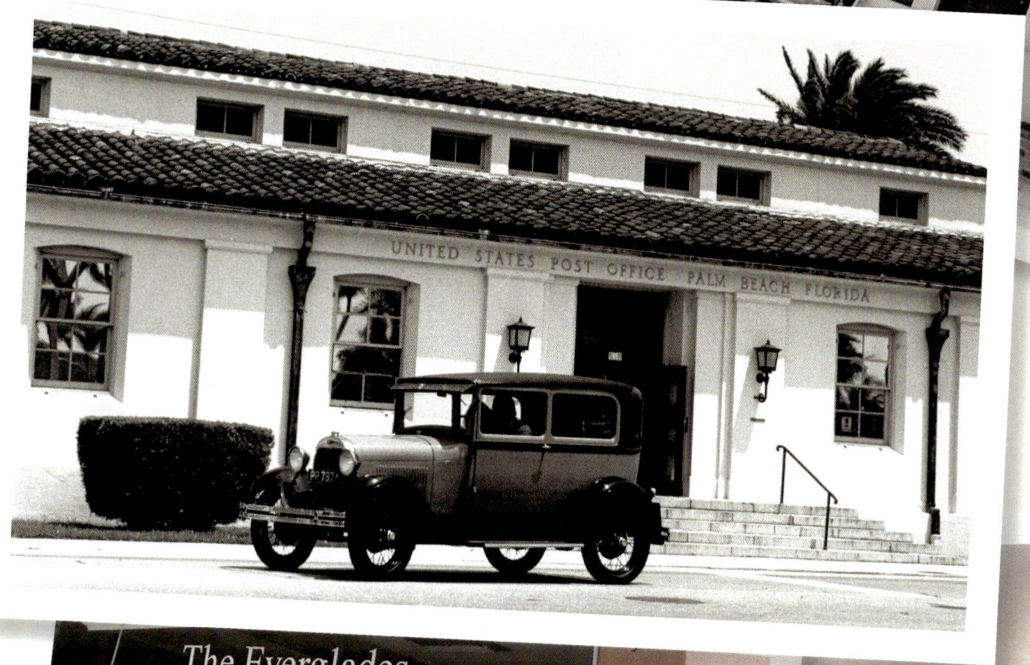

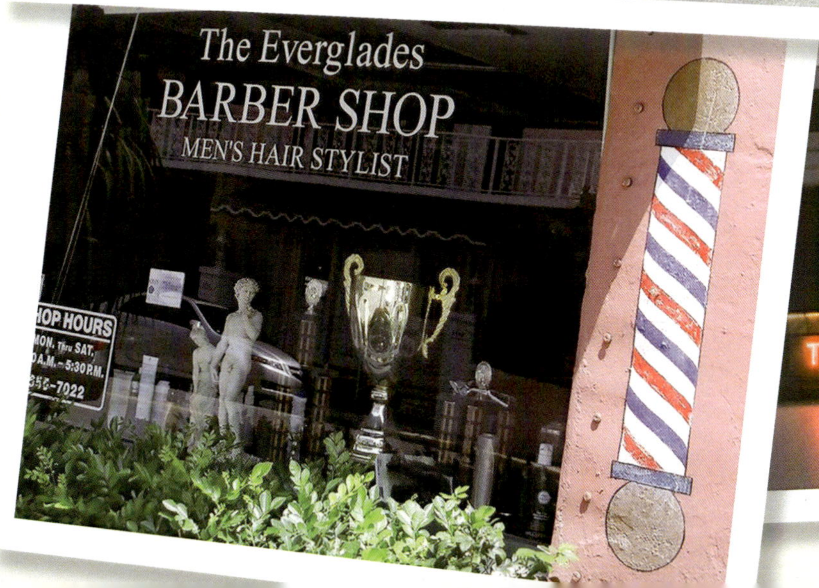

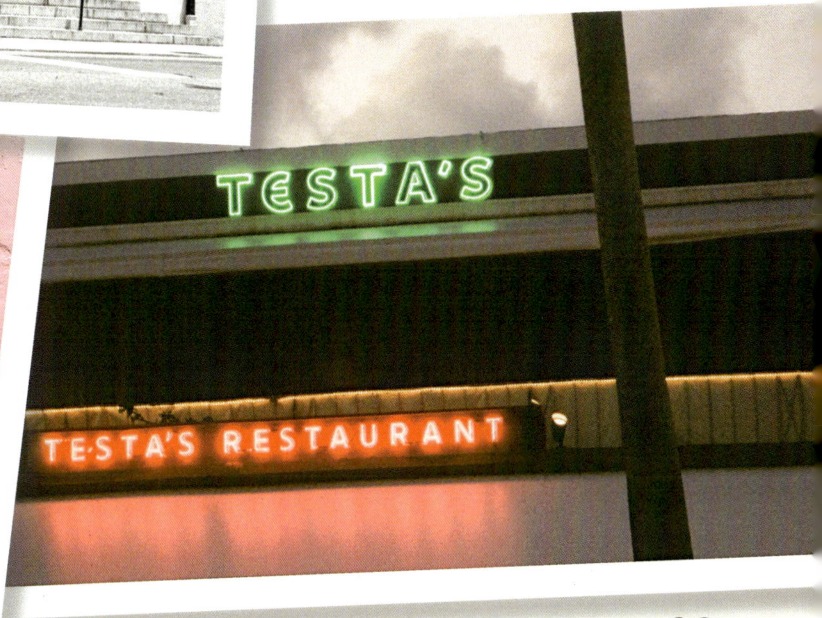

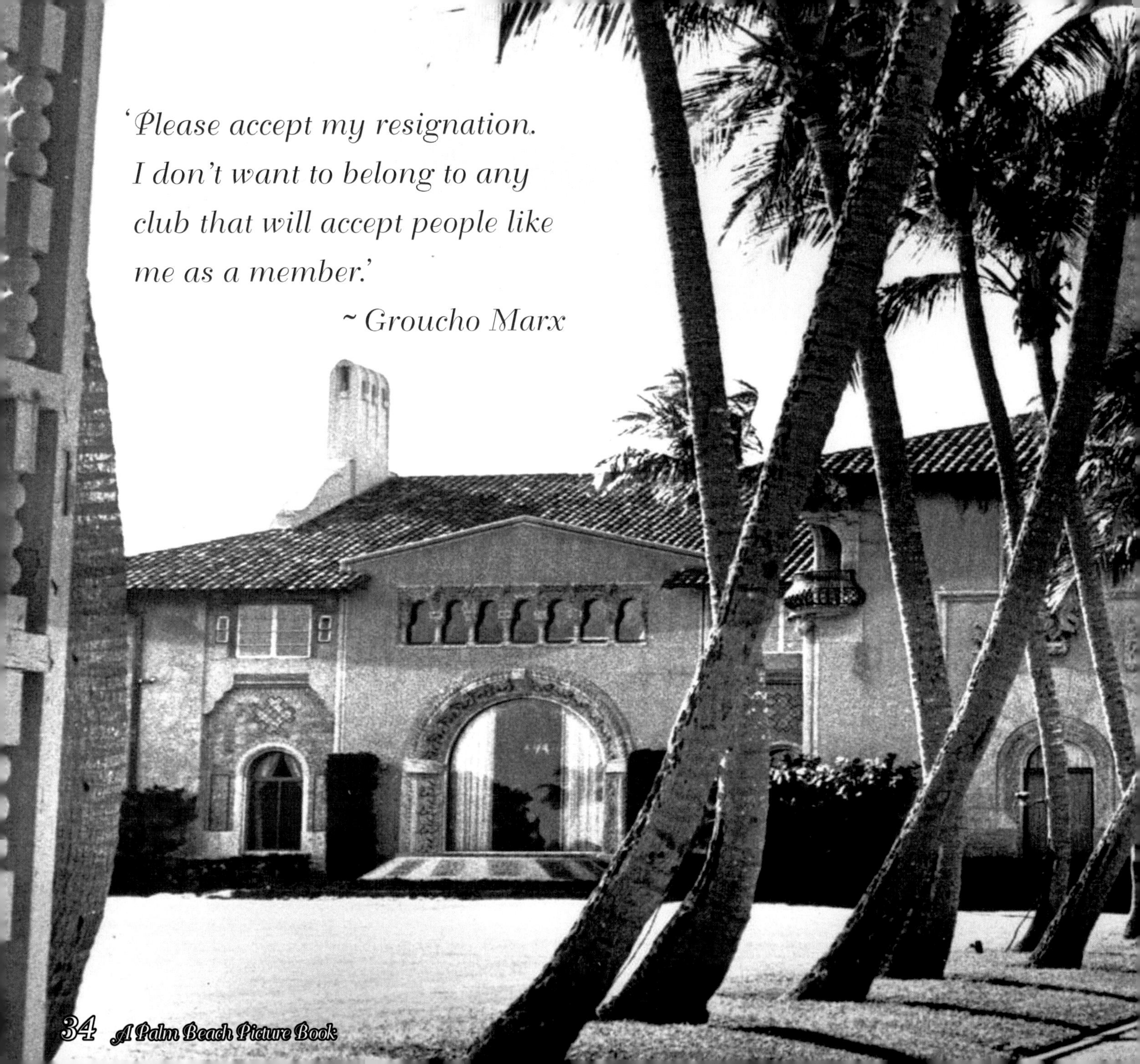

'Please accept my resignation. I don't want to belong to any club that will accept people like me as a member.'

~ Groucho Marx

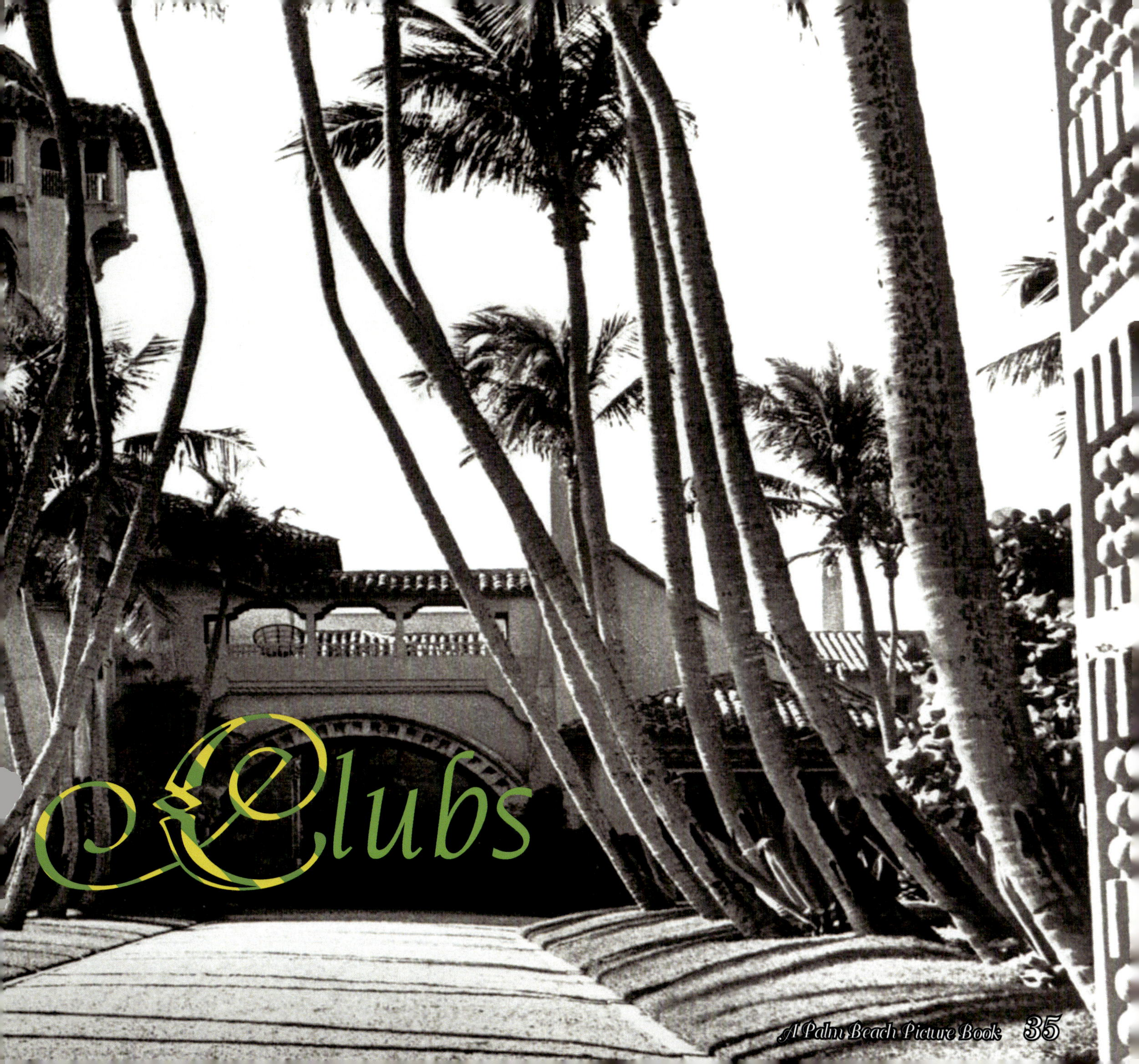

Clubs

Mar-a-Lago

PEOPLE DID GREAT ENTERTAINING in the Mediterranean villas because they were very spacious. Unfortunately, a lot of them have been torn down. The ones still standing are great. Mar-a-Lago, for instance, was built in the mid-twenties by another great architect, *Marion Sims Wyeth*. In fact, Marjorie Merriweather Post wanted Mar-a-Lago to be the 'Winter Whitehouse,' so that when foreign dignitaries came down they would have somewhere suitable to stay.

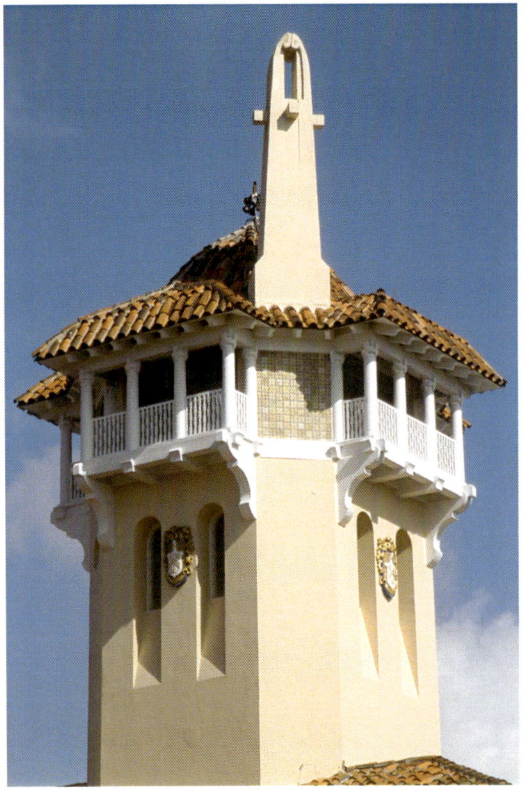

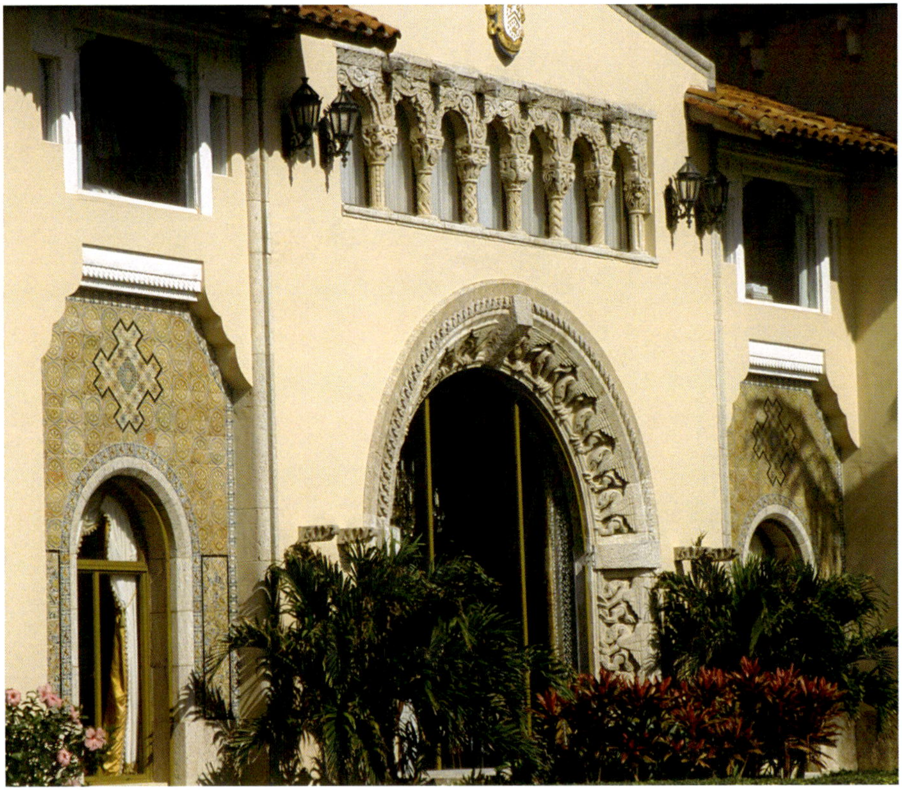

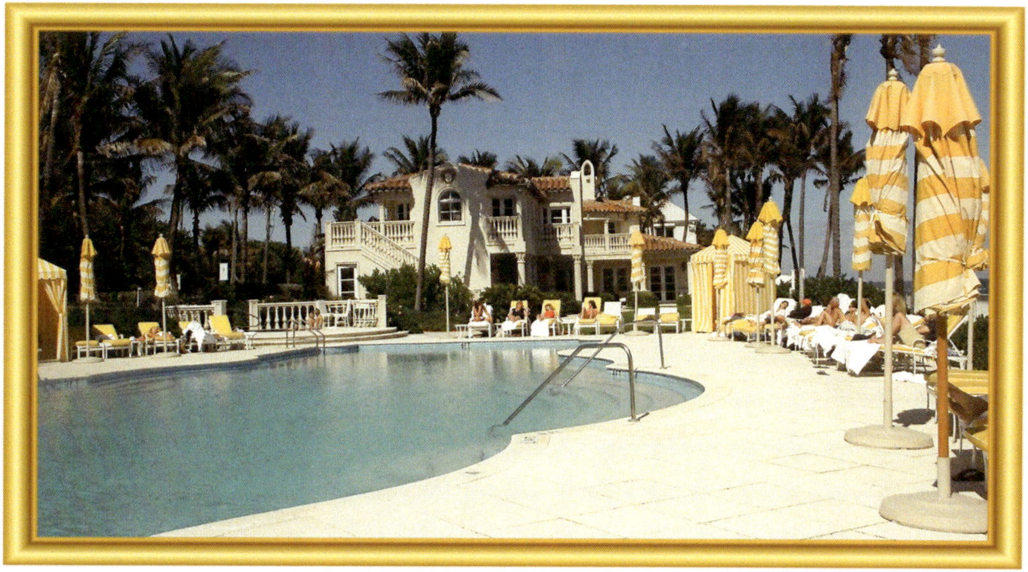

Mar-a-Lago Beach Club

"WHEN DONALD TRUMP BOUGHT MAR-A-LAGO and turned it into a private club, it was one of the most amazing houses in the world! He really has infused Palm Beach with an excitement because going to Mar-a-Lago is like going to a giant private home, not like going to The Breakers where you're going to a hotel. When going to Mar-a-Lago, you're going to see Marjorie Merriweather Post's house. He's always attracted a high end group of people there because everyone knows to go there you have to be a member. And the memberships are really expensive. He's maintained a certain strata of people. Now, people are noticing that he's allowing a lot of other people to come in. But he brings in a lot of big name entertainers too, which socialites enjoy."

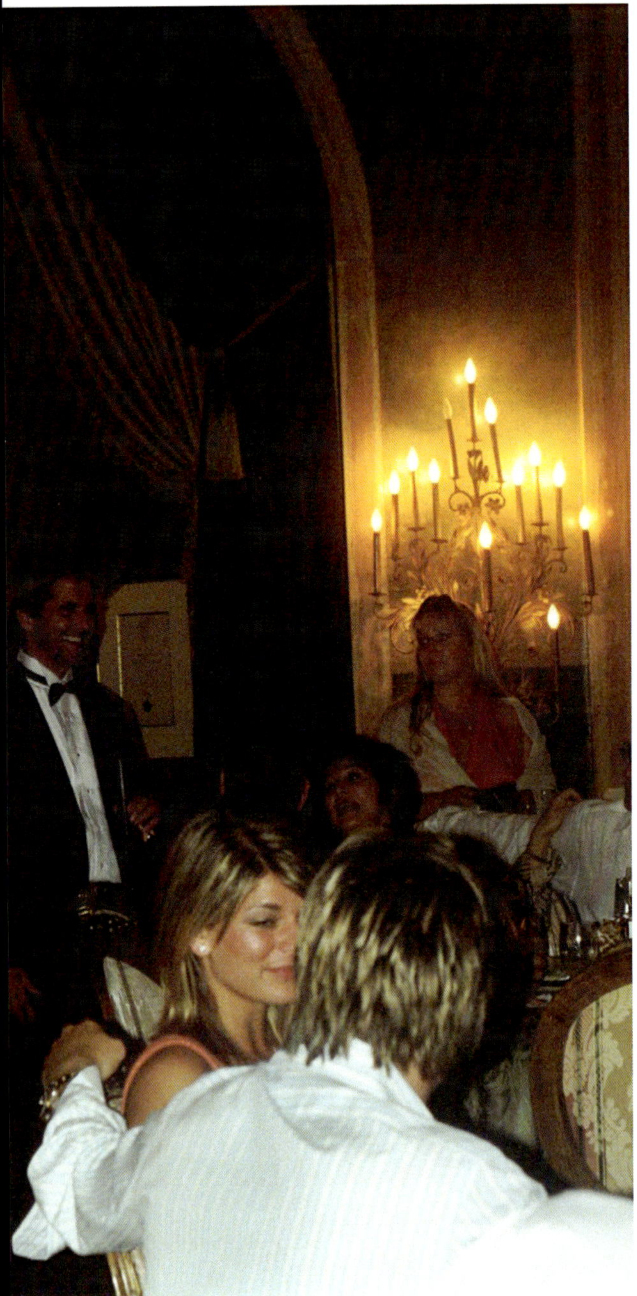

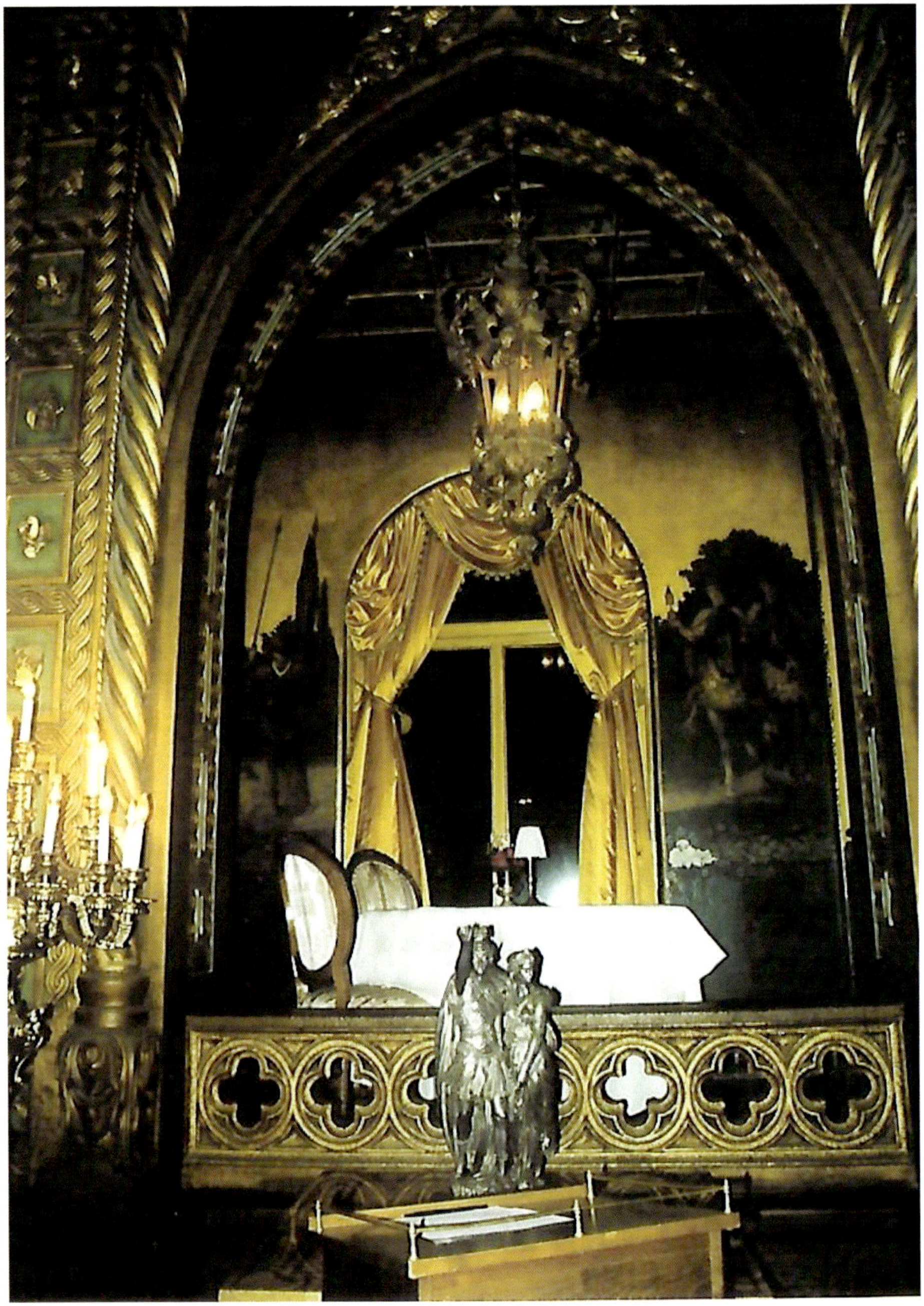

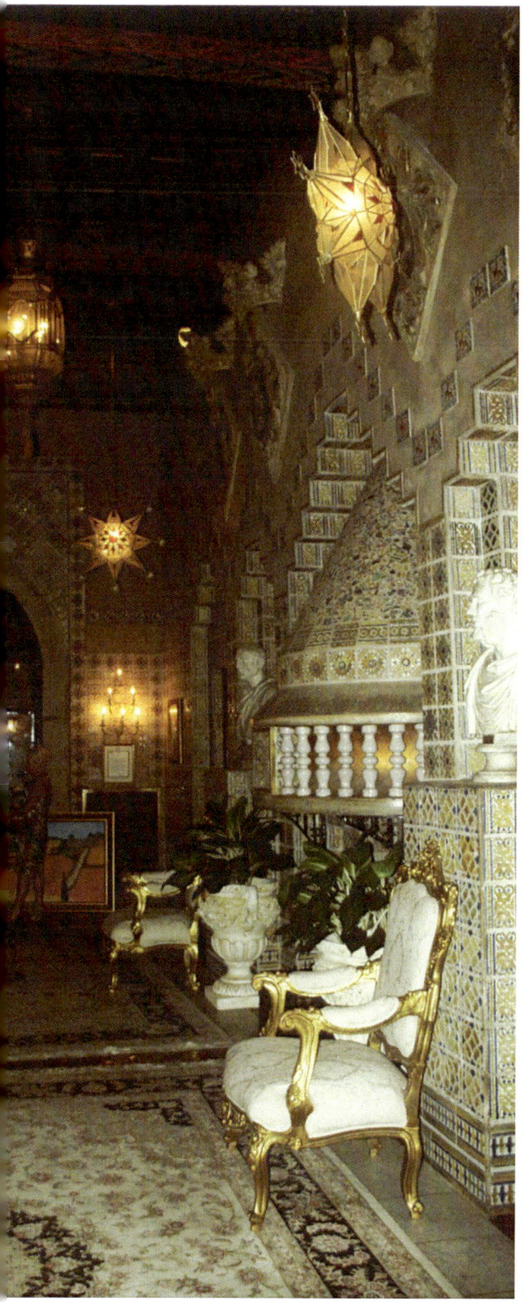

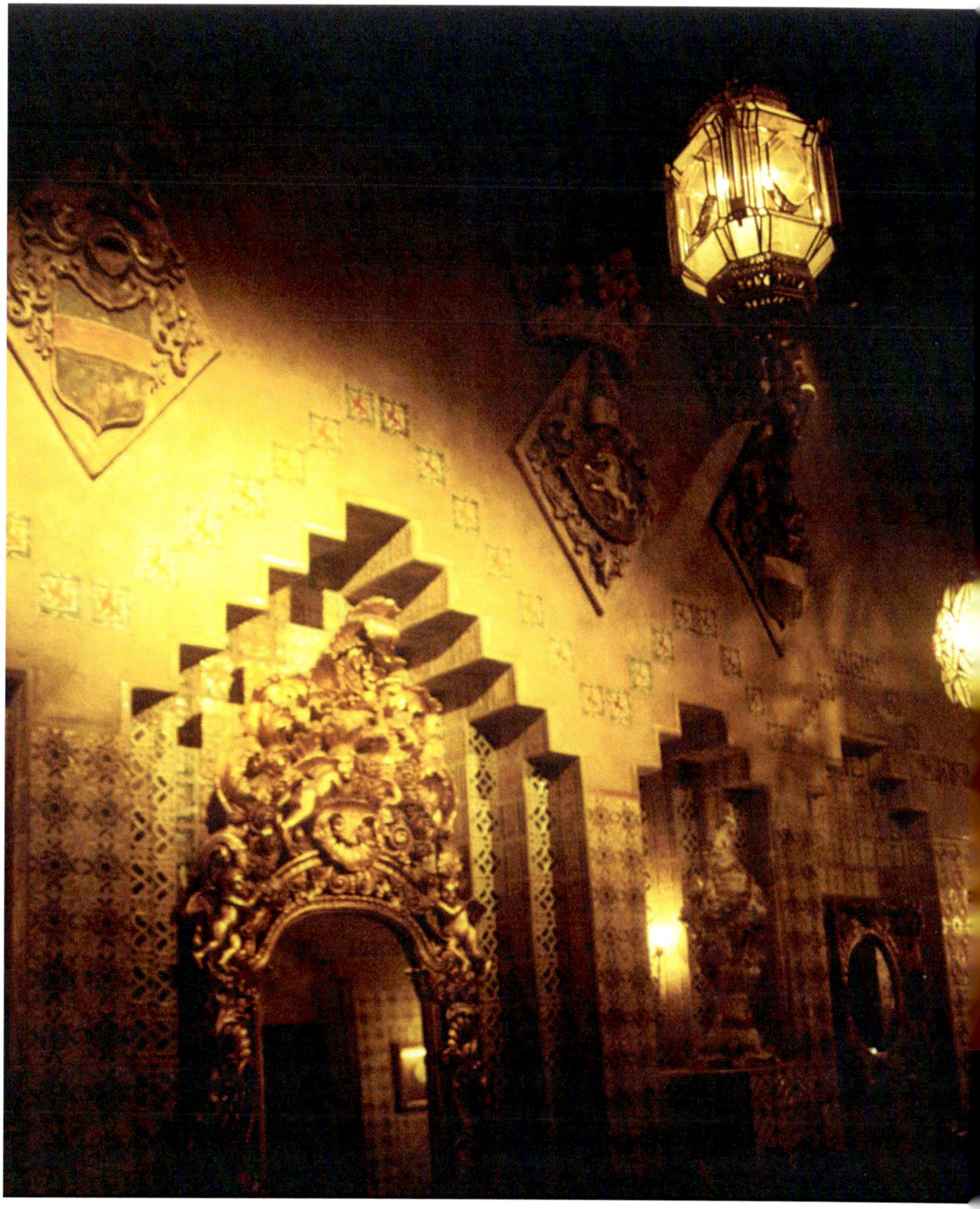

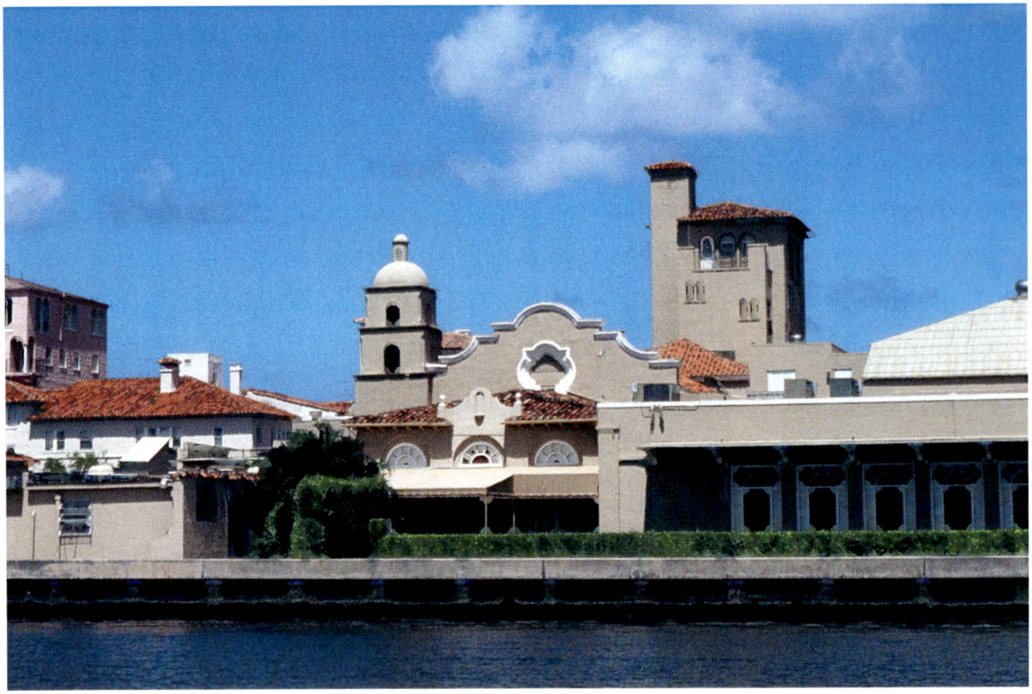

Everglades Club

BY THAT TIME WWI HAD STARTED and Palm Beach had grown to Worth Avenue, Singer was in his money. What he wanted to do was to create a private club. Addison Mizner was going to design it, but anything built had to be for the war effort. So, Mizner's commission was to build a facility to be used as a convalescent place for soldiers injured in the war. The plan was, that when the war was over, they could convert it into a club. Of course it took them so long to build it that the war was over and it never opened as a hospital. Some people thought that they had never really intended to use it as that. Oddly enough, they had purchased a lot of medical equipment which was donated to start what is now Good Samaritan Hospital in West Palm Beach, and the Everglades club opened in 1919.

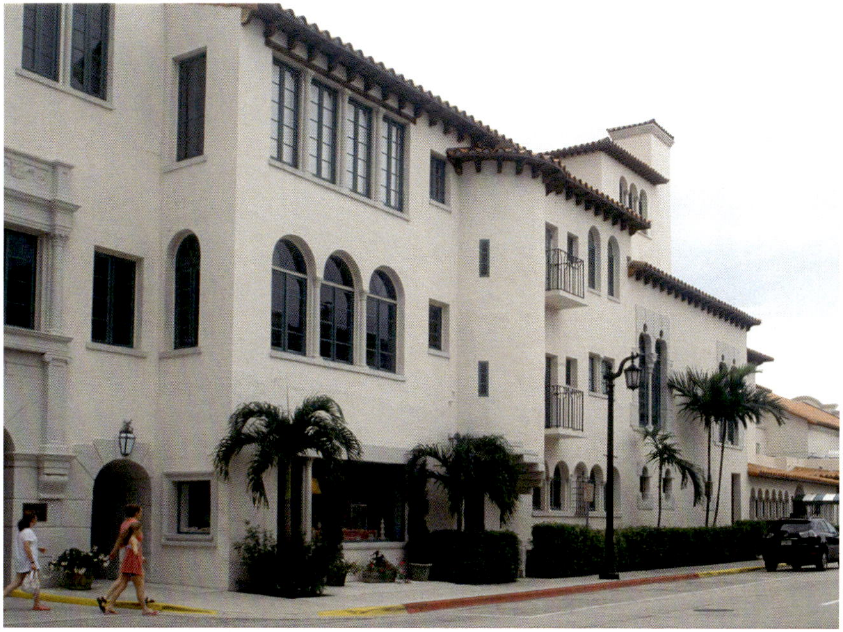

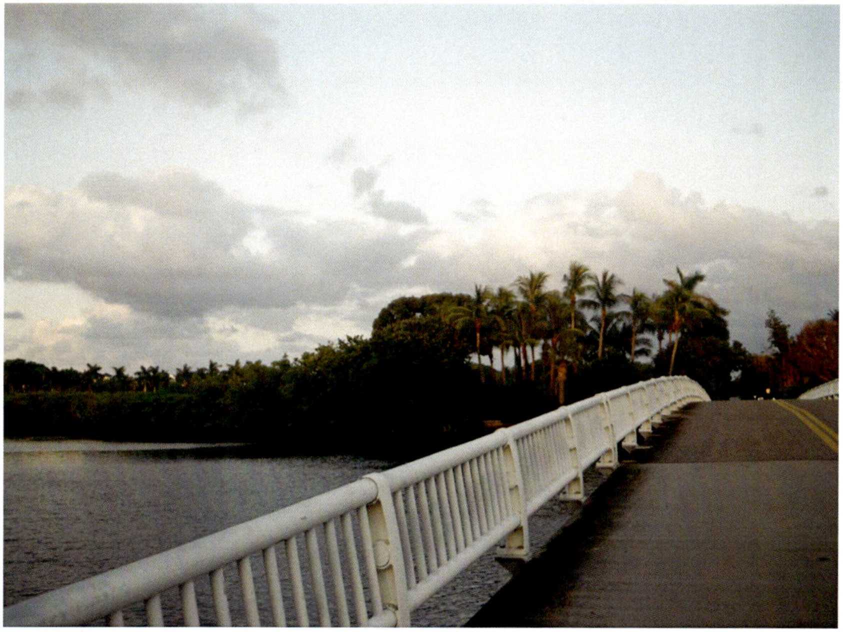

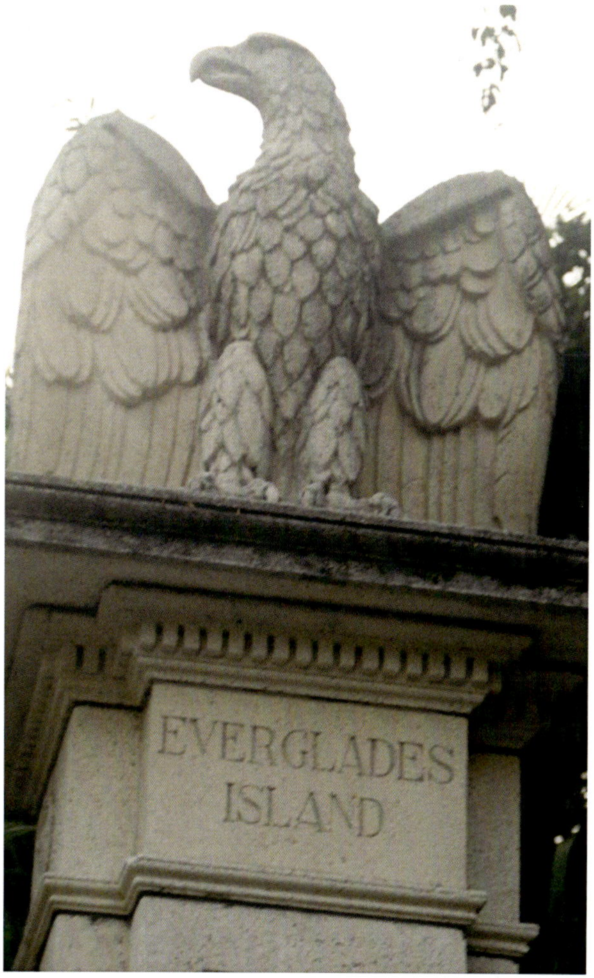
EVERGLADES
ISLAND

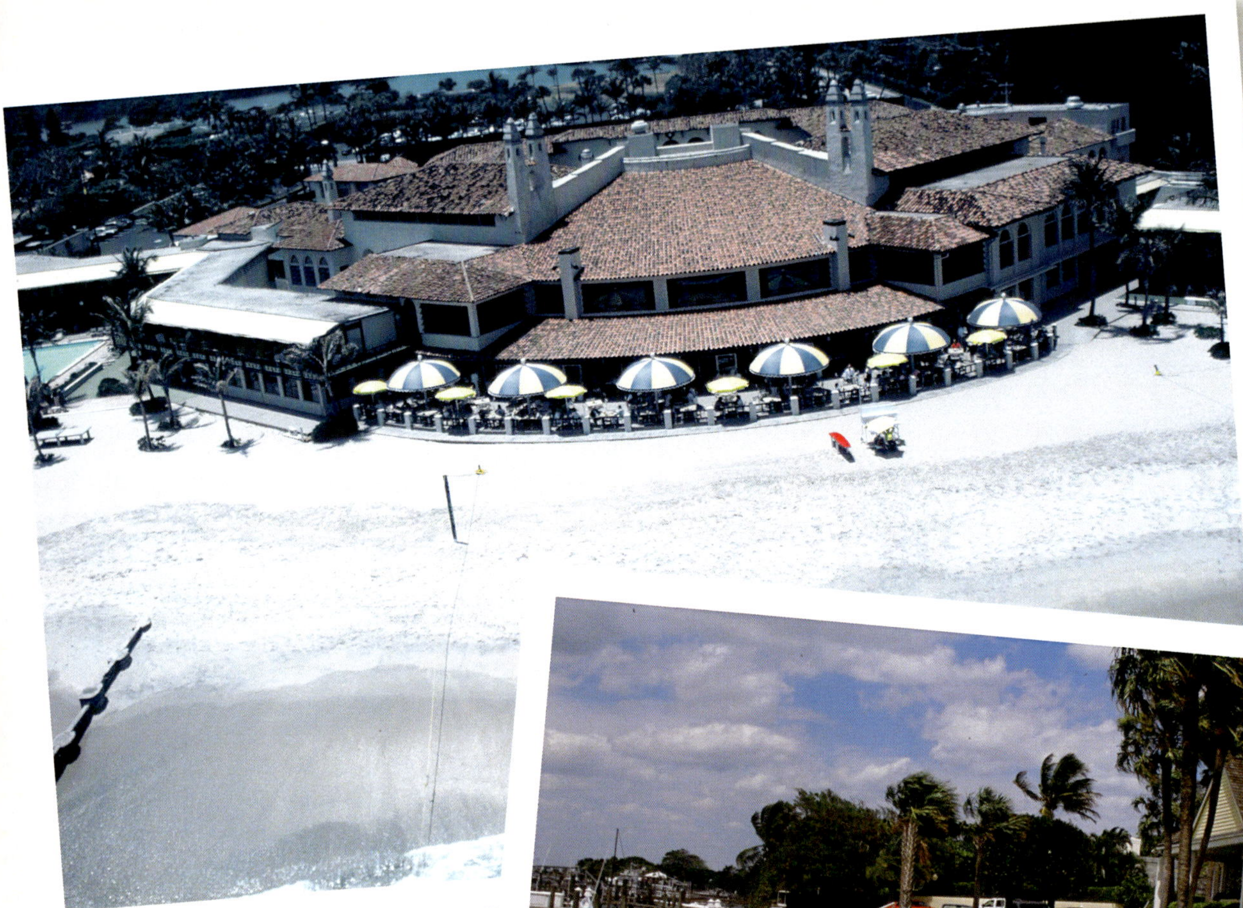

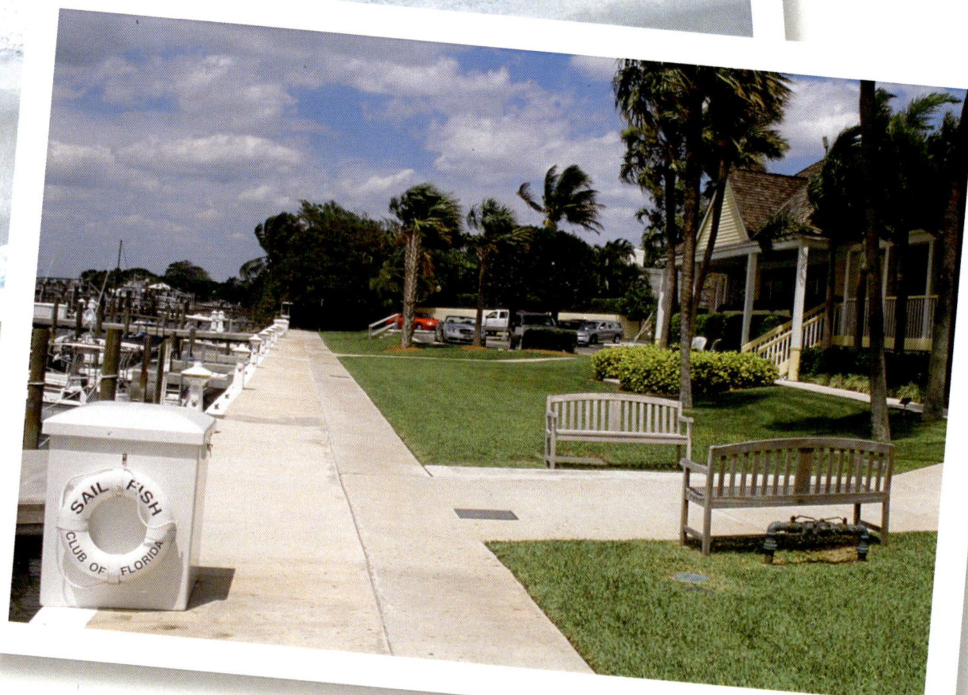
SAIL FISH
CLUB OF FLORIDA

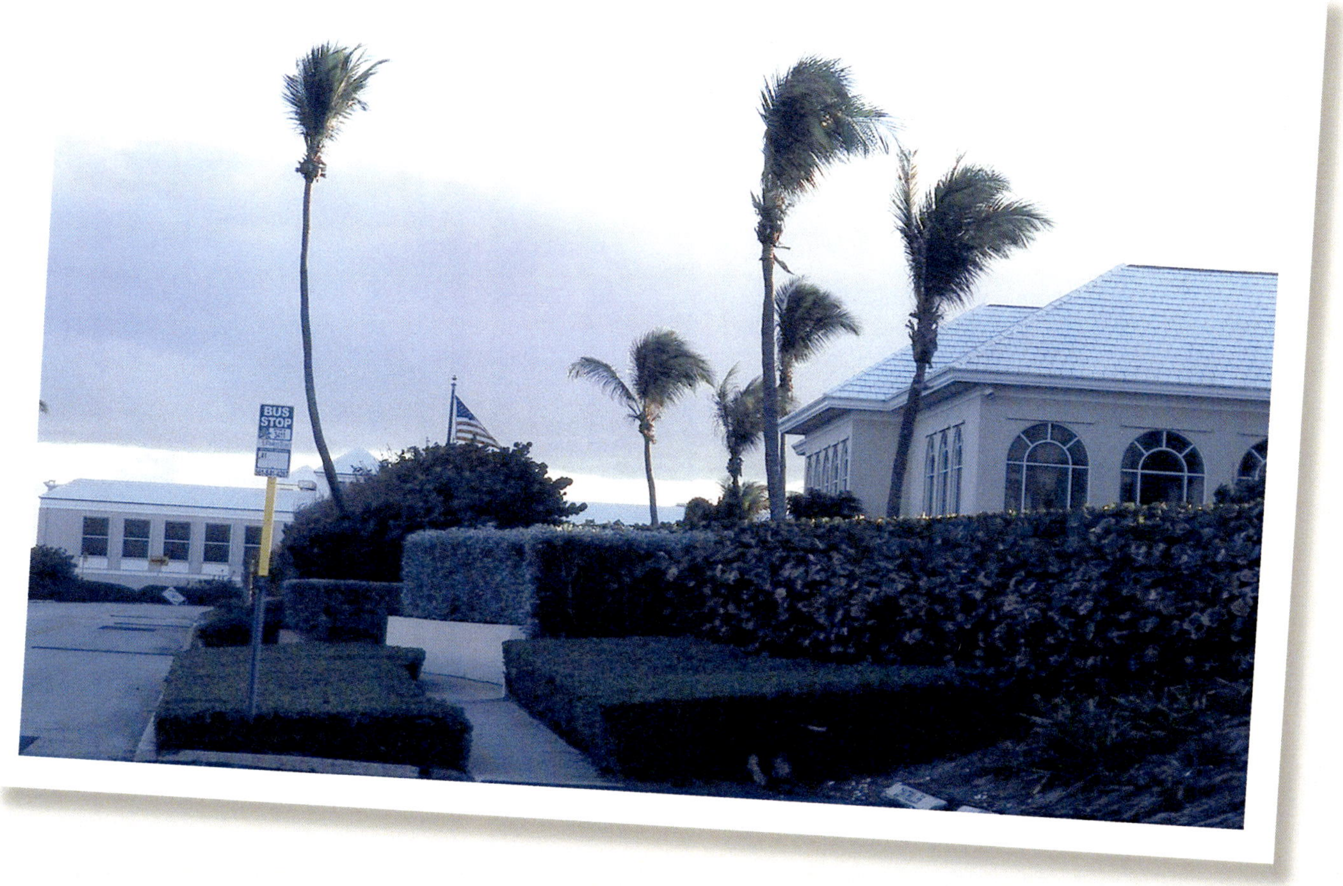

The Palm Beach Country Club

:he only Jewish country club on the island, has endured even after Bernie Madoff swindled fortunes from nany of the club's high profile members. In the early 1960s, it was the only club on the island that welcomed President John F. Kennedy, a Catholic, to play golf. Ironically, The Everglades Club, still a bastion of WASPs, vas built by Paris Singer who was a Jew.

Sports

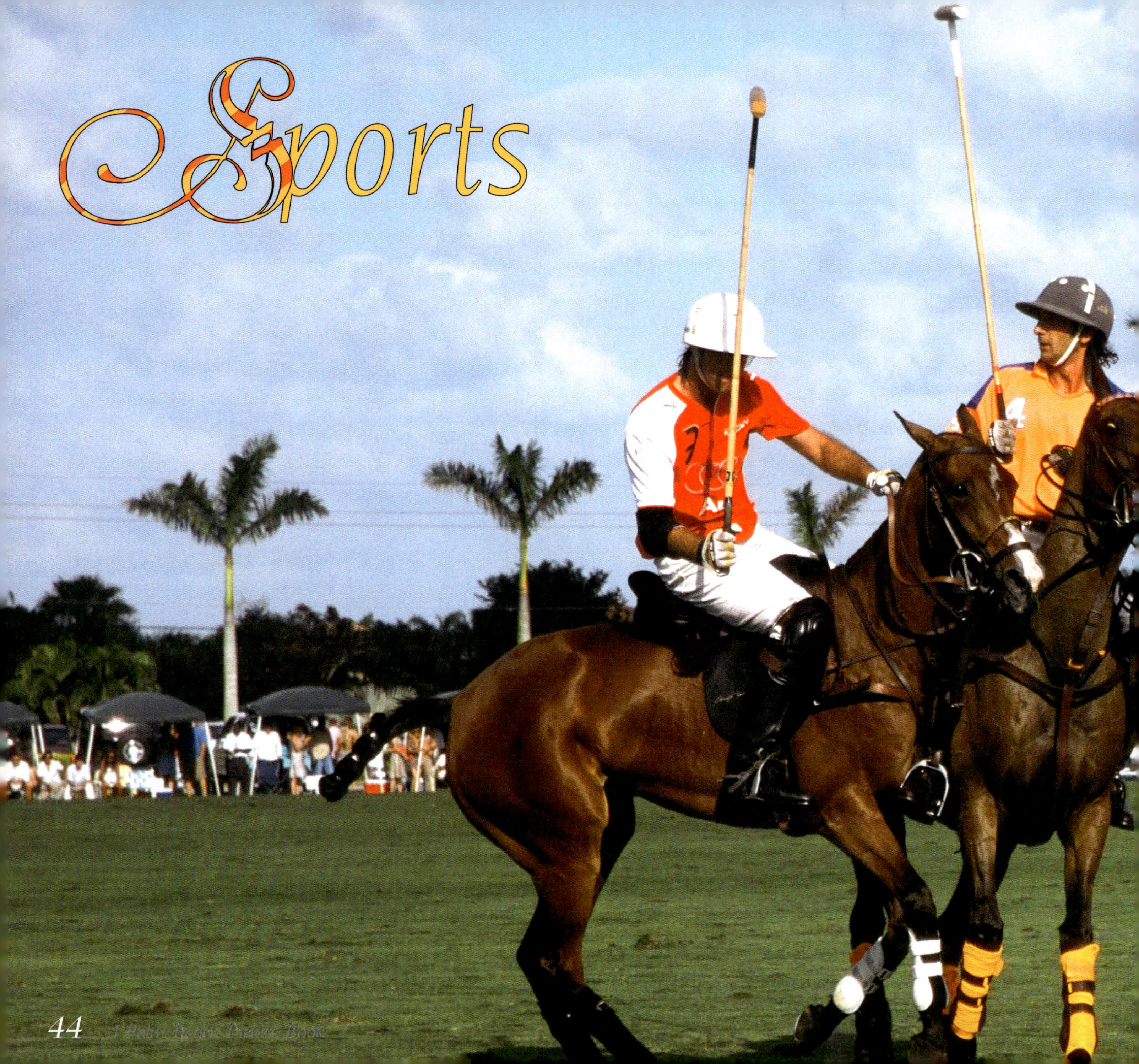

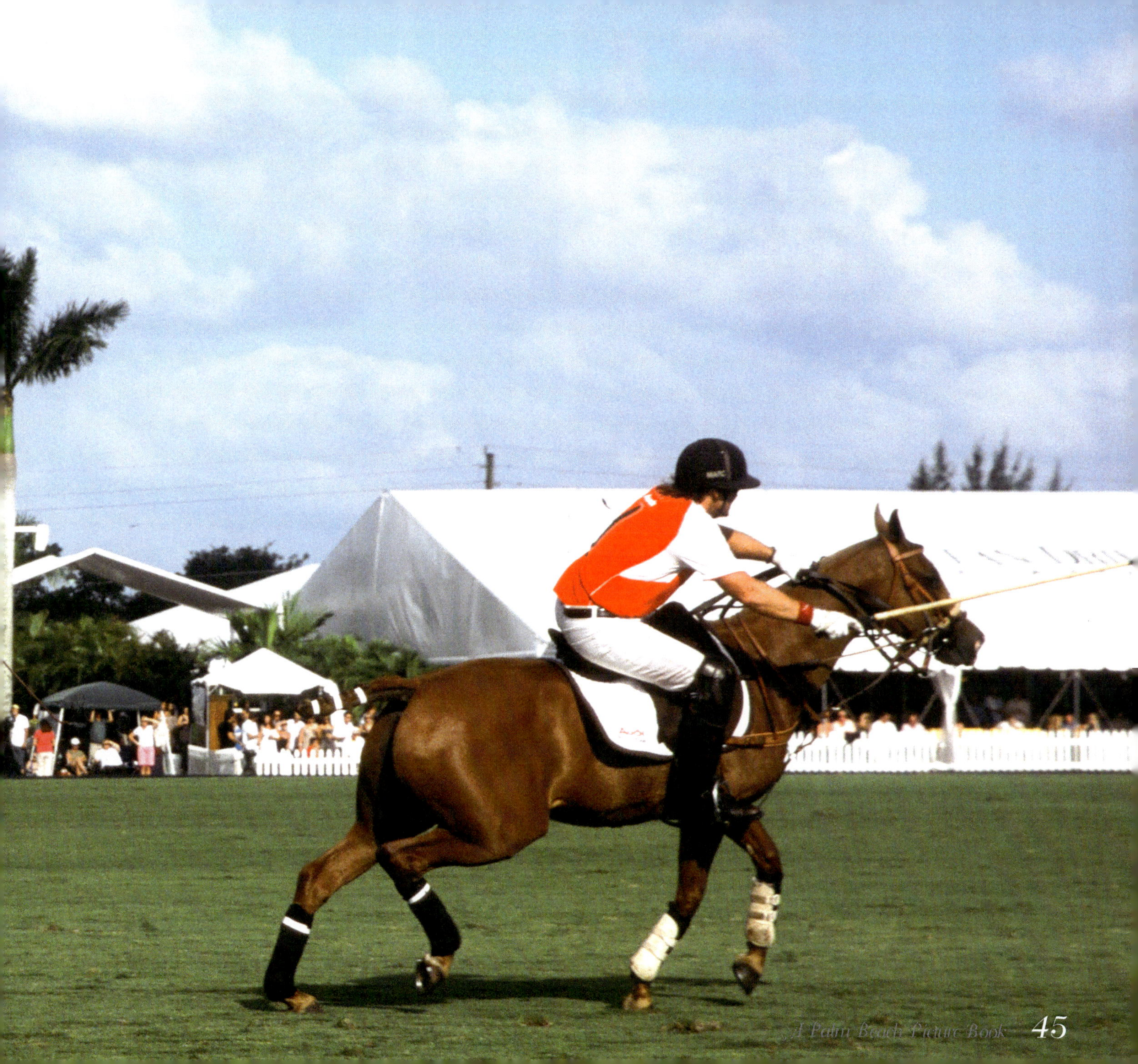

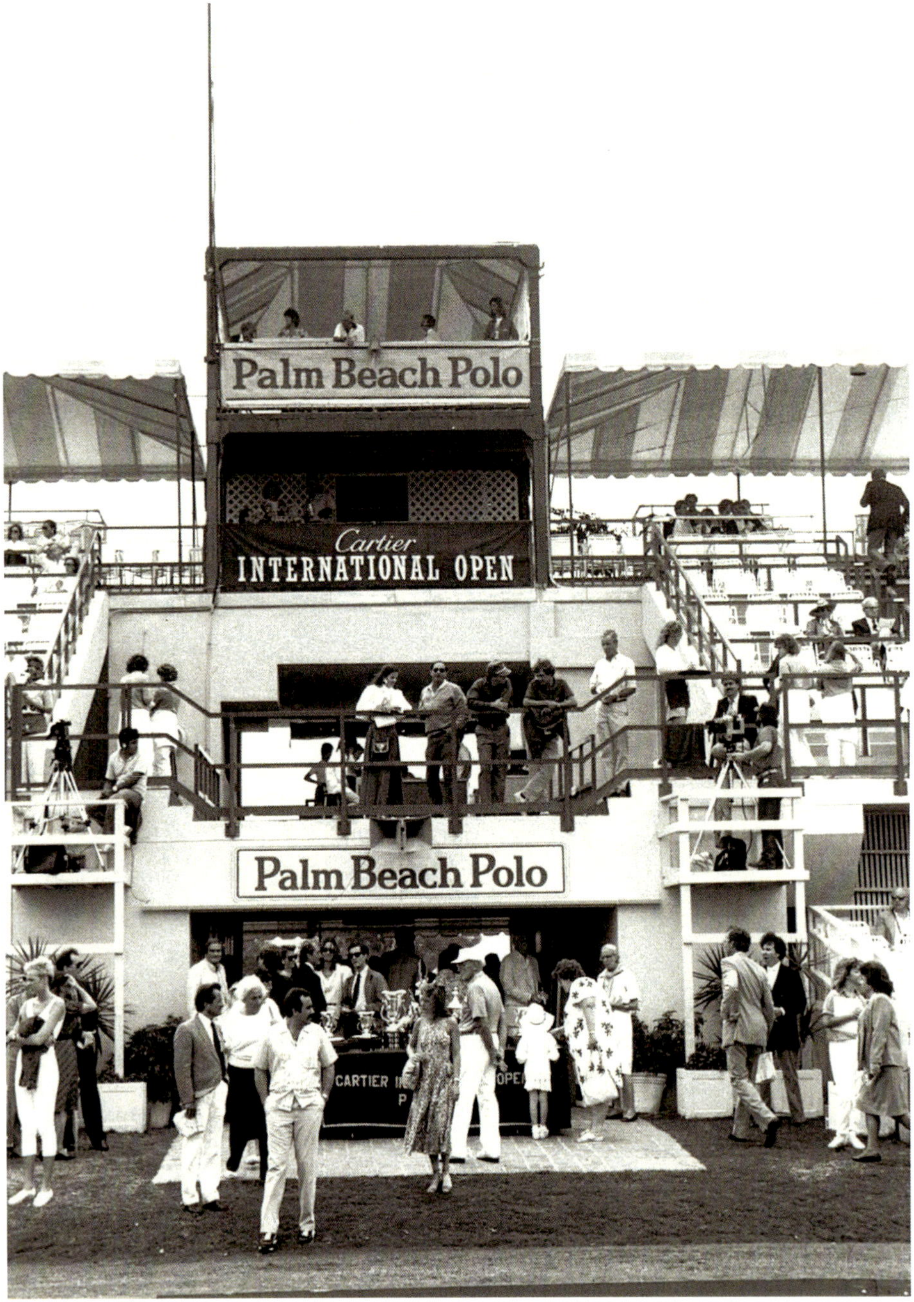
Palm Beach Polo
Cartier
INTERNATIONAL OPEN
Palm Beach Polo

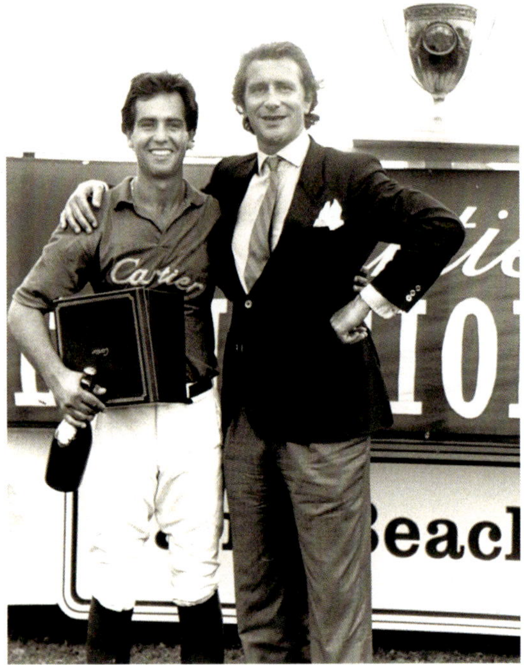
Cartier

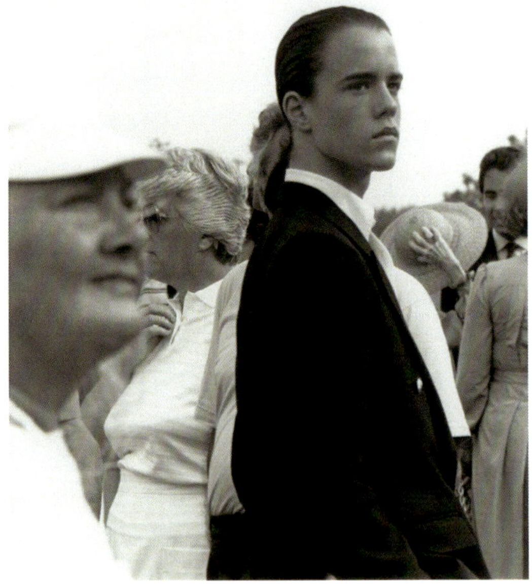

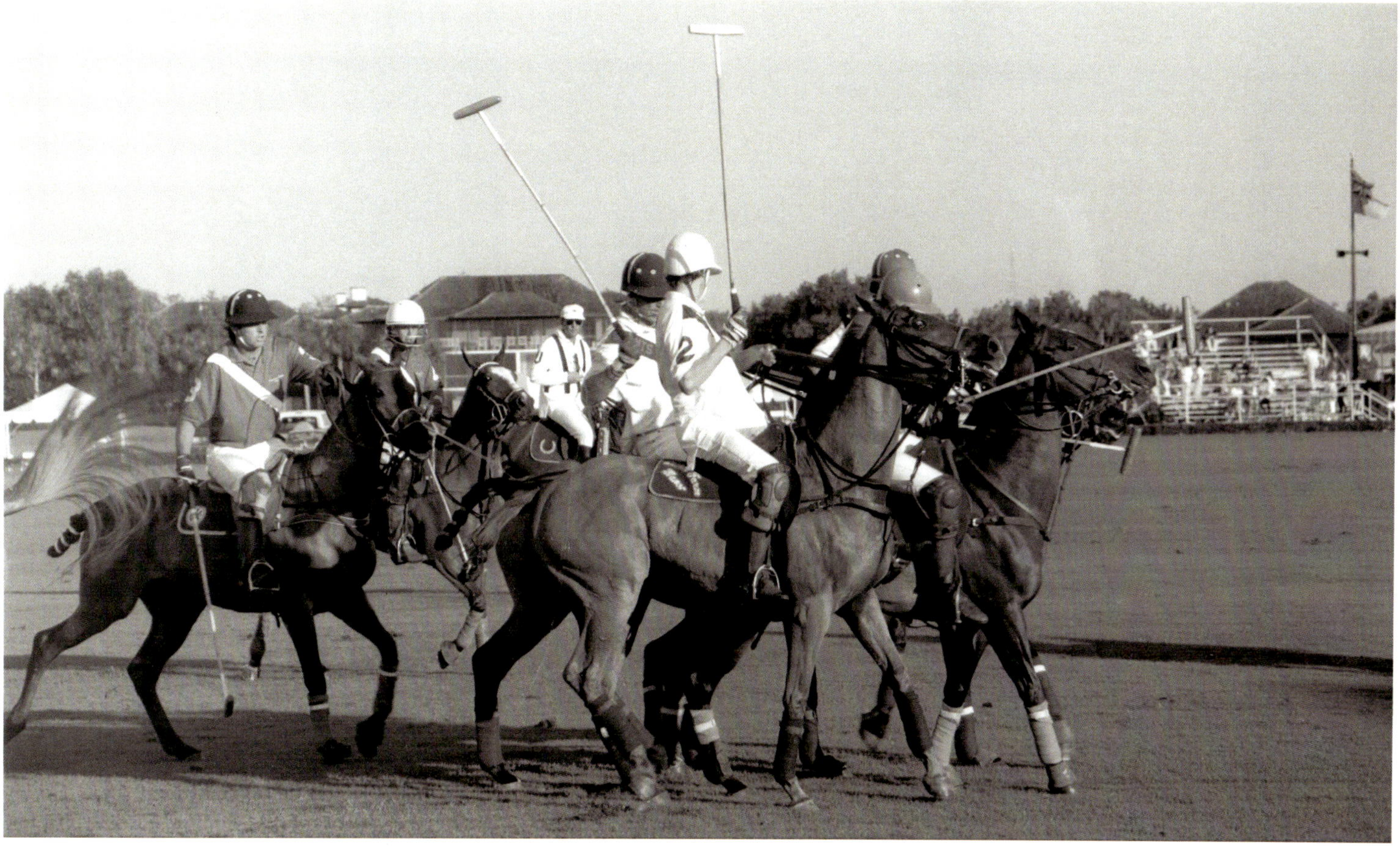

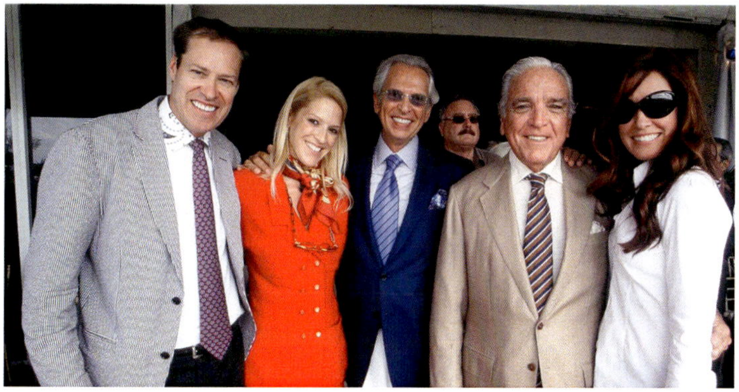

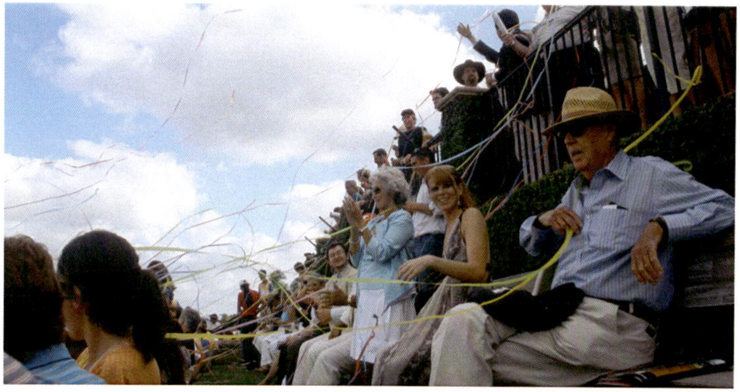

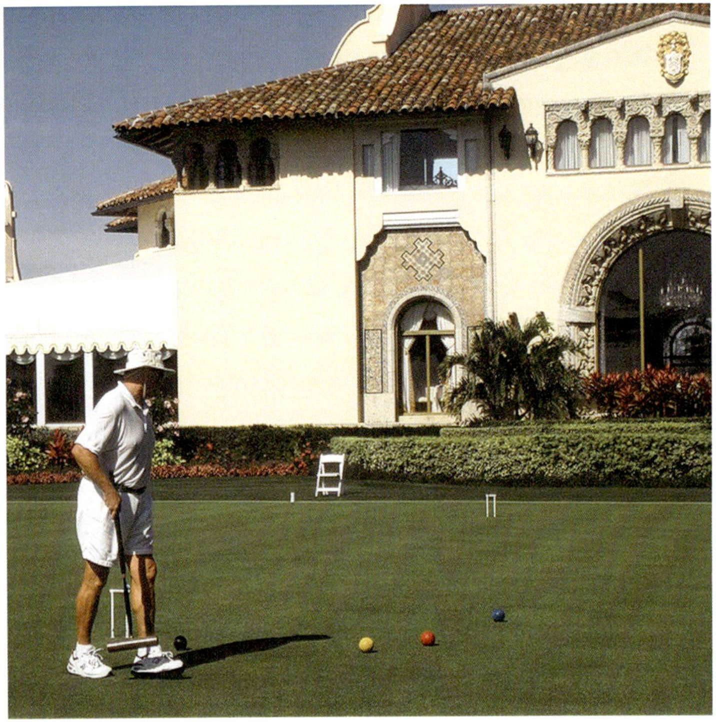

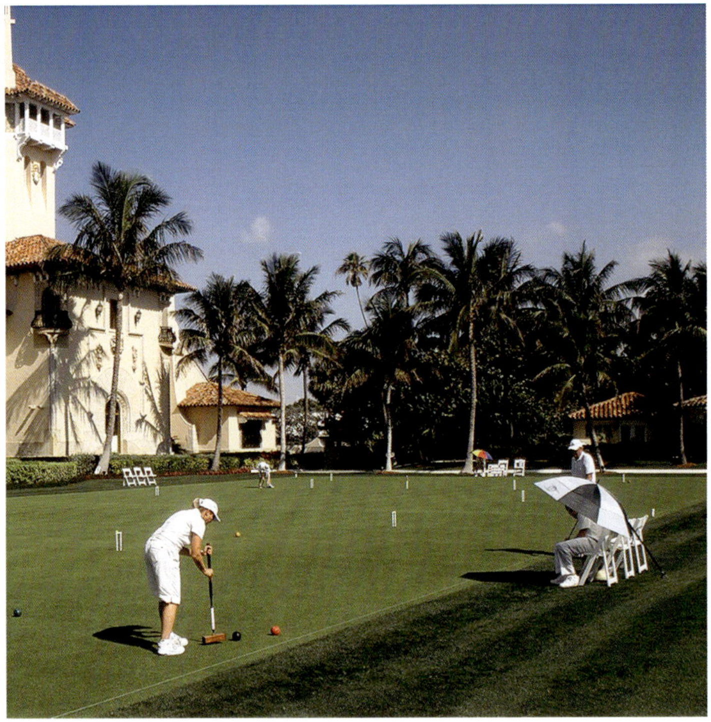

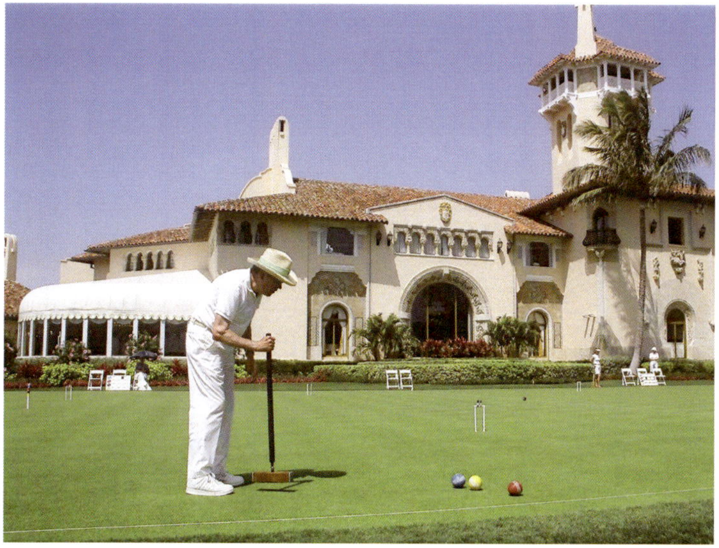

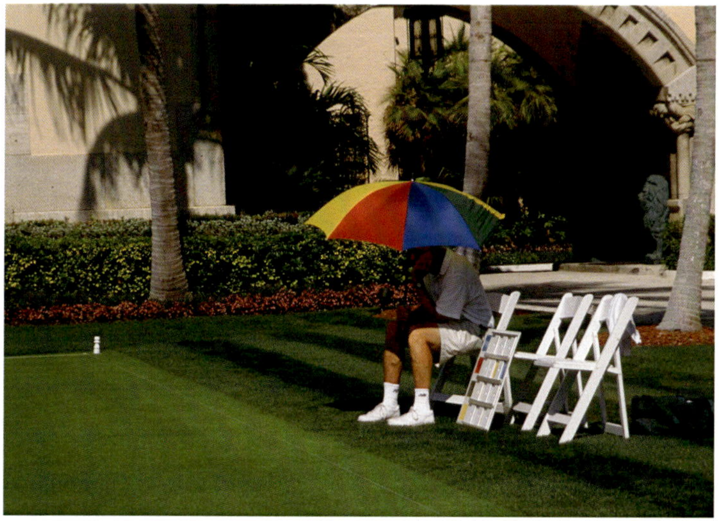

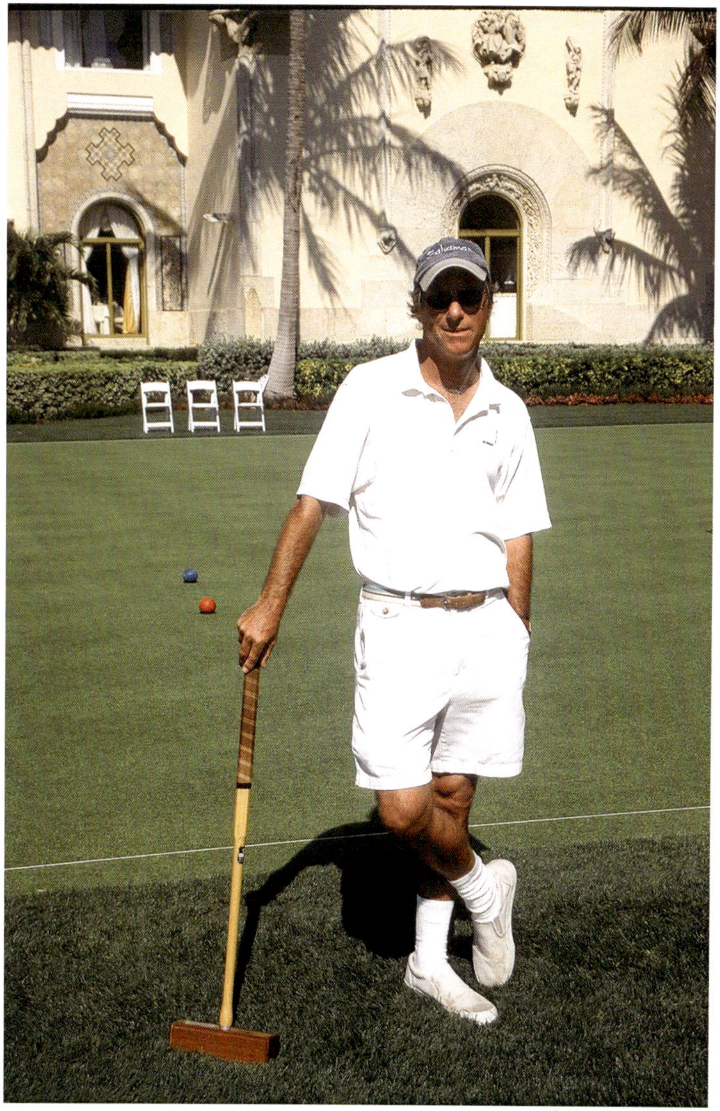

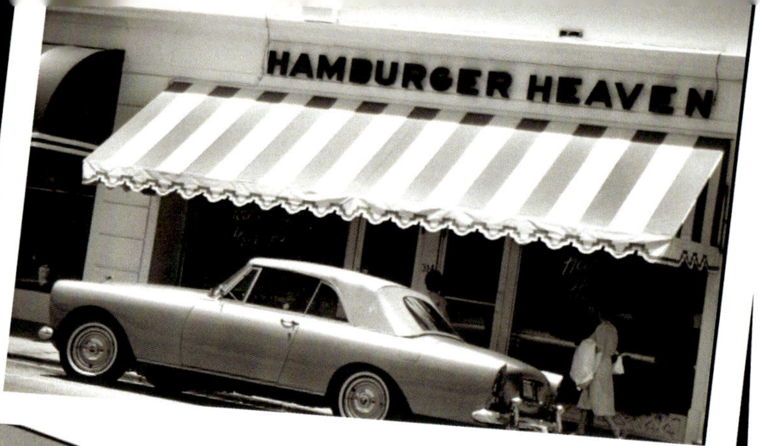
HAMBURGER HEAVEN

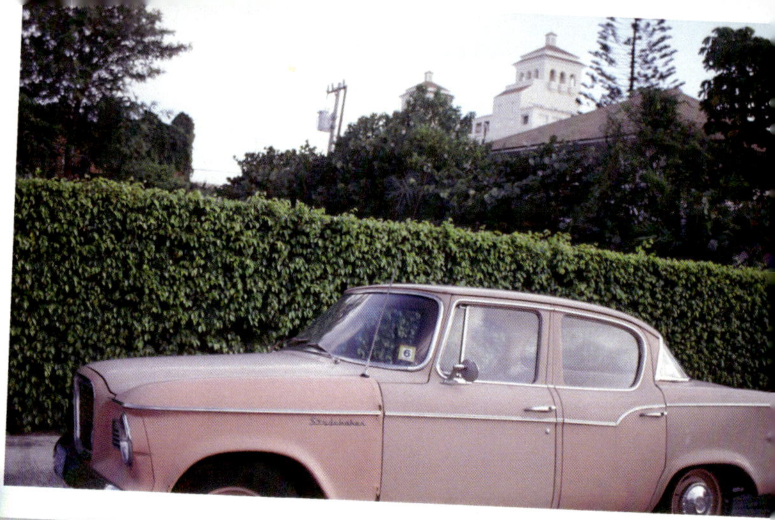

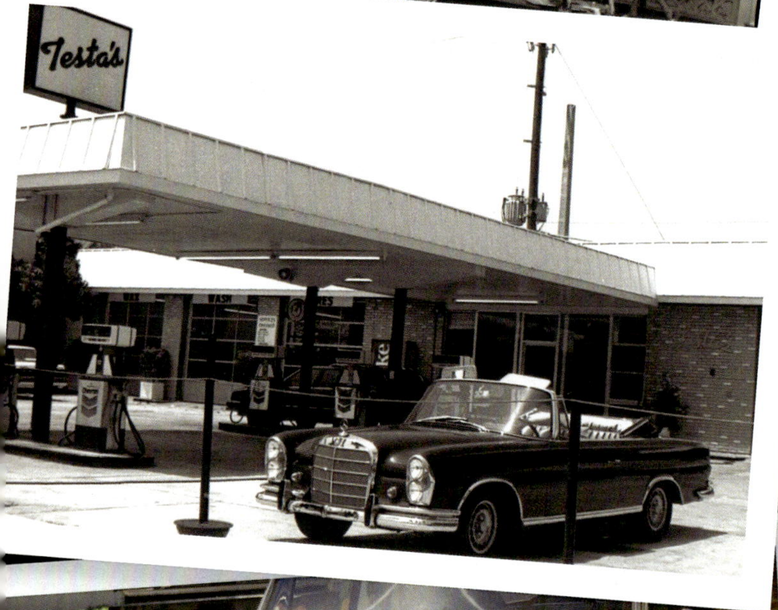
Testa's

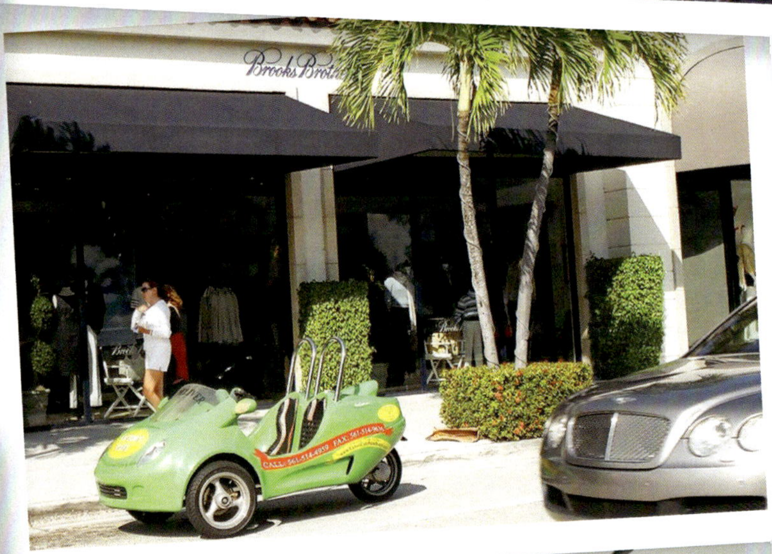

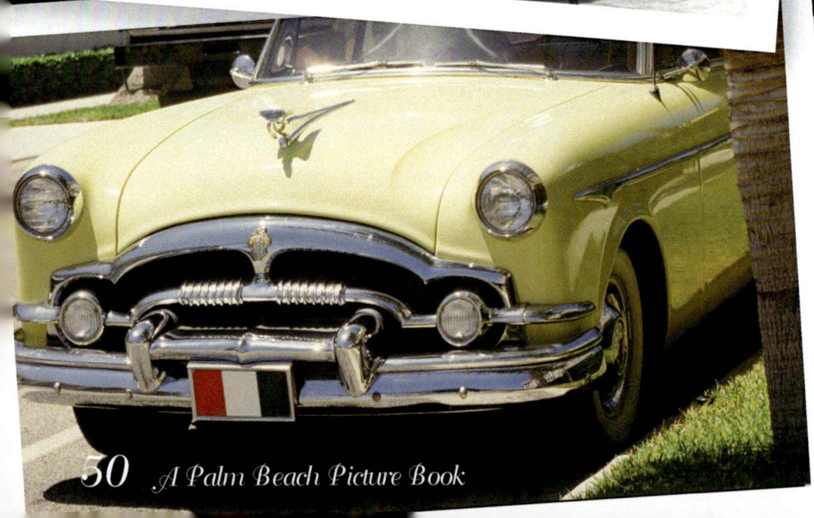

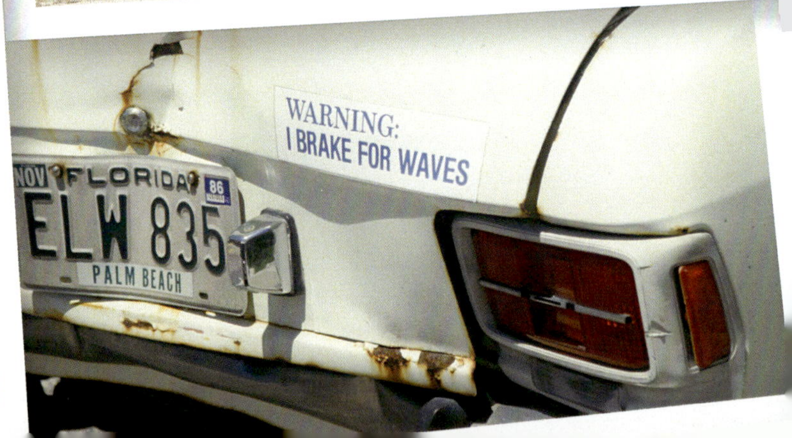
WARNING:
I BRAKE FOR WAVES
NOV FLORIDA 86
ELW 835
PALM BEACH

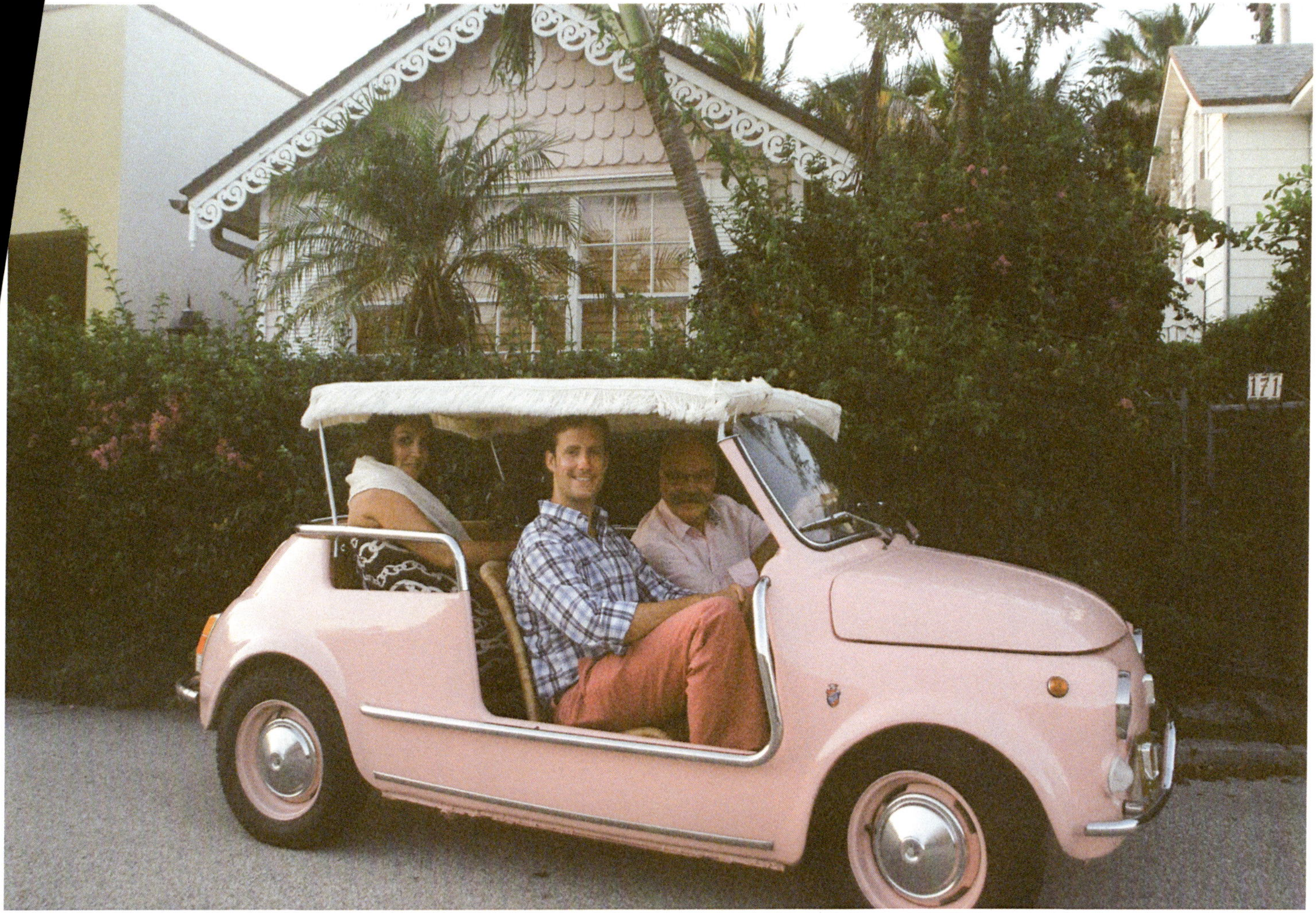

Cars

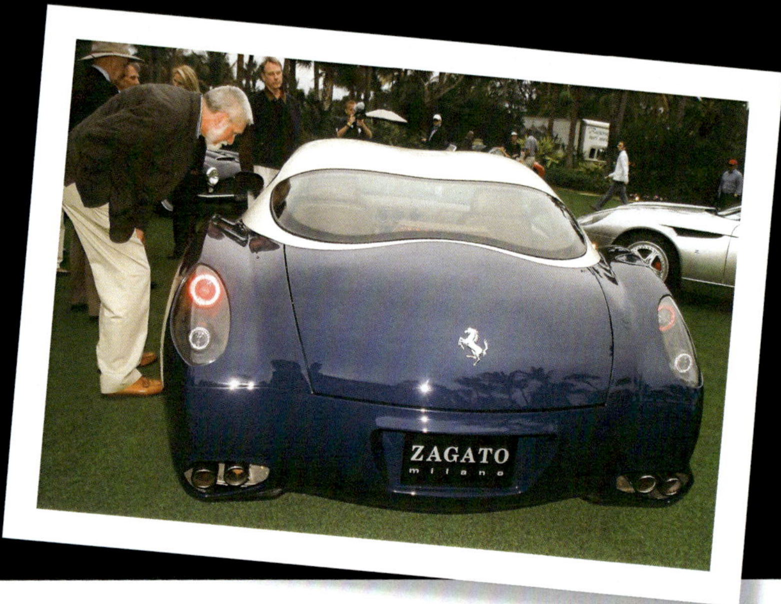
ZAGATO
milano

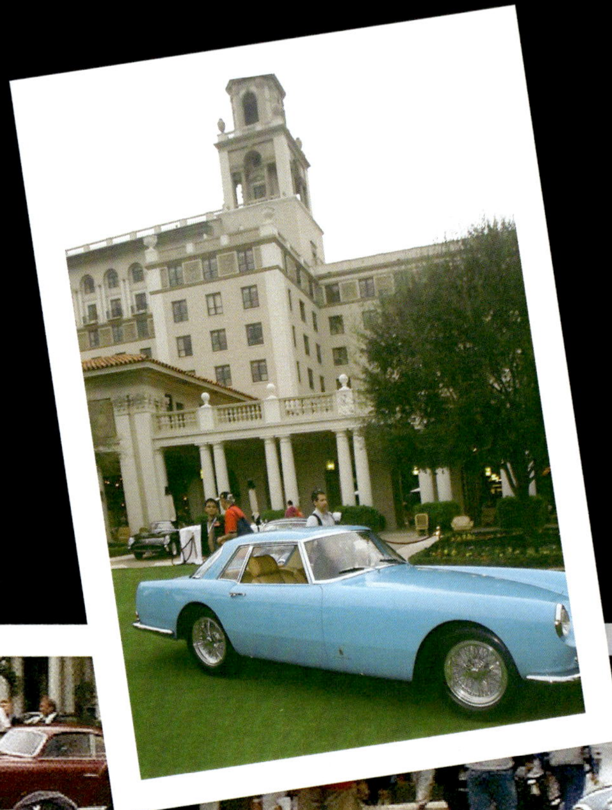

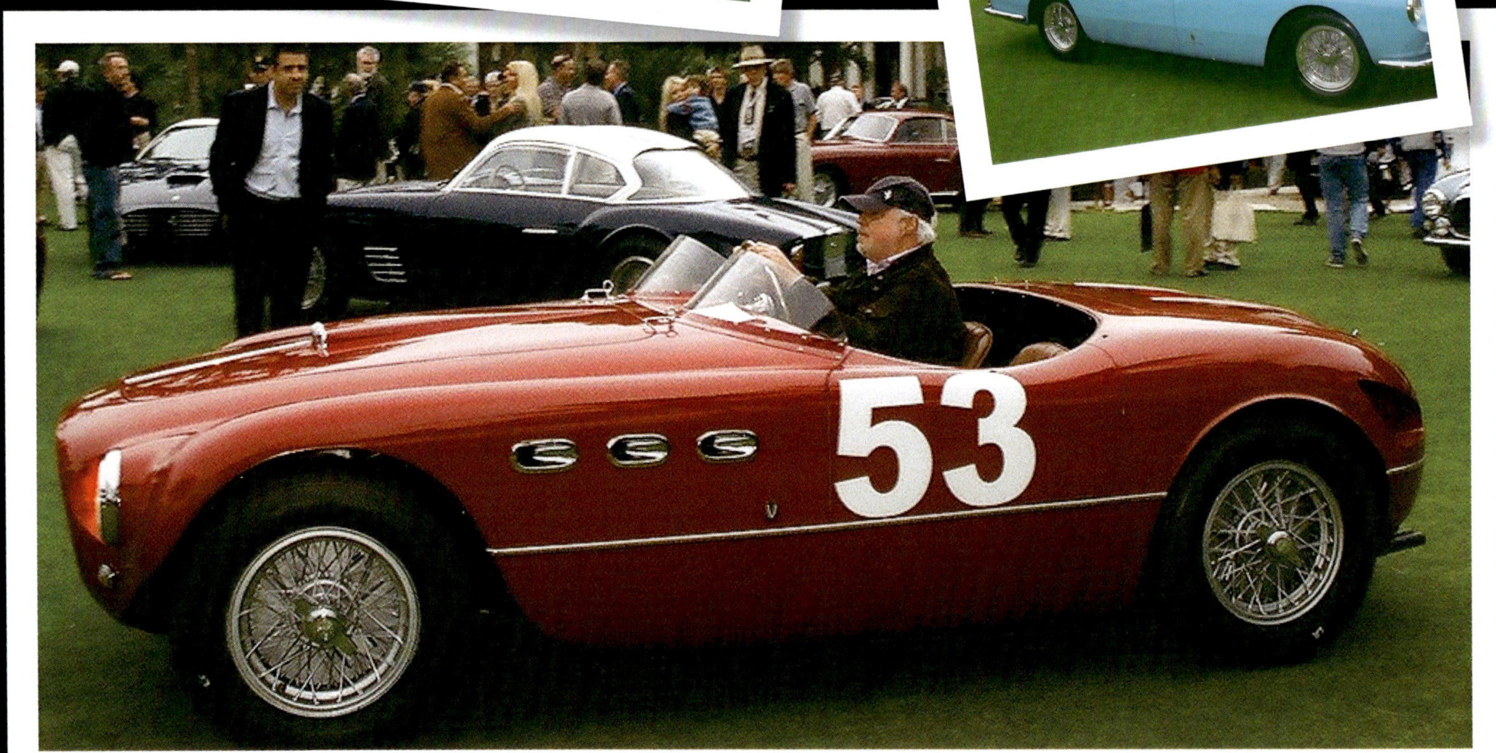
53

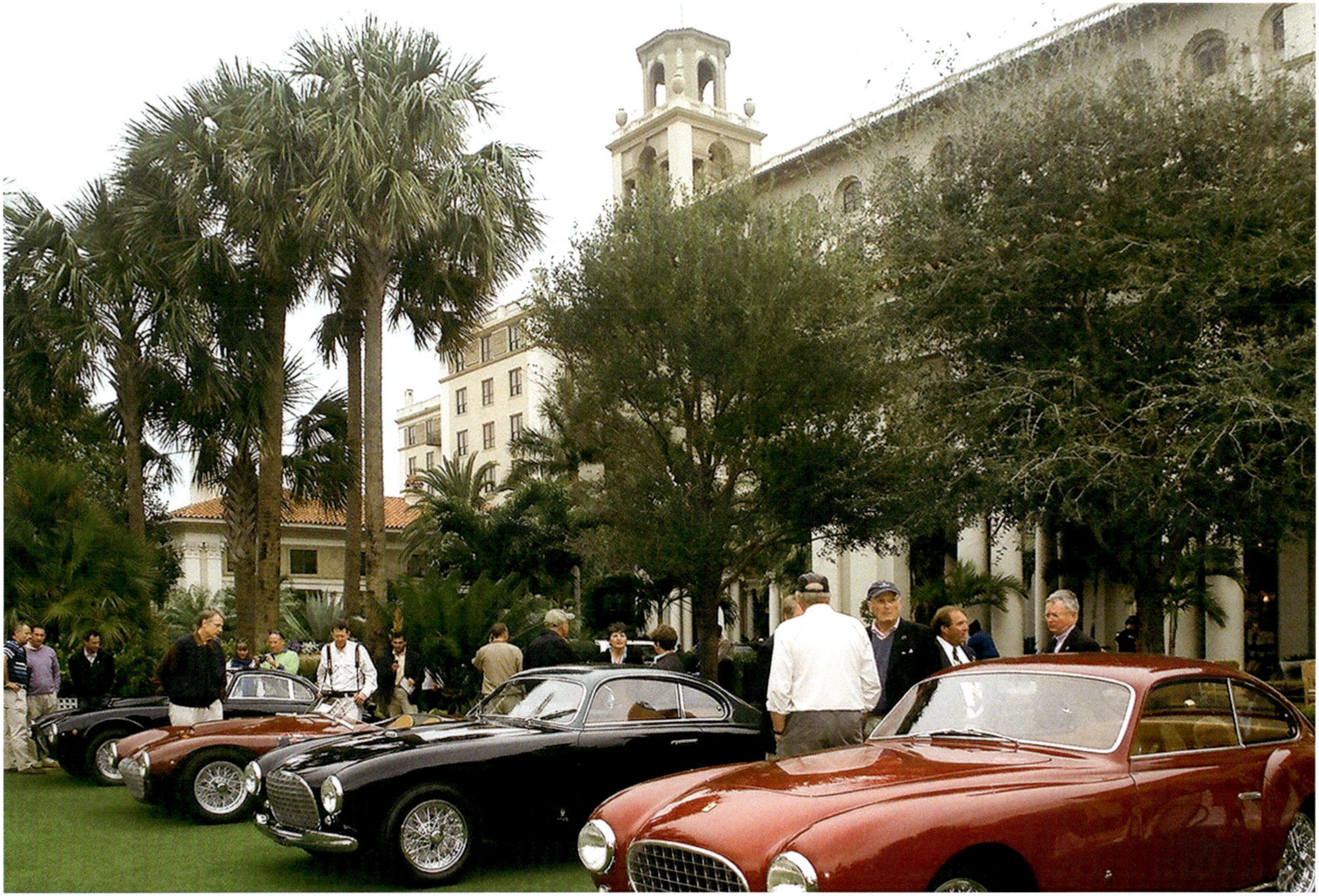

Ferrari Envy at The Breakers

DAZZLED BY SPARKLING HAND-BUFFED CHROME, a coterie of car-lovers gather at the Breakers Hotel once a year for the Cavallino Classic Car Show. There, Palm Beachers ruminate over vintage Ferraris restored to perfection, just the thing to drive to Green's Pharmacy.

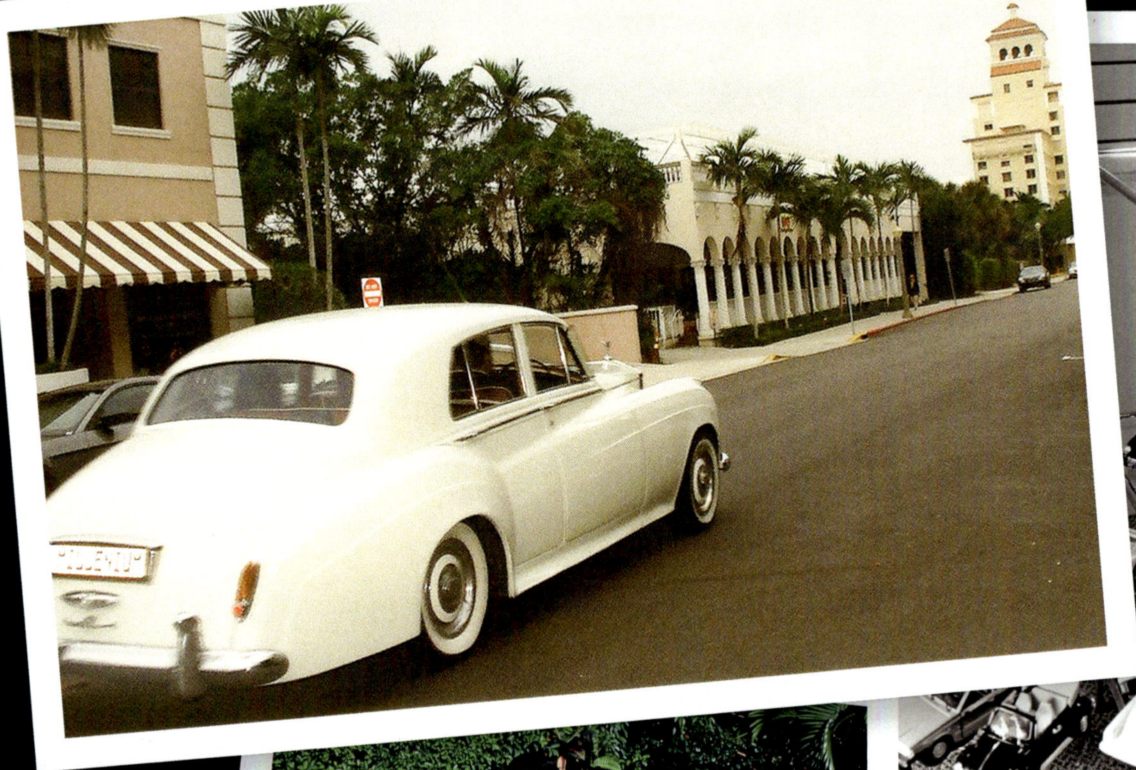

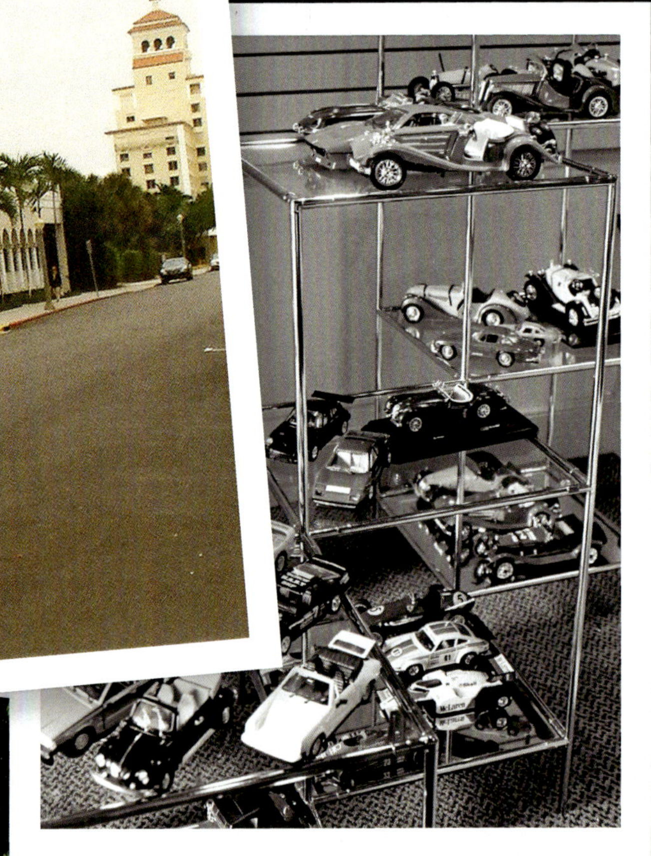

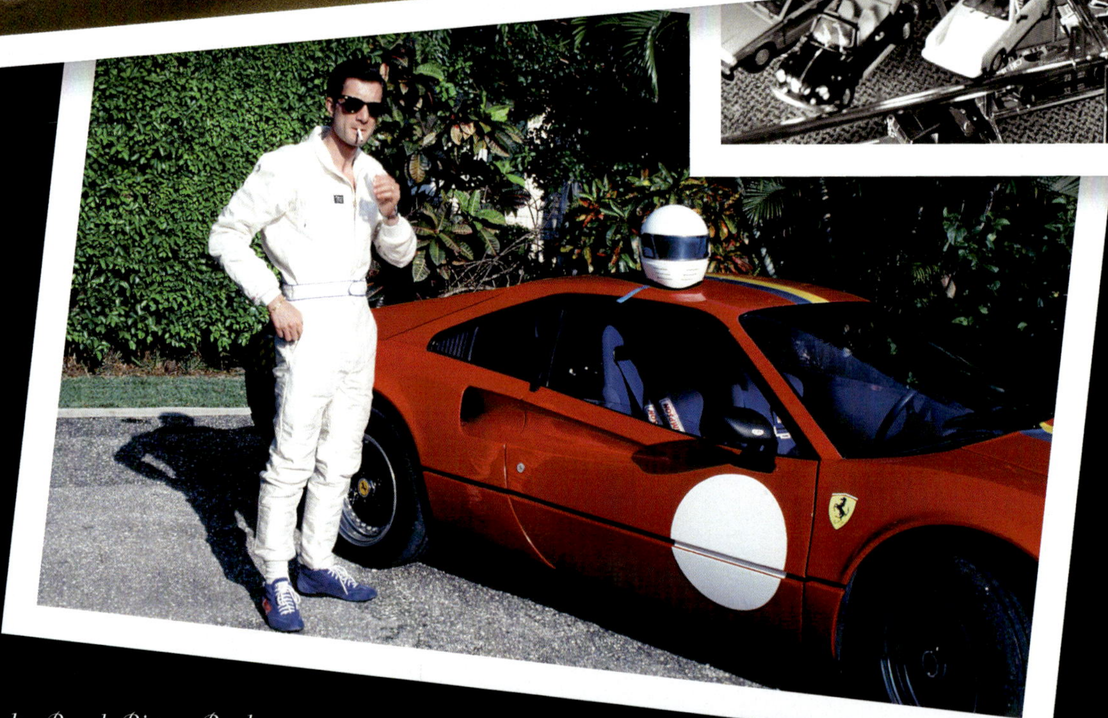

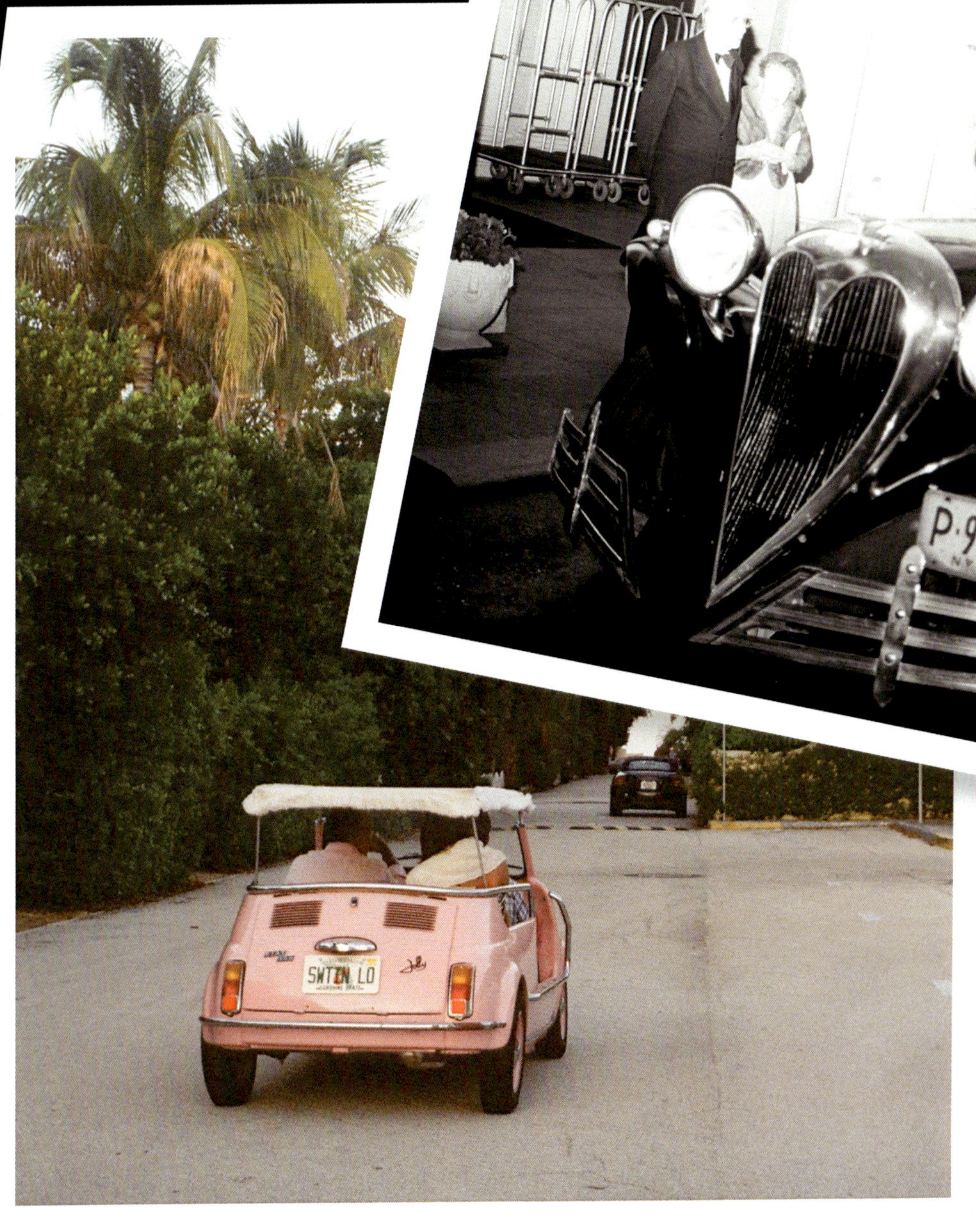
SWTIN LO

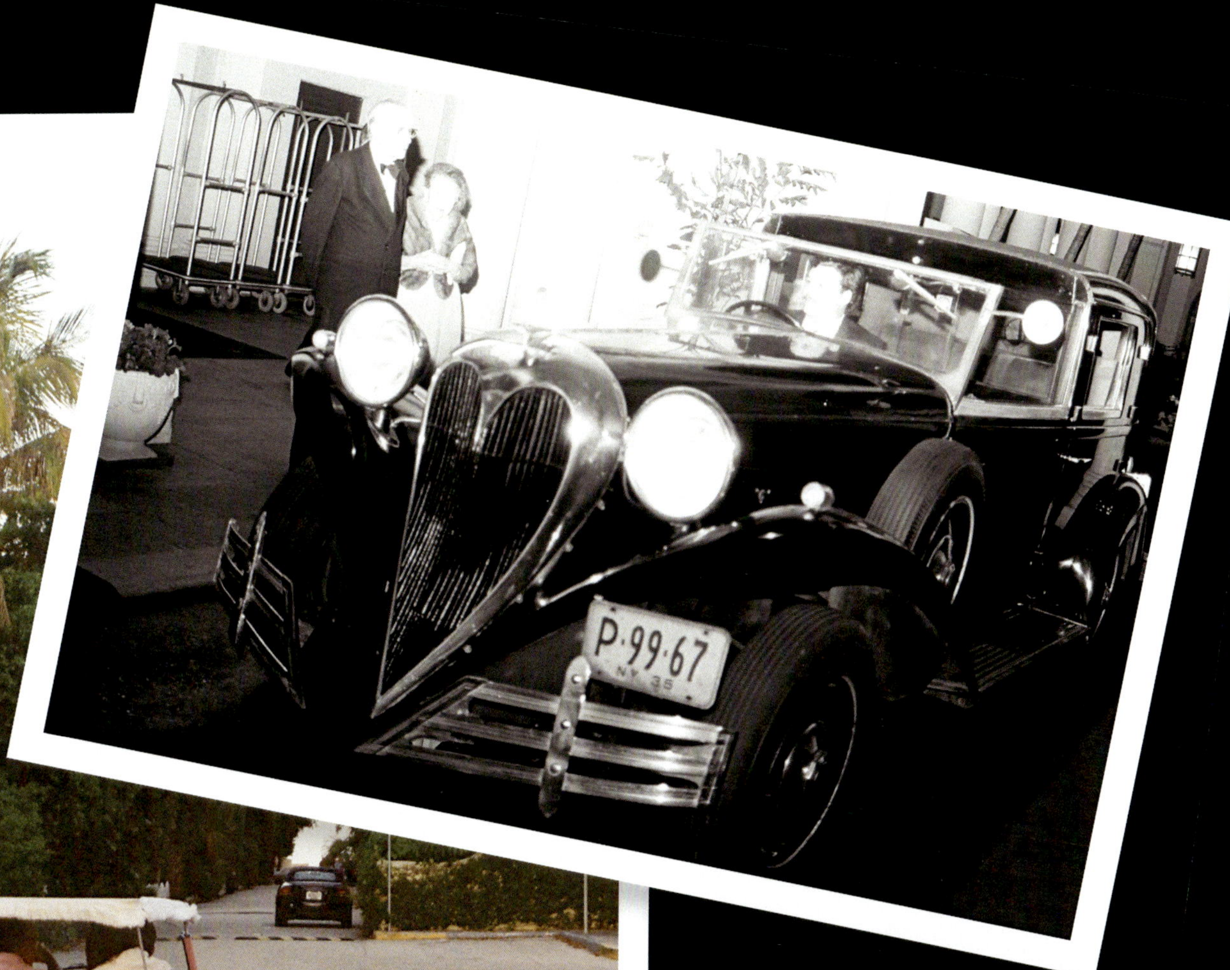
P·99·67
NY 35

'A woman needs four animals in her life:
A mink in the closet,
A jaguar in the garage,
A tiger in bed,
And an ass to pay for it all.'

~Ann Slater

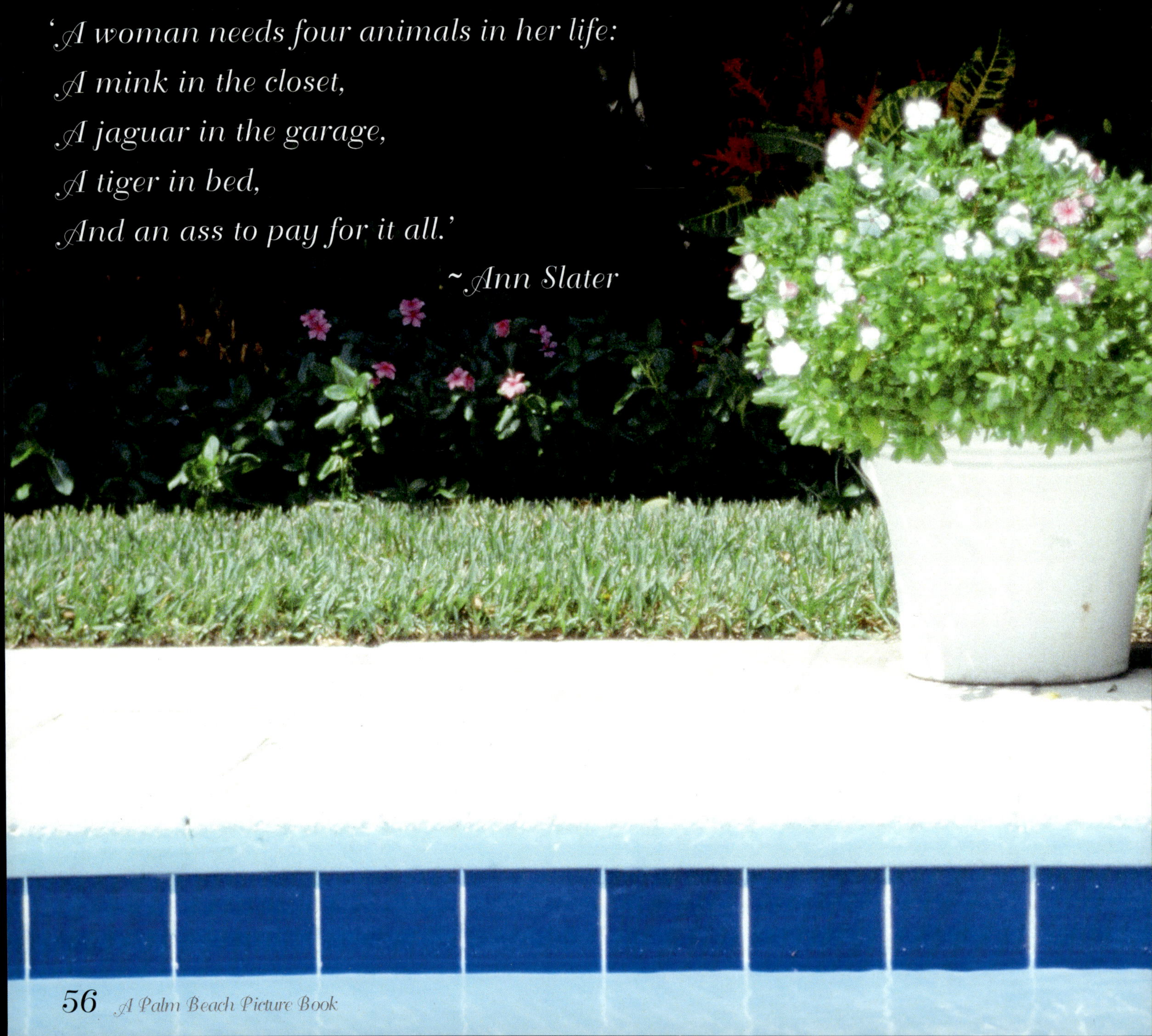

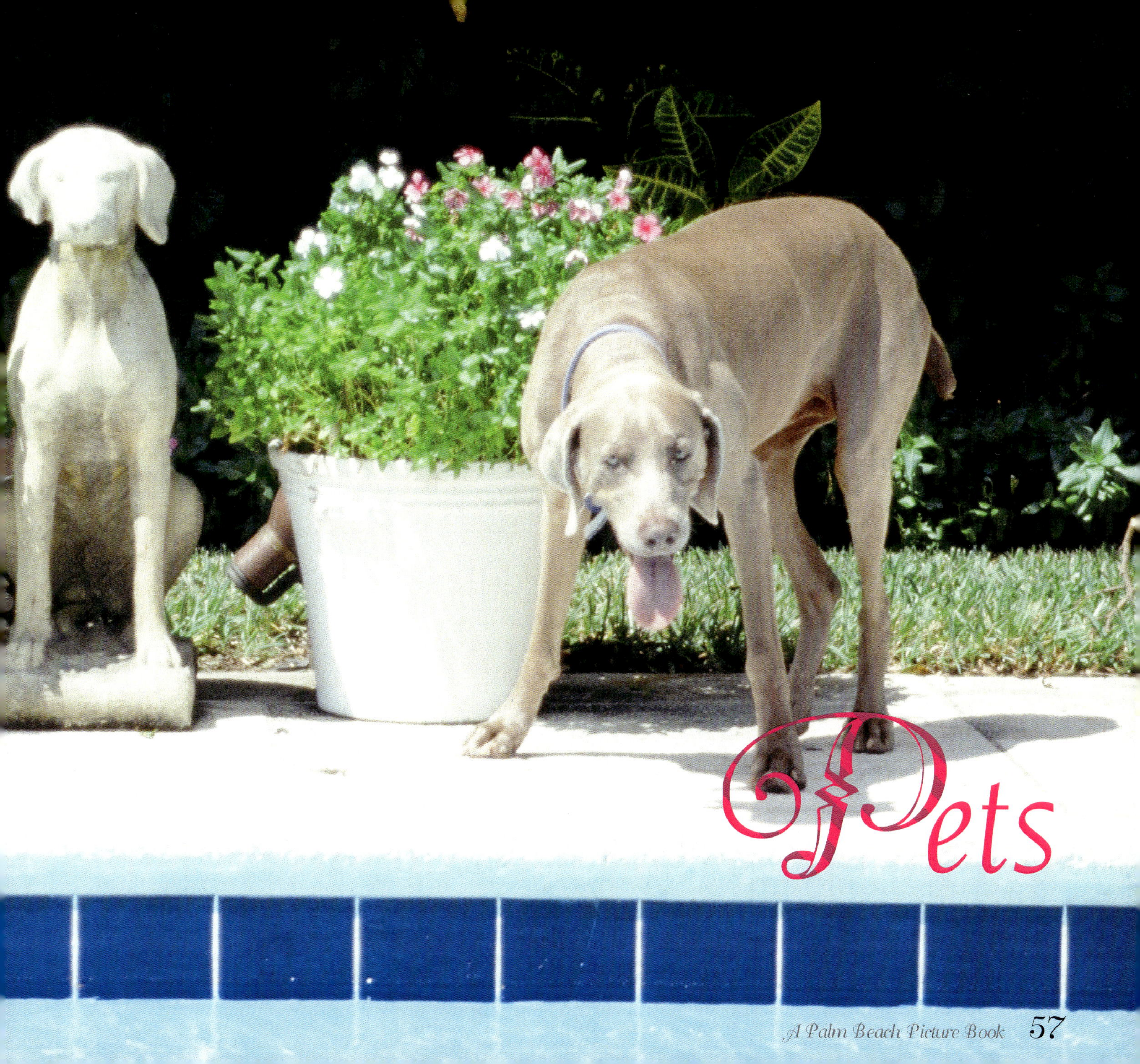

Pets

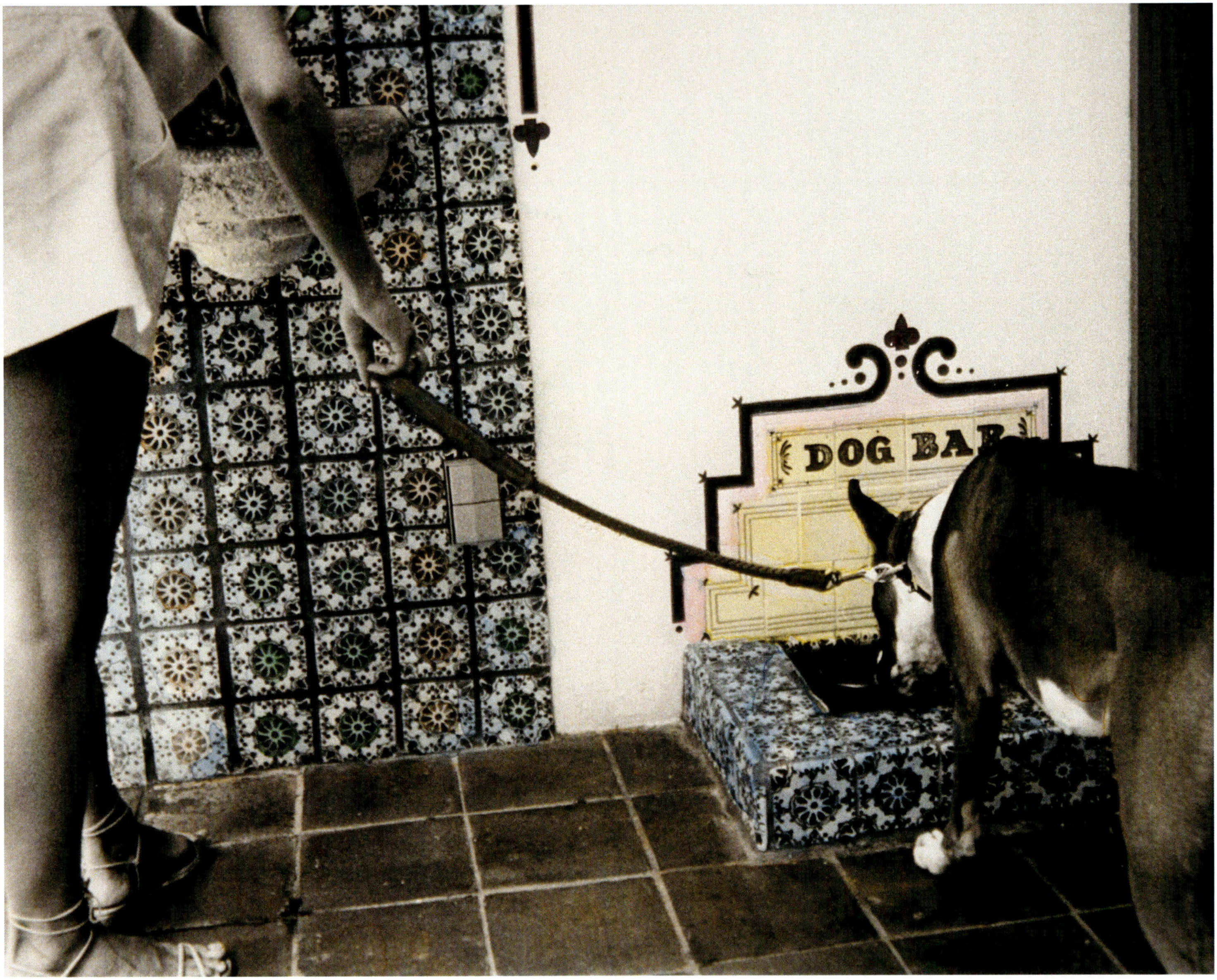
DOG BAR

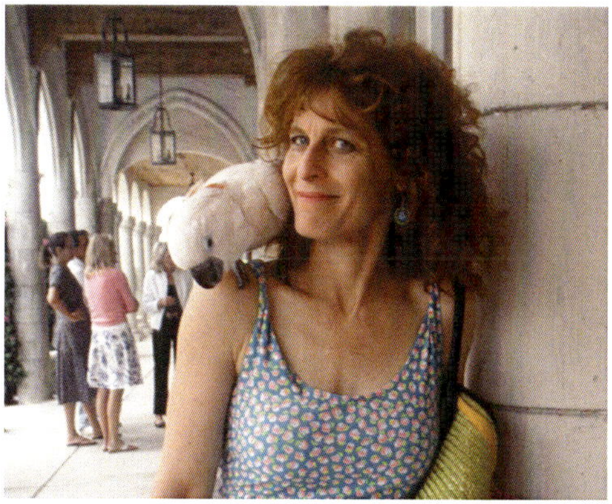

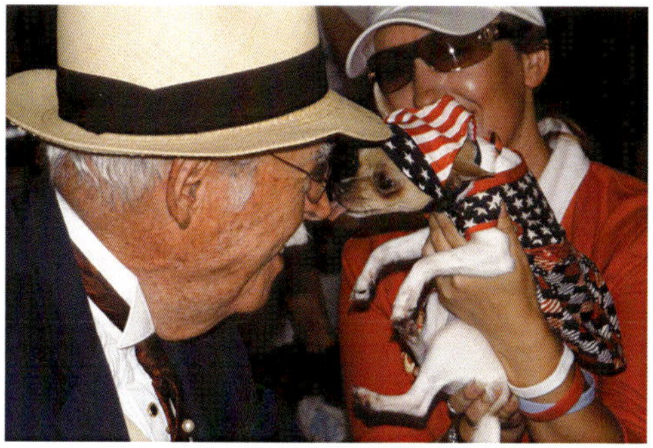

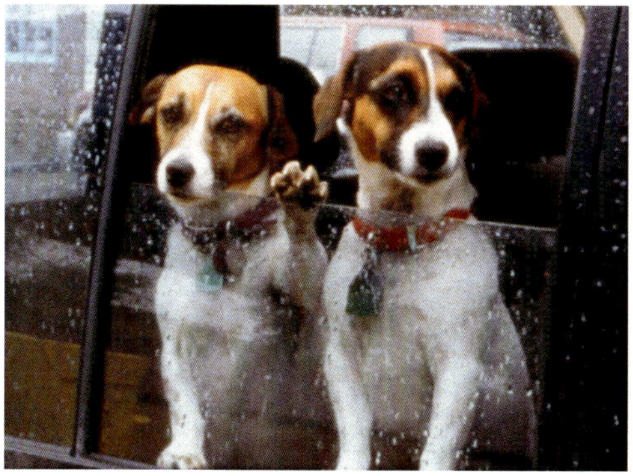

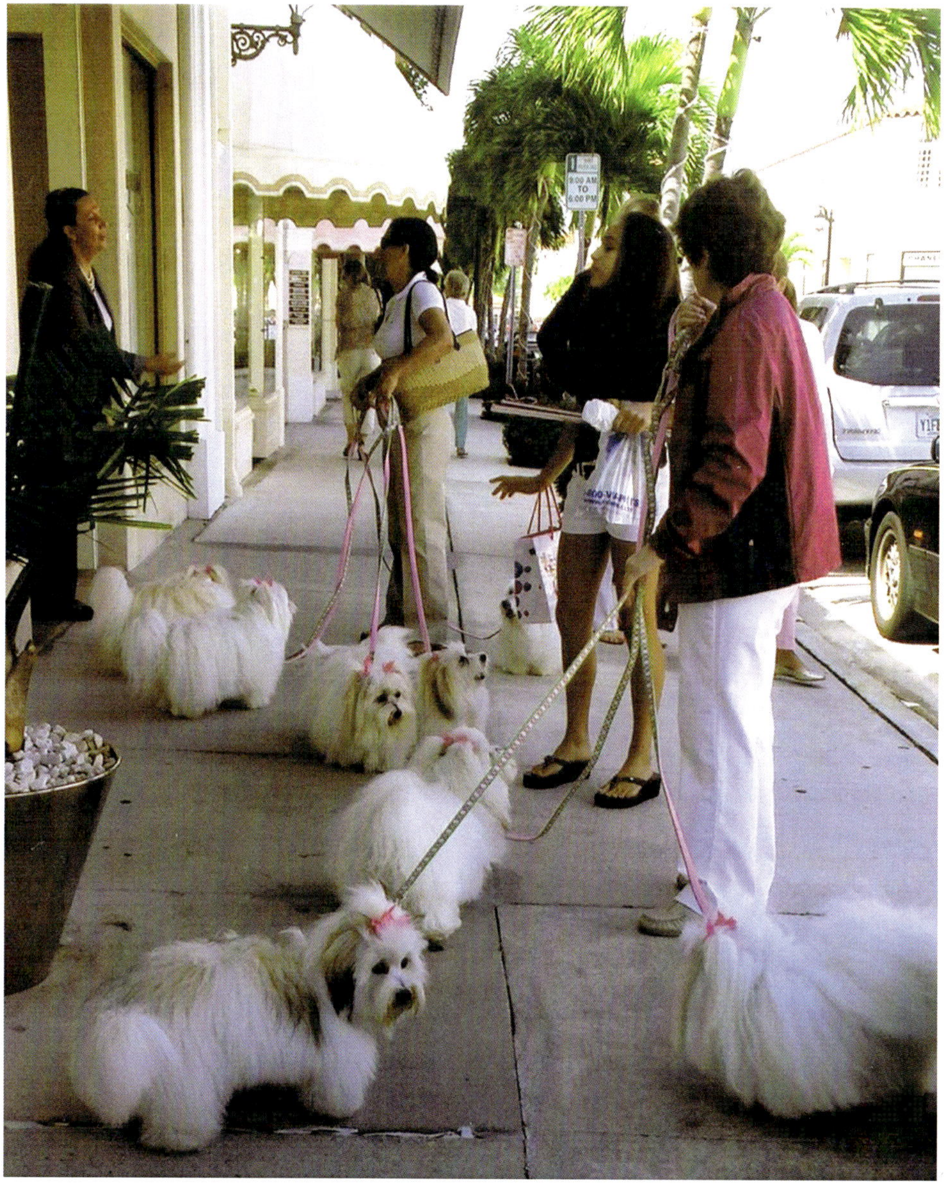
9:00 AM
TO
6:00 PM

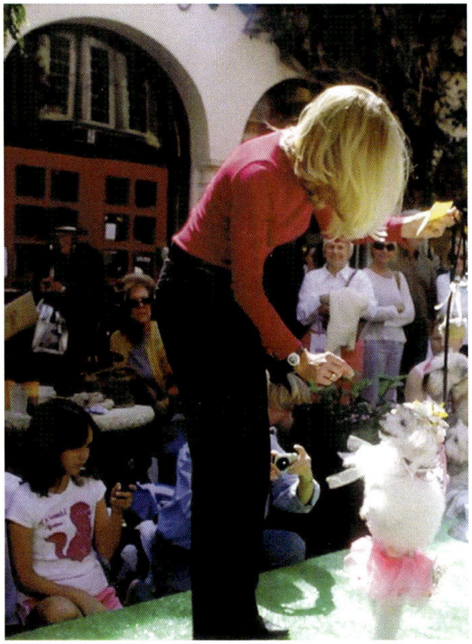
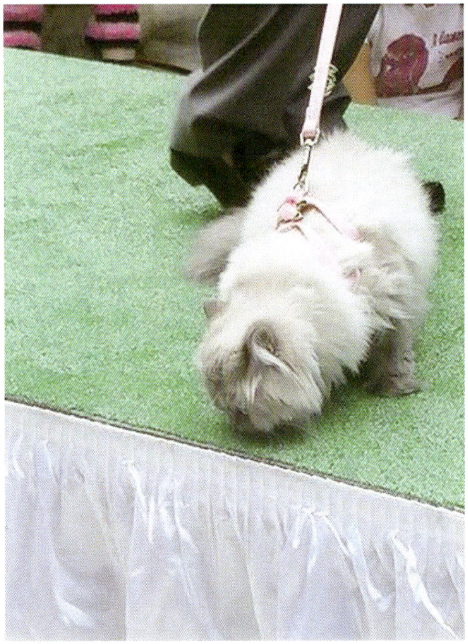
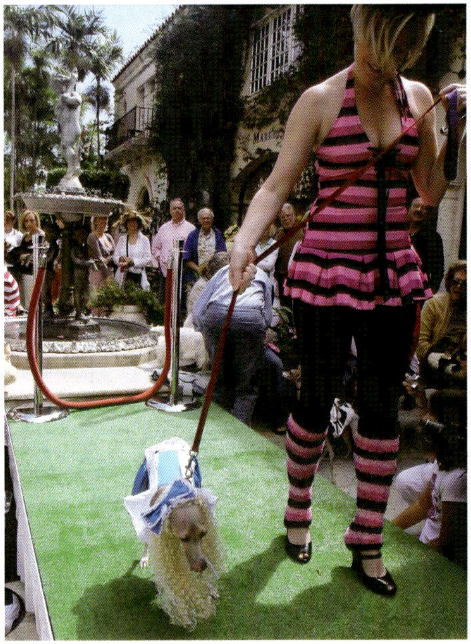
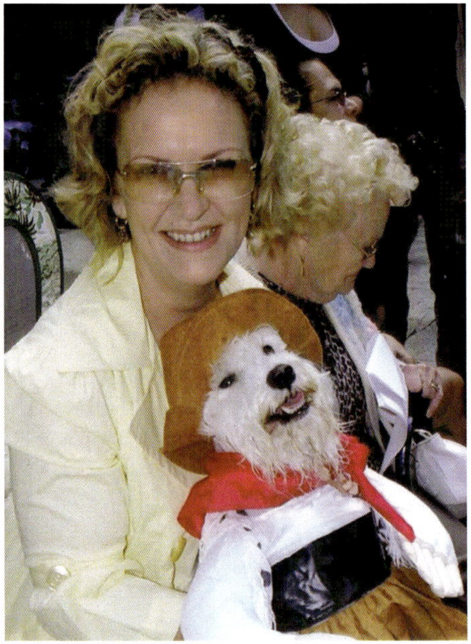
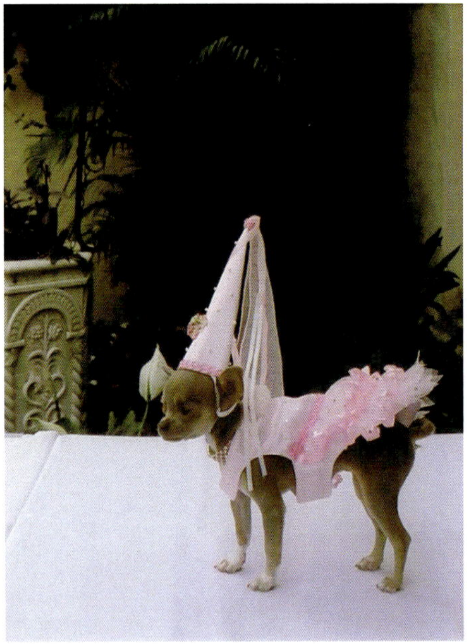
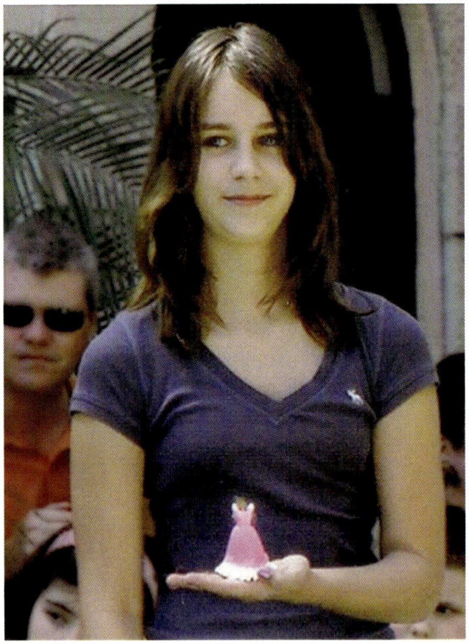

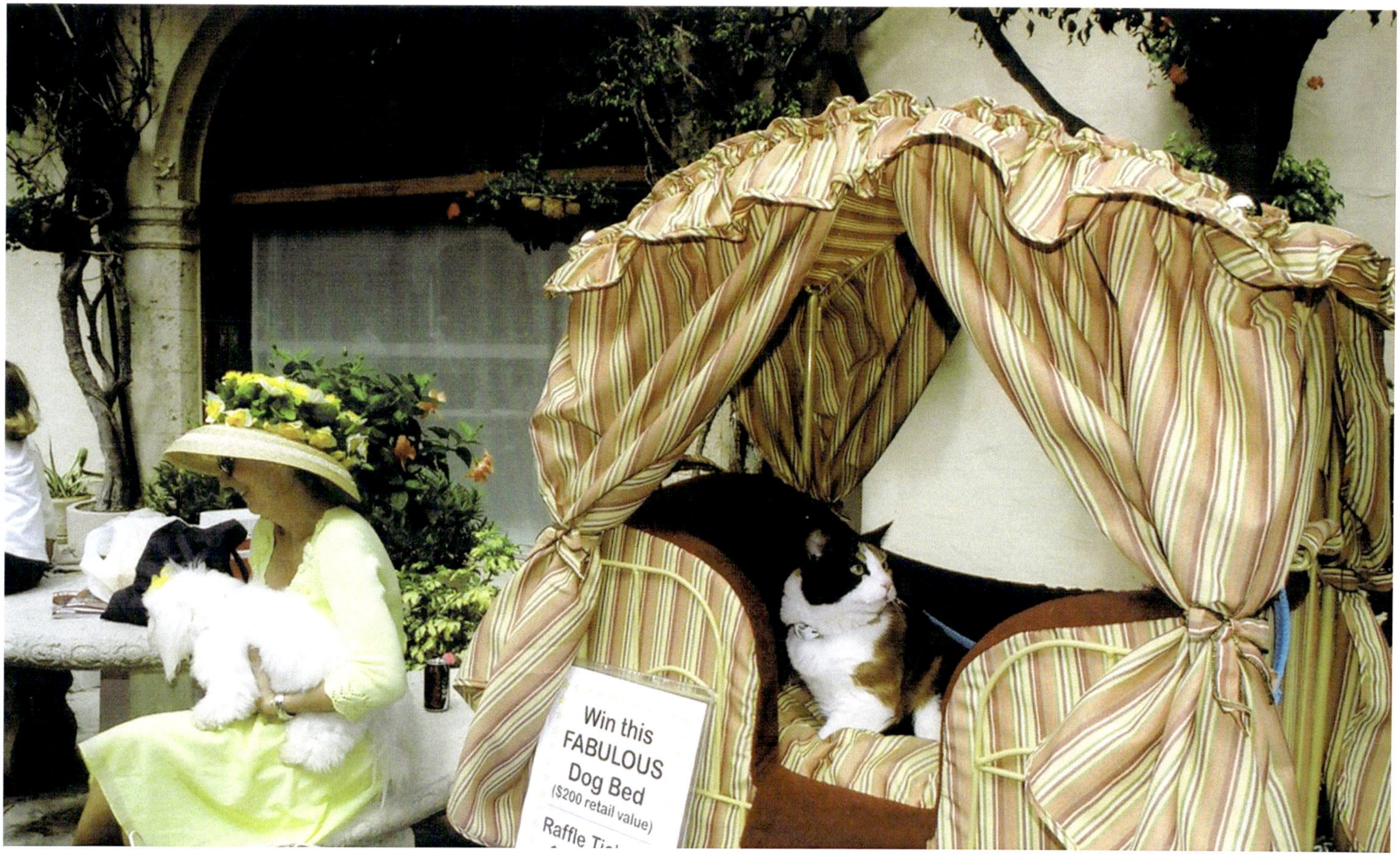

PALM BEACHERS TAKE PRIDE in celebrating their animals. The Worth Avenue Association has an annual pet fashion show which is attended by island residents who dress up with their pets to promenade down the catwalk in Via Gucci. Occasionally, other animals appear on the catwalk, such as a lizard or even a rare cat.

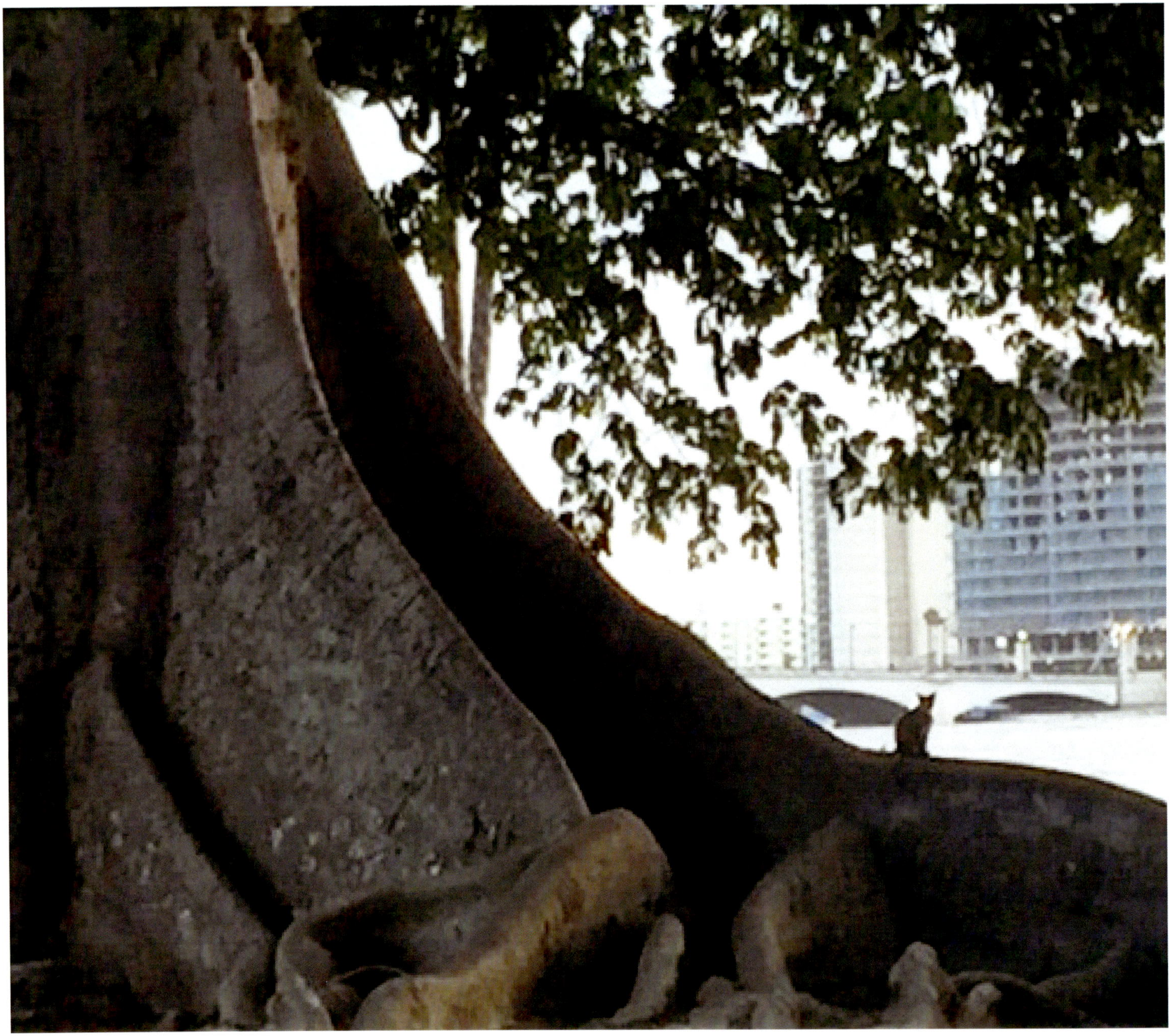

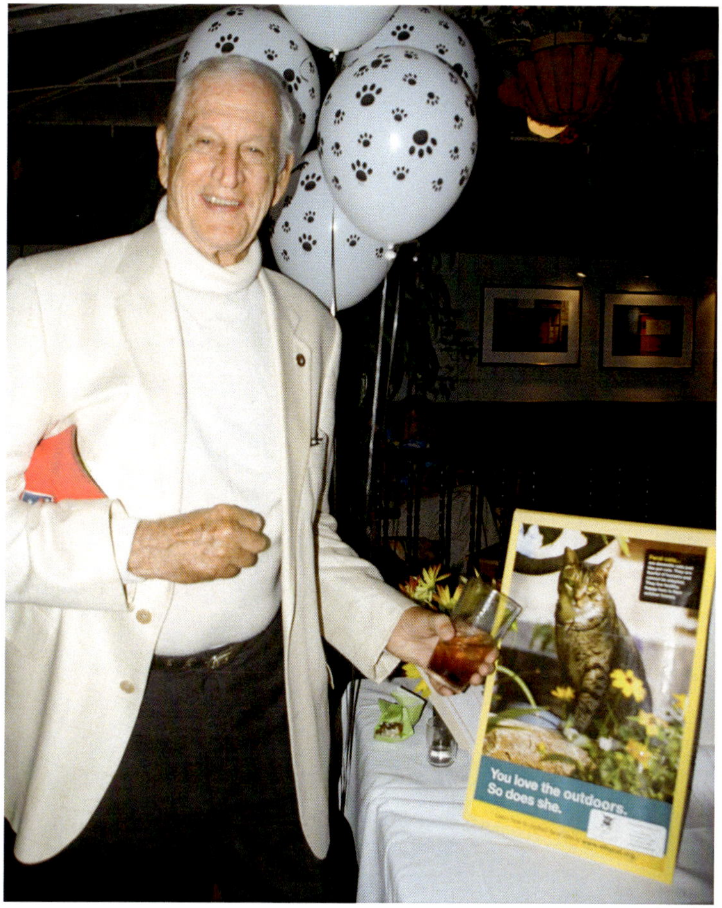

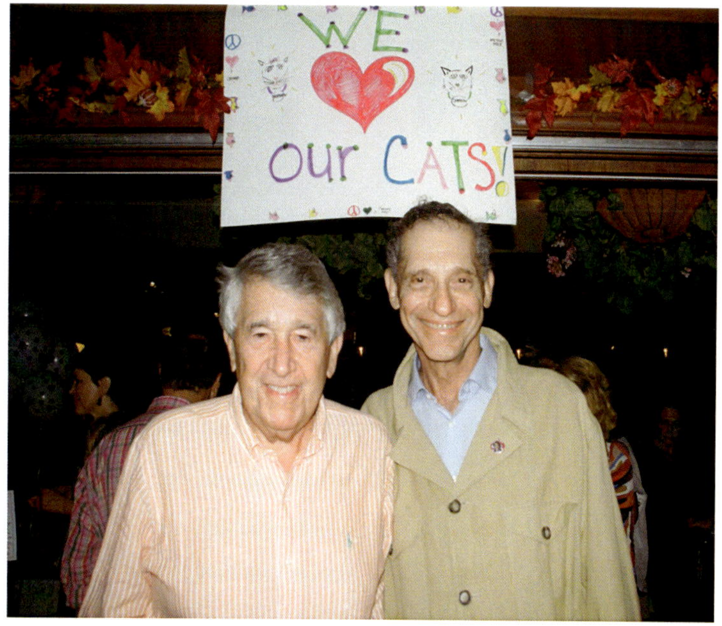

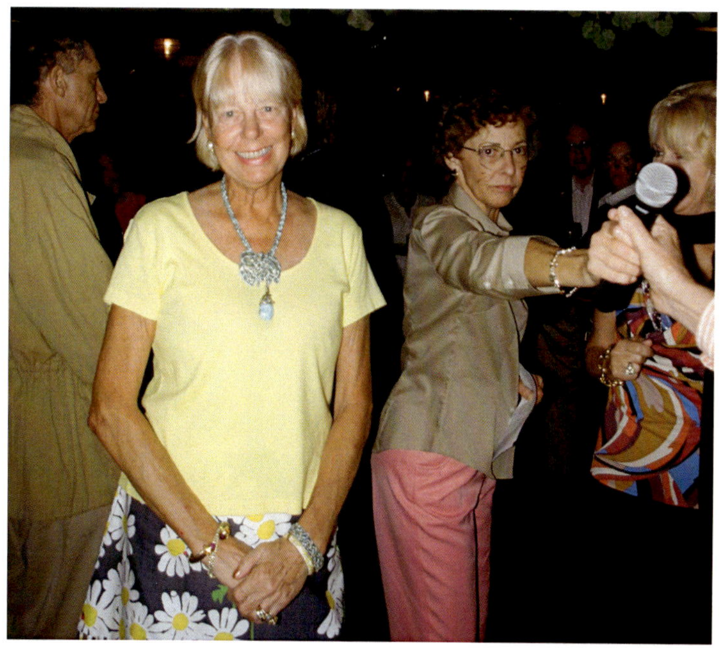

THE ISLAND CAT SOCIETY, one of the many philanthropic groups in Palm Beach, has raised a quarter million dollars to care for a colony of about seven hundred feral cats on the island, preventing them from being euthanized. They spay and neuter the felines, as well as vaccinate and provide food and water for the animals at feeding stations throughout the island.

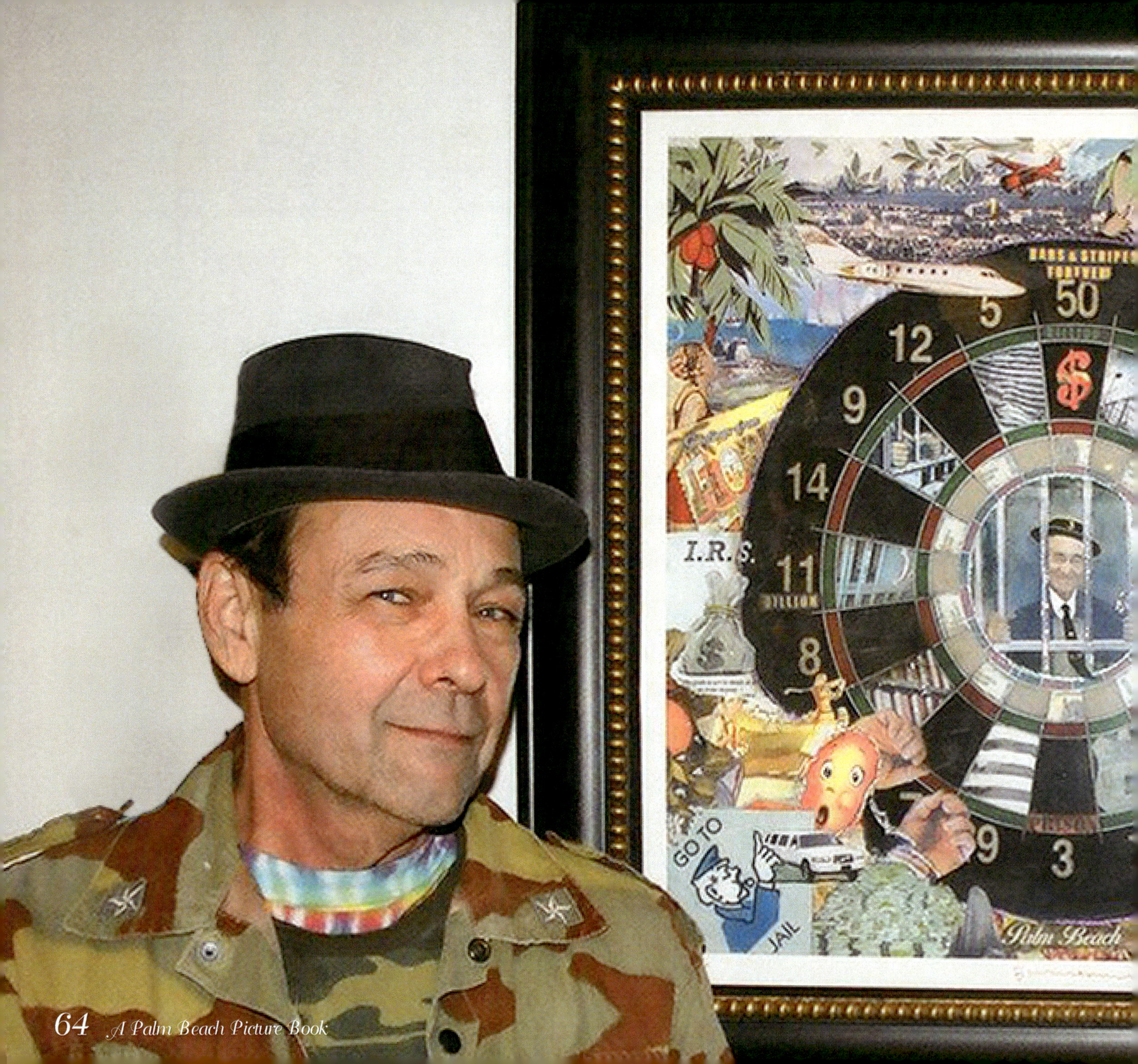
I.R.S.
GO TO
JAIL
Palm Beach

Art Scene

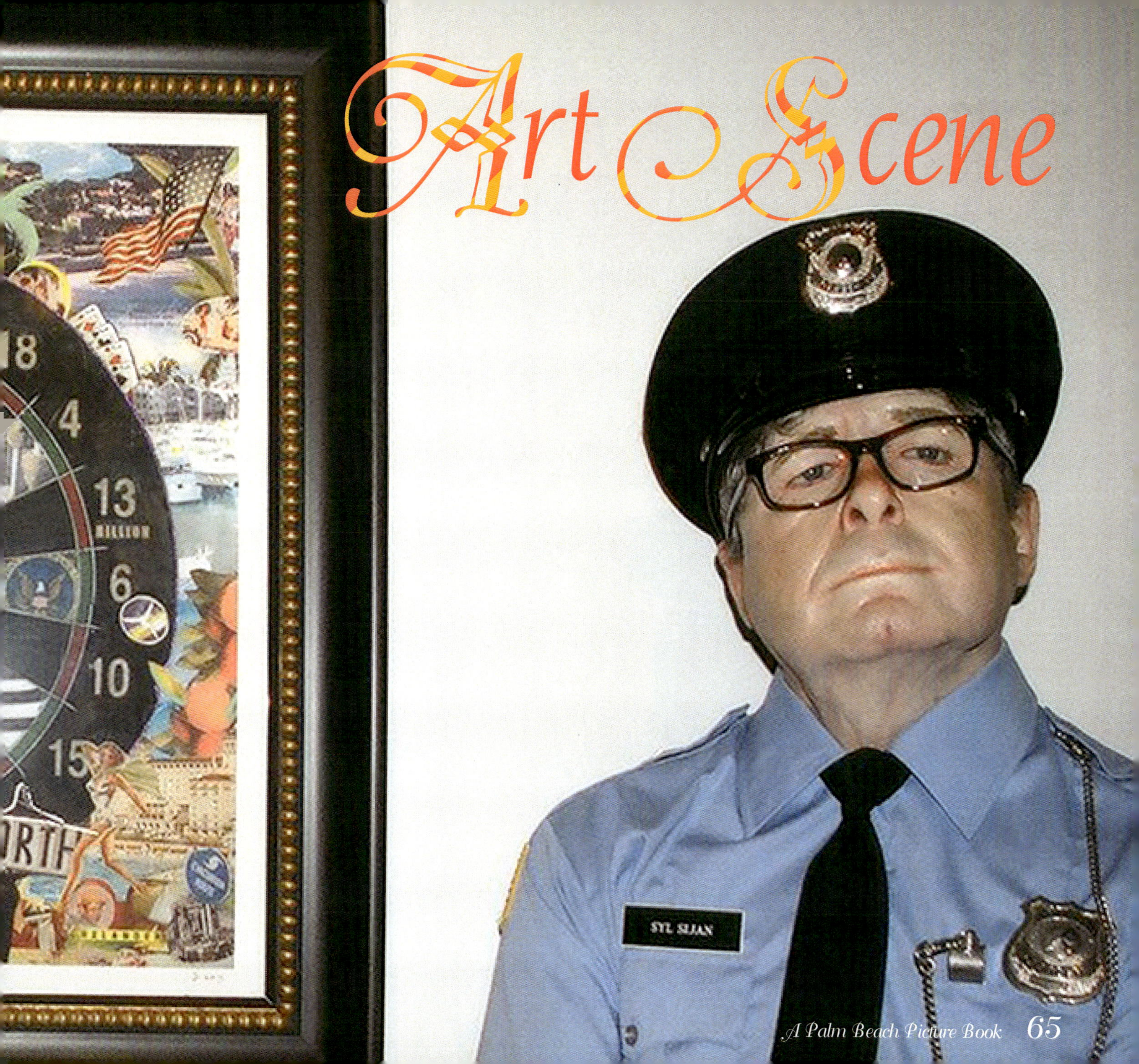

A Brief History of the Palm Beach Art Scene

BY BRUCE HELANDER

Art Historian and renowned Collage Artist

AT THE TURN OF THE 20TH CENTURY, Palm Beach was lucky to find an original painting hung prominently in the lobby of any major hotel on this thin strip of an island. Anything of value would have been lost in the multiple fires and hurricanes that eventually brought down every wooden hotel east of the Intracoastal. For a time, Henry Flagler's white house probably took the prize for best art collection, but those works were no doubt acquired on the streets of Paris and from a few obscure galleries on the Upper East Side of New York City. Flagler's vision of bringing down a crowd of important people on his own railroad from the frozen mean streets of Manhattan ultimately materialized into one of the most unique communities in America. As houses began to go up, the decorators moved in to create glamorous, expensive-looking interiors that required original

works of art. It didn't take long for an ambitious gallery to open a storefront on Worth Avenue to sell paintings, sculpture and antiques to a seriously wealthy selection of residents. One of the first truly successful galleries was Wally Findlay, who showed decorative works accented with pastel colors that would find favor in beach houses. Later, as Worth Avenue began to flourish, several top notch gallery owners, such as Irving Luntz or Grace Hokin, began introducing contemporary works of art that needed a little more education to be appreciated. Both galleries made small fortunes as the south end condo projects swallowed up art as fast as could be produced and delivered.

I came on the scene in the winter of 1982 by invitation from Frank Rubinstein, a serious local collector, to consider starting a really cutting edge art gallery. He wanted a gallery reflecting his taste for adventure with new imagery that would require some independent thought and risk. I had never been in Florida before and was a little suspect about whether I was wasting my time, compared to the built-in audience in Manhattan and my familiarly with the art market there. After I landed in West Palm Beach, I asked the taxi driver to, 'take me to Worth Avenue, wherever that is,' and I could immediately see the potential. Ten days later, we opened the gallery at 125 Worth Avenue. Jesse Newman, President of the Palm Beach Chamber of Commerce and my first visitor, put his arm around me and advised that the secret of success on 'The Avenue' was to display the very best of the product in which you specialize. The formula worked, as we operated a gallery that became famous and often controversial for over fifteen years. My early days were full of enthusiasm and exciting events with respected artists.

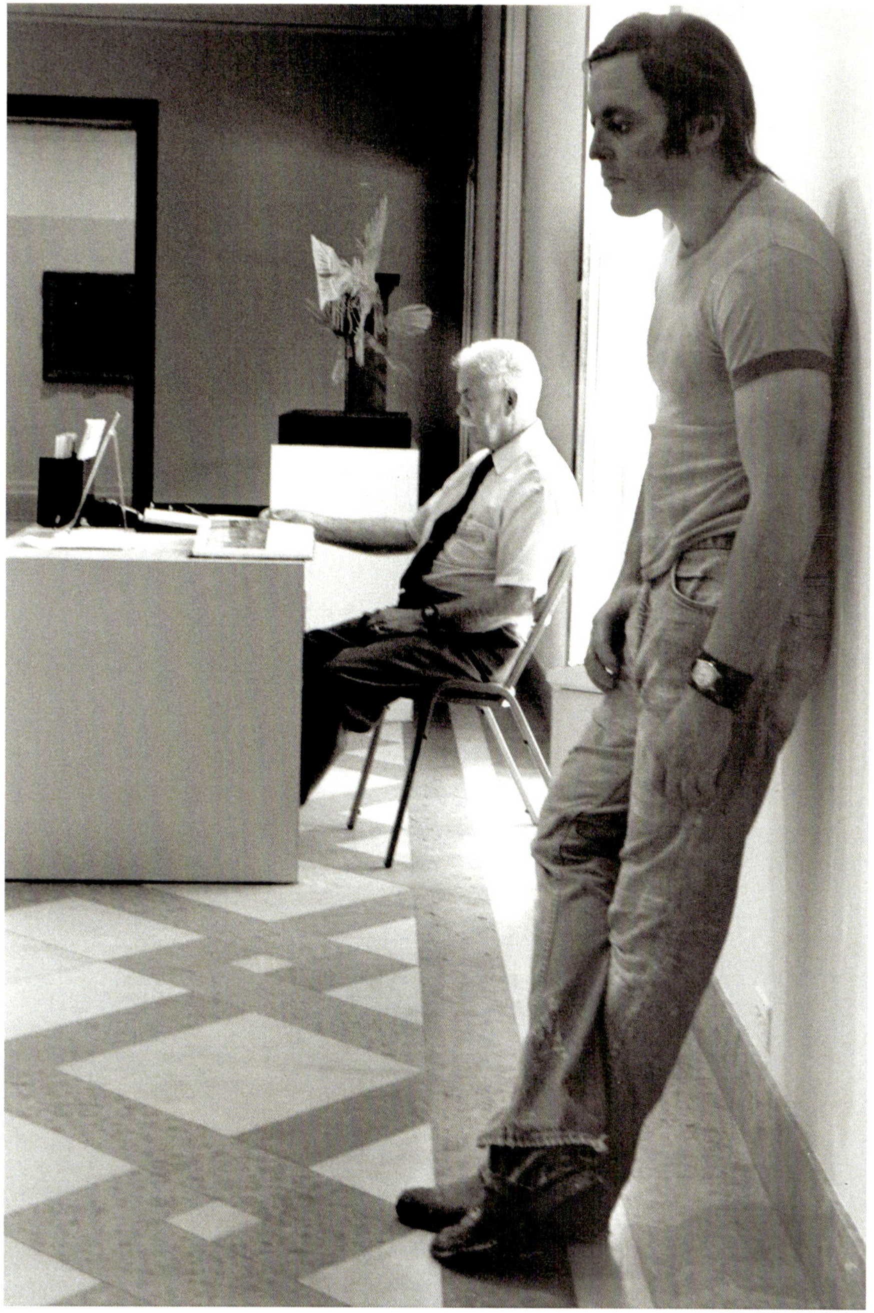

THOSE WERE THE DAYS when artists I dealt with visited the gallery and would stay with us on the island. We had a ball! I went about searching for top artists who lived in South Florida. Our first big break was seeing Robert Rauschenberg in his studio on Captiva Island. I had given him an honorary degree while I was dean of the Rhode Island School of Design, so he had a hard time refusing my requests. We then set out to represent a host of blue chip artists, and our clients kept getting more significant from Henry Ford and Senator Howard Metzenbaum to Jane Holzer and Sidney Kimmel. Our show, titled *Five Floridians*, which included Rauschenberg, Rosenquist, Chamberlain, Poons and Duane Hanson,

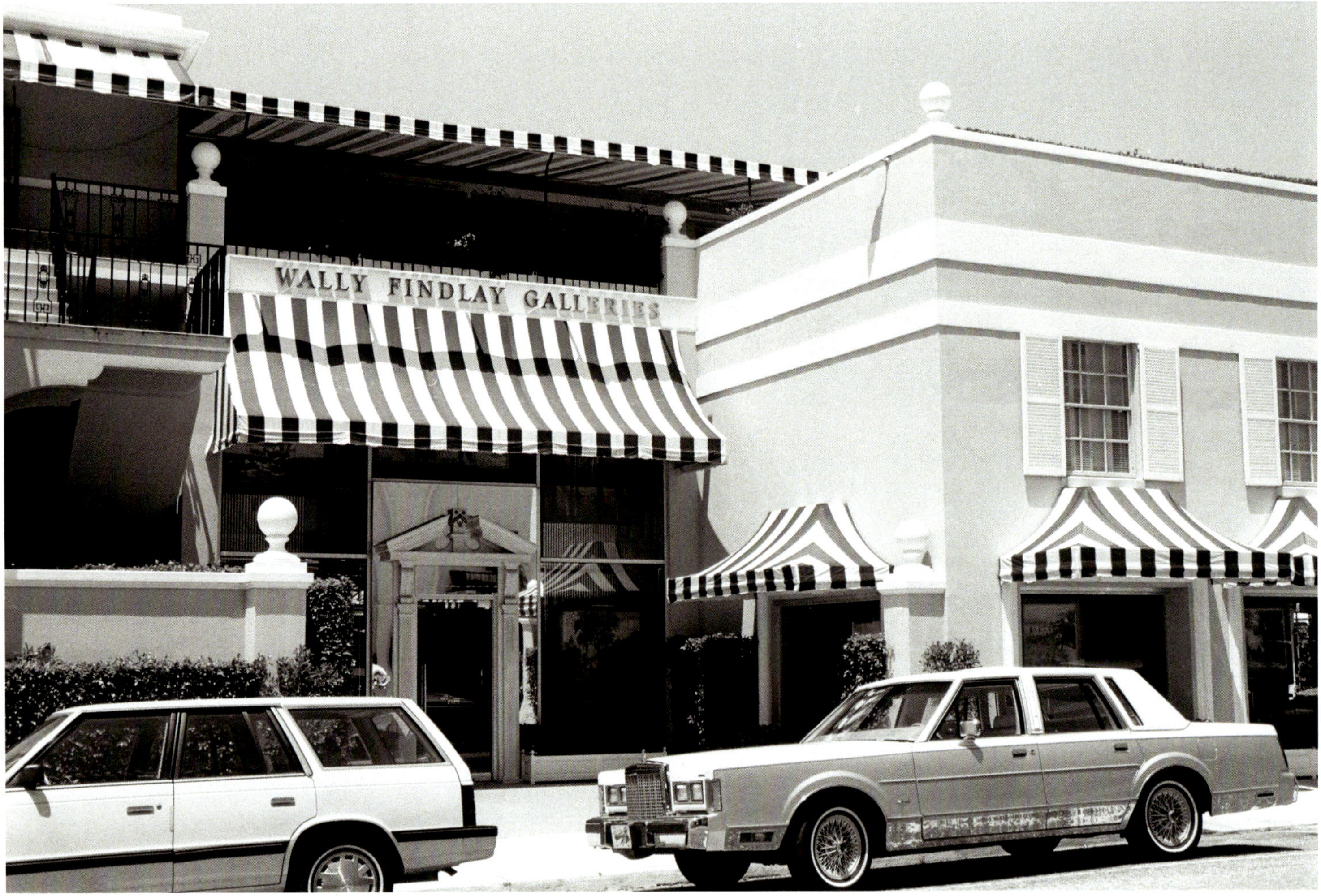

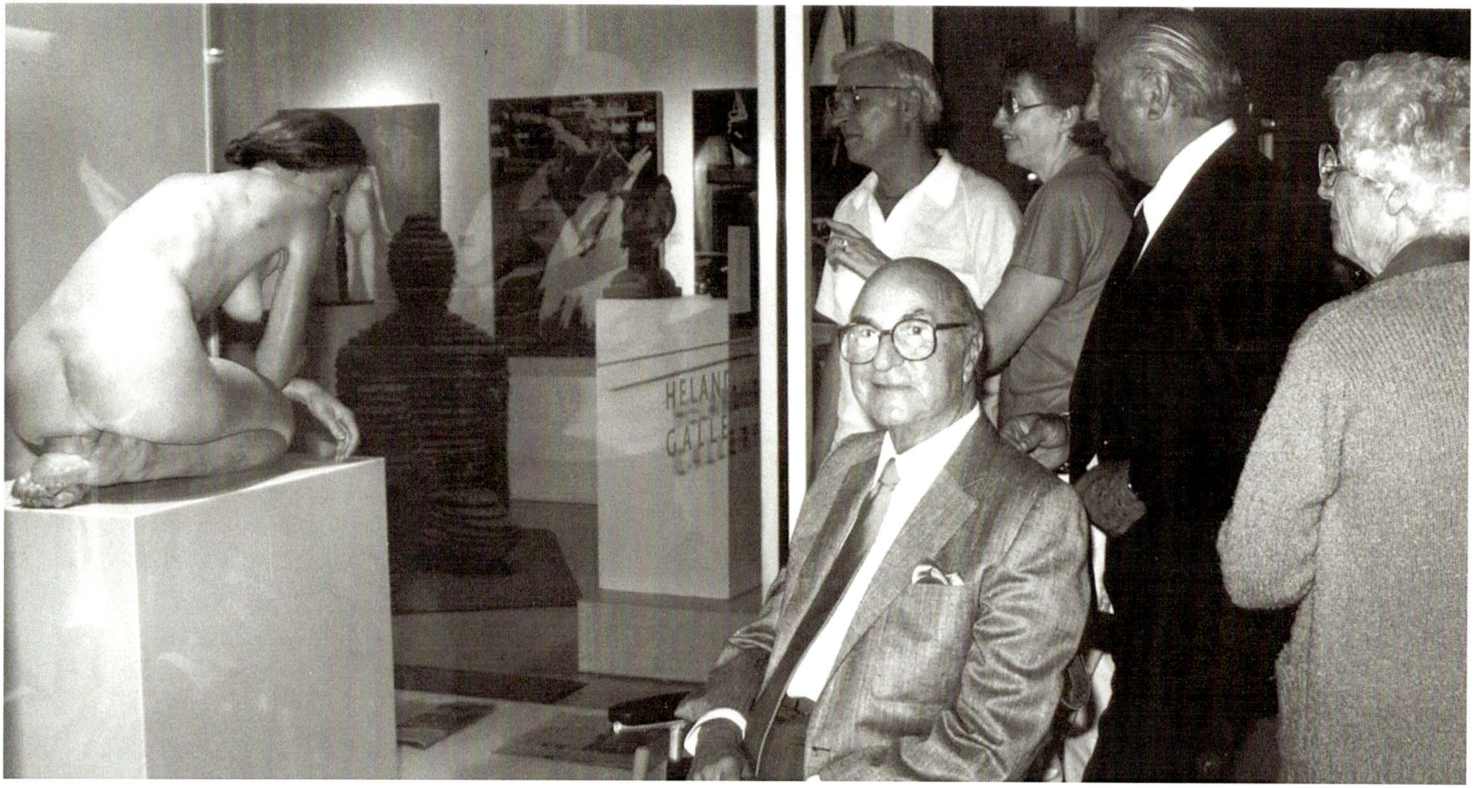

remains to this day the greatest museum quality exhibition in Worth Avenue history, with dozens of reviews and numerous accolades from major publications. Second place was a multi-million dollar retrospective of large paintings by Kenneth Noland. The first man to come in the door on the day of the show was Si Newhouse. Perhaps our greatest and most infamous highlight was an exhibition titled *Figure It Out~Visual Body Language*, where we decided to place a completely nude hyper-realistic polyvinyl figure by John DeAndrea in the window at our new location, 210 Worth Avenue, a well-traveled section of the street. The work became an overnight sensation, with dozens of newspapers and magazines including Playboy, reporting on the piece and the reaction to it. A full-time traffic cop was assigned to keep traffic from slowing to a halt in front of the gallery.

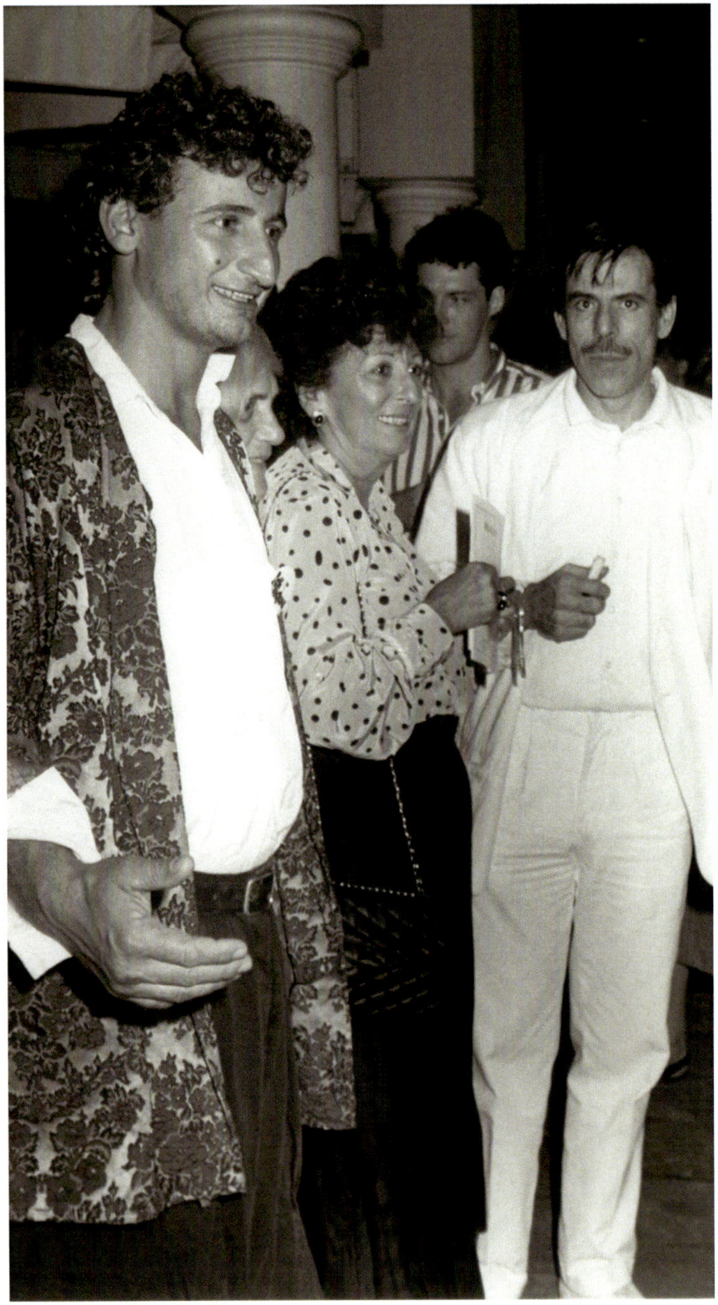

The Norton Museum of Art also is responsible for the continuing interest in and vitality of the art scene by showing inventive and cutting edge contemporary art. The two great art fairs just over the middle bridge bring to Palm Beach a remarkable exuberance and quality that few cities of this size enjoy. This commercial and scholarly energy has encouraged and supported many artists on the Island and beyond to continue working in their studios, and indeed encourages other superior artists to harness the energy and financial resources of the collecting community.

(Bruce Helander)

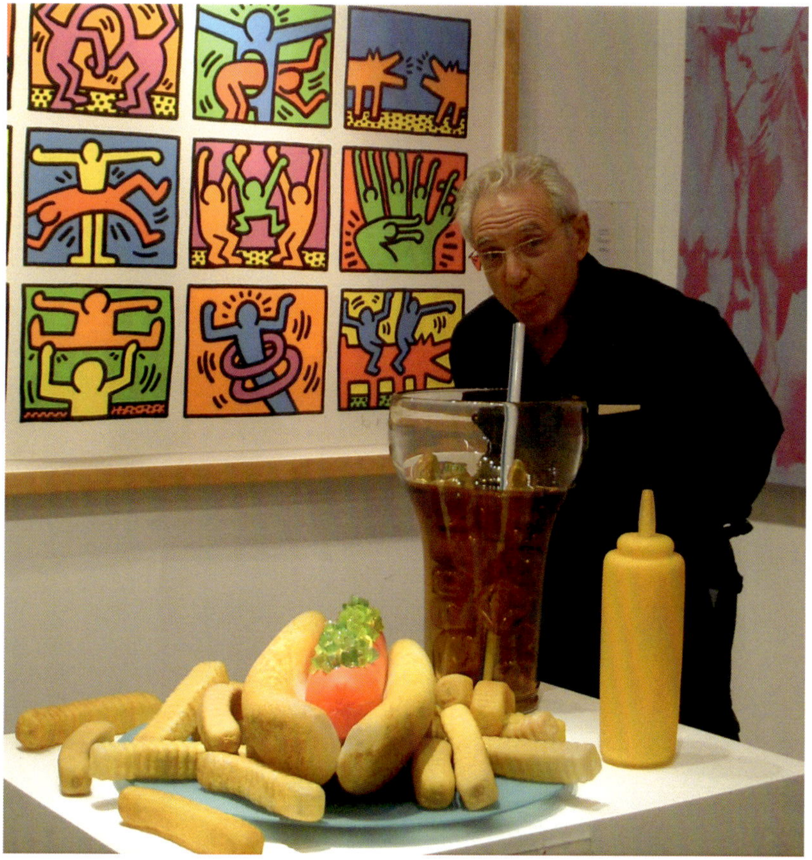

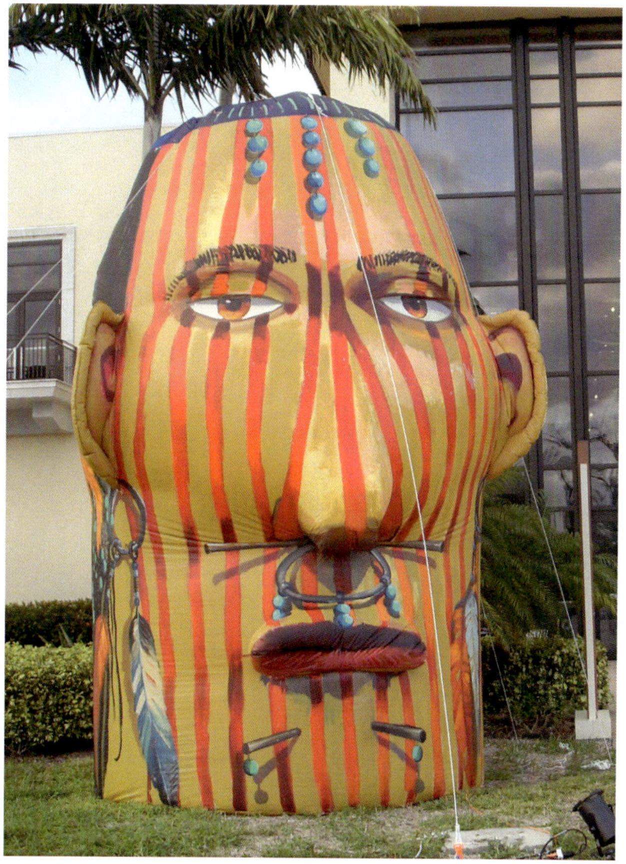

Seen at the Opening

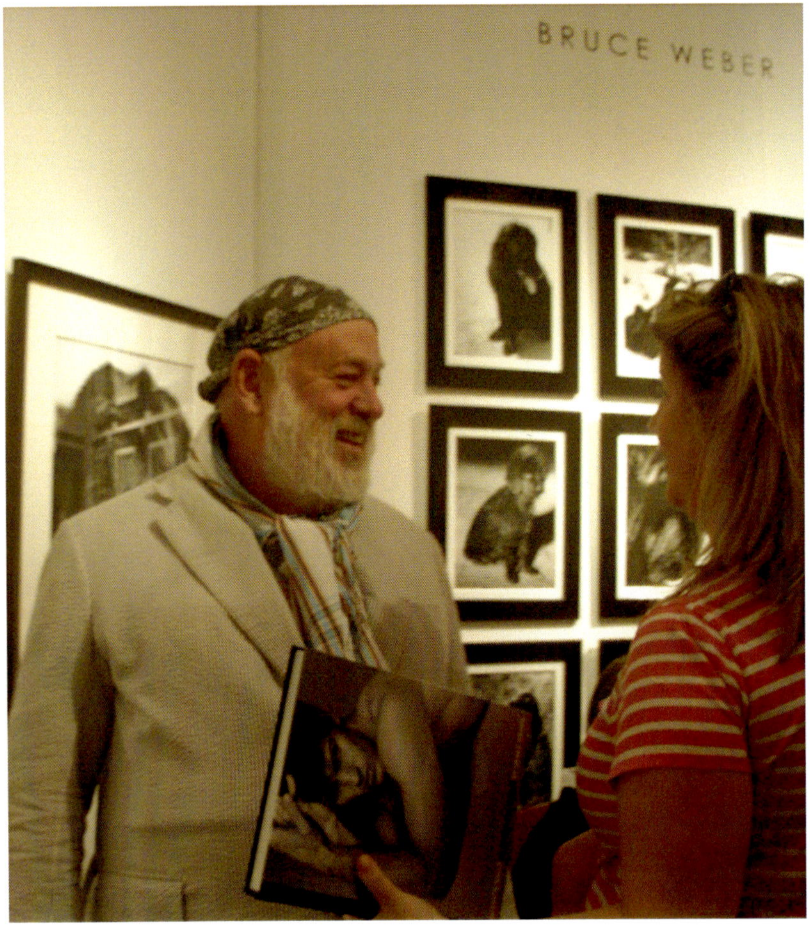

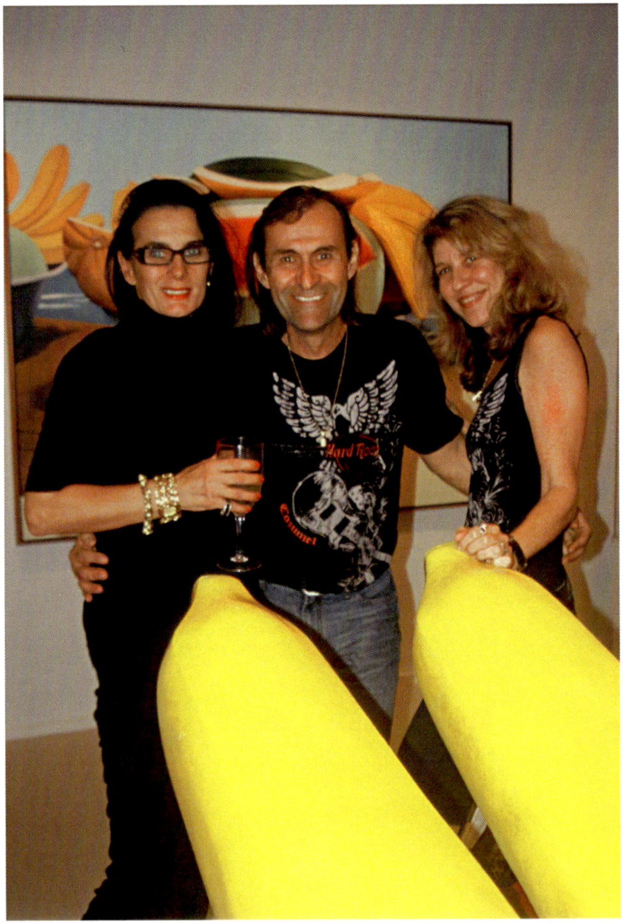

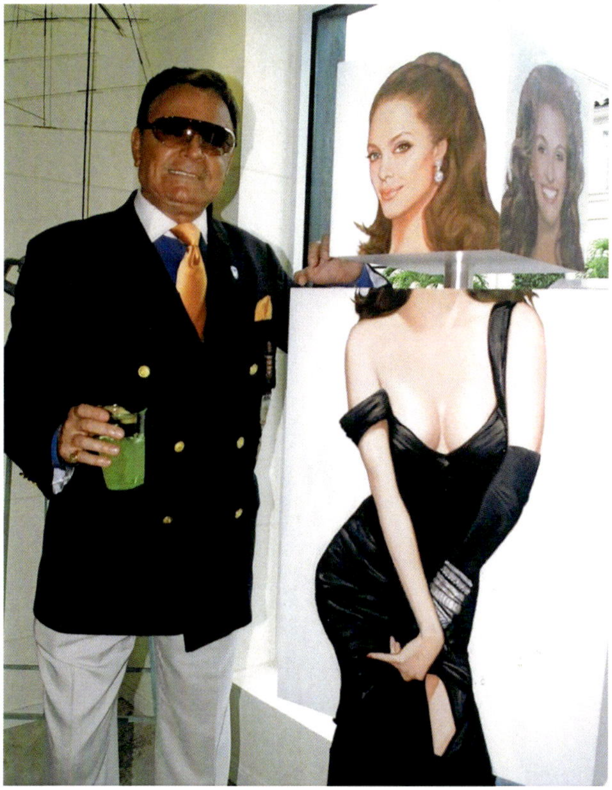

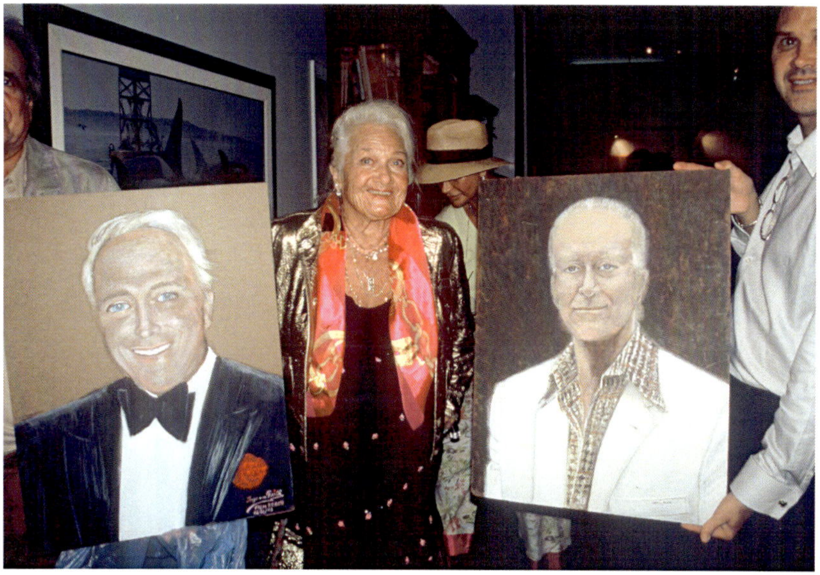

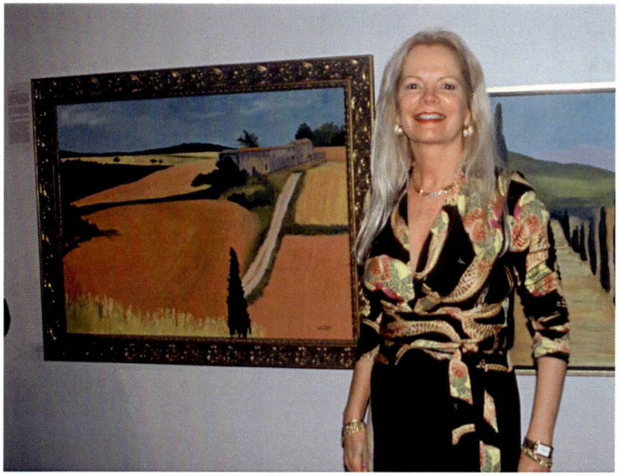

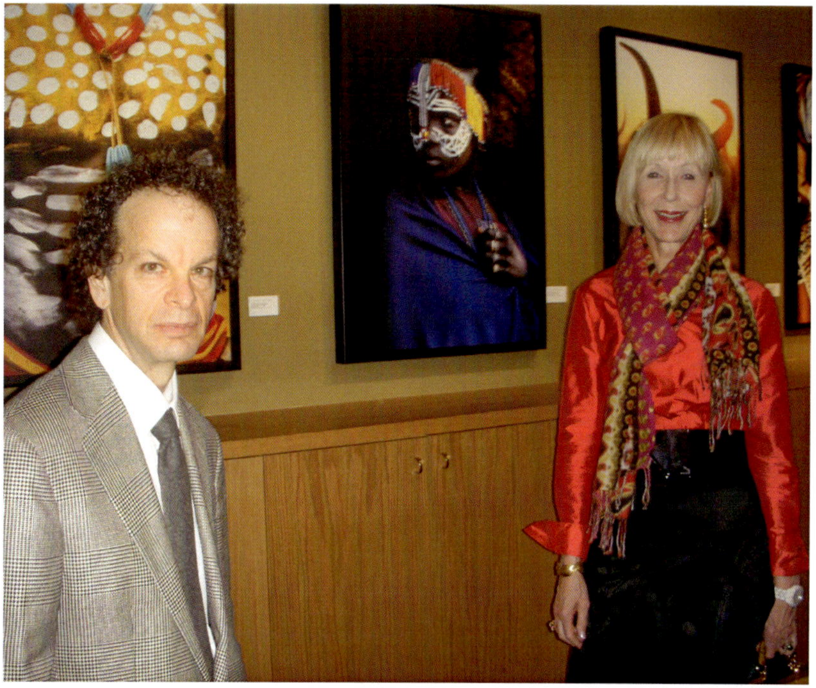

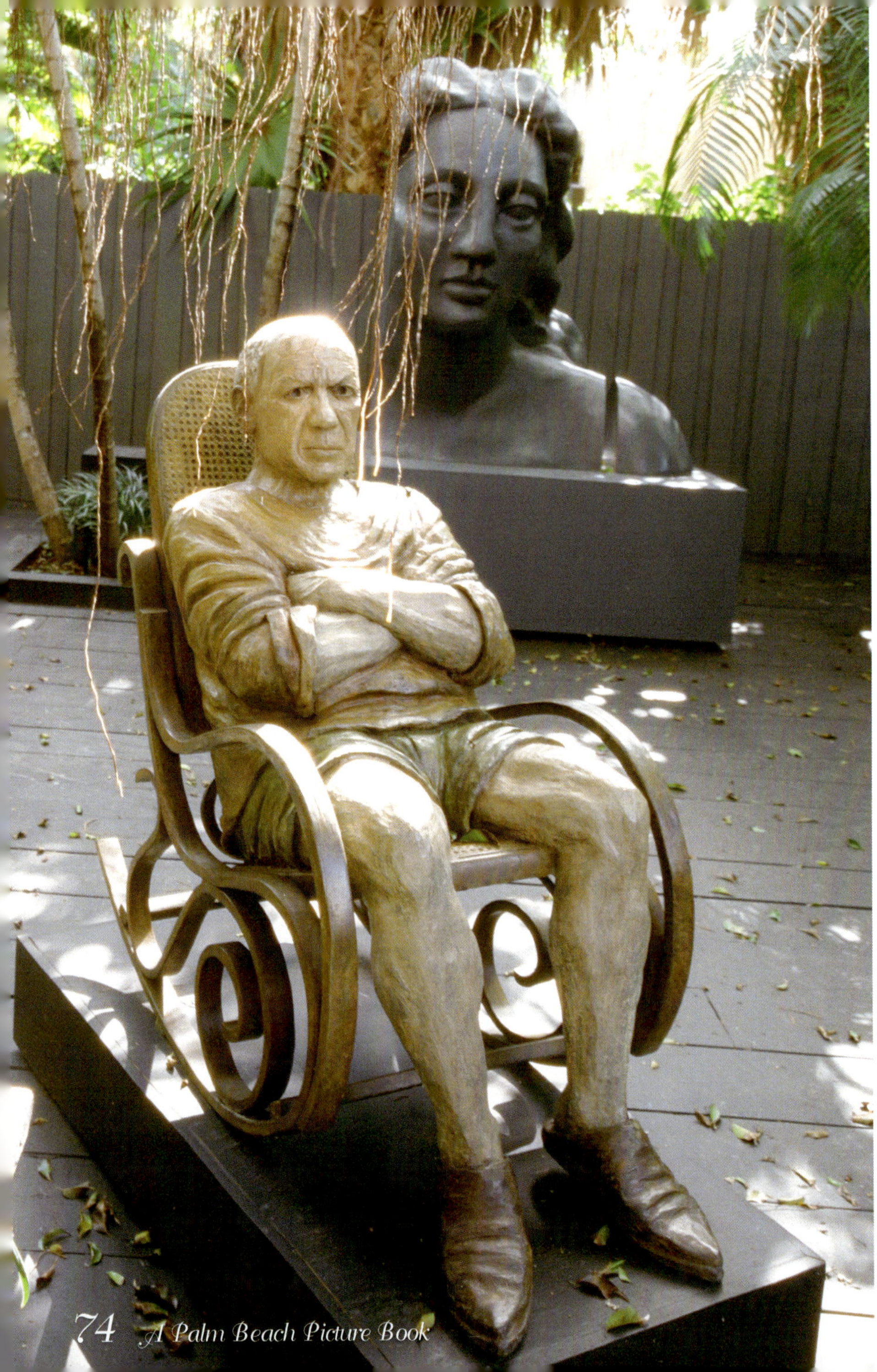

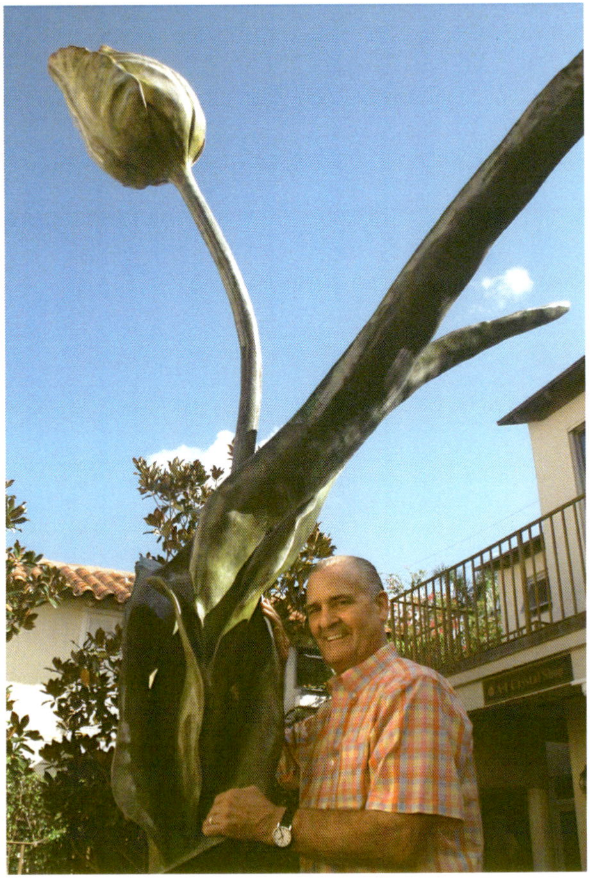

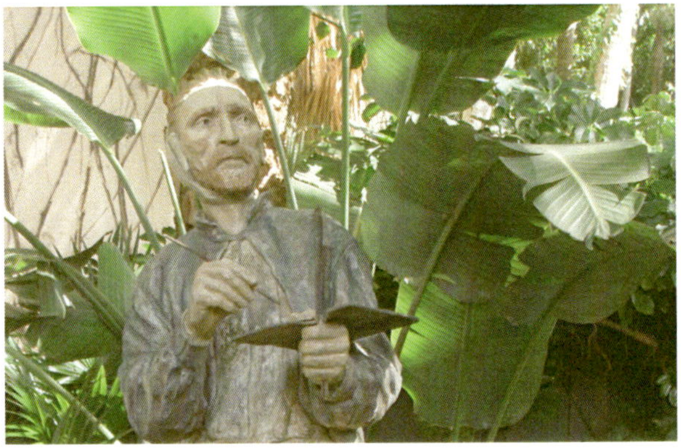

Robert St. Croix SCULPTURE GARDEN

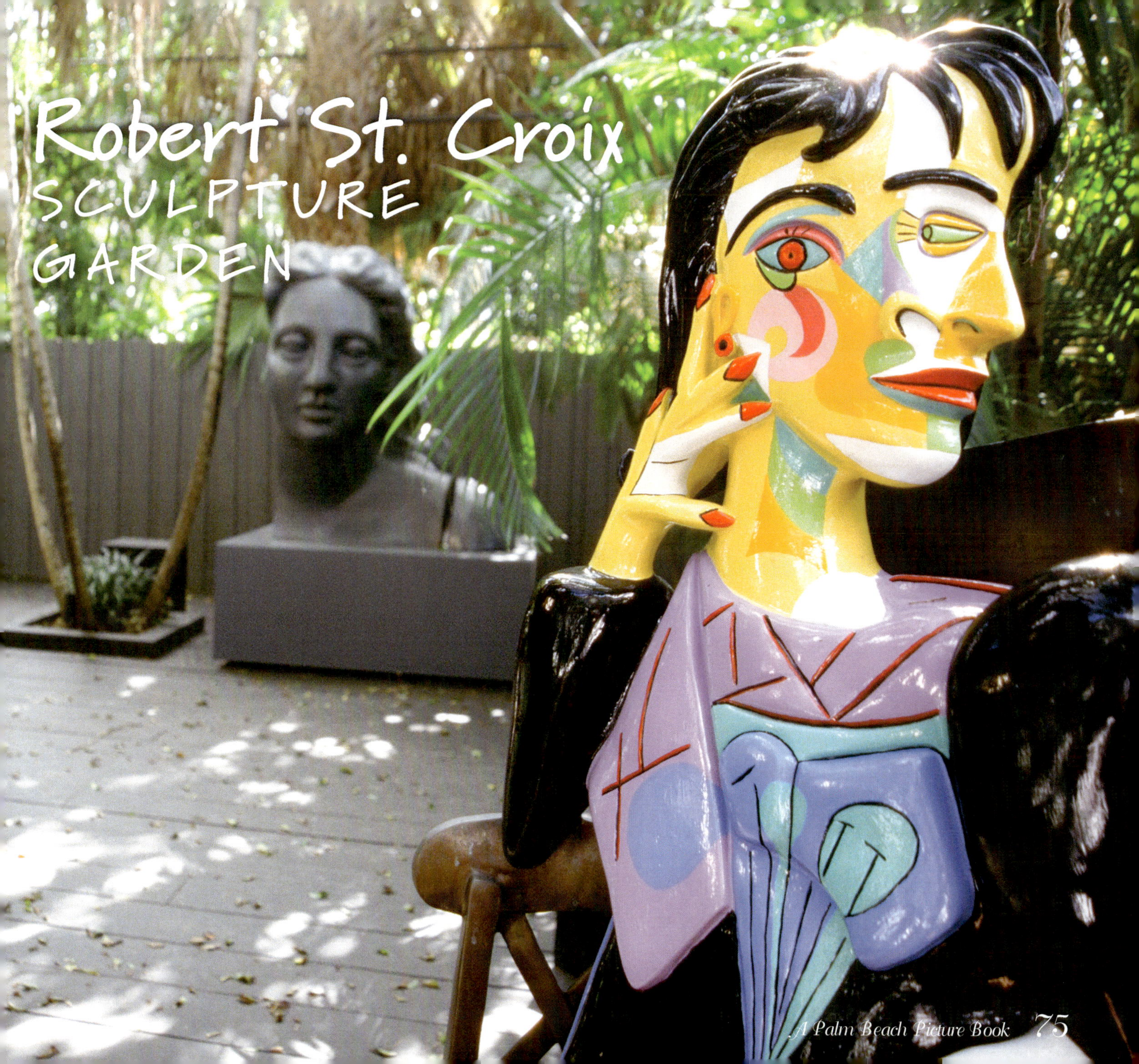

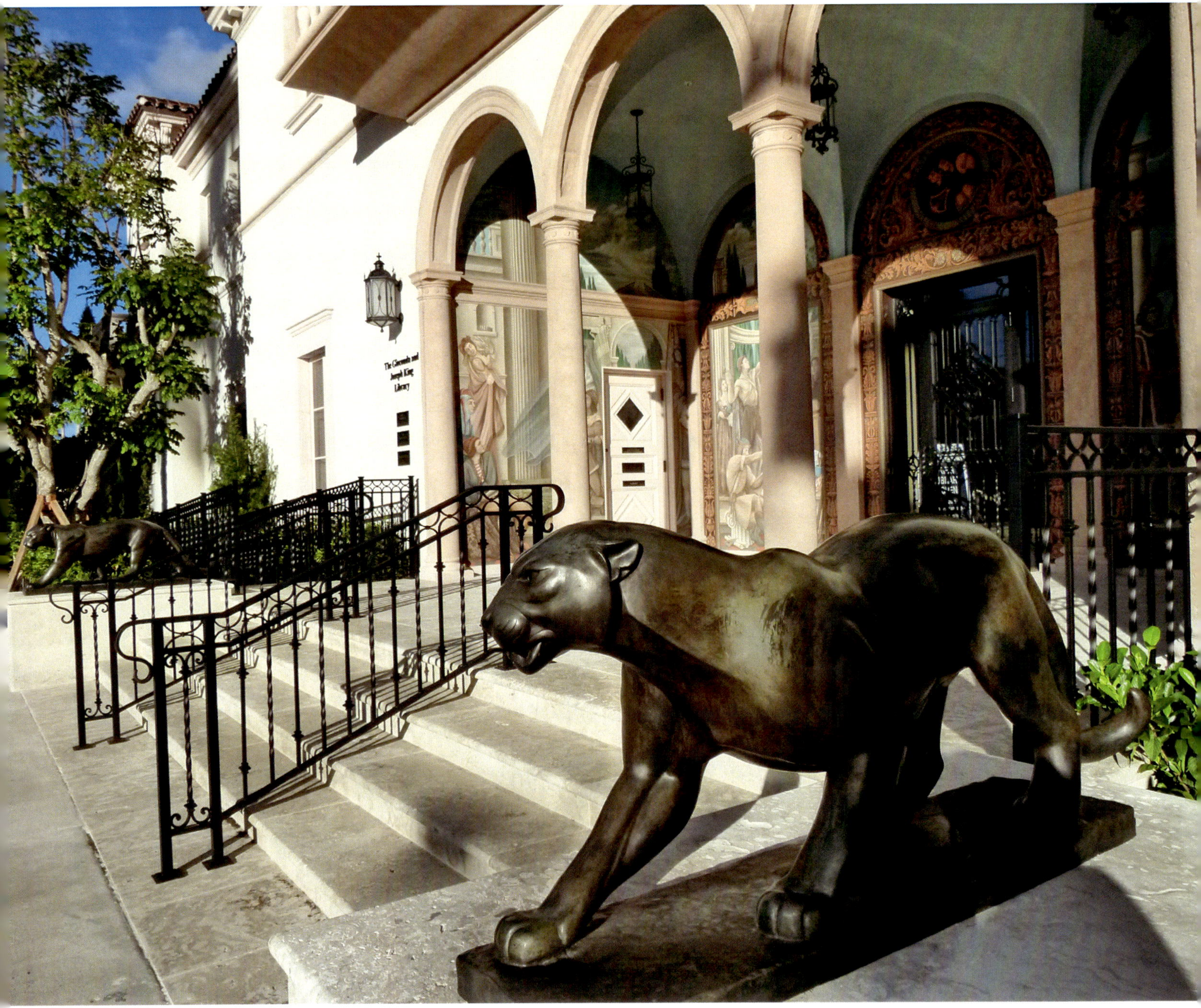

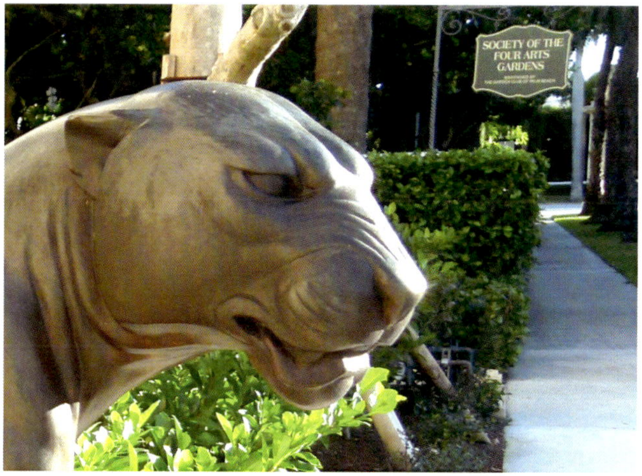

British artist Edwina Sandys loaned her painted aluminum sculpture, Eve's Apple, to the Society of the Four Arts sculpture garden. The sculpture is displayed near the watchful eye of her grandfather, Sir Winston Churchill who happens to be perched on a nearby bench in the garden with President Roosevelt.

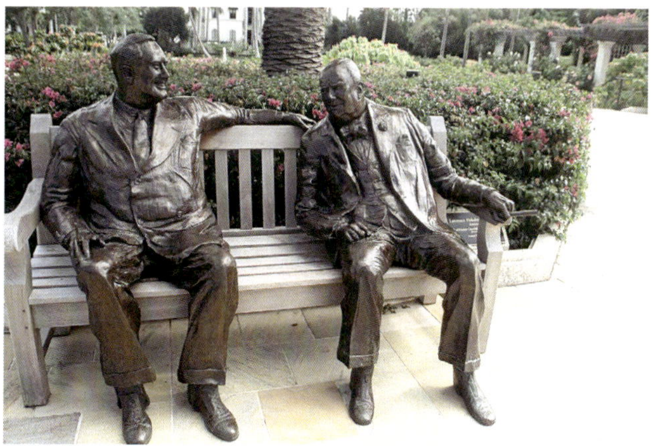

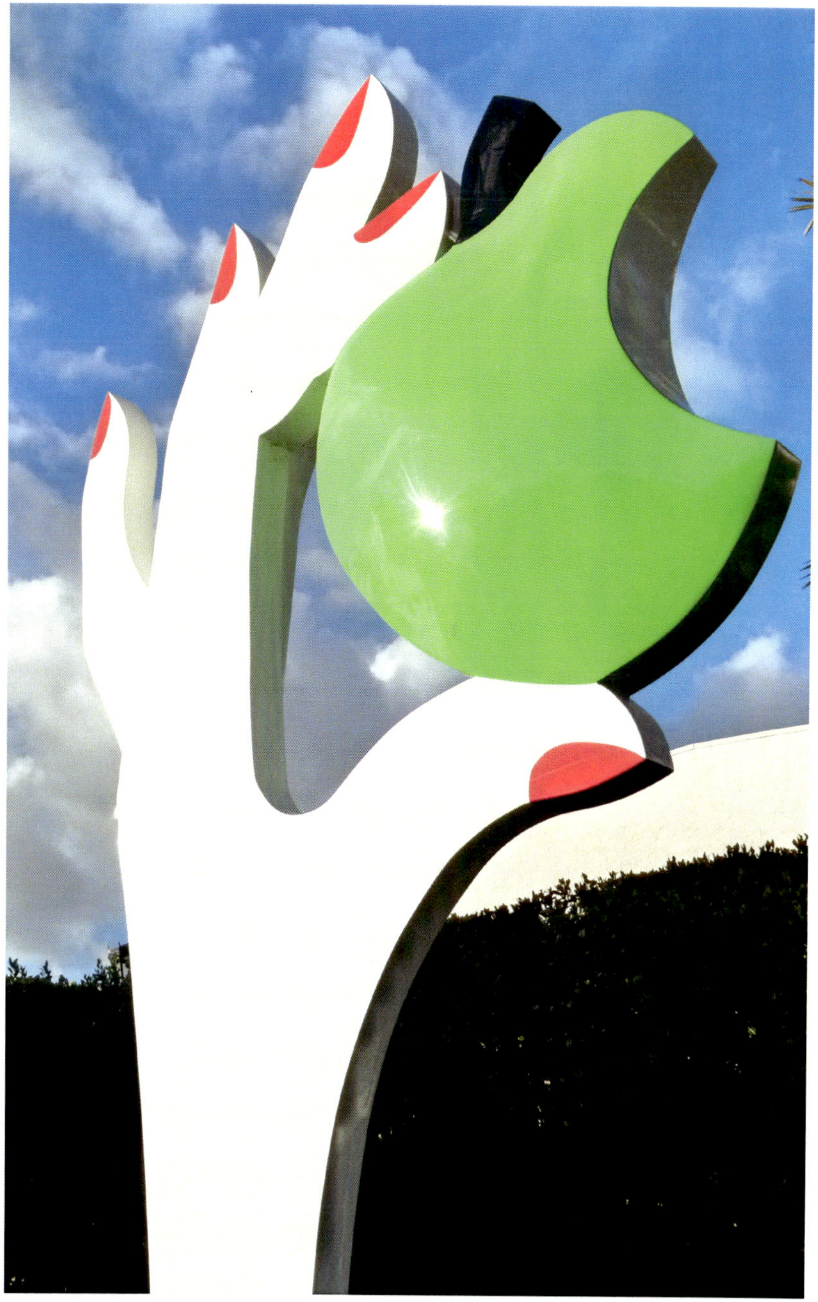

FASHION ICONS

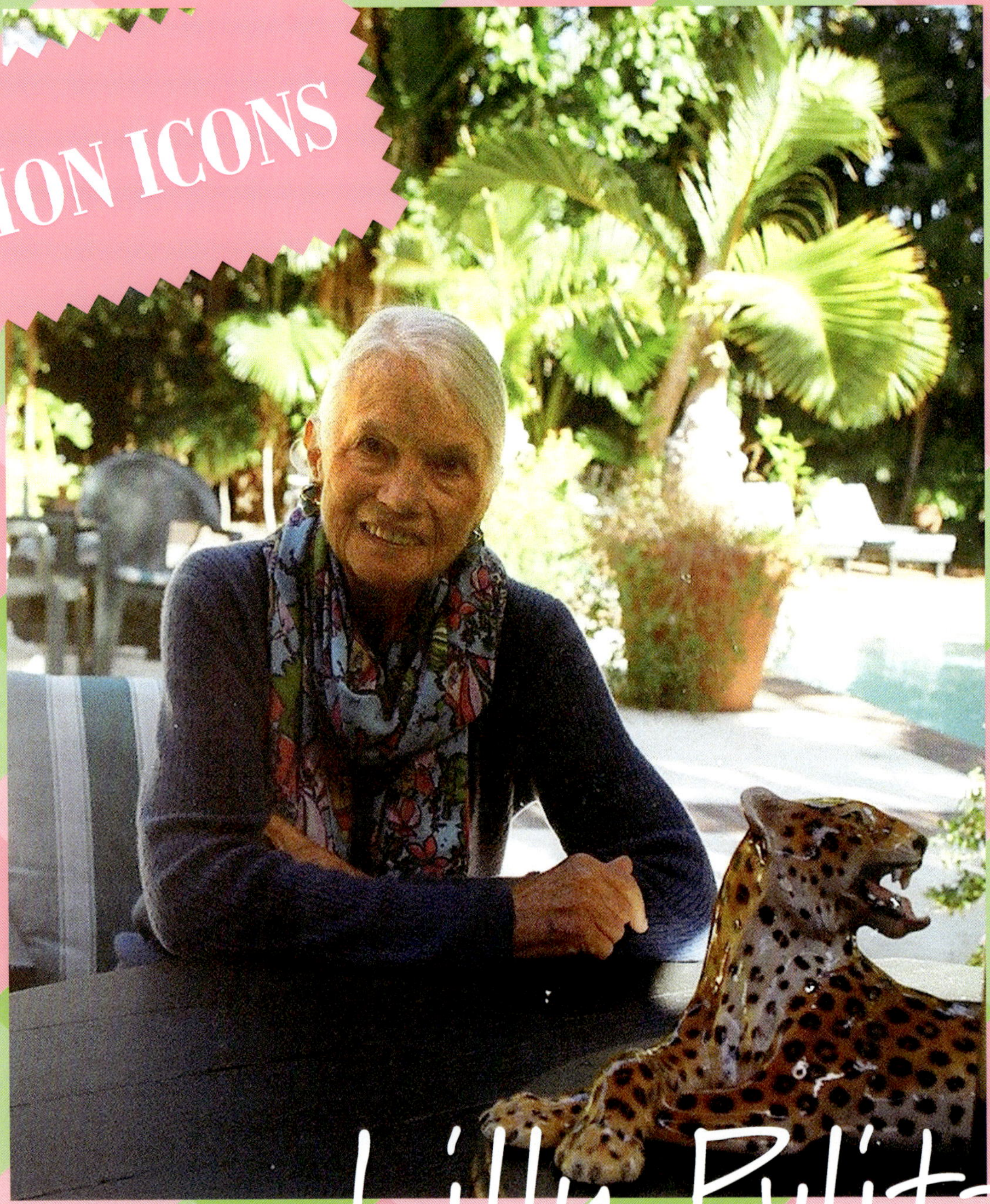

Lilly Pulitzer

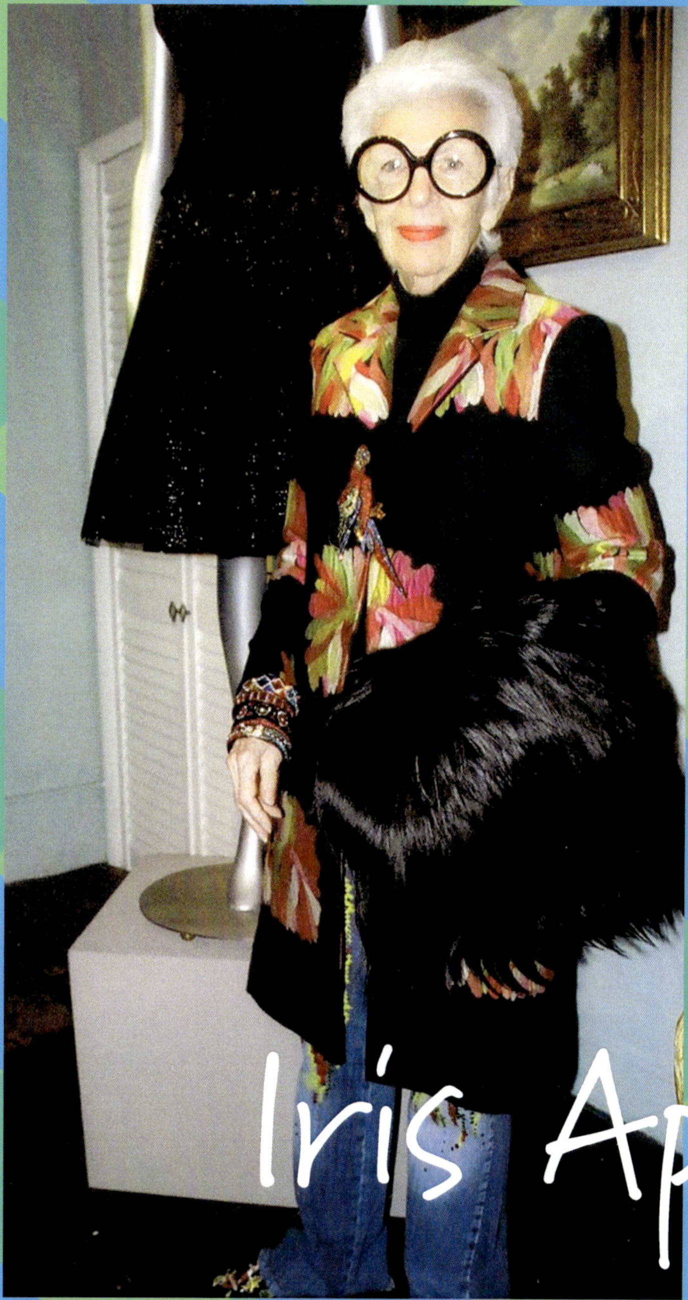

Iris Apfel

Michael Volbrecht

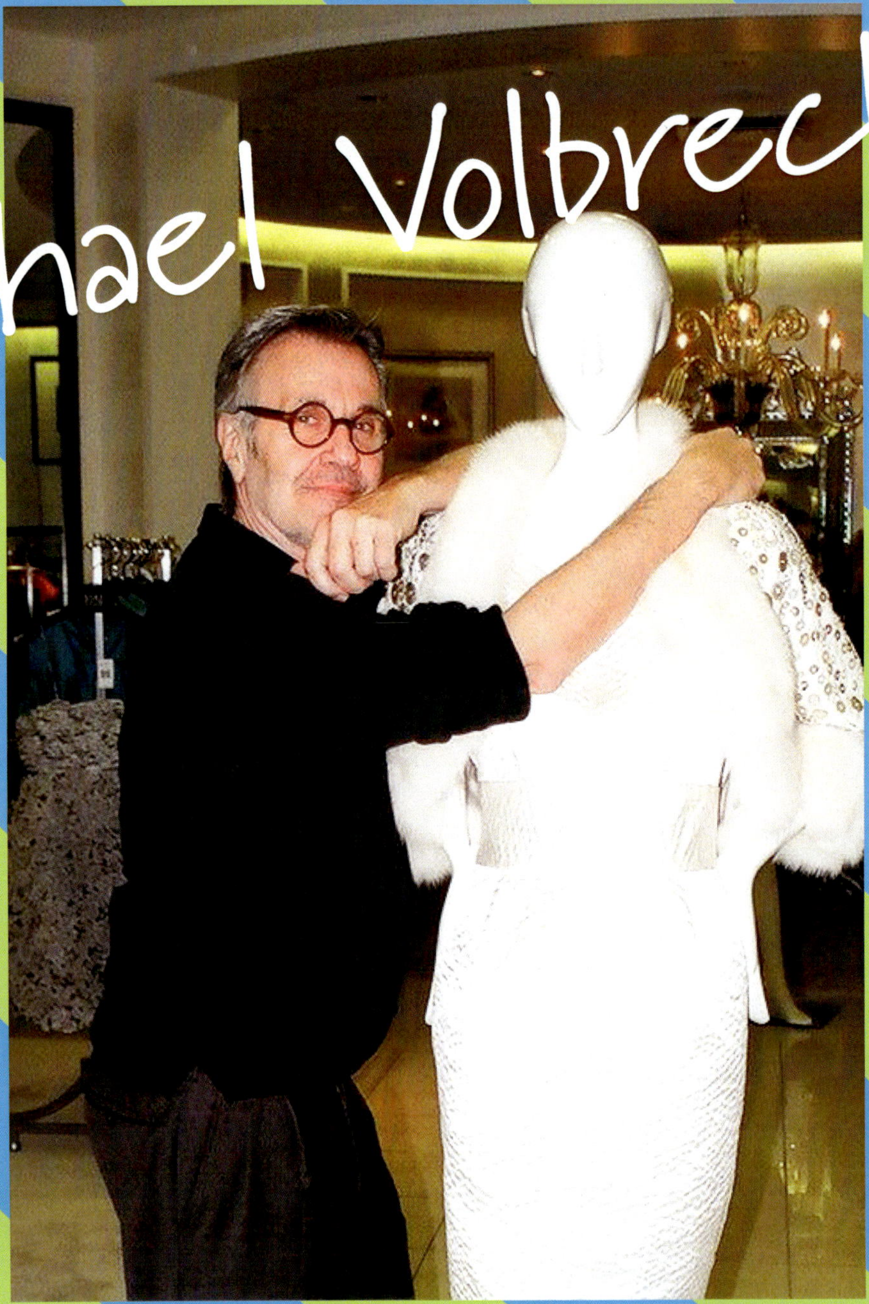

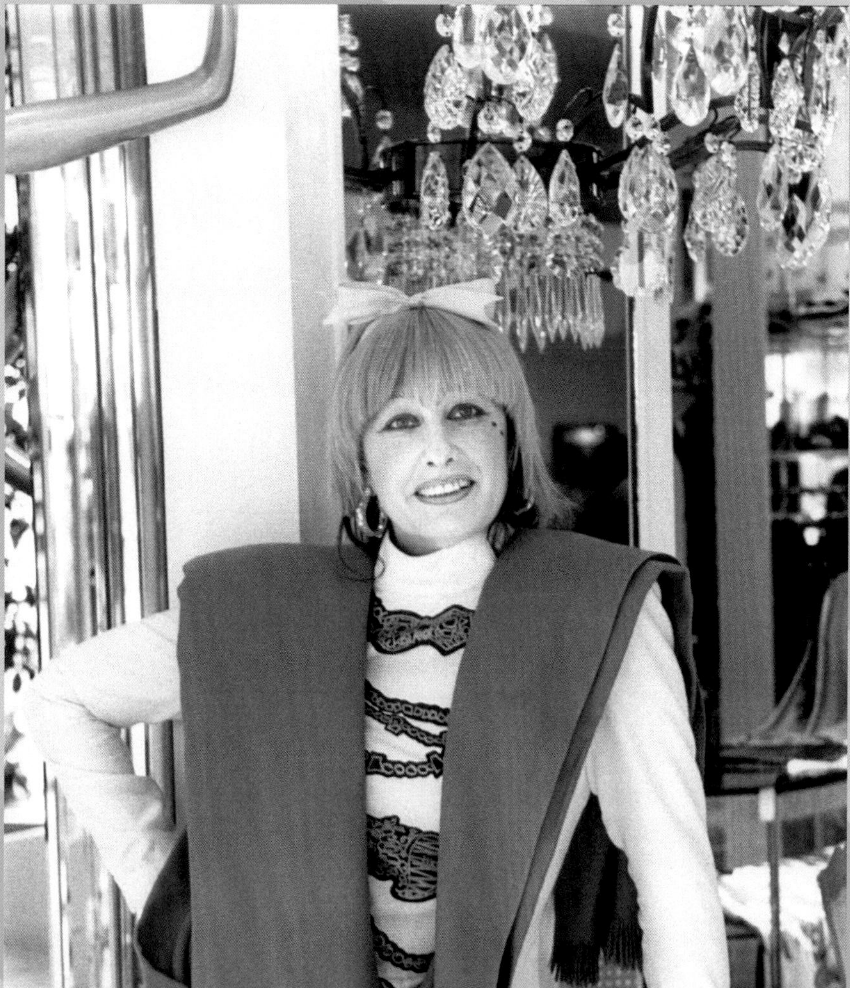

Zandra Rhodes

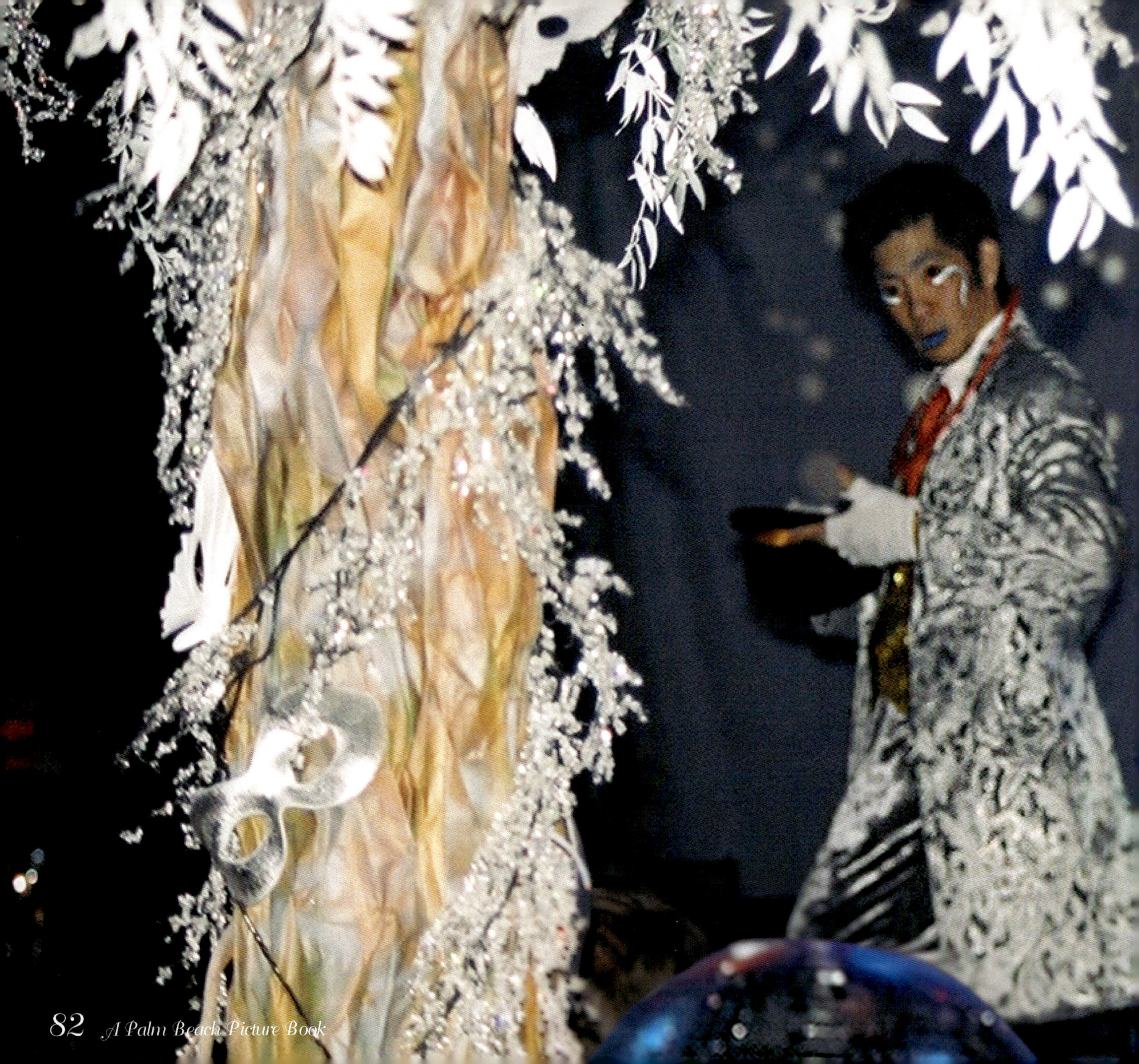

People & Parties

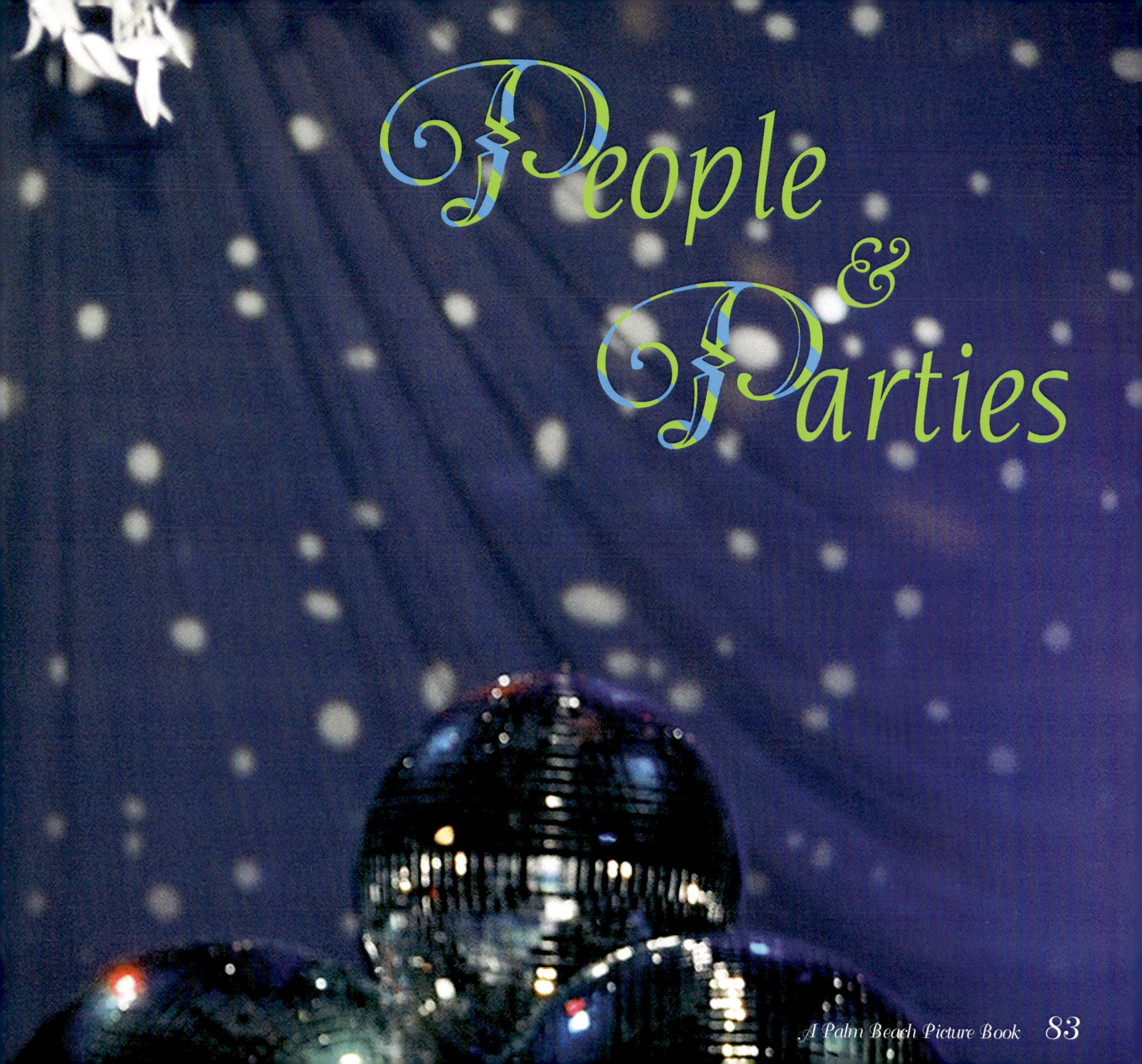

CONFESSIONS OF A PALM BEACH PARTY PLANNER

BY BRUCE SUTKA

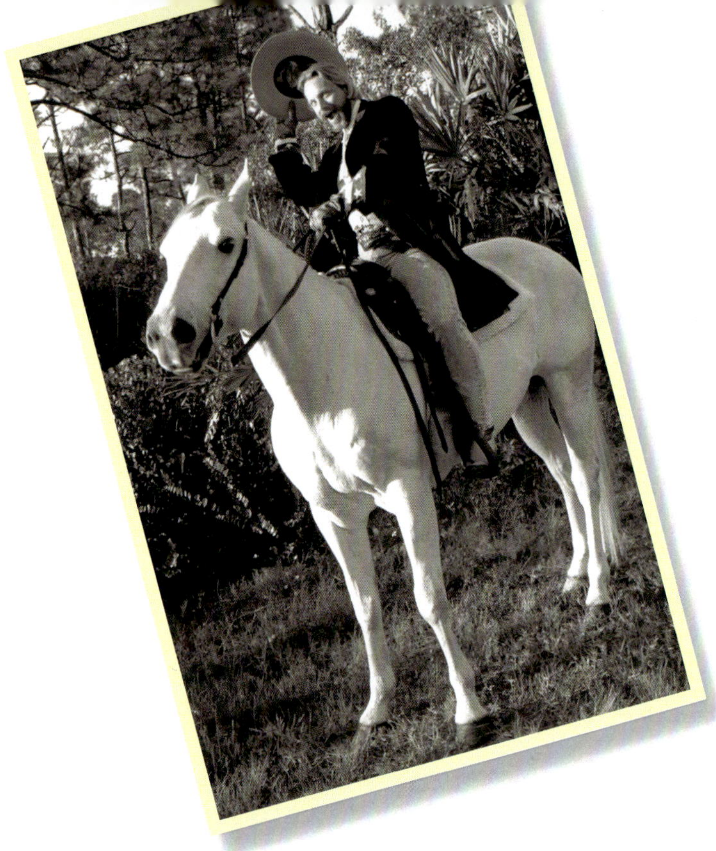

WHEN I STARTED CREATING PARTIES, we were at a time in our cultural history when the whole disco era was happening, Studio 54, Le Palace in Paris, and Les Mouches in New York. You had clubs all over the world that were really allowing people to shed their inhibitions and have a great time with their friends. That's exactly what happened in Palm Beach. I found myself at the right place at the right time. The people I was friends with were all young jet setters. They thought it was time that Palm Beach change the face of partying, and they invited me to help. I brought my ideas from what I was seeing in New York, and my imagination was unleashed for them. They wanted a New Year's Eve party that would attract people from all over the world.

I did a lot of things as an artist, a sculptor, interior designer, furniture painter and window designer. We got written up all over the country because of these parties in Palm Beach. It was such a departure from your regular charity event where you'd get to your table and they didn't have any décor and no fancy table cloths or good lighting. There was never any real excitement to these things.

Then we took the party to another level. We wouldn't let them know what was happening. My parties were shocking and entertaining, and had an element of surprise. I never really told them exactly what they were getting.

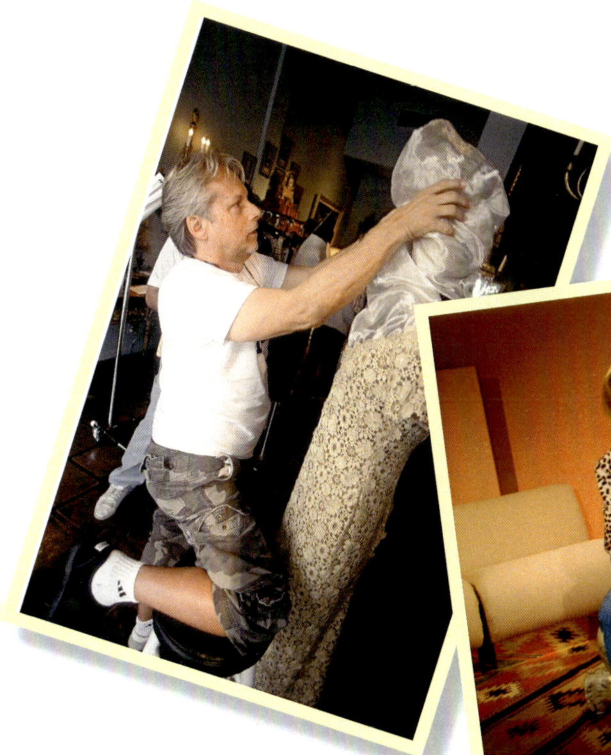

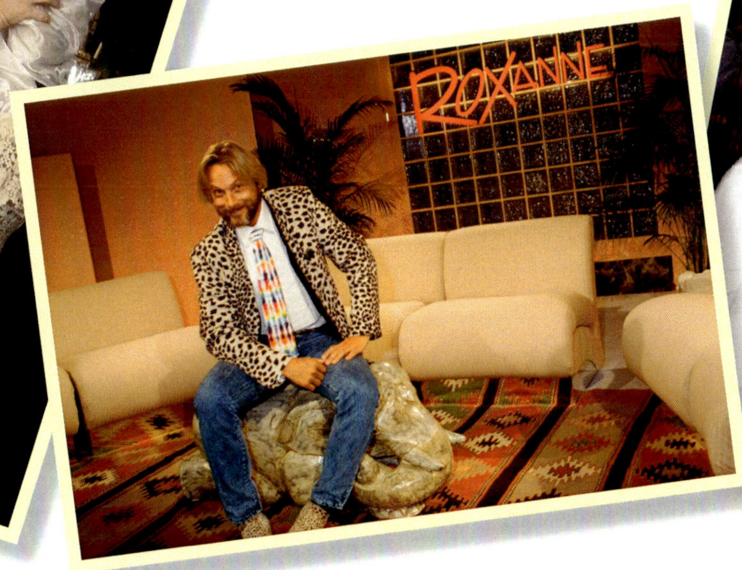

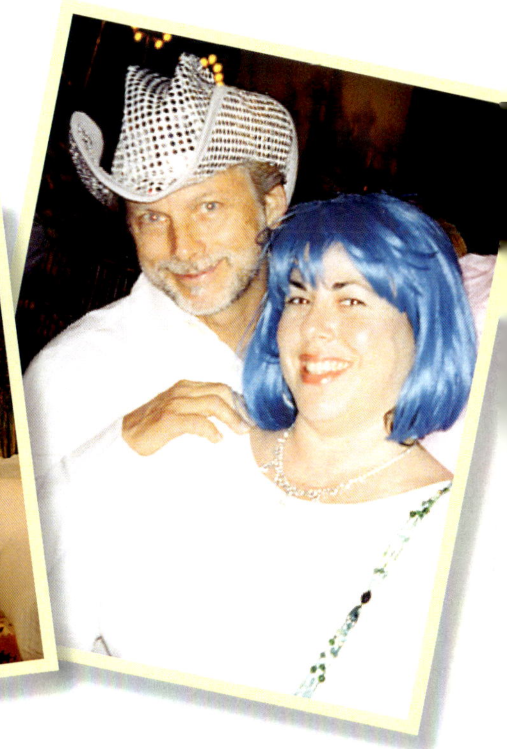

They knew the gist of it, but the New Year's Eve reveal was top secret.

Sometimes we would have lions and tigers on the pathway to the museum, or there would be an elephant brought in and trapeze artists. Or, we would have Joey Arias come from New York singing "Devil with the Blue Dress On," and he'd tear the blue dress off wearing a G-string on stage. Once Jimmy Buffett jumped on stage with the band. It was always one surprise after the next. One year, we flew 19 drag queens in from New York for New Year's Eve and let them run rampant. Those are the things that people never forget. I totally broke the mold in Palm Beach. And that was because of the people I was working with here.

The young socialites in Palm Beach at the time wanted to have fun! They'd had enough of these boring parties. All of a sudden everybody wanted me to do their event because they felt that I had a following of people. They wanted all the young cool people there instead of the same old same old. We kind of started a trend.

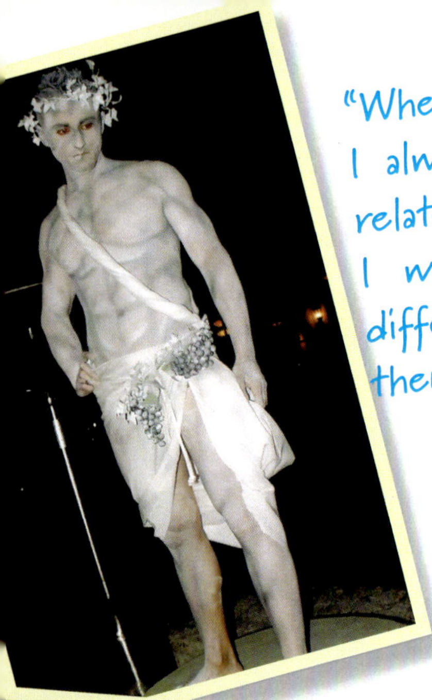

"When I put these parties together, I always tell a story that people can relate to, a story that's not too abstract. I want people experience something different than what they're used to."

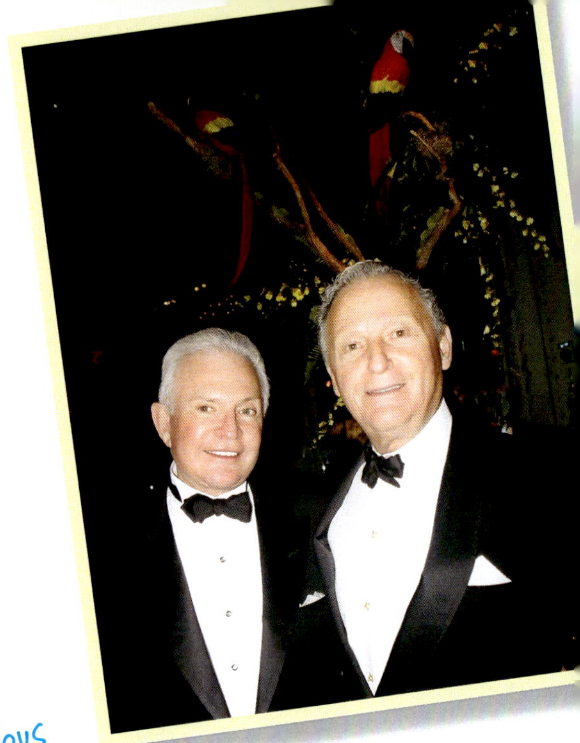

PARTIES

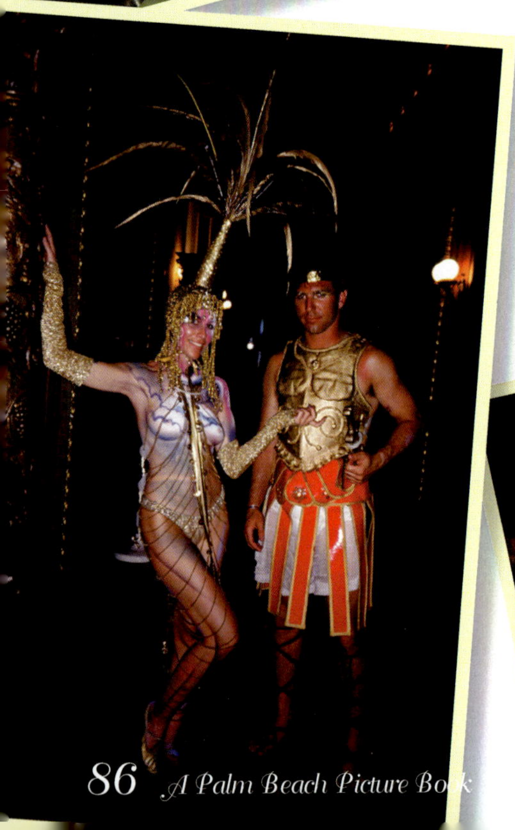

"I think people like vicarious thrills. I don't care what level you're living at, you like being around celebrity and stars."

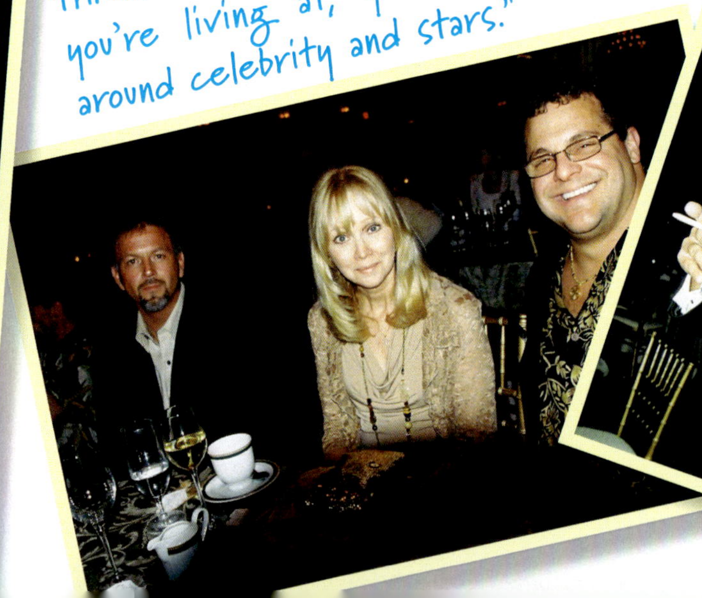

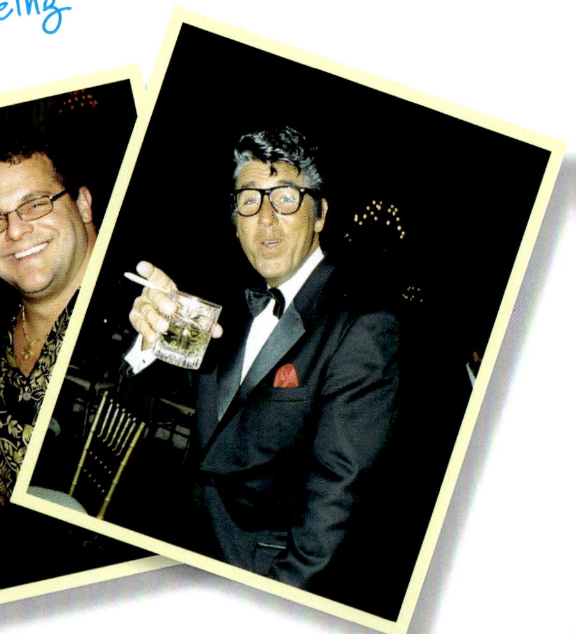

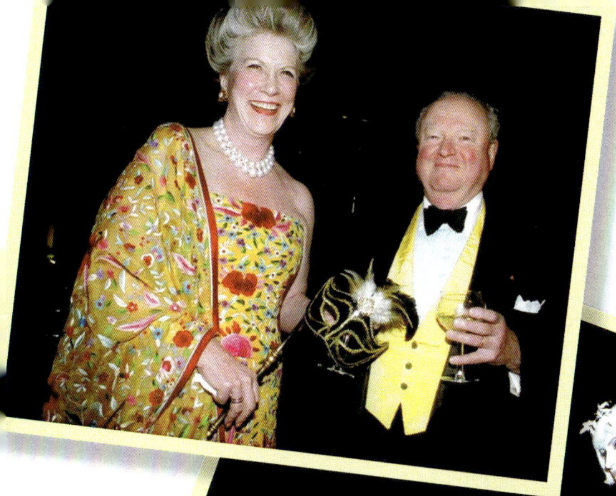
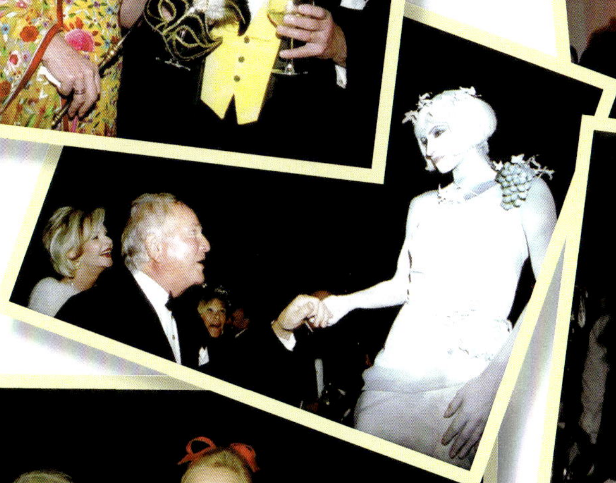
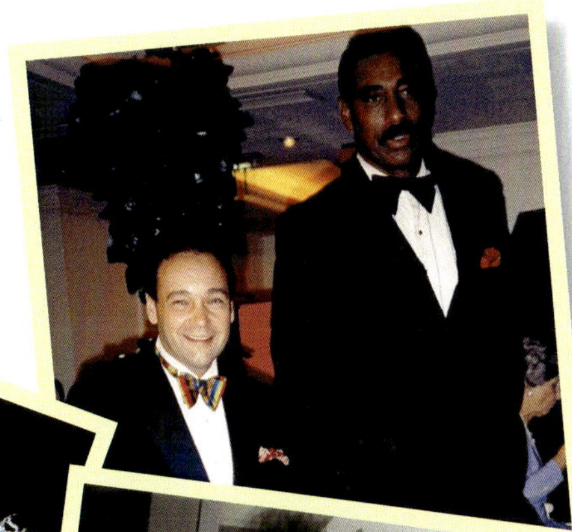
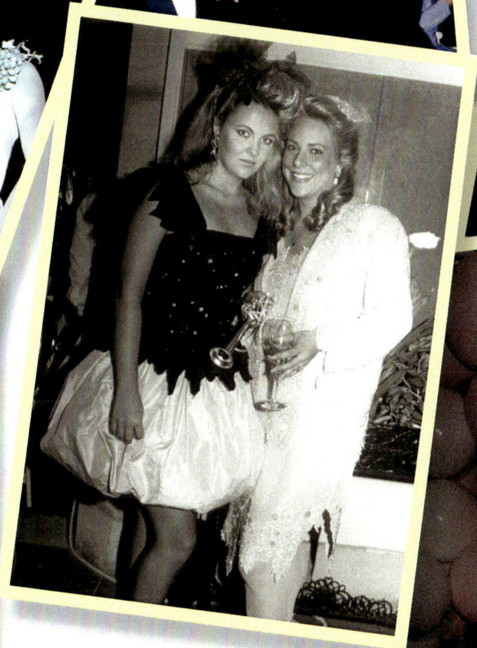
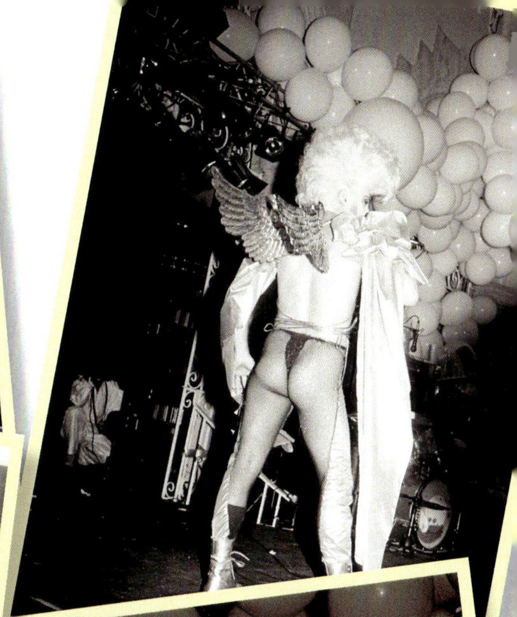
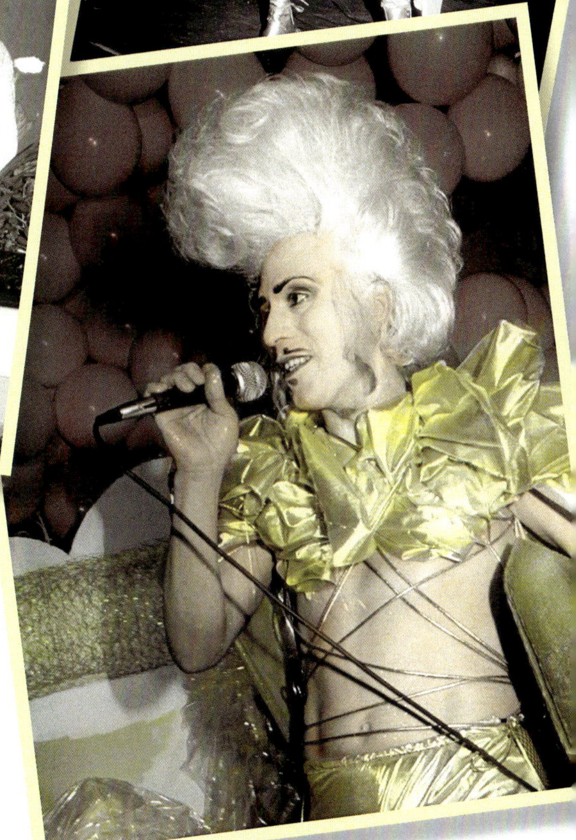
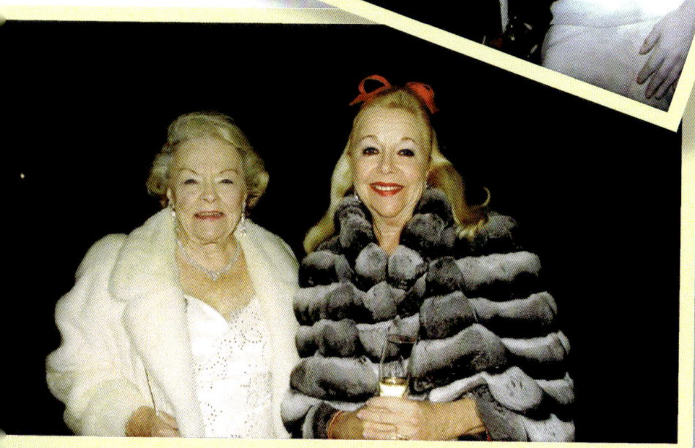
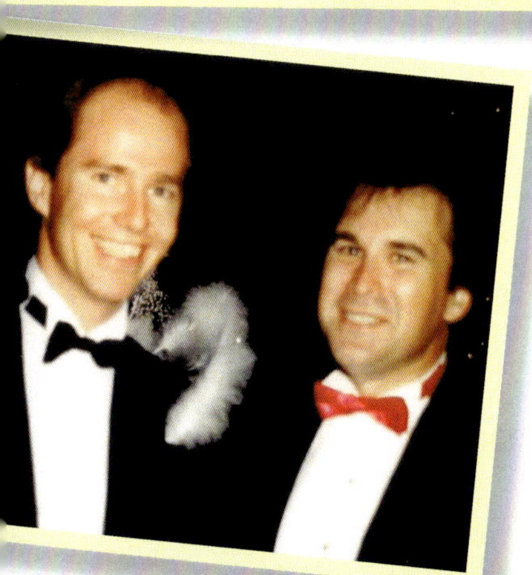

"People want creativity. They want something unusual with a different slant on something. They don't want old same old. In this time, I think we're into escapism."

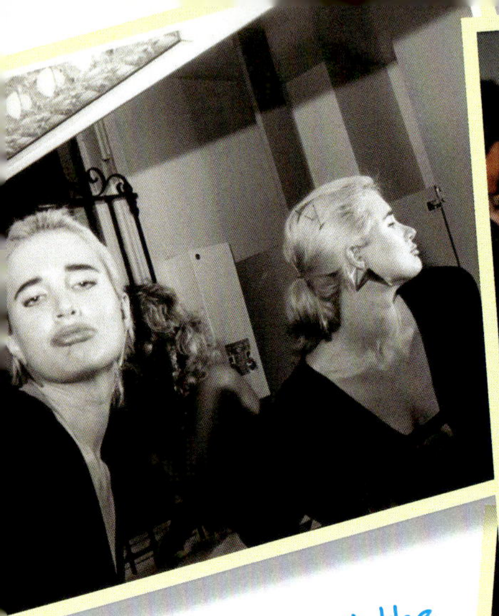

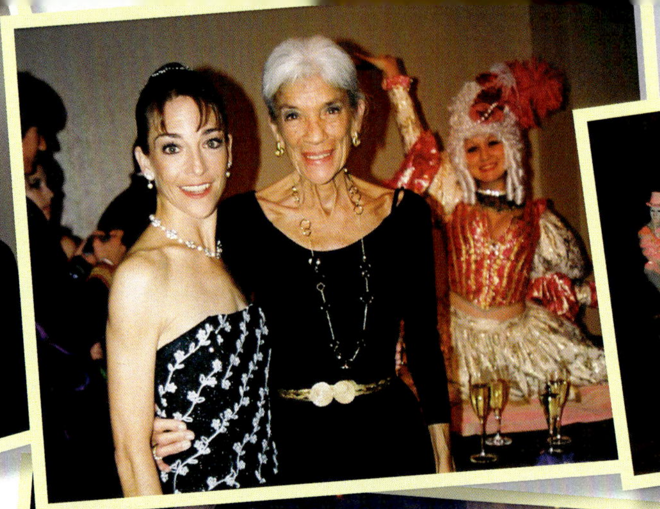

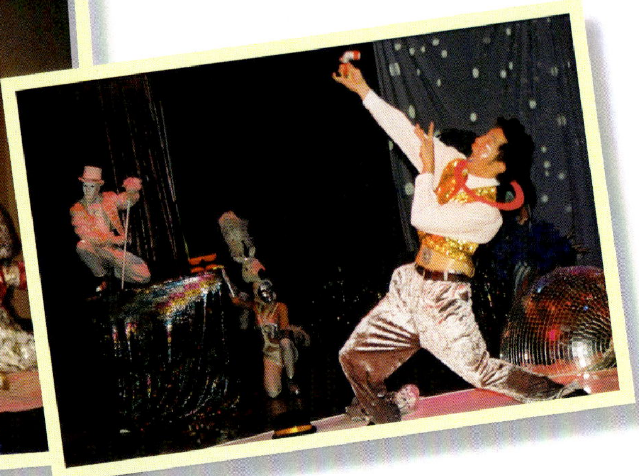

think we've raised the ar for parties here in Palm Beach."

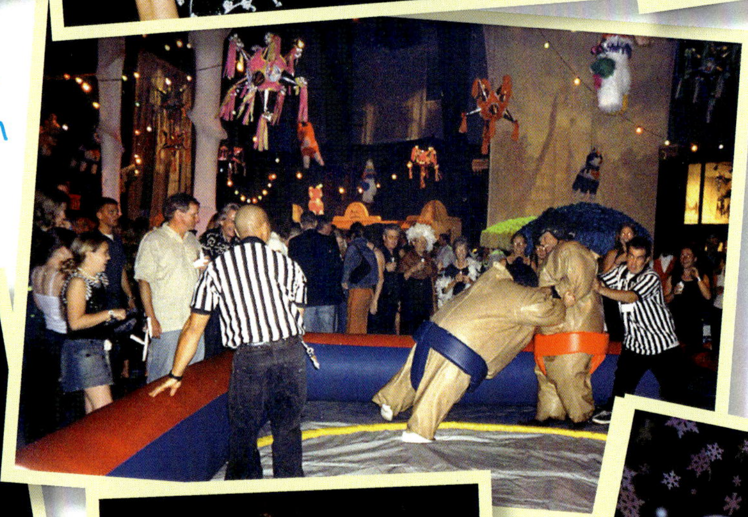

"Palm Beach was built and predicated on the idea of fun and that's what we're still doing here during the season."

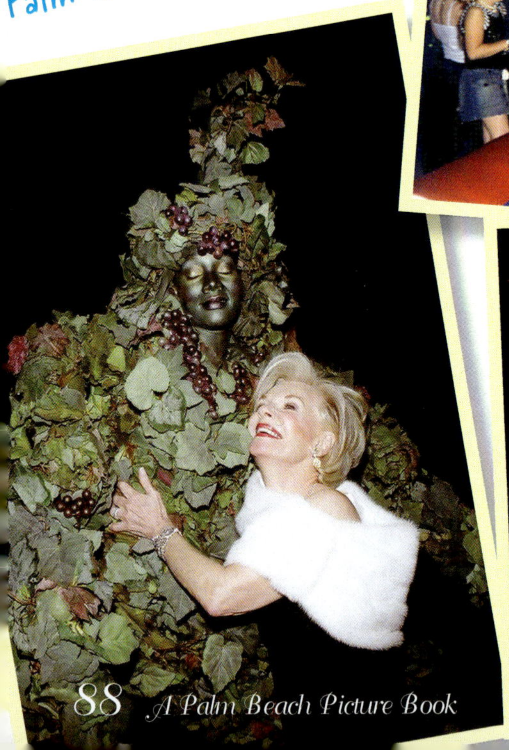

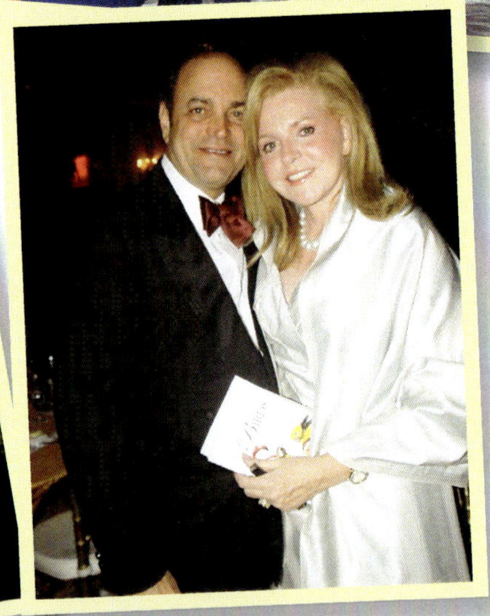

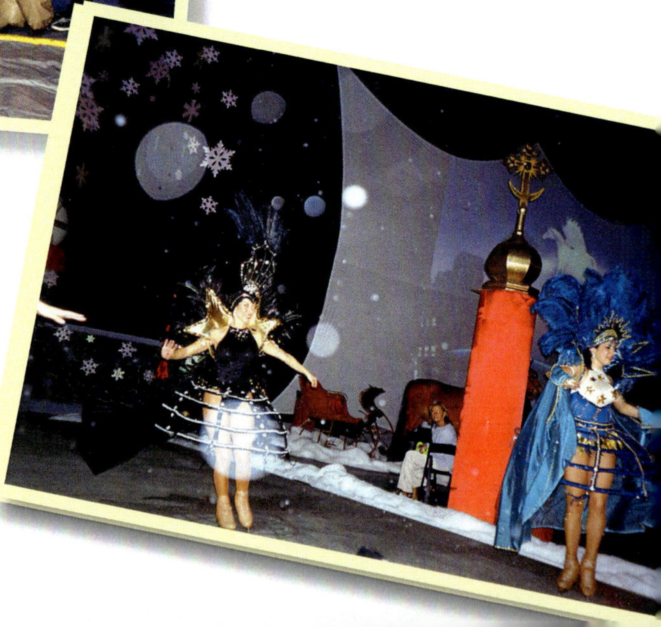

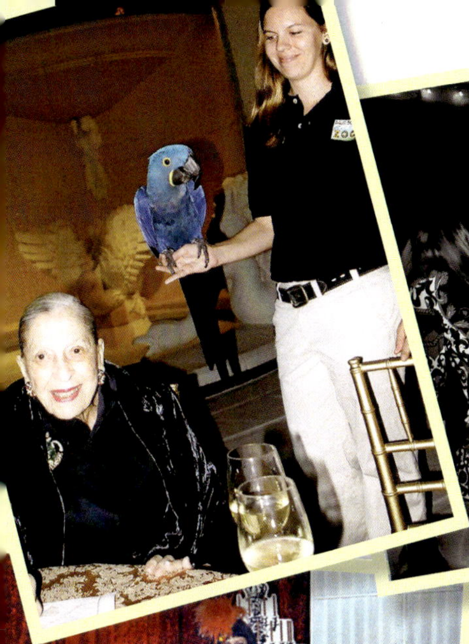

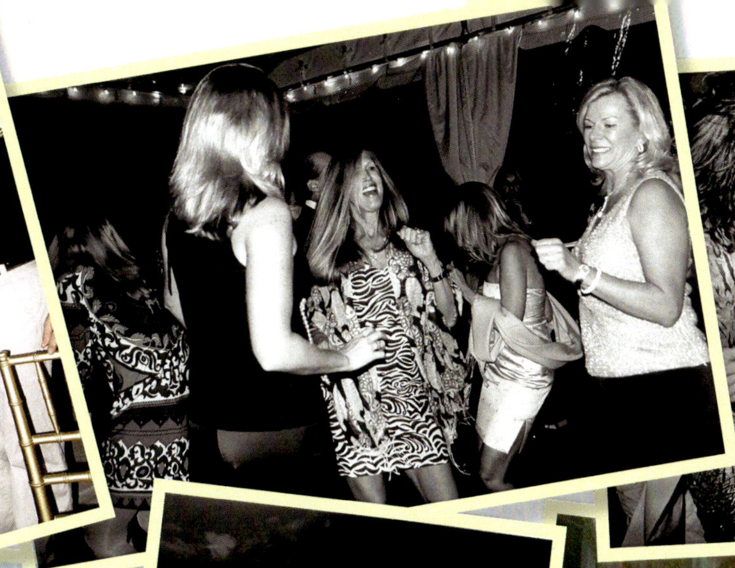

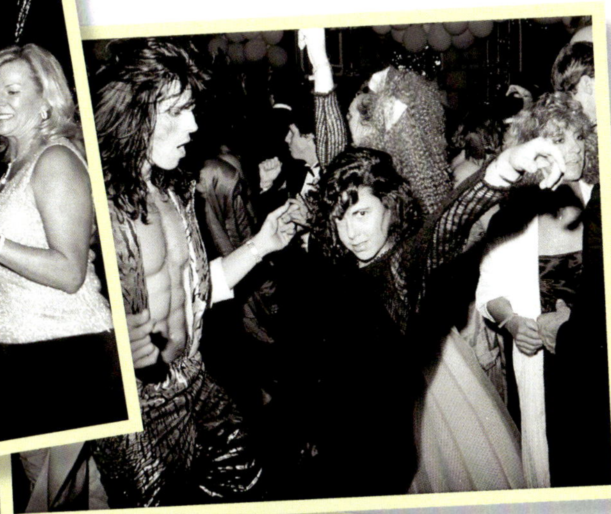

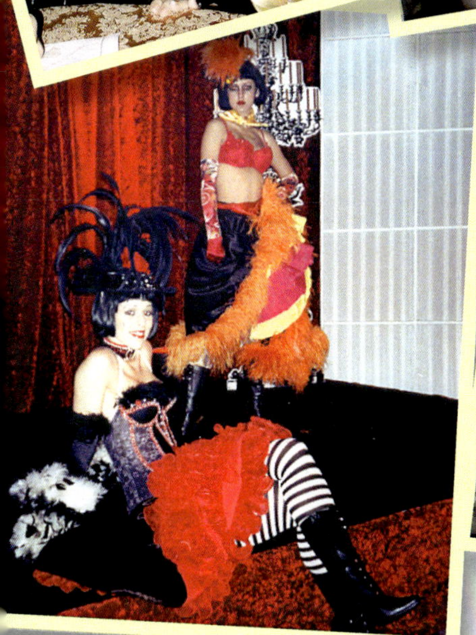

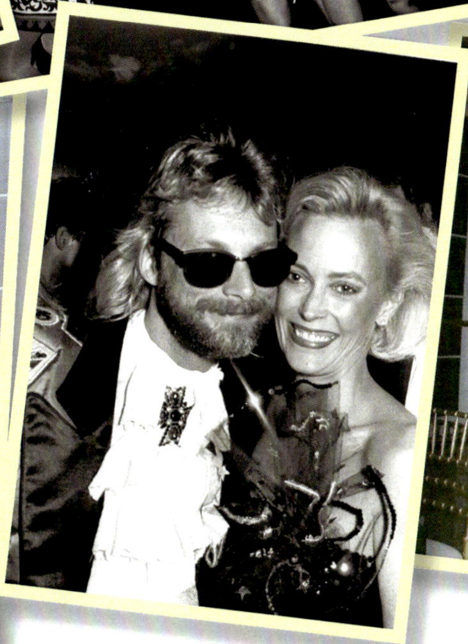

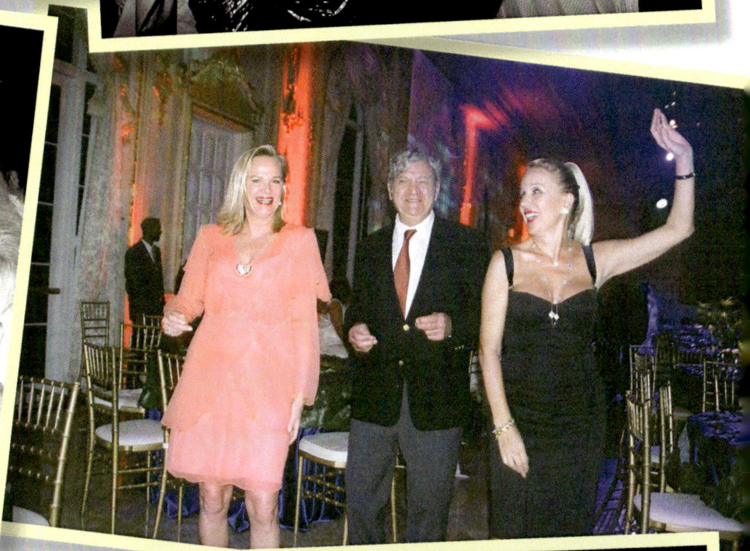

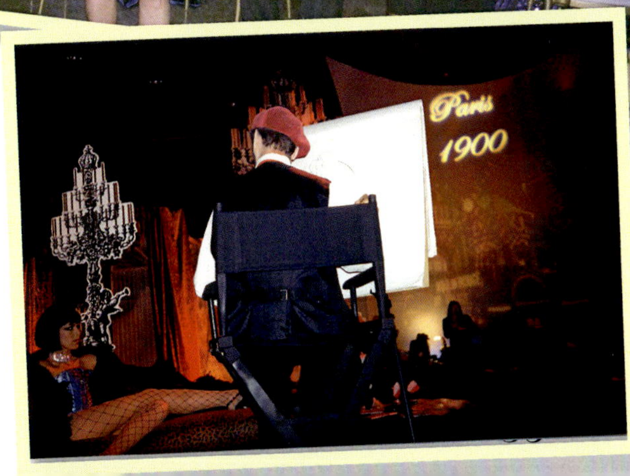

"It's not just a party. I think there should be things that people look at all night that go on in a certain flow which increases the energy level of the room."

FAMOUS FACES

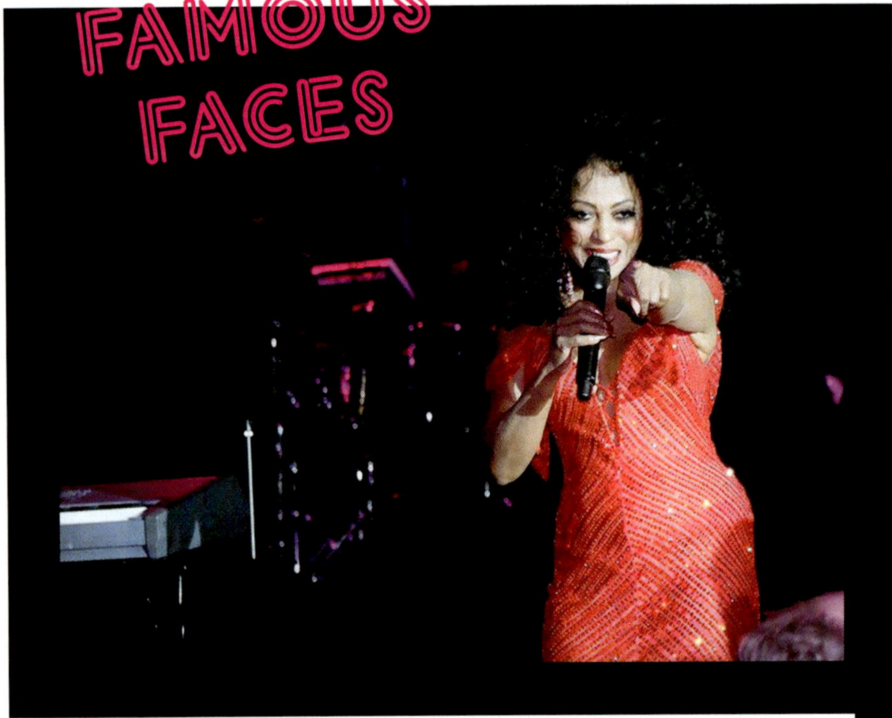

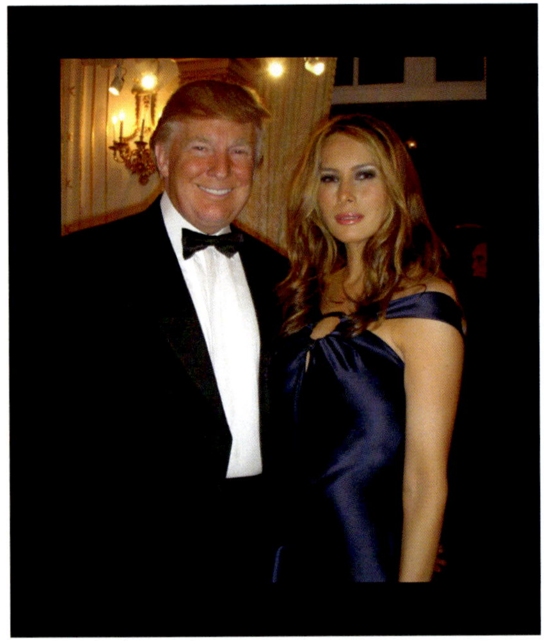

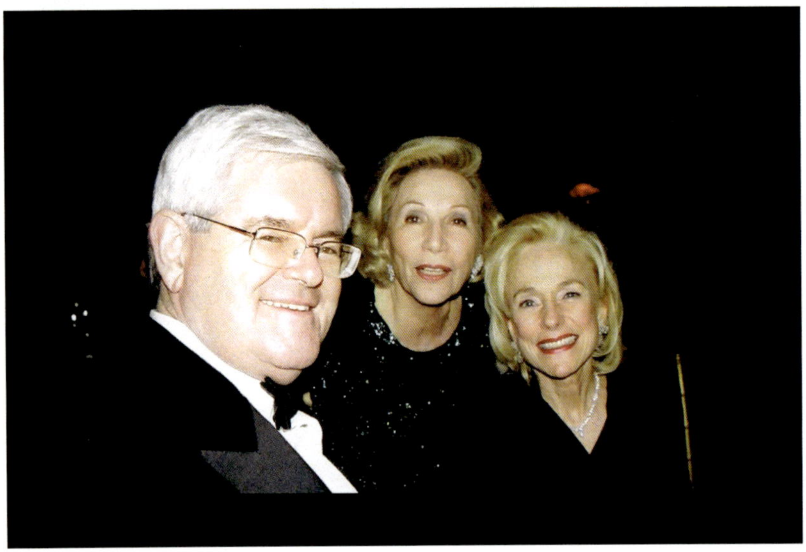

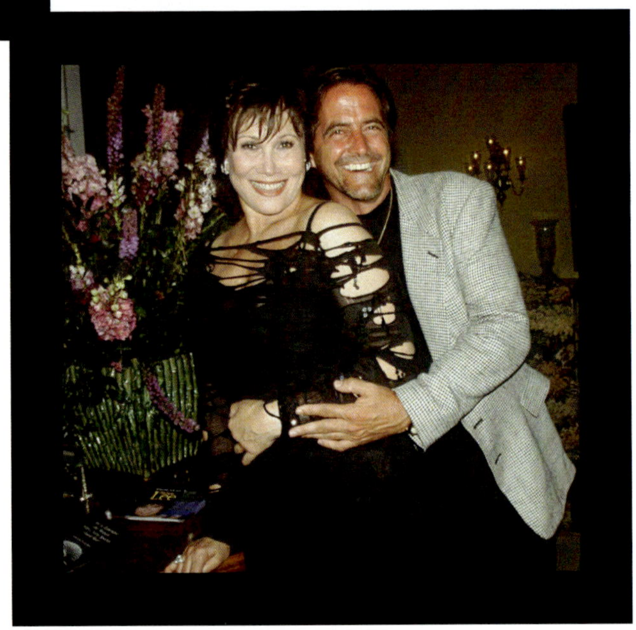

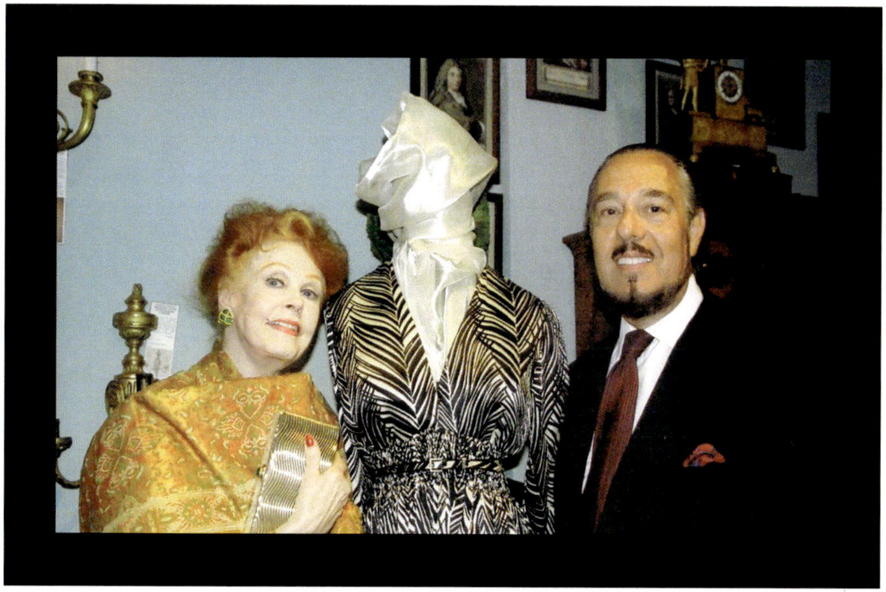

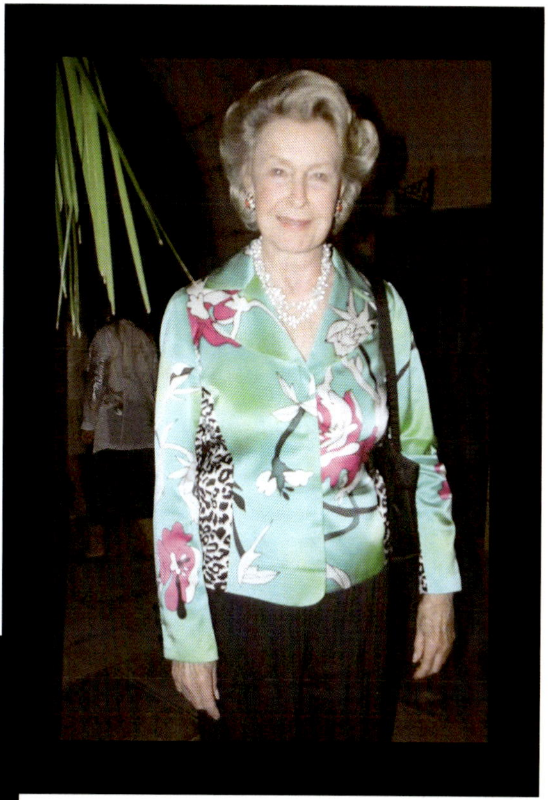

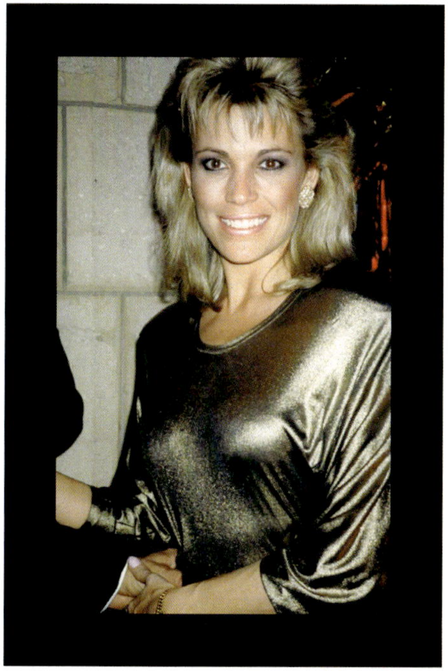

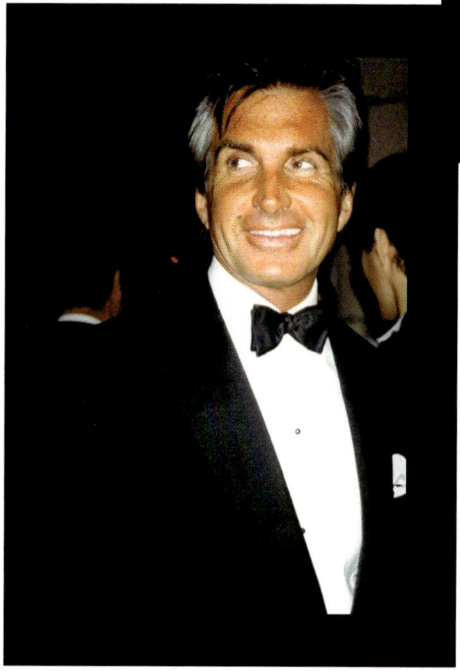

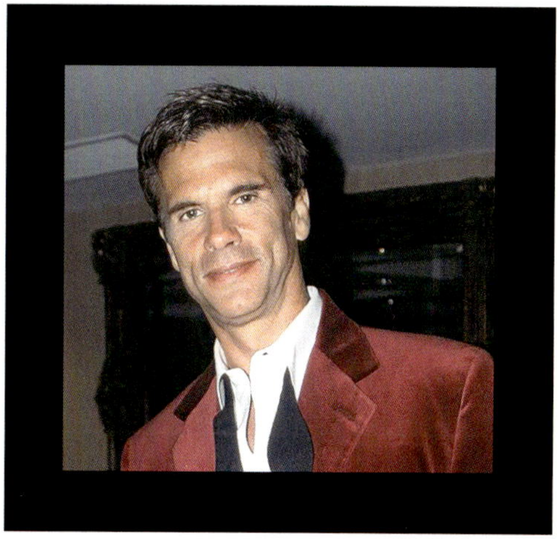

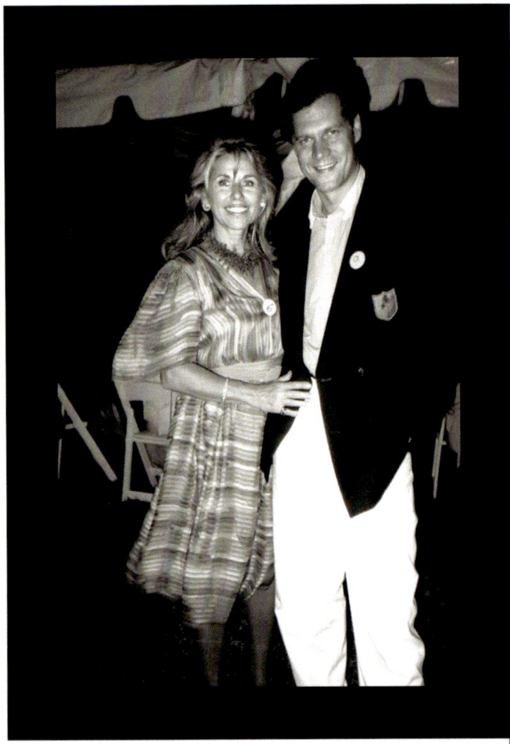

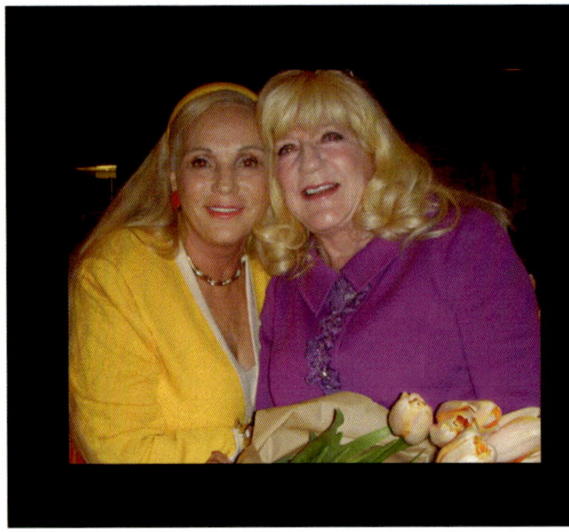

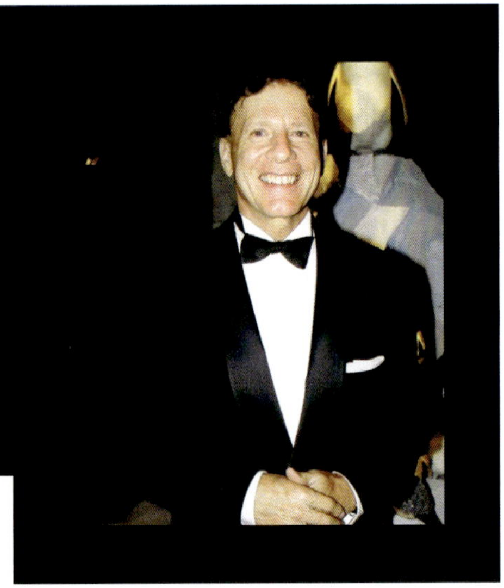

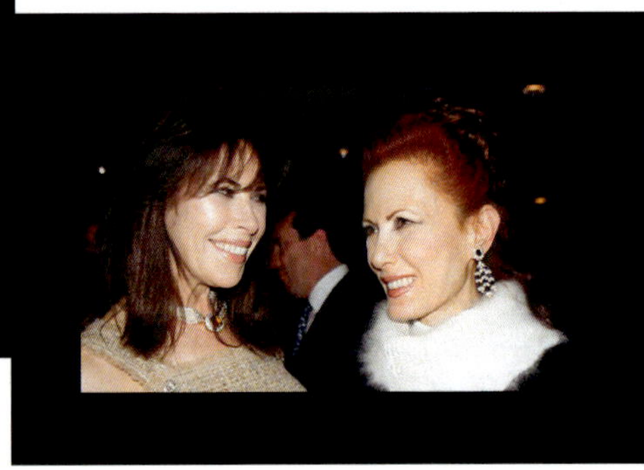

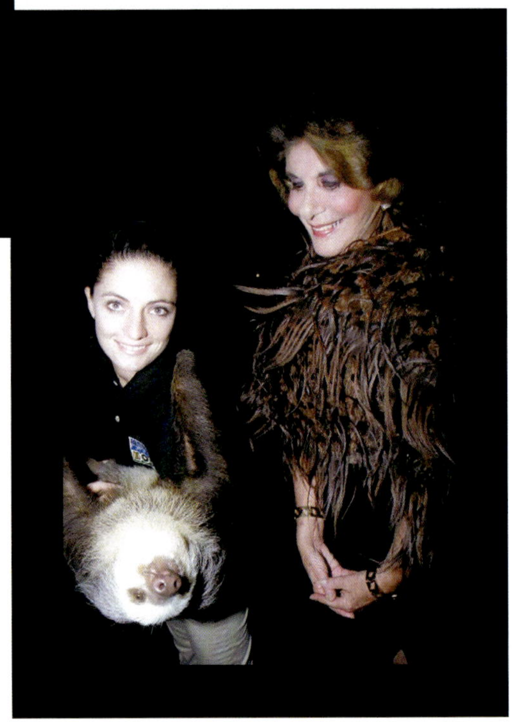

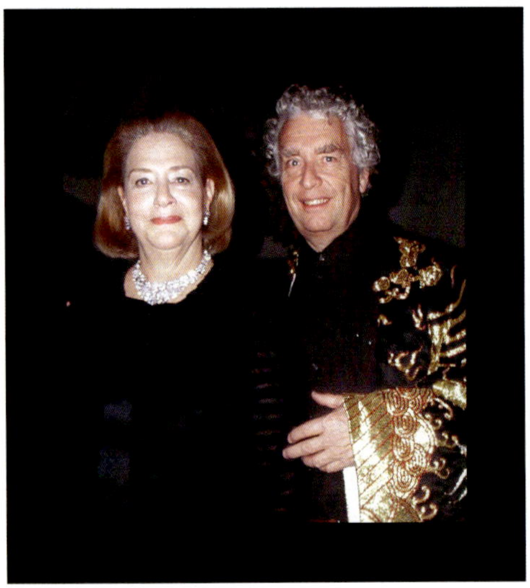

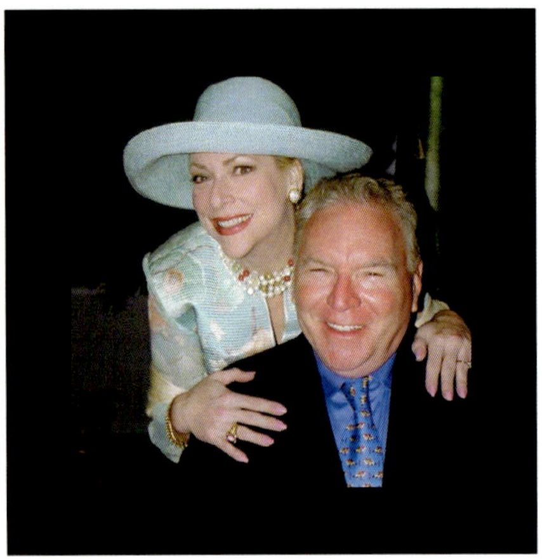

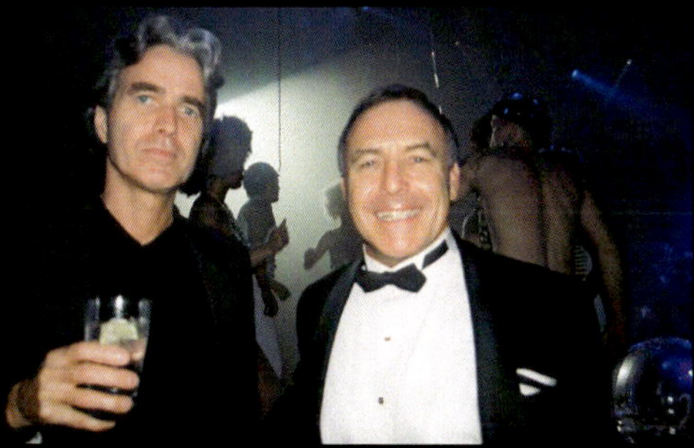

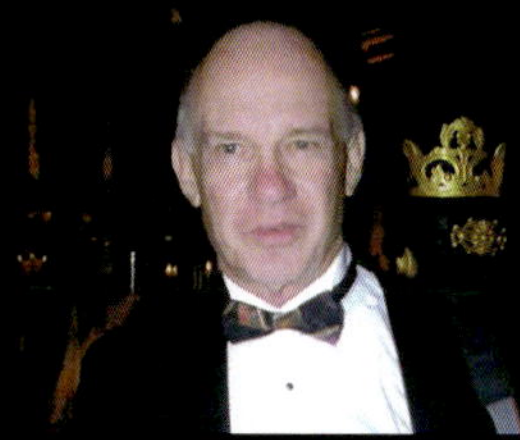

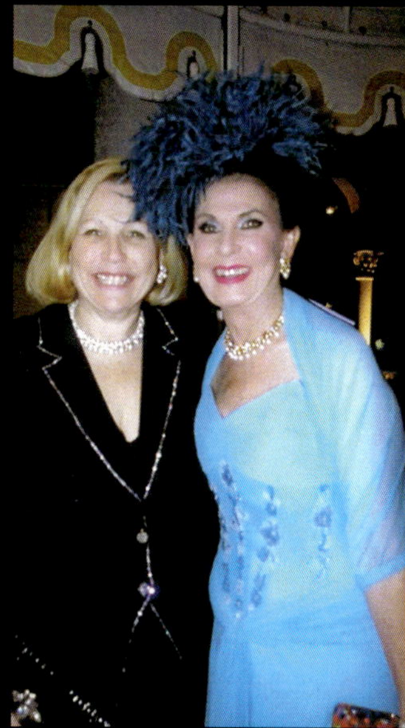

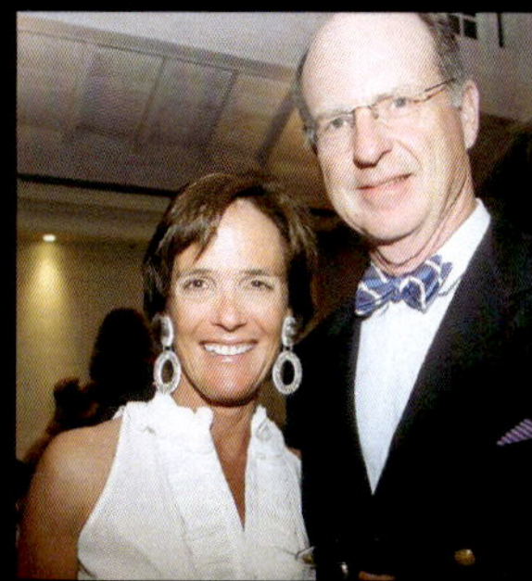

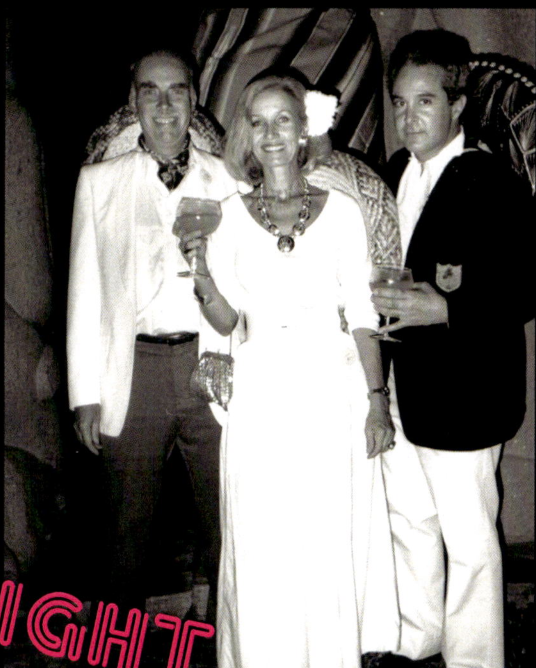

NIGHT OWLS

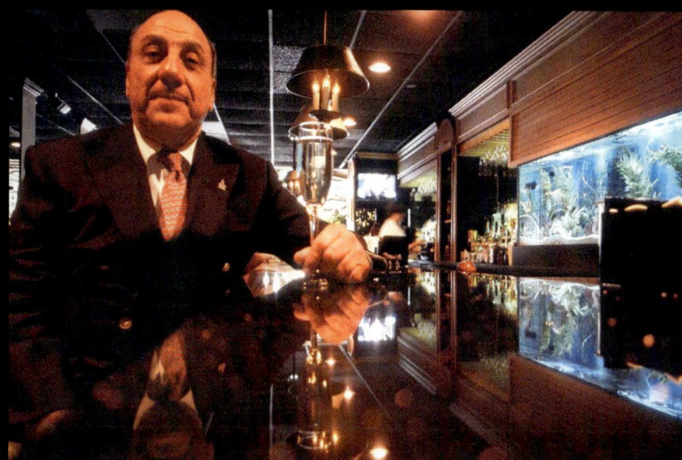

AFTERNOON TEA

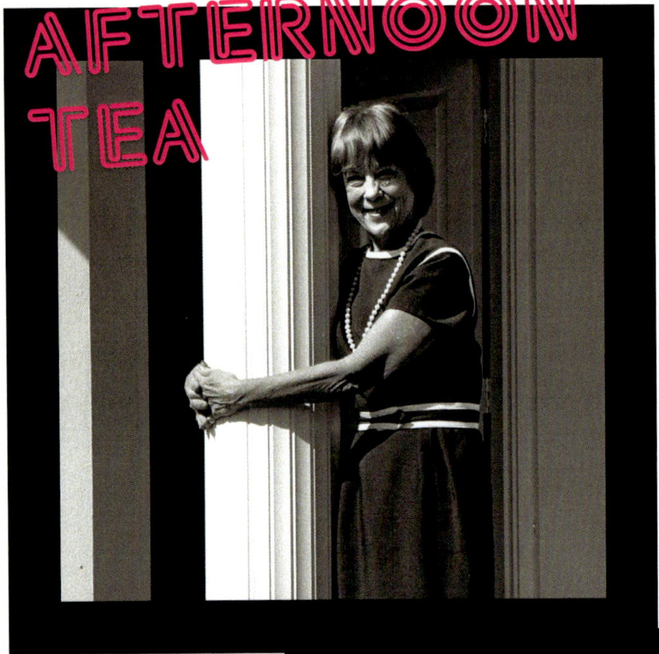

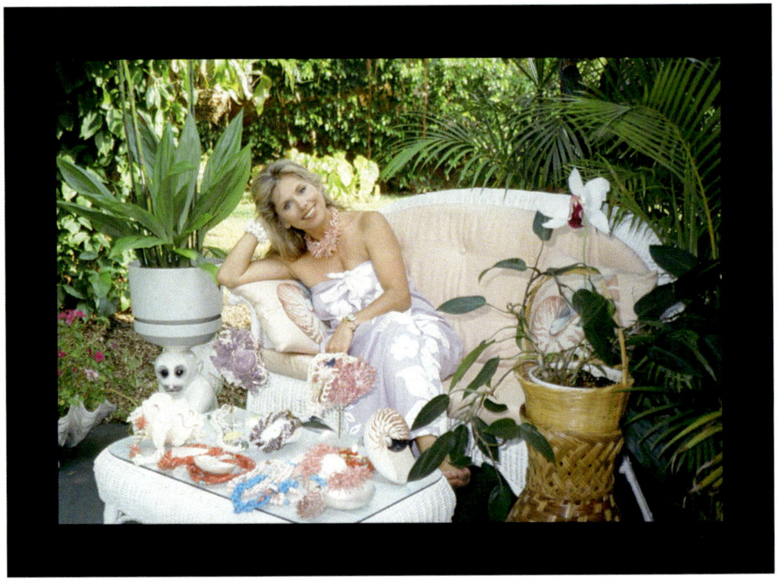

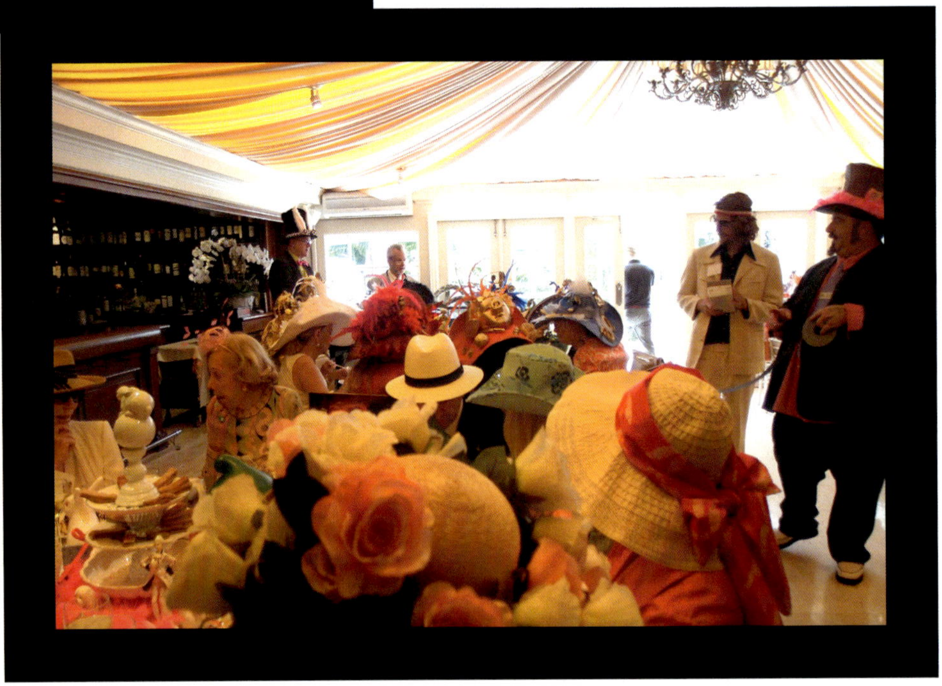

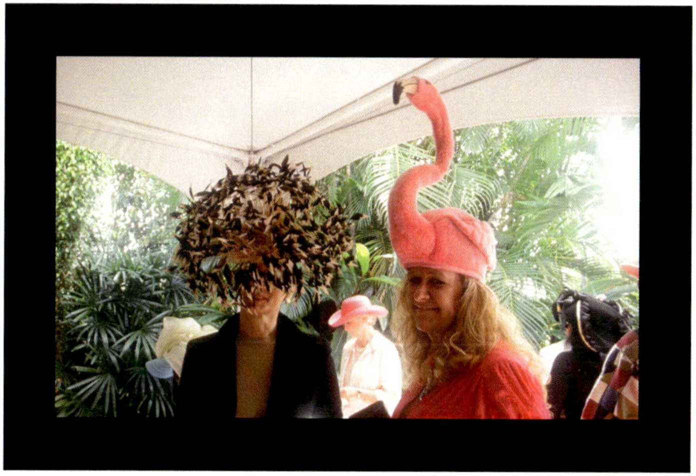

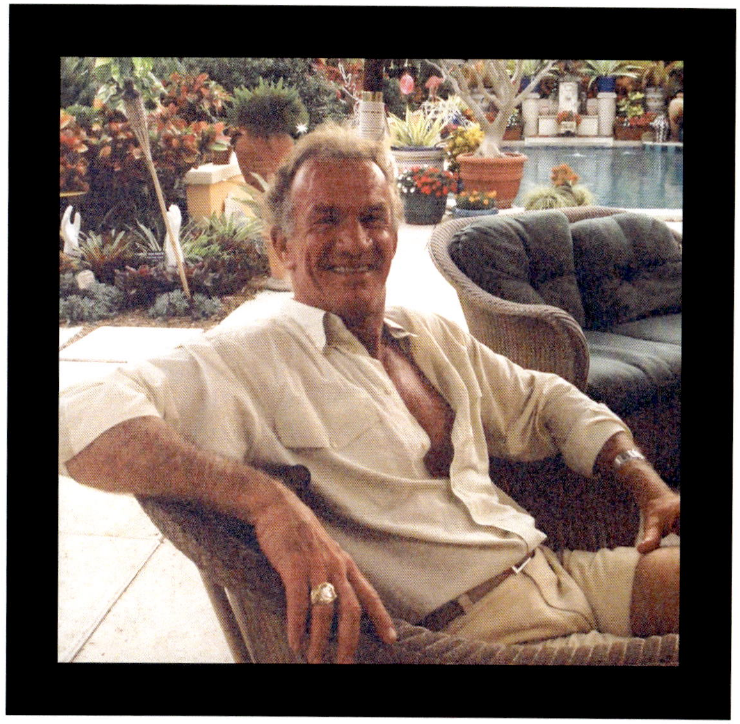

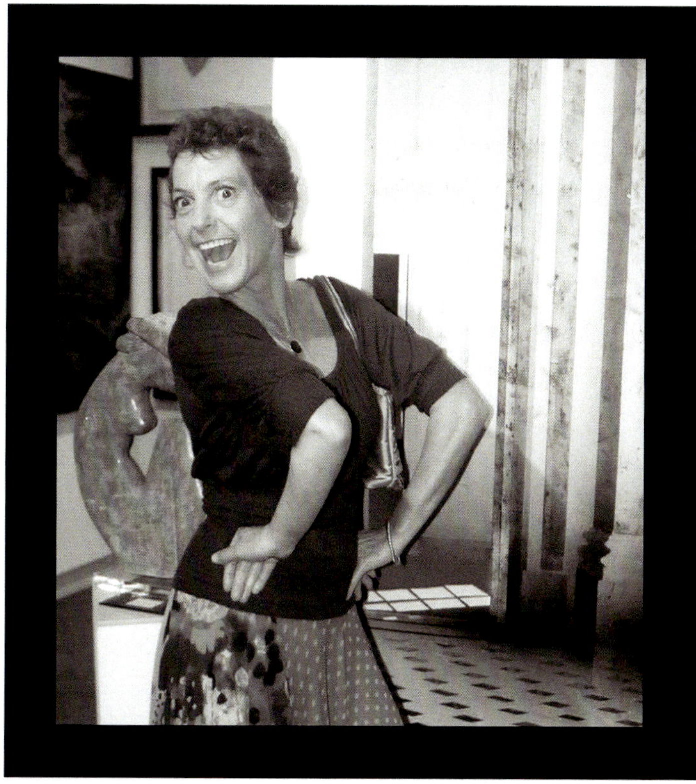

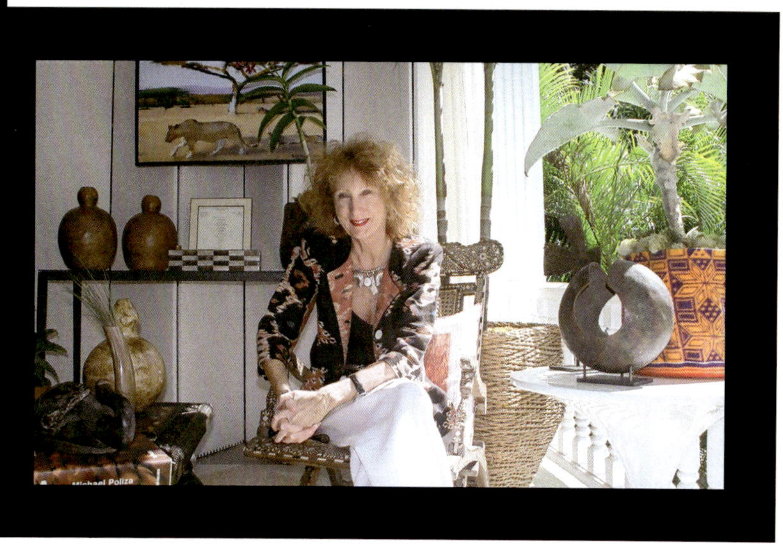

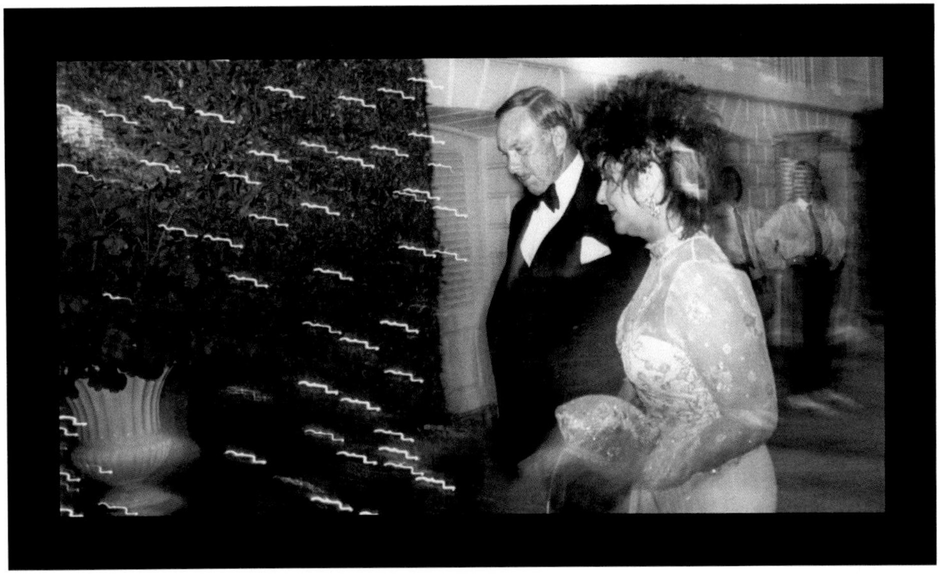

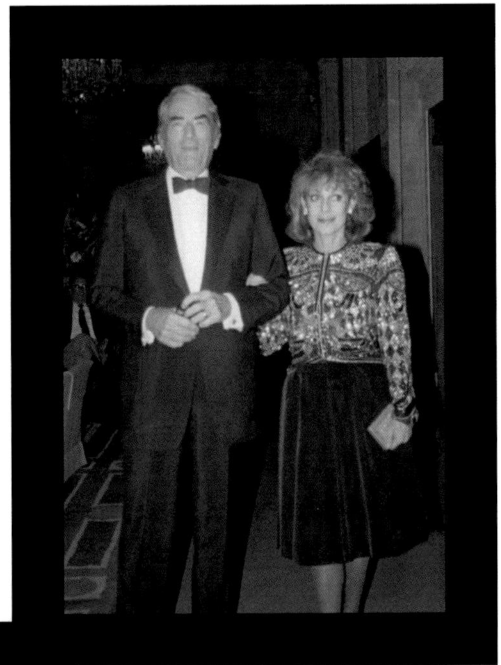

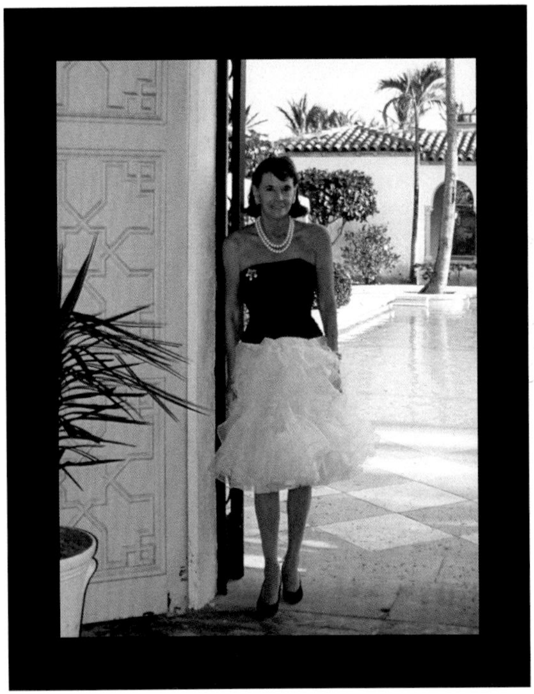

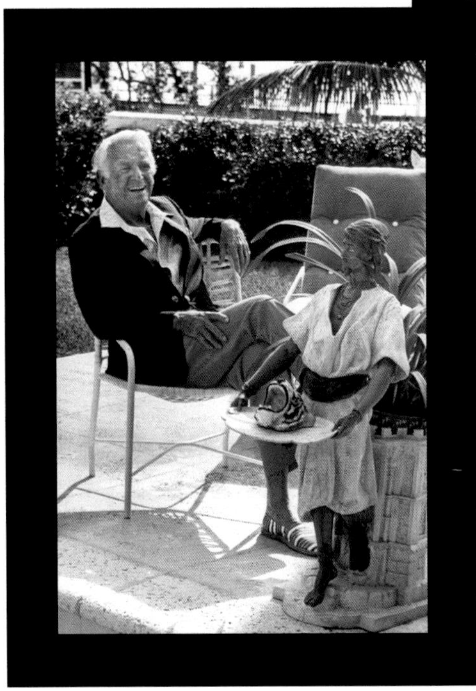

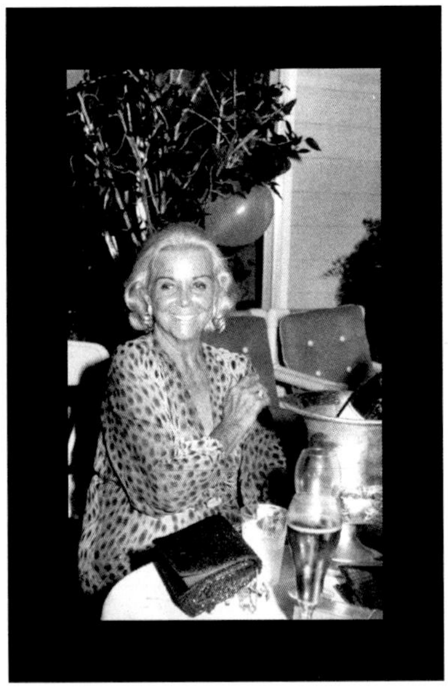

LOVED & REMEMBERED

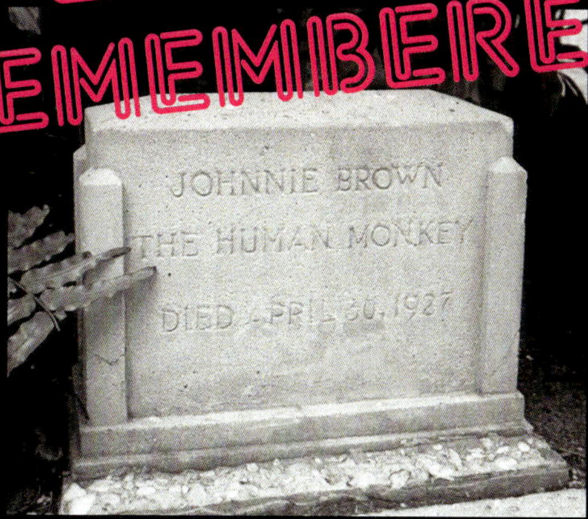

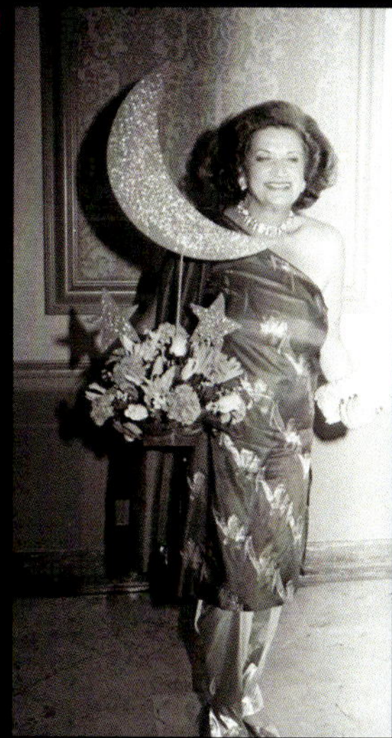

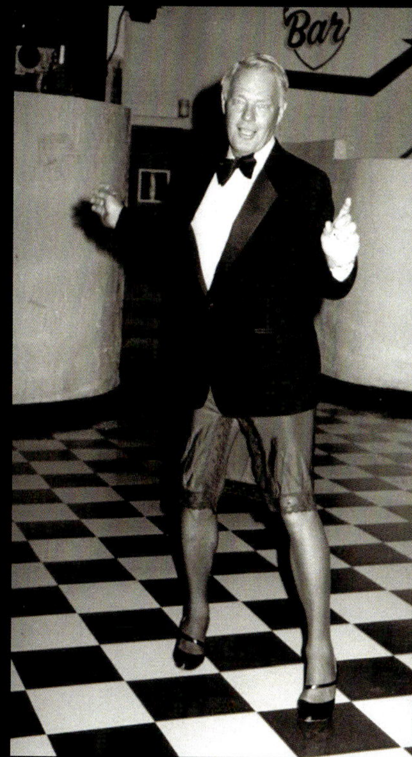

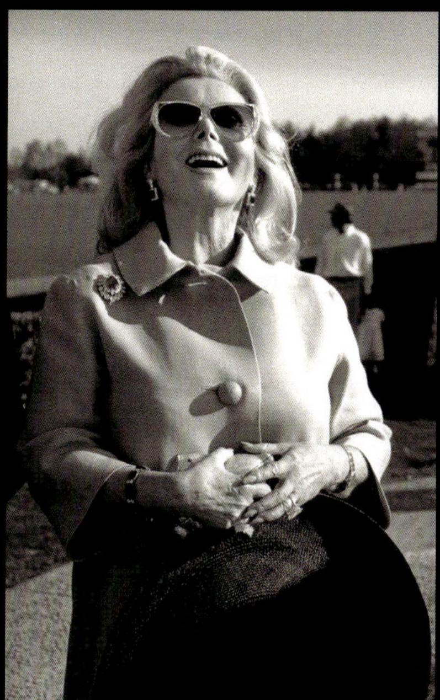

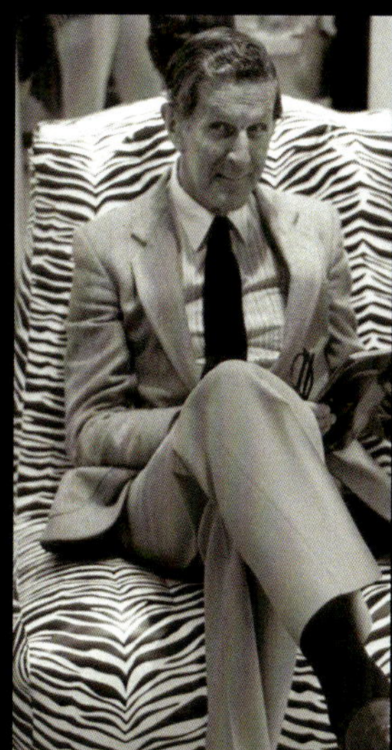

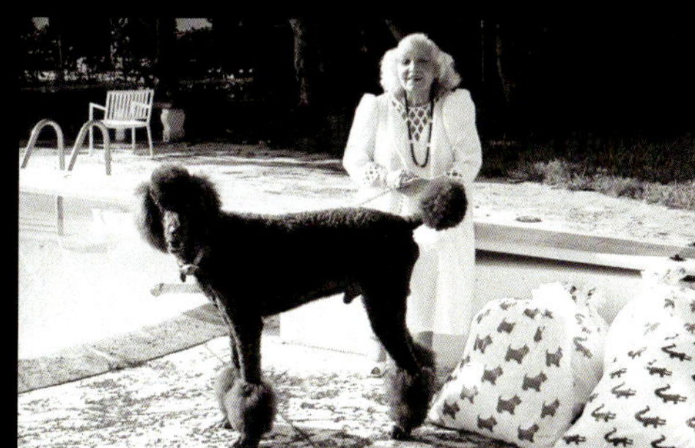

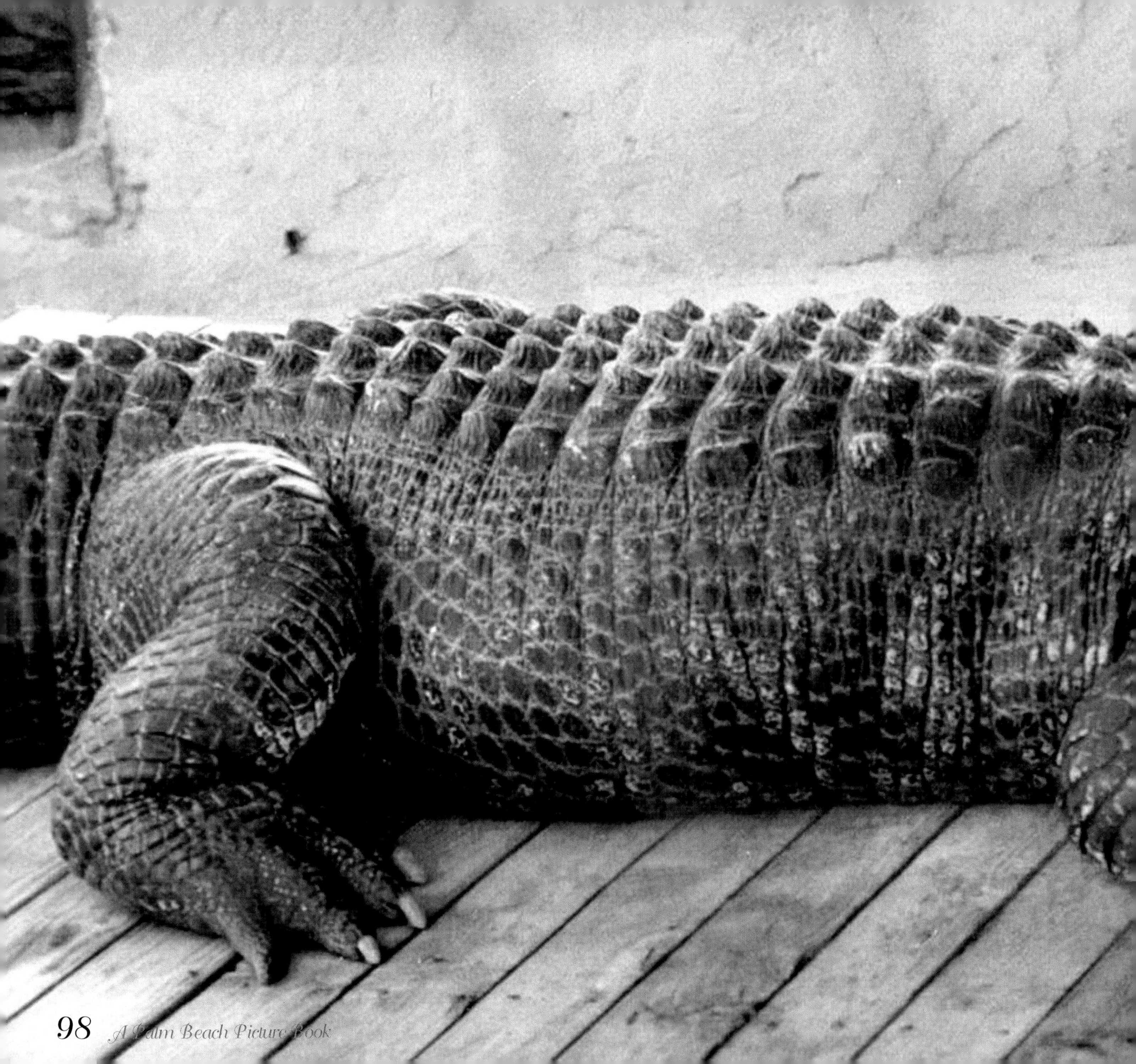

Nature

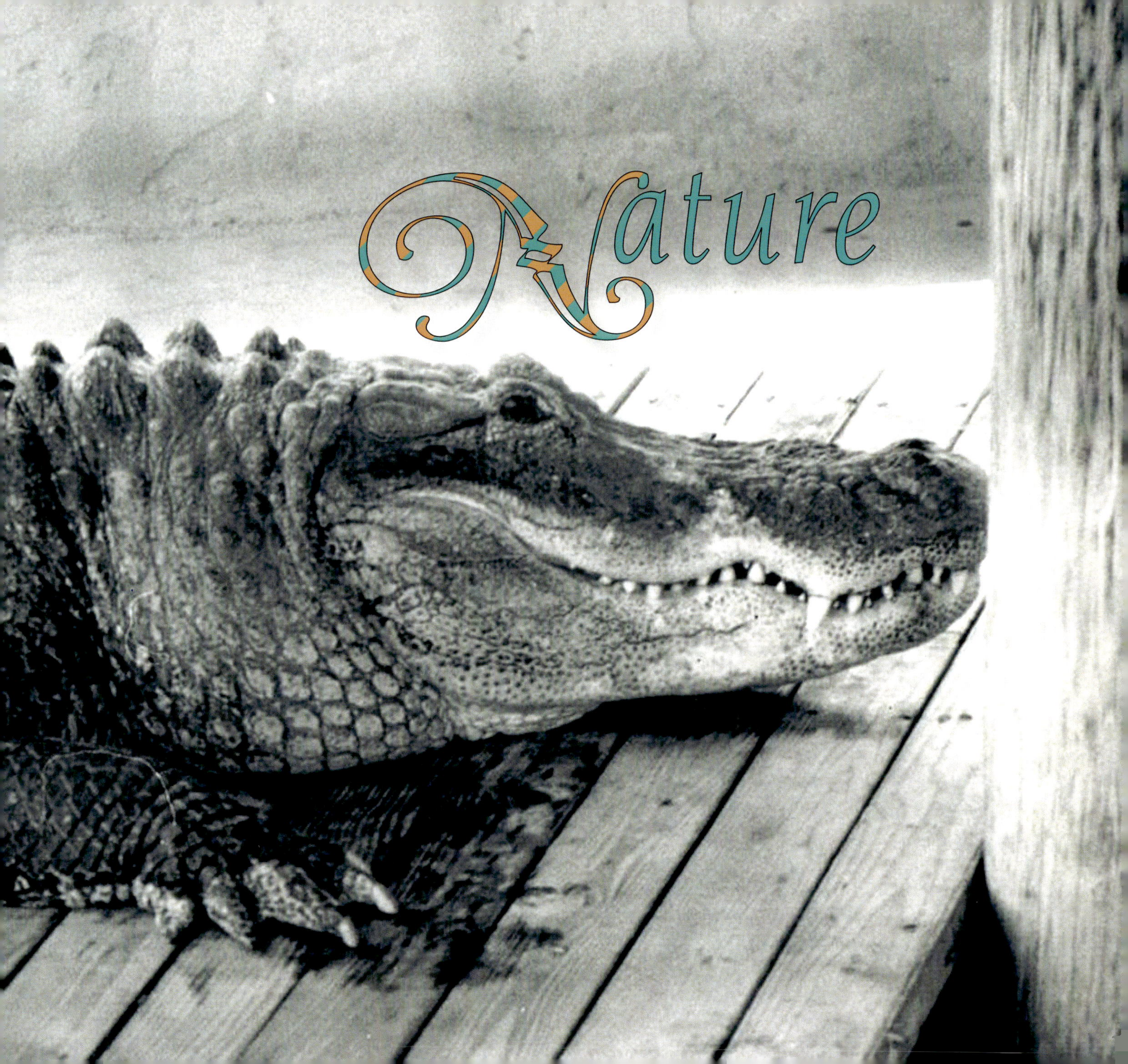

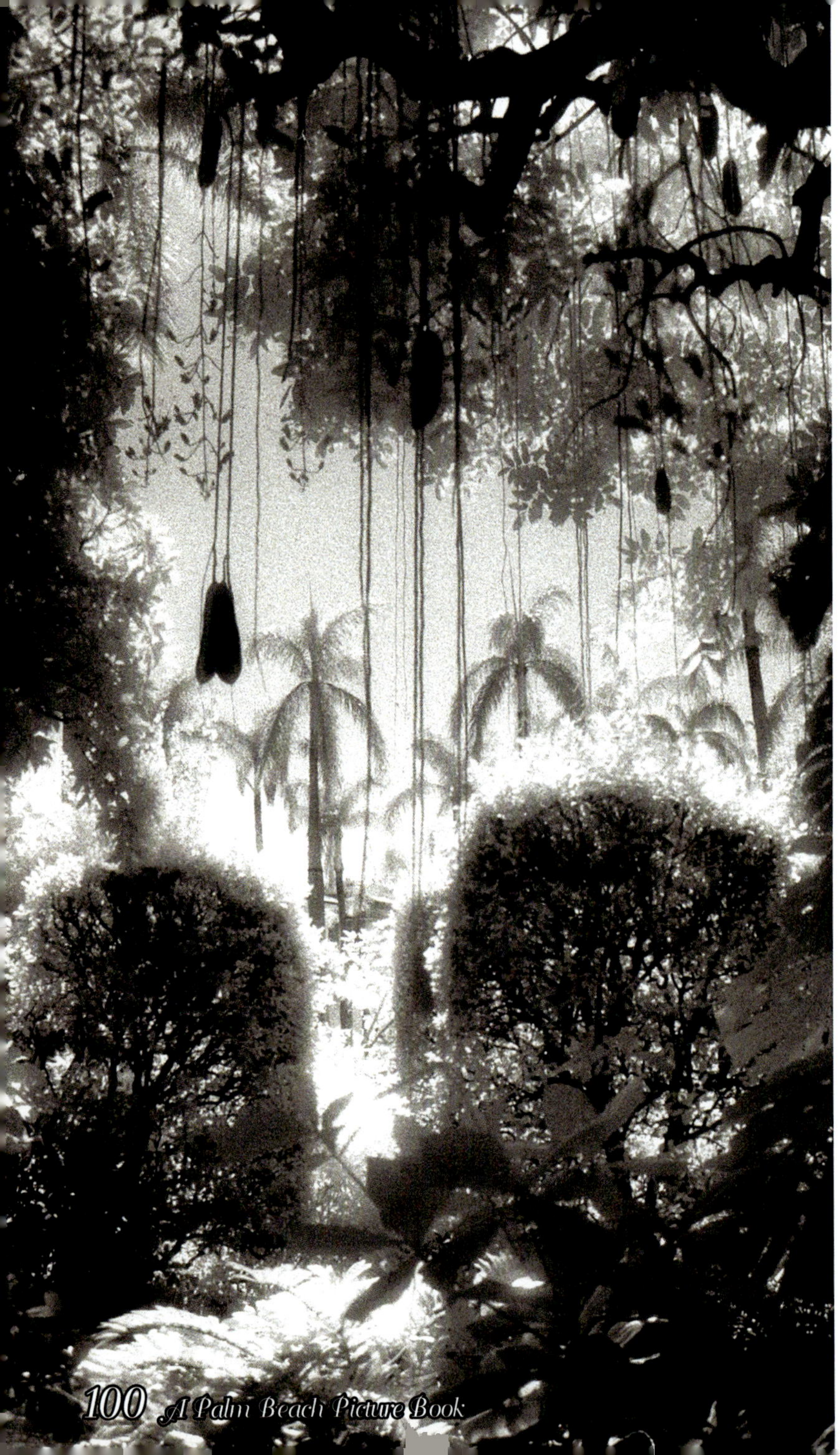

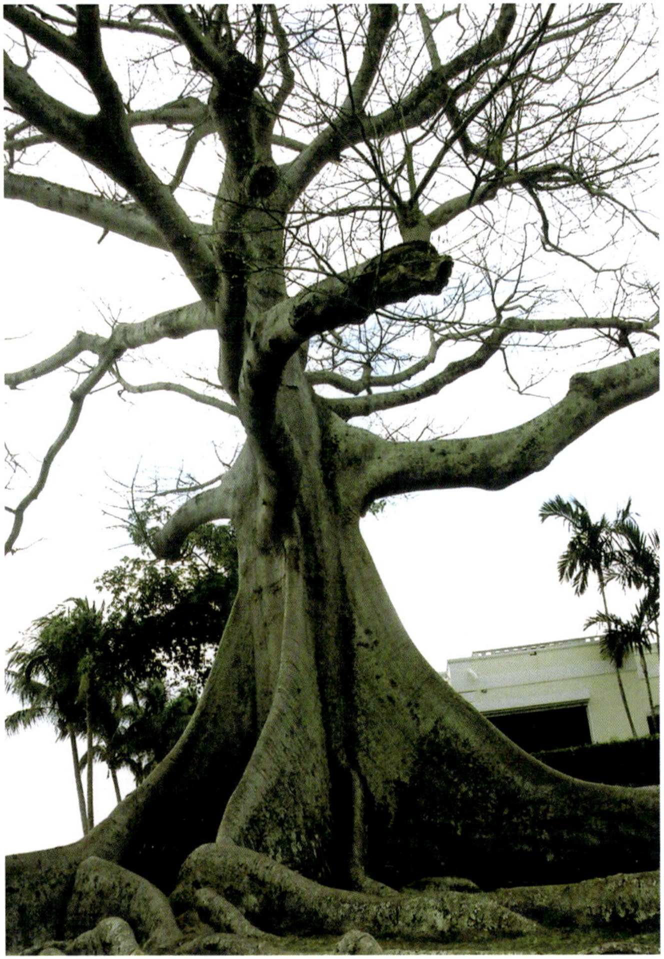

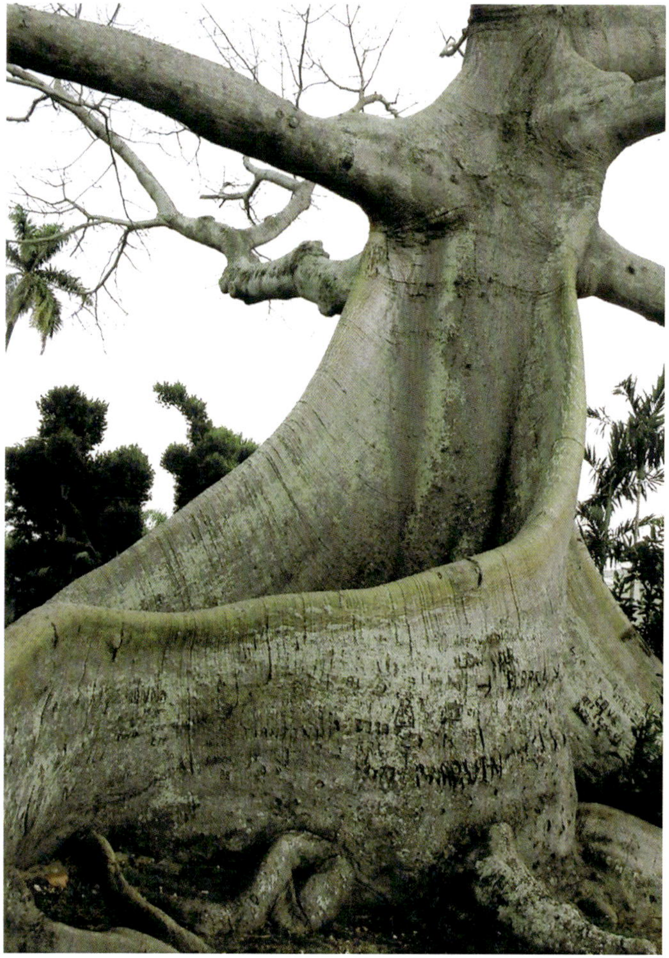

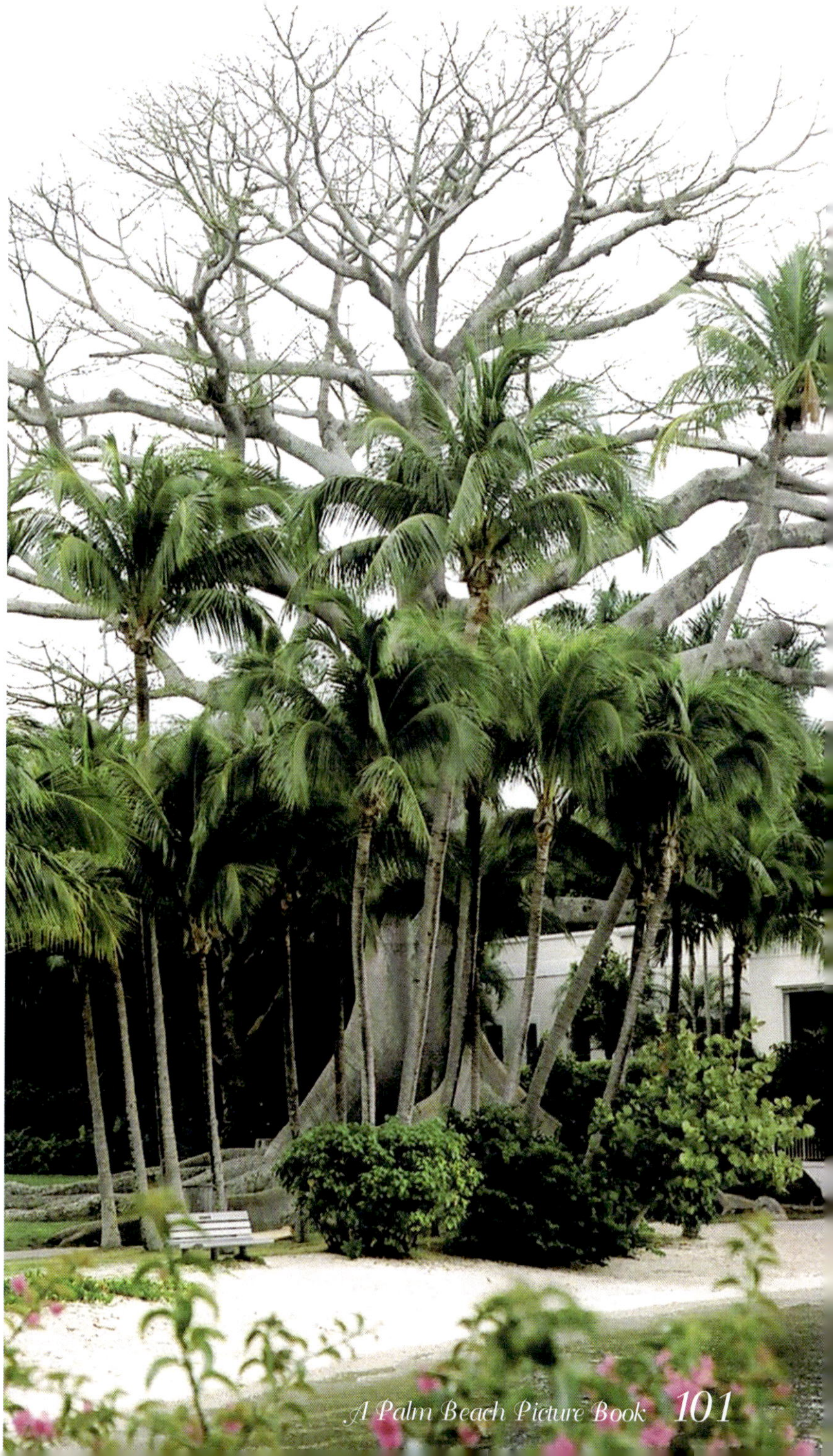

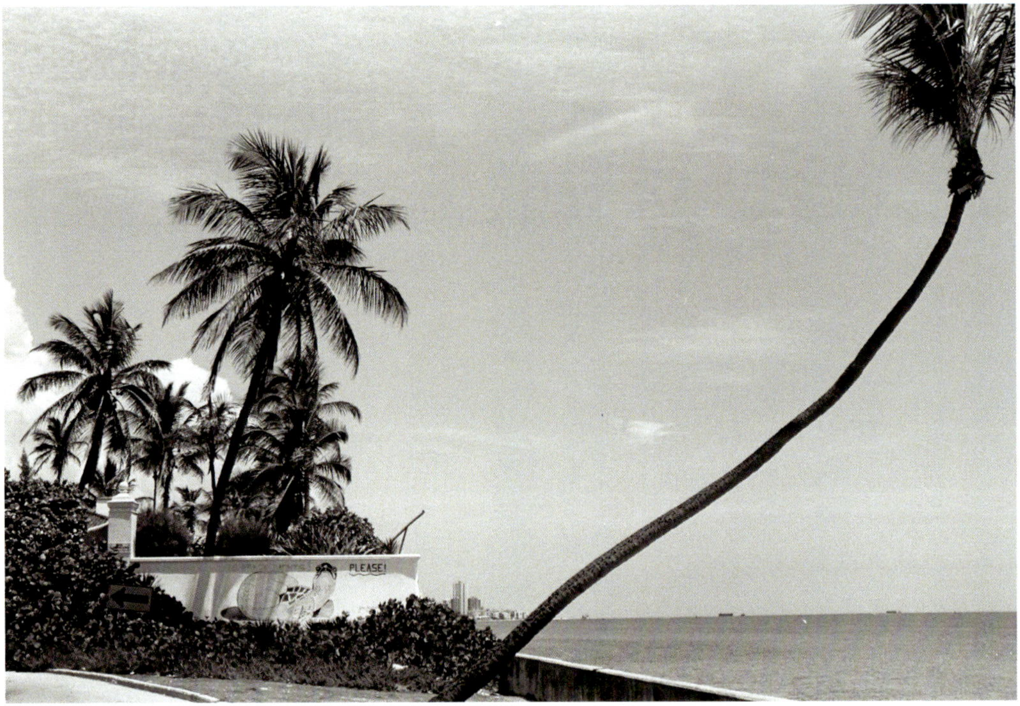
PLEASE!

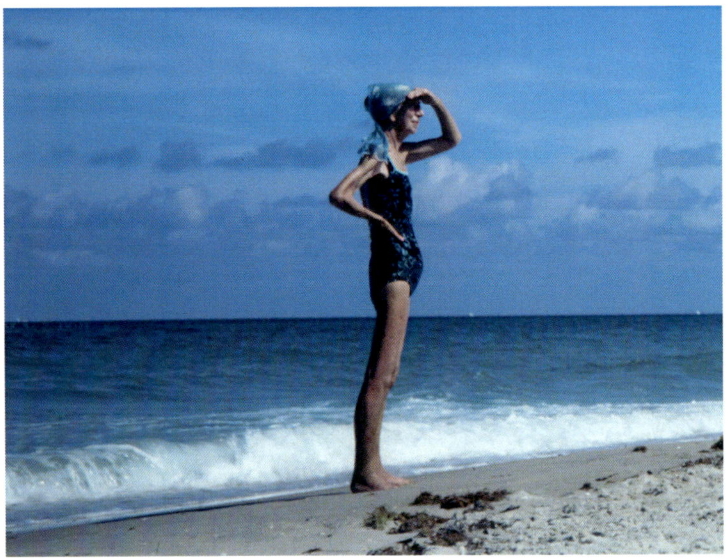

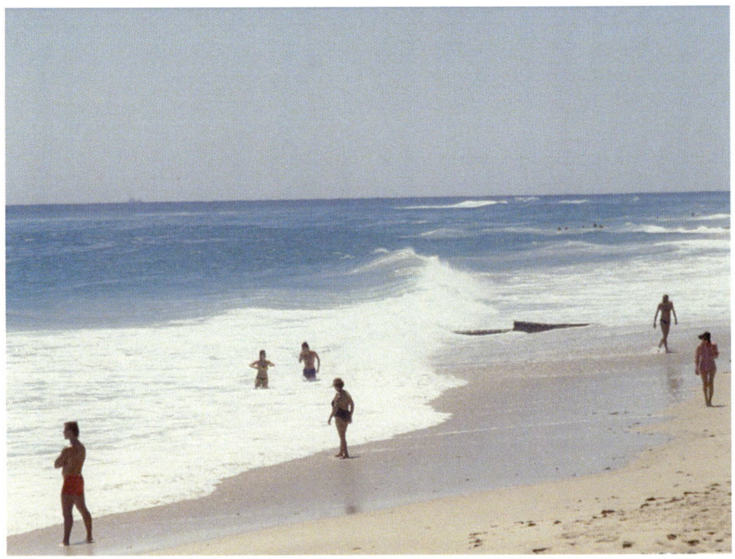

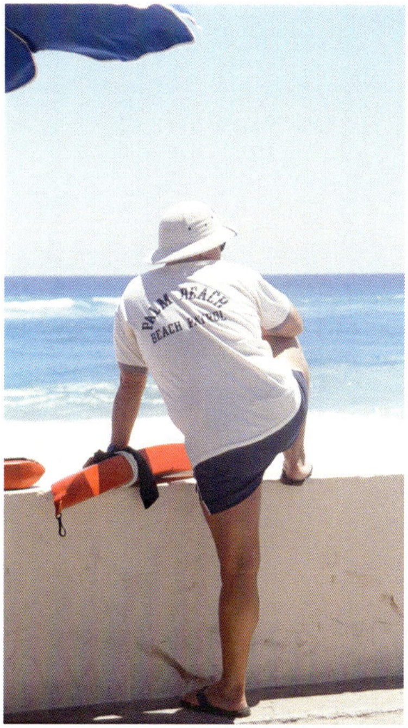
PALM BEACH

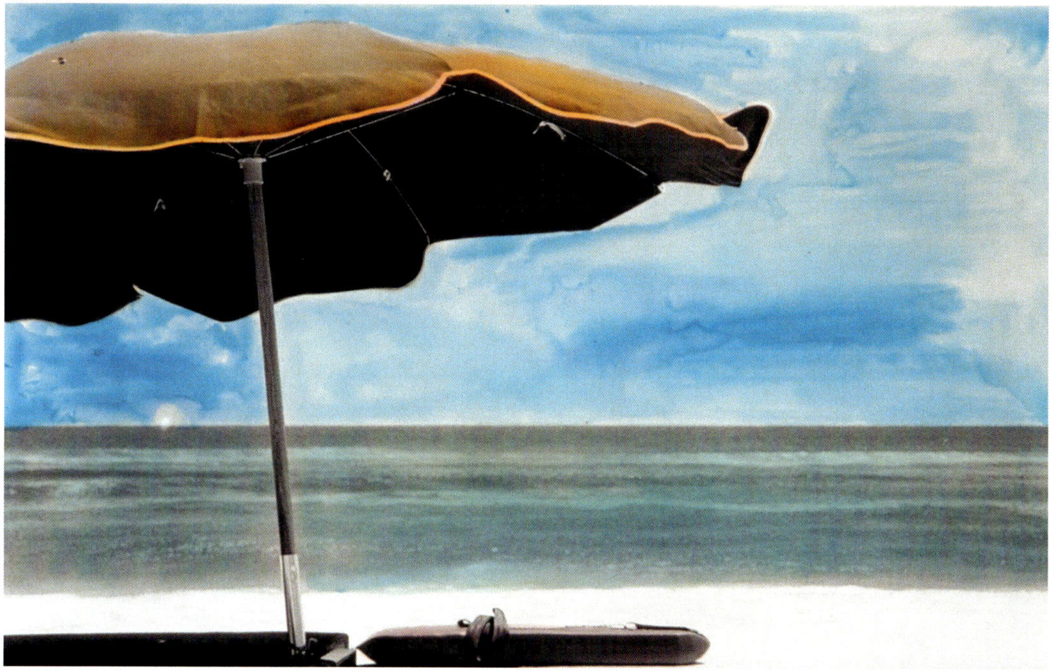

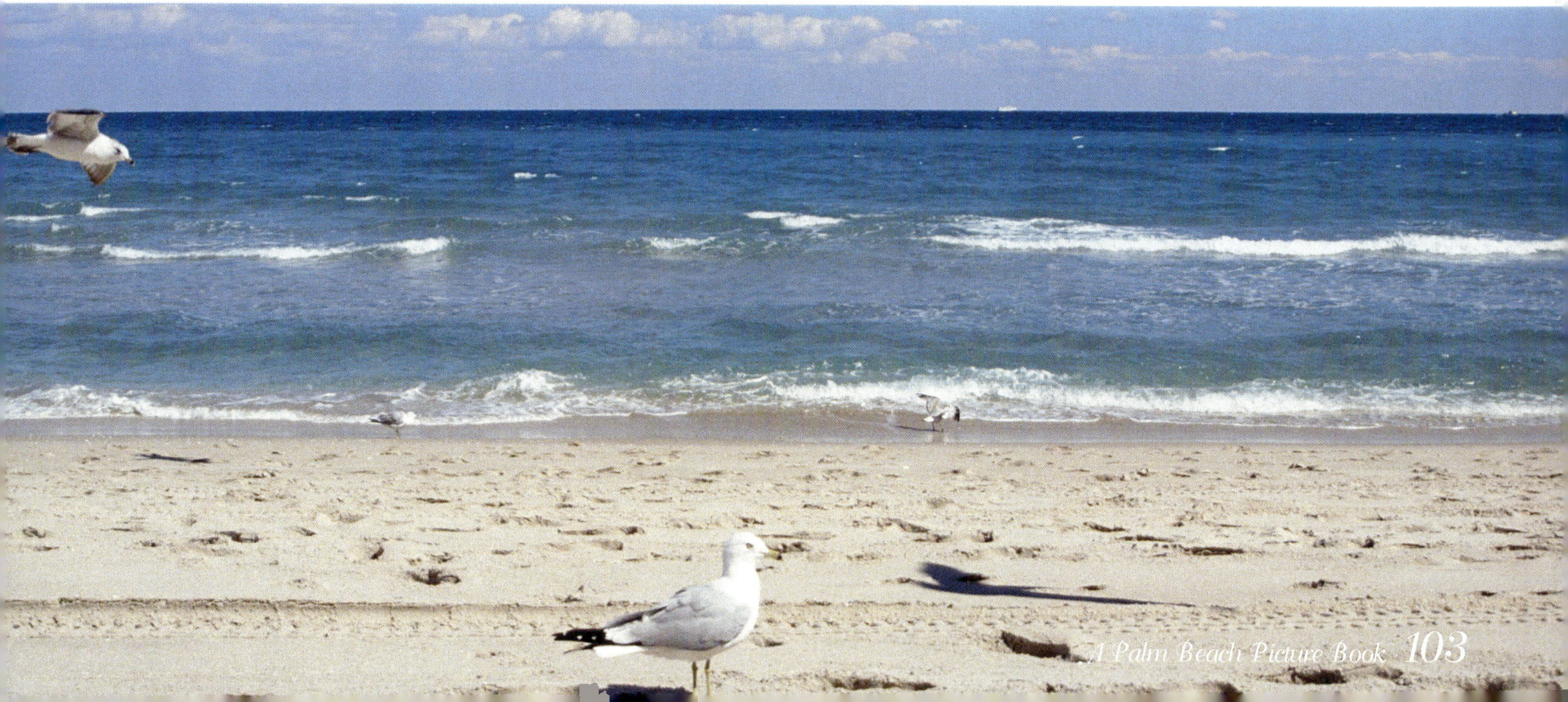

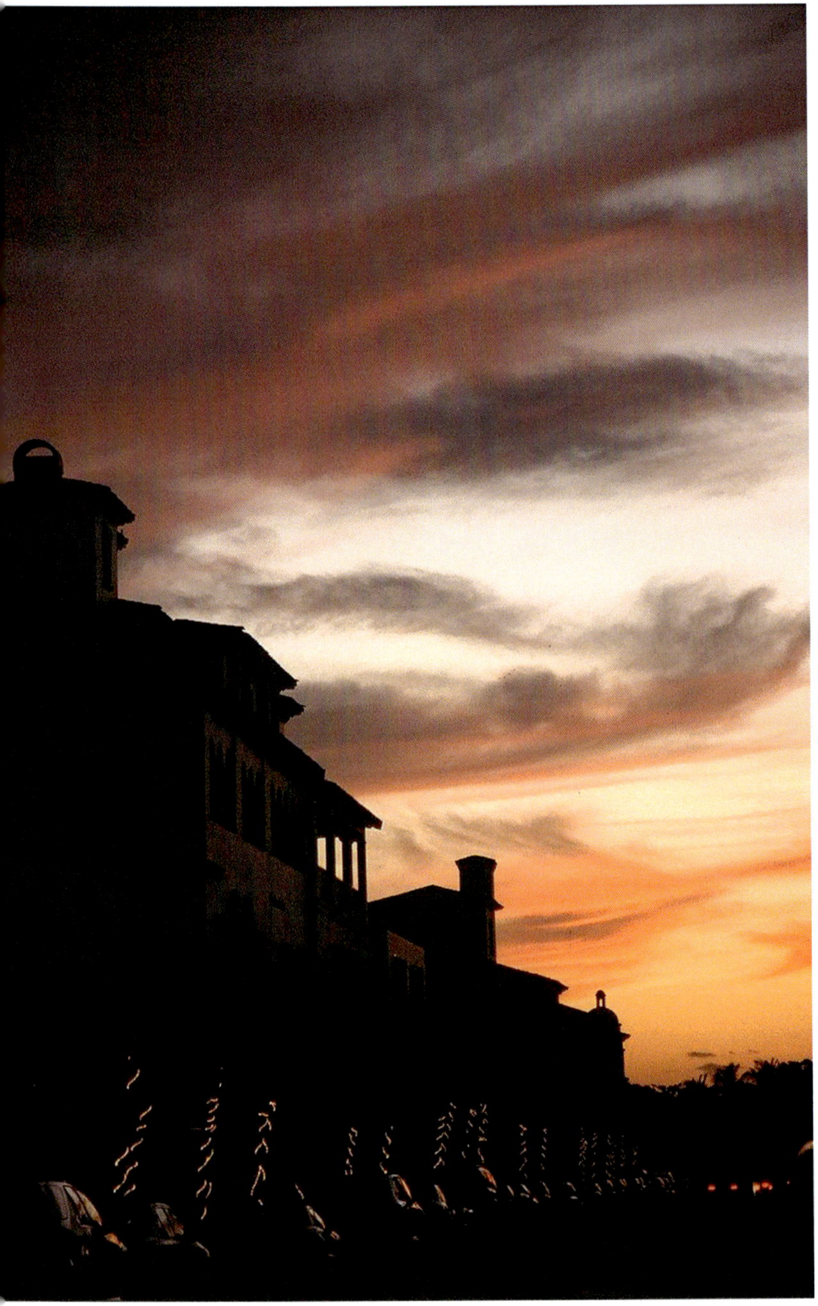

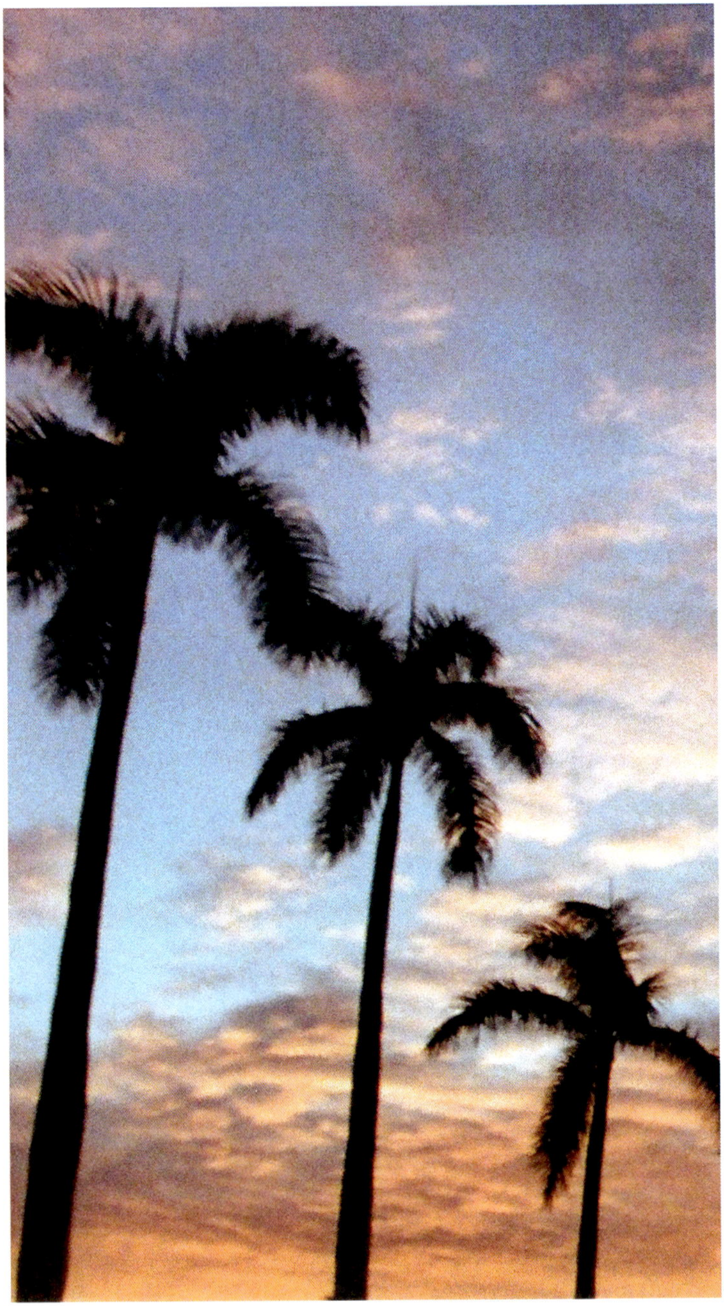

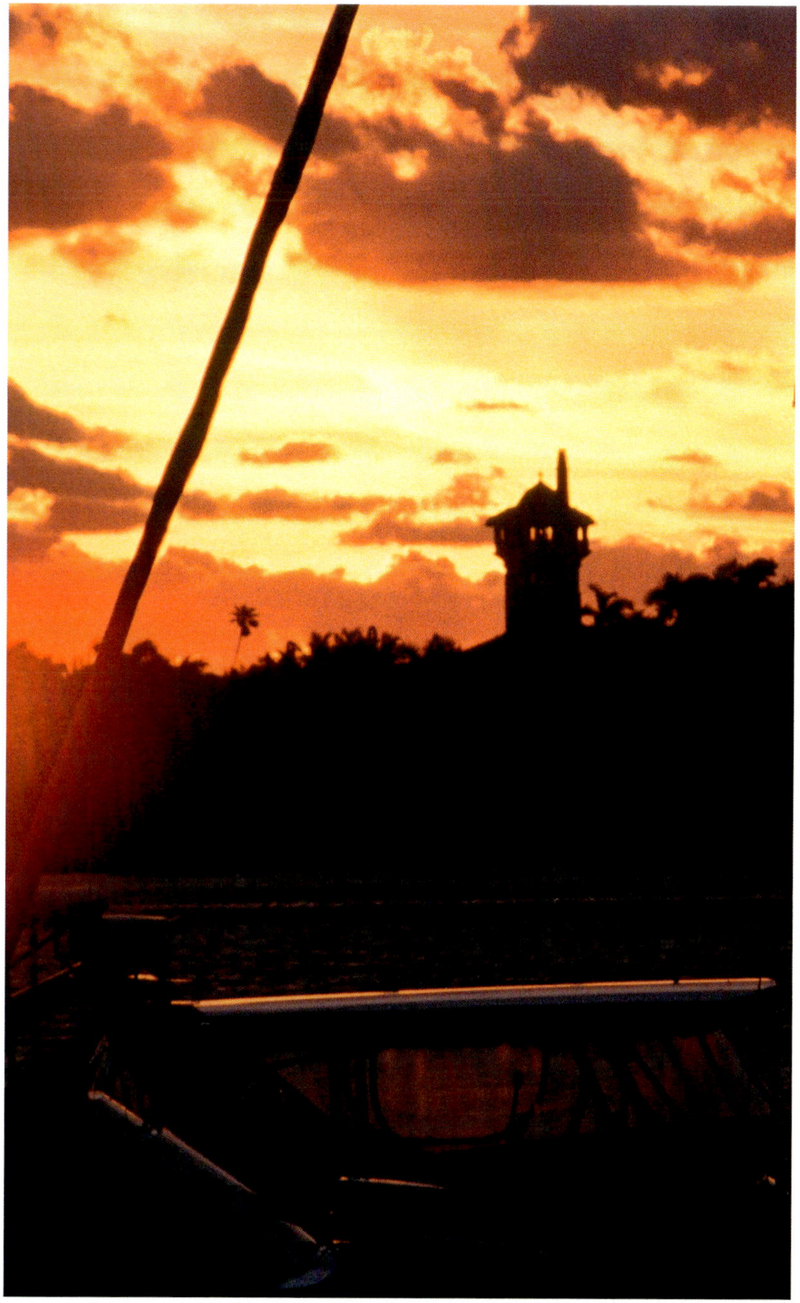

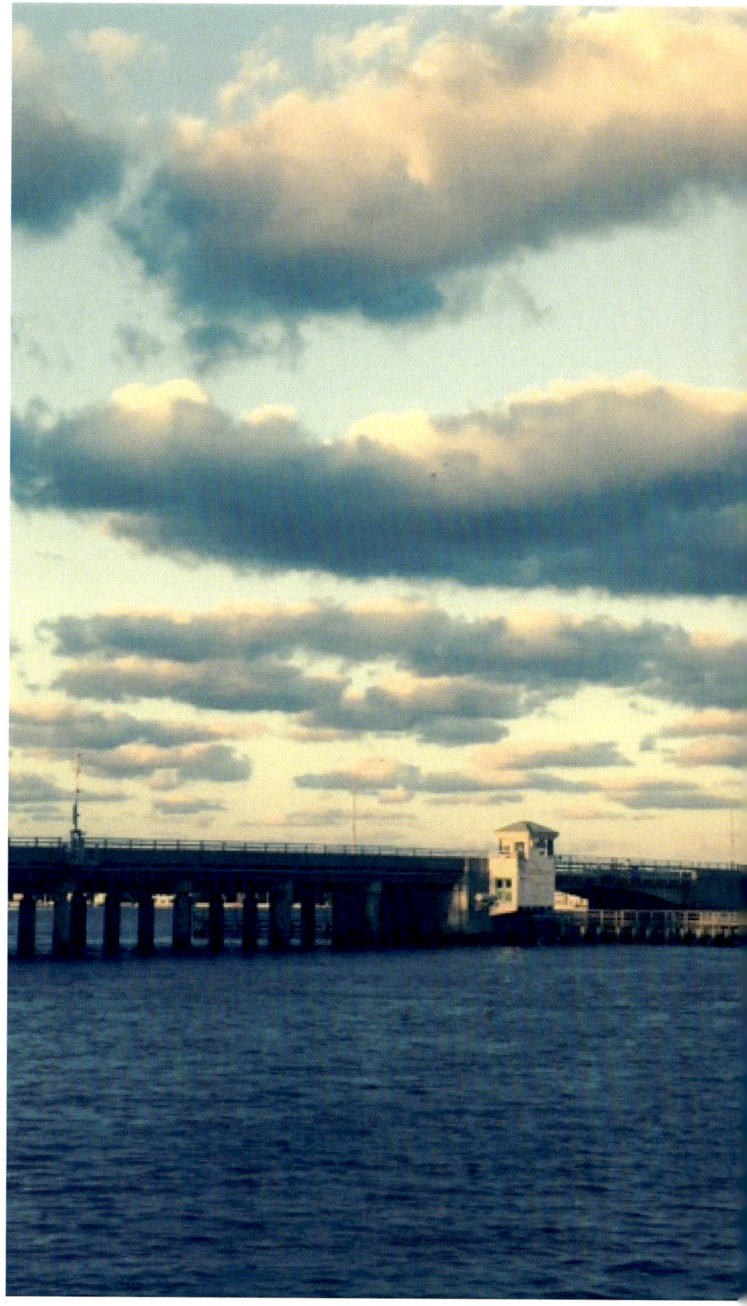

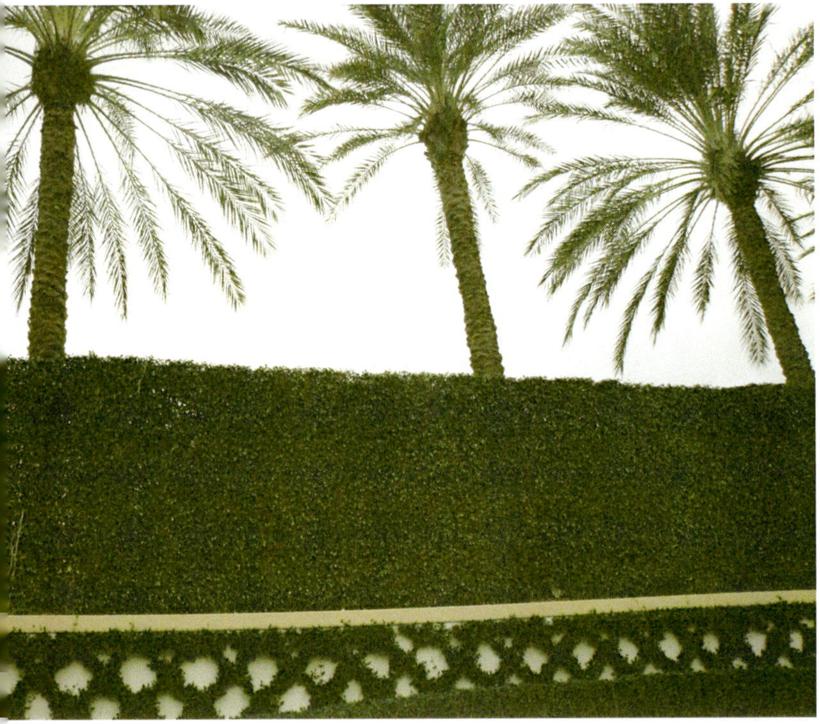

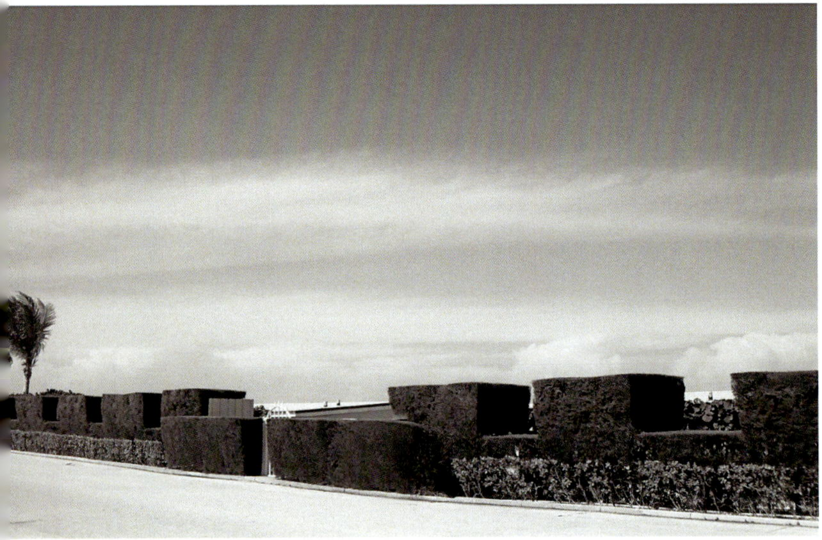

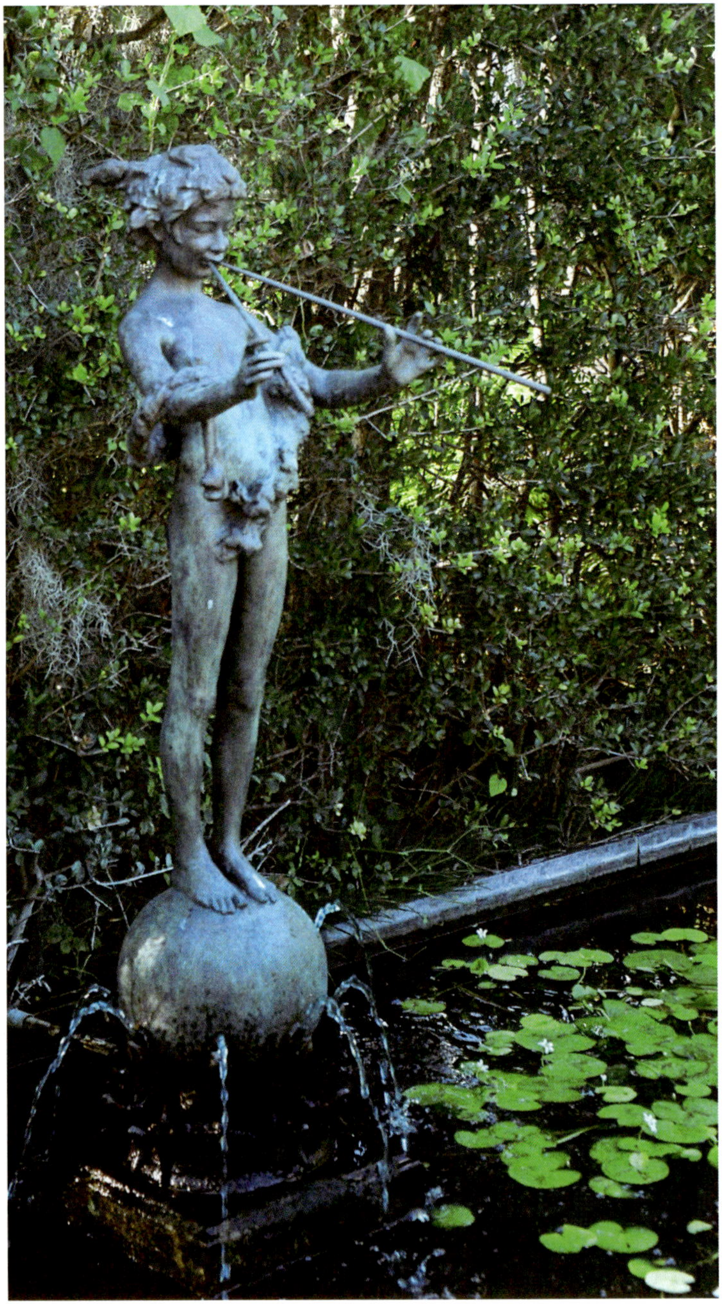

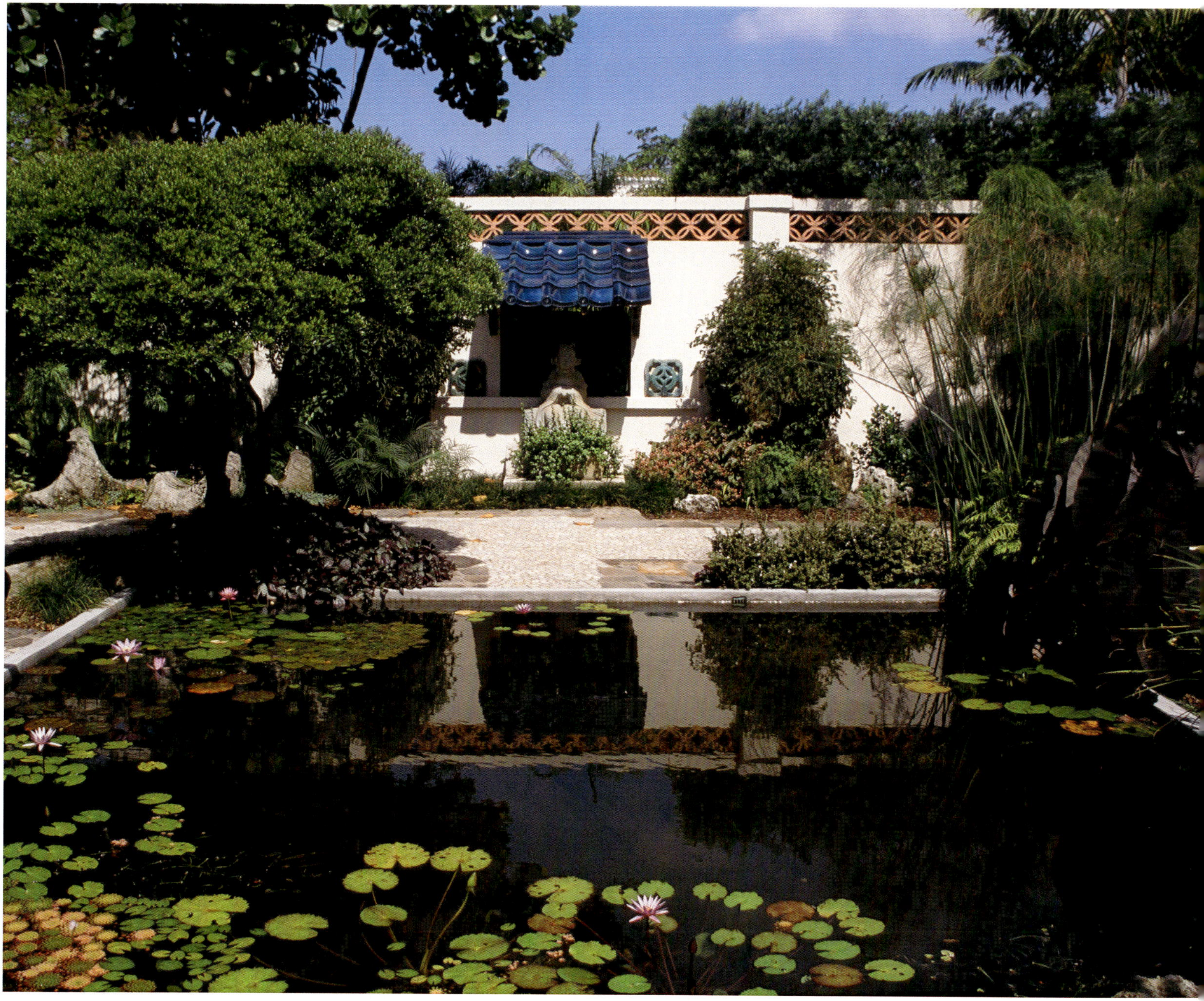

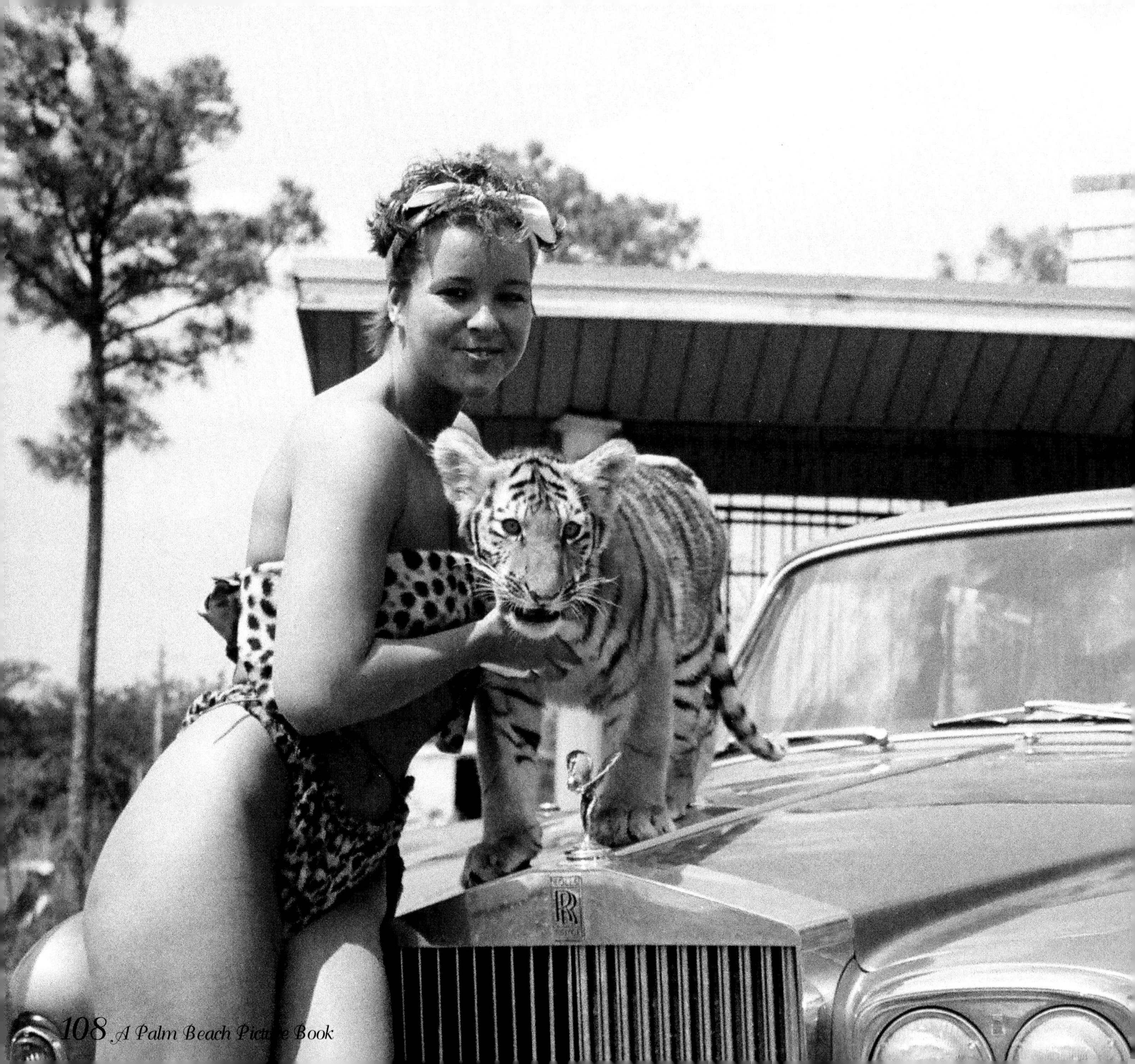

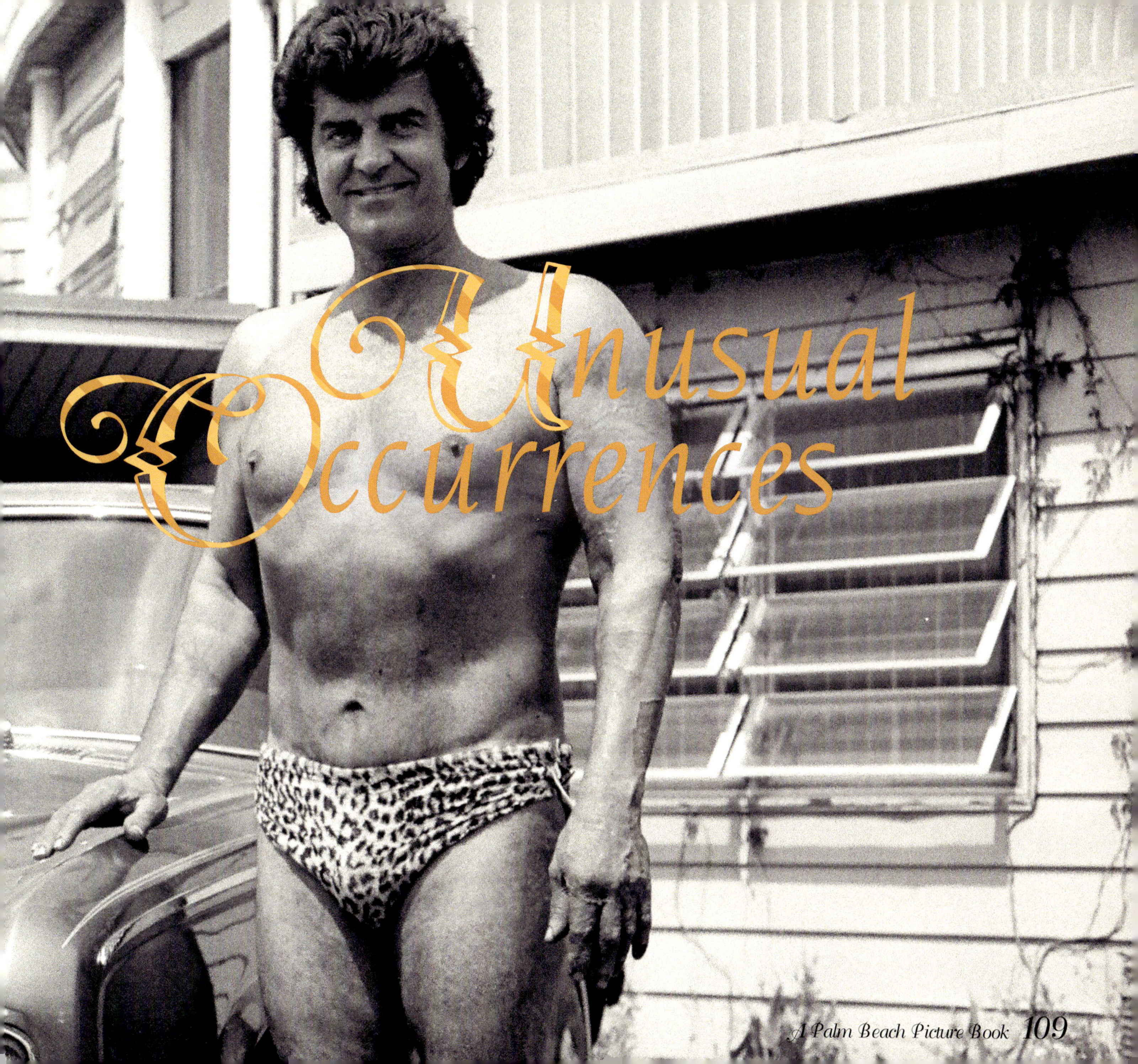

Unusual Occurrences

SHIP LANDS IN SOCIALITE'S YARD

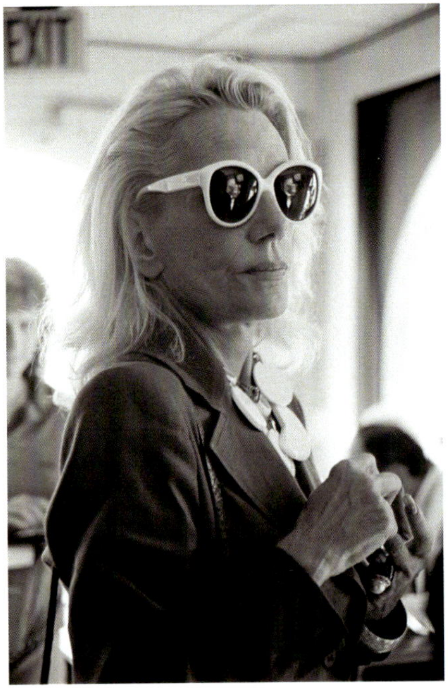

THE PROVIDENCIA WASN'T THE ONLY SHIP to wreck upon the shores of Palm Beach. In 1984, the day after Thanksgiving, a 197-foot Venezuelan freighter appropriately named "Mercedes" crashed through the seawall and onto socialite Mollie Wilmot's oceanfront property next door to the Kennedy estate. It was the very day that Town & Country was supposed to arrive for a photo shoot at her home. The unexpected visitor remained on her property during that entire season. Ms. Wilmot played hostess to international journalists and friends and neighbors who gathered every day in her beach cabana to have caviar and champagne while enjoying the spectacle.

"She also fed the ship's cat, which the crew later gave to her. The cat, by then known as Mollie Mercedes, was passed on to her neighbors, the Pulitzer family, who sent it to the beauty parlor for a thorough fluffing and then outfitted it in velvet collars decorated with gold." ~ New York Times

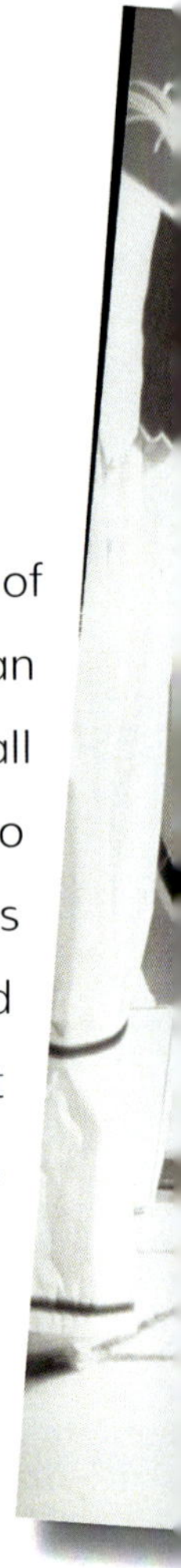

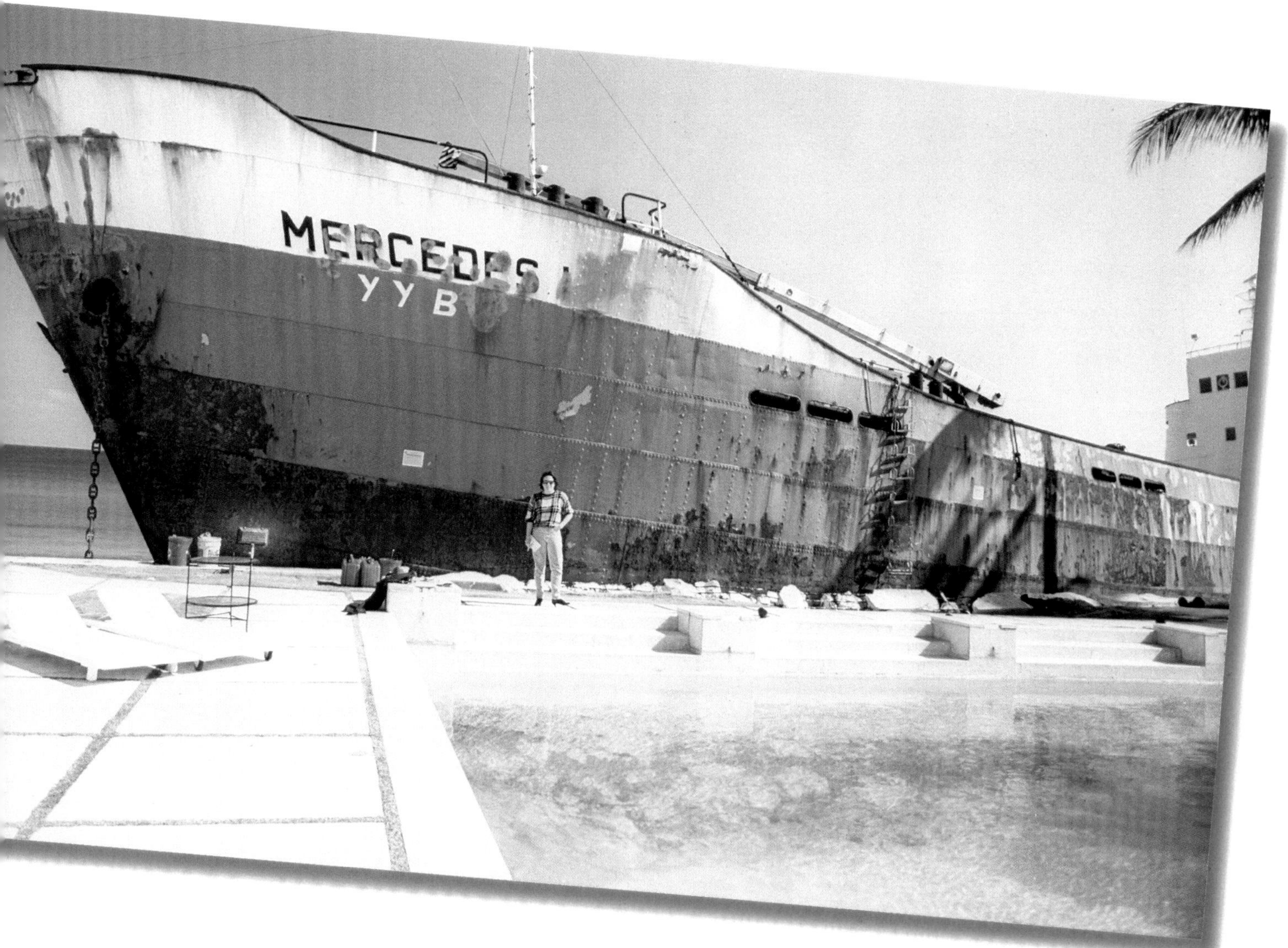
MERCEDES
YYB

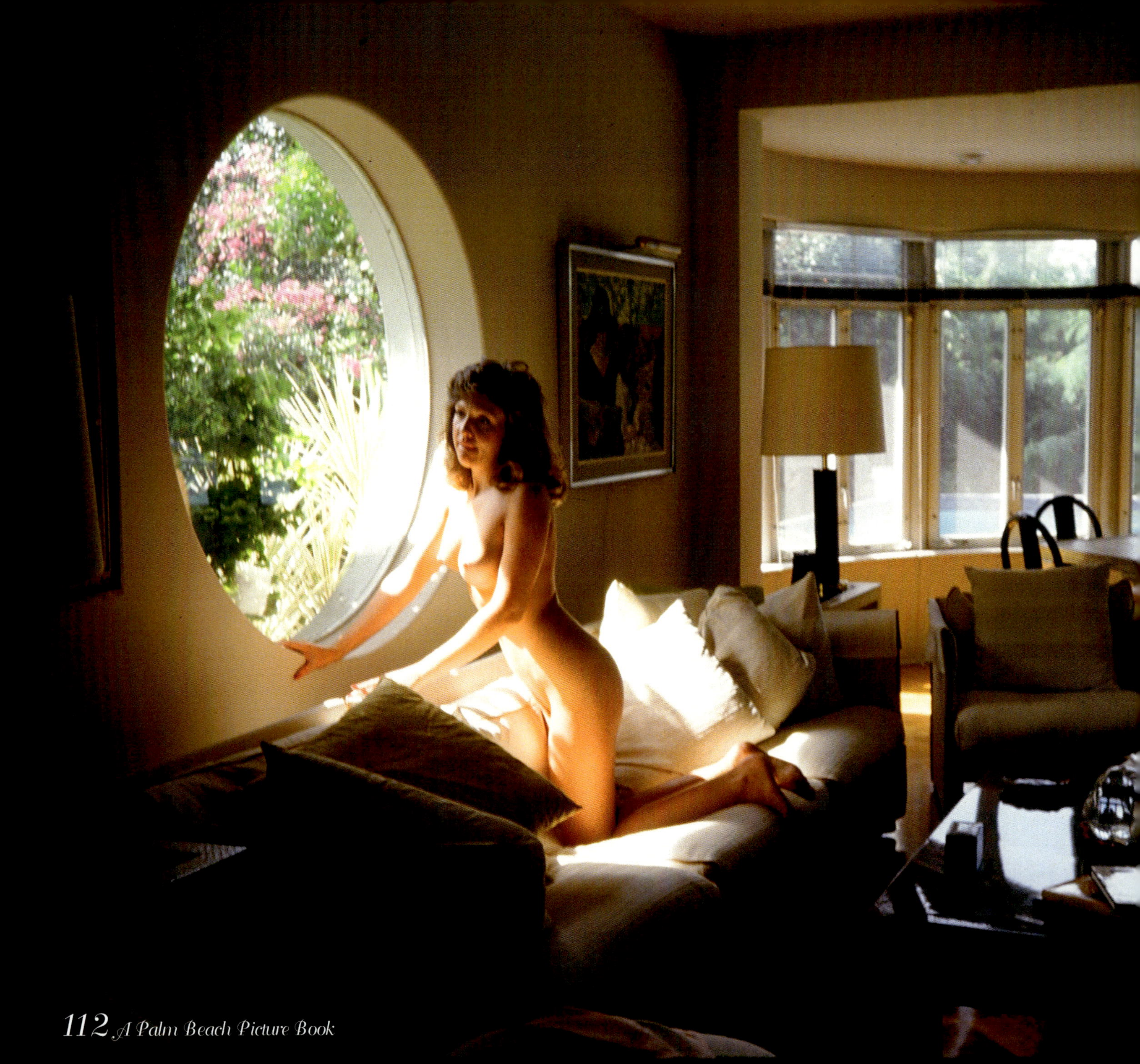

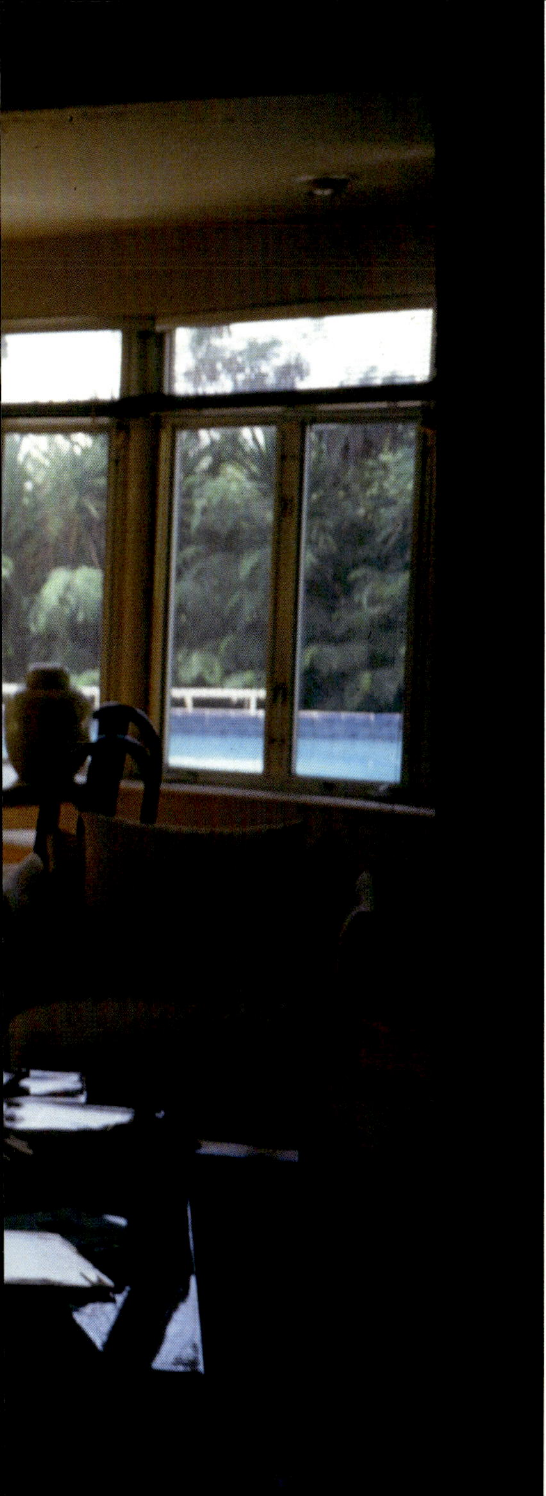

NUDE FLAUNTS IT IN PARLOR

IN THE SEXY SUMMER OF 1989, dozens of nude models and photographers descended upon the home of Kirby Kooluris at his Historic Landmark Deco house, Fore and Aft (see p.22.) Author and student Leslie D. Weinberg volunteered Kirby's home for the photo shoot in exchange for a nude photography class with celebrated French photographer Lucien Clergue. Kirby, a photographer and aesthete himself, hosted a get-together on the upper deck of his 'ship on land' to gaze at nudes draped all around his home. While neighbors enjoyed the spectacle, beautiful art was made, and a good time had by all.

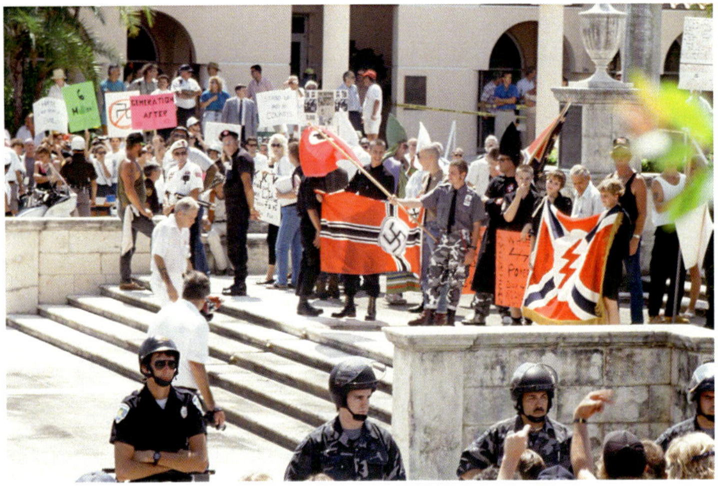

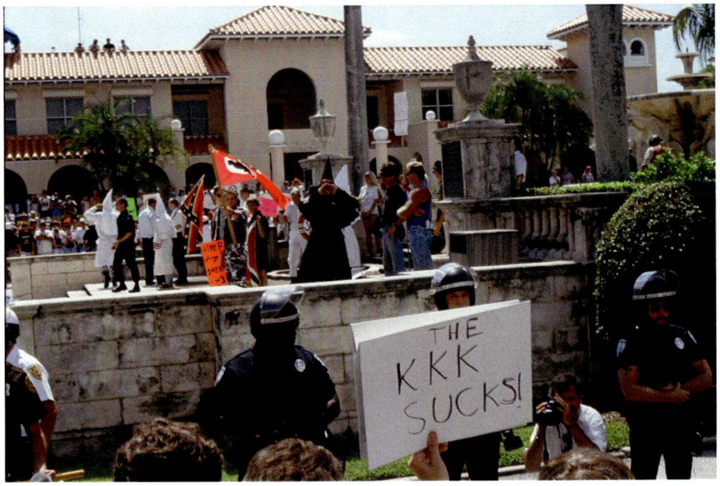

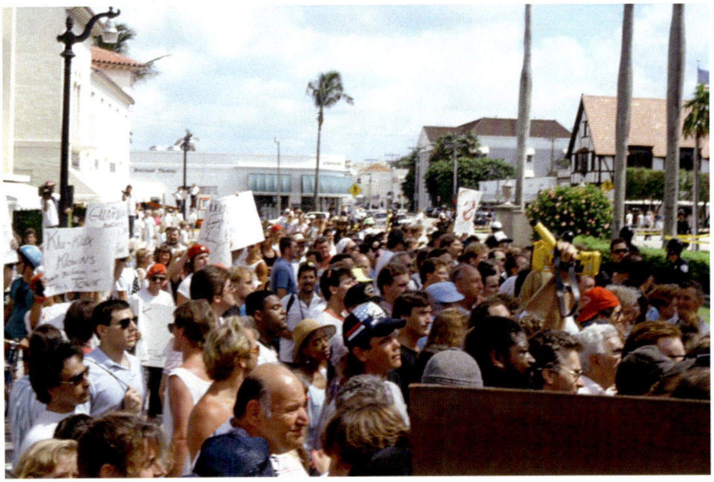

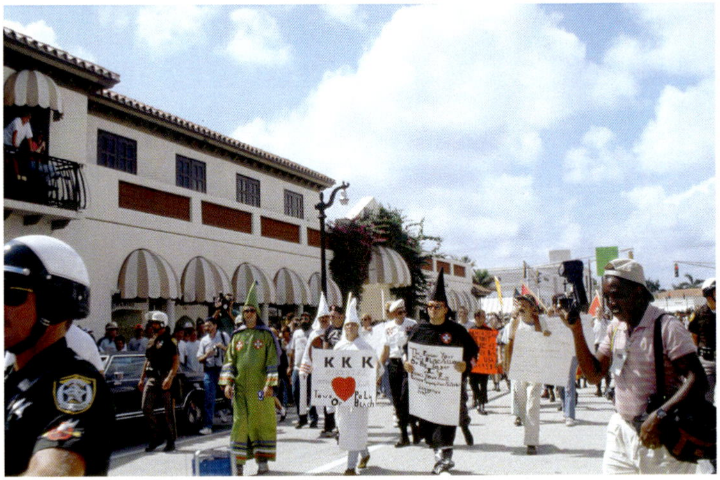

CROWD JEERS AT KLAN RALLY

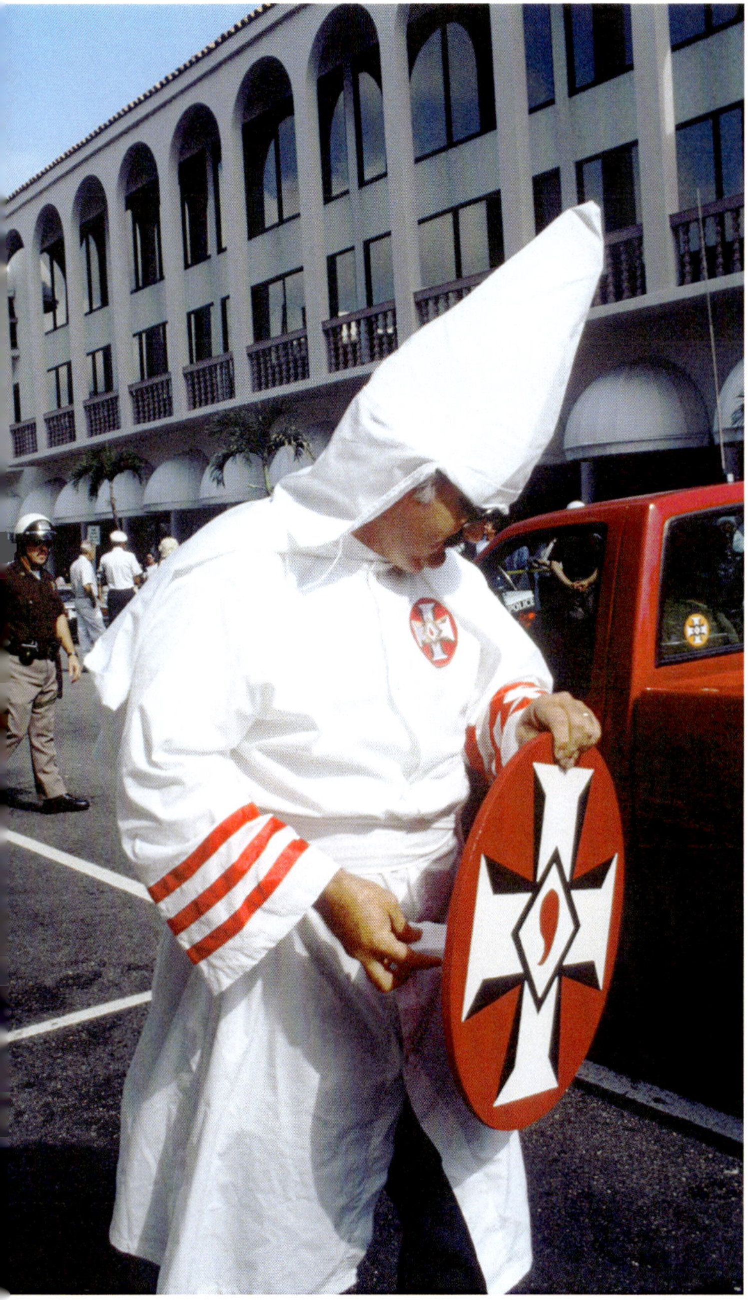

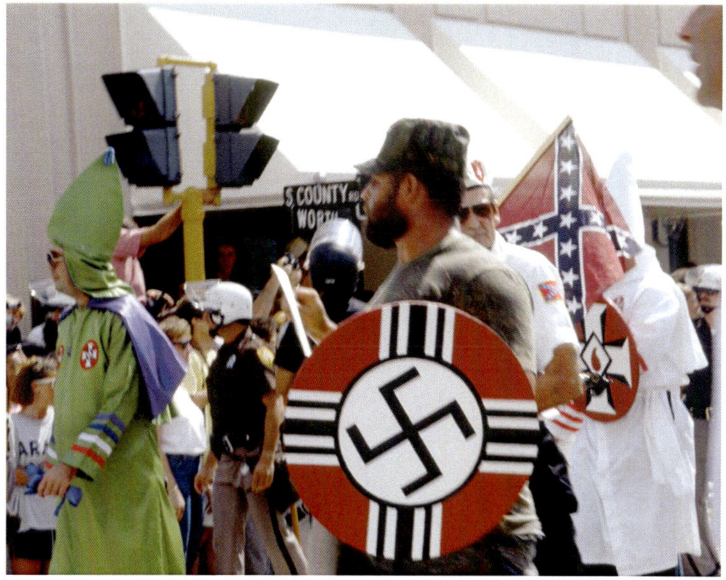

IN THE SWEATY SUMMER OF 1990, the KKK decided to march down Worth Avenue. There was little the town could do to block their first amendment rights, and they were issued a permit. They were in for a surprise when the townspeople rose up against the Klan and came out with signs and banners expressing that they were unwelcome visitors to the island. Protected by the Palm Beach Police in riot gear, only a handful of white hooded Klansmen dared to show up at the rally. The white supremacists were no match for the thousands of residents who turned out in droves protesting their presence.

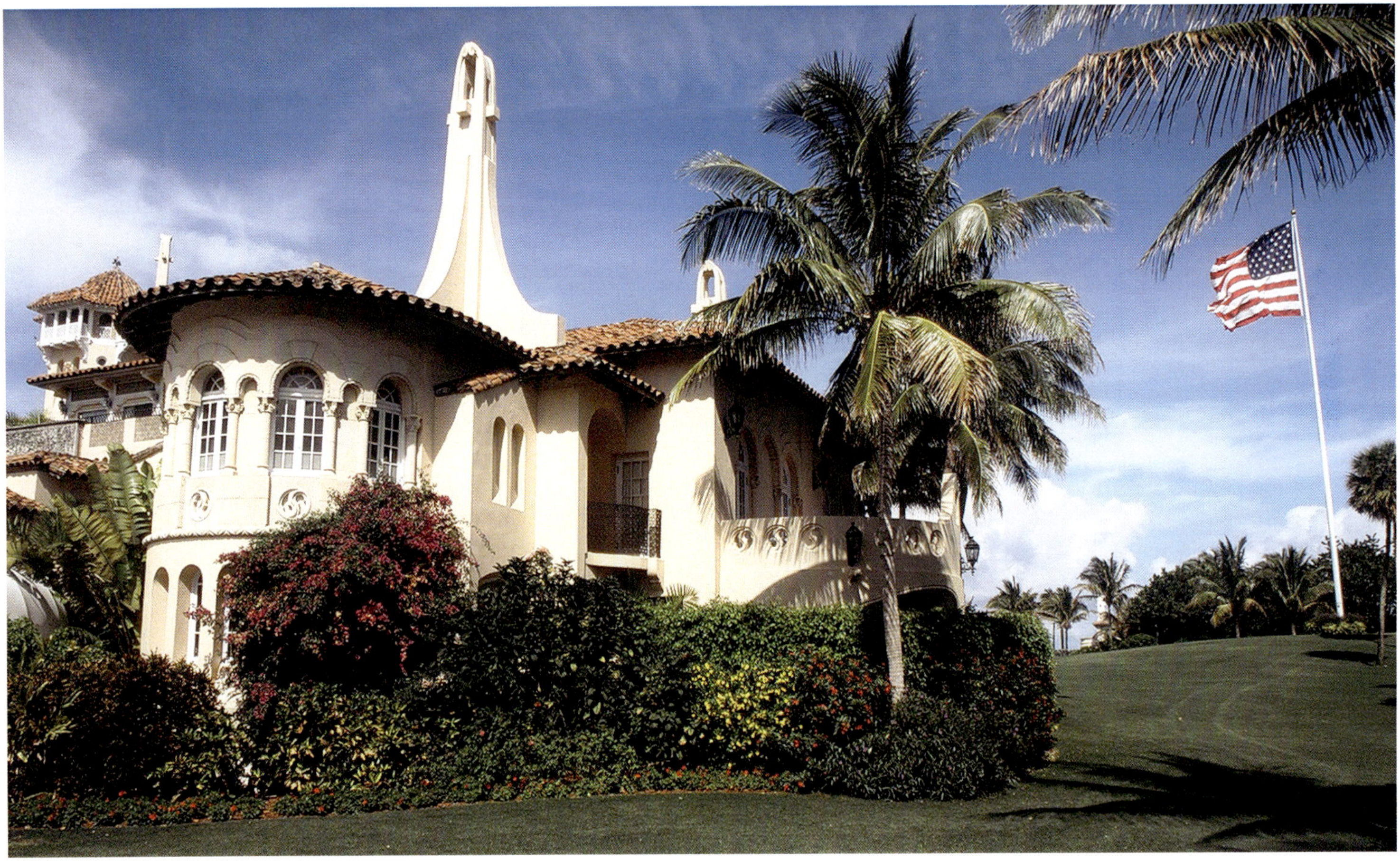

IN A PATRIOTIC STATEMENT IN 2006, Donald Trump erected the most enormous flag ever flown on the shores of Palm Beach at the Mar-a-Lago Club. With apparent disregard for the town's size regulation, Mr. Trump was charged $1,250 for each day he violated the codes. After a few weeks, this pesky tab was starting to add up.

TRUMP refused to move Old Glory. Instead, he slapped a lawsuit back at the Town of Palm Beach for $25 million, claiming they were selectively enforcing their codes and violating his constitutional right of freedom of speech to display the American flag, causing an annoyance to the Billionaire.

FLAG FLAP

IT WASN'T THE FLAG as much as the flagpole that the town considered disproportionately large. The towering 80-foot pole was almost double the size of the enforced code limit. Trump's defense? His flag was the same size as the one that flies over the Capital, and they don't need a permit in Washington. Perhaps Mr. Trump was only dreaming of his 'Winter Whitehouse.'

In the end, a settlement was reached. The town waived all fees, provided the lawsuit was dropped. As a good will gesture, Trump donated $100,000 to charities pertaining to war veterans and American flag.

'The rules are
There are no rules.'
~Aristotle Onassis

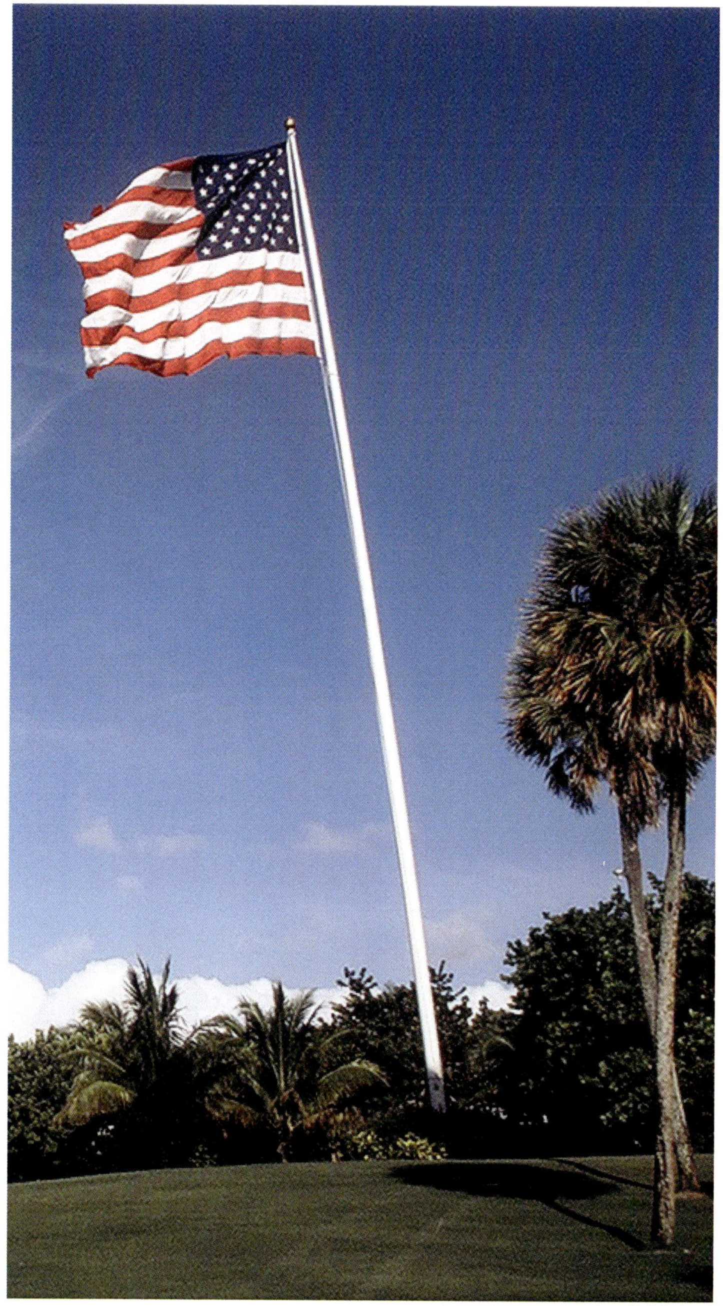

Palm Beach in

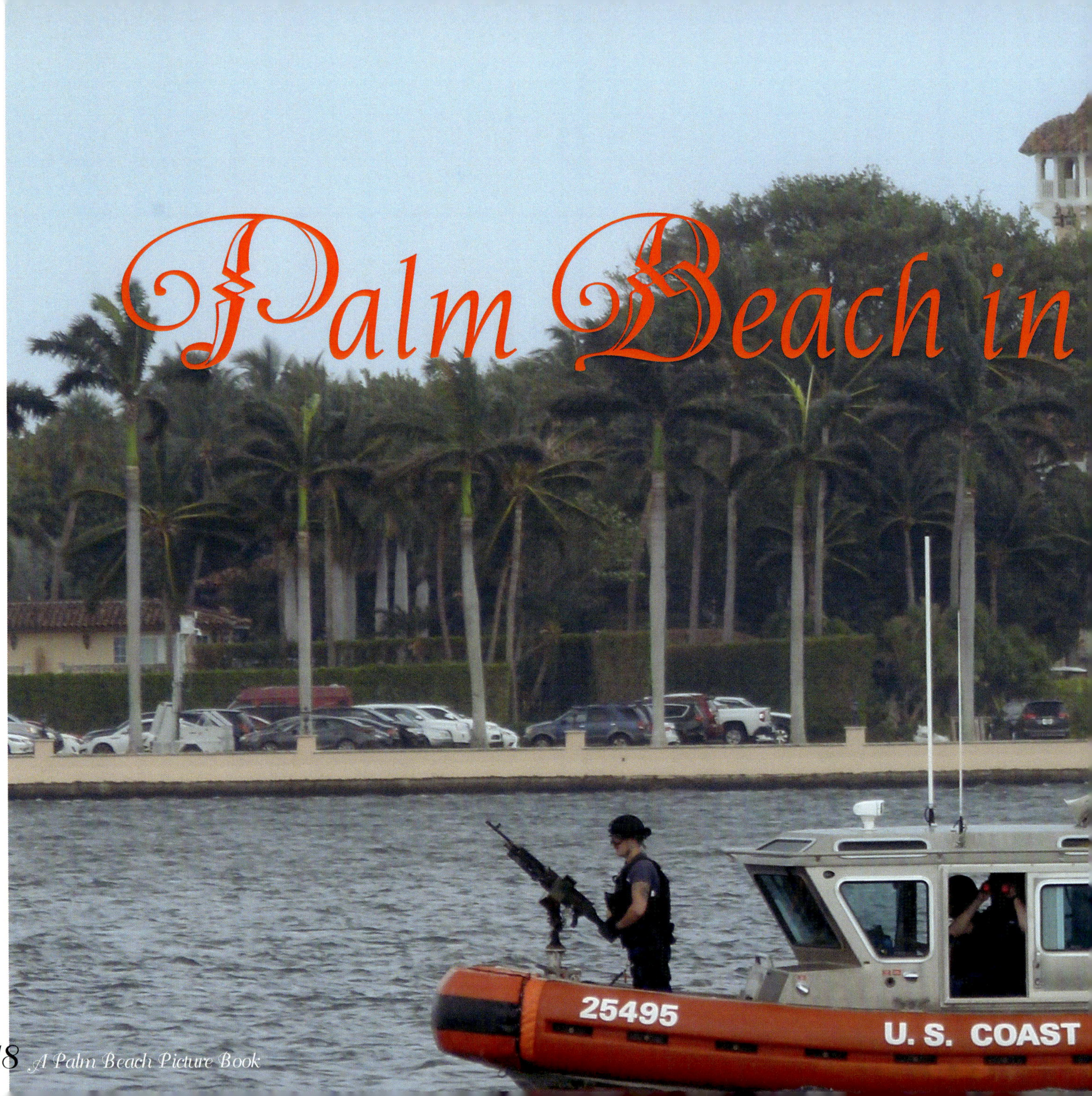

the Trump Era

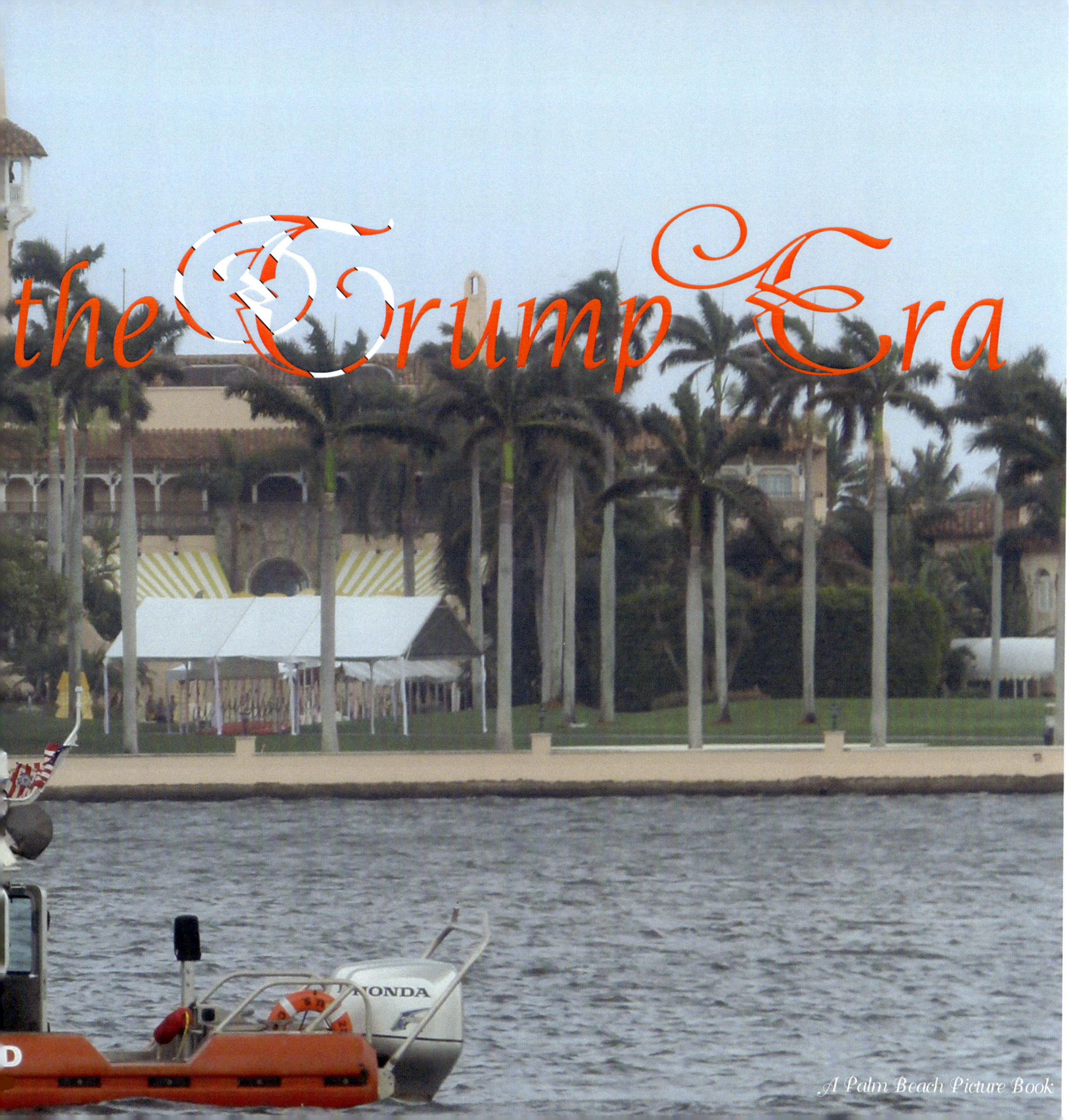

Palm Beach resident Donald Trump was sworn into office as President of the Unite

Since then he has traveled from the White House to the 'Pink House' a total of seventeen times in fifteen costs of Air Force One, Secret Service personnel, multiple motorcades, road closures and local law enforcement the clock Coast Guard protection on the Intracoastal waterway, Florida residents have paid a high price. Its grounded at the private airports in the area on days the President is in town, not to mention the fact that all flying over Mar-a-Lago.

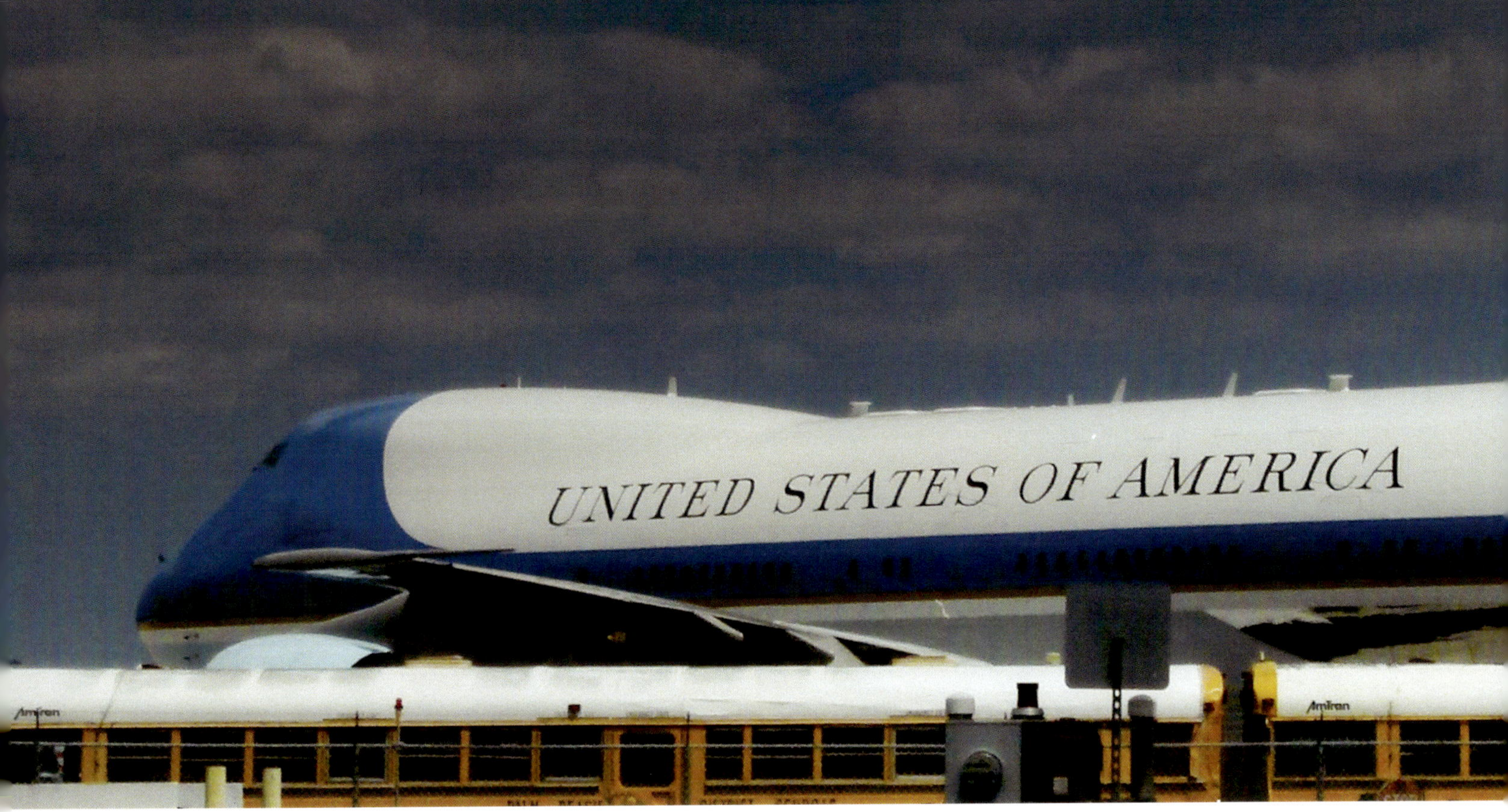

States on January 20, 2017.

nonths. In addition to the operational
vorking overtime on land and round
stimated that hundreds of flights are
ight patterns must be shifted to avoid

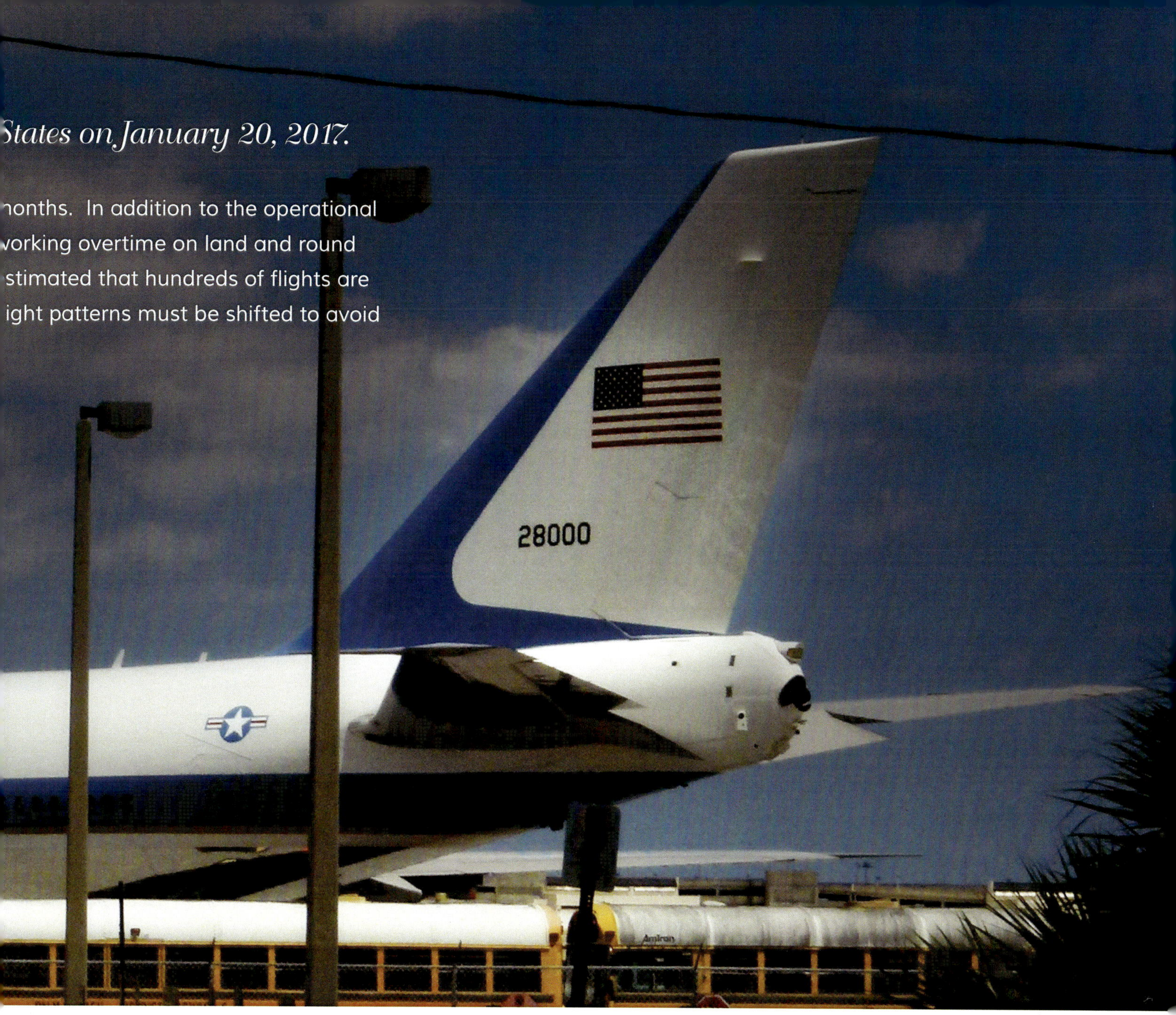

Two-Thousand seventeen was

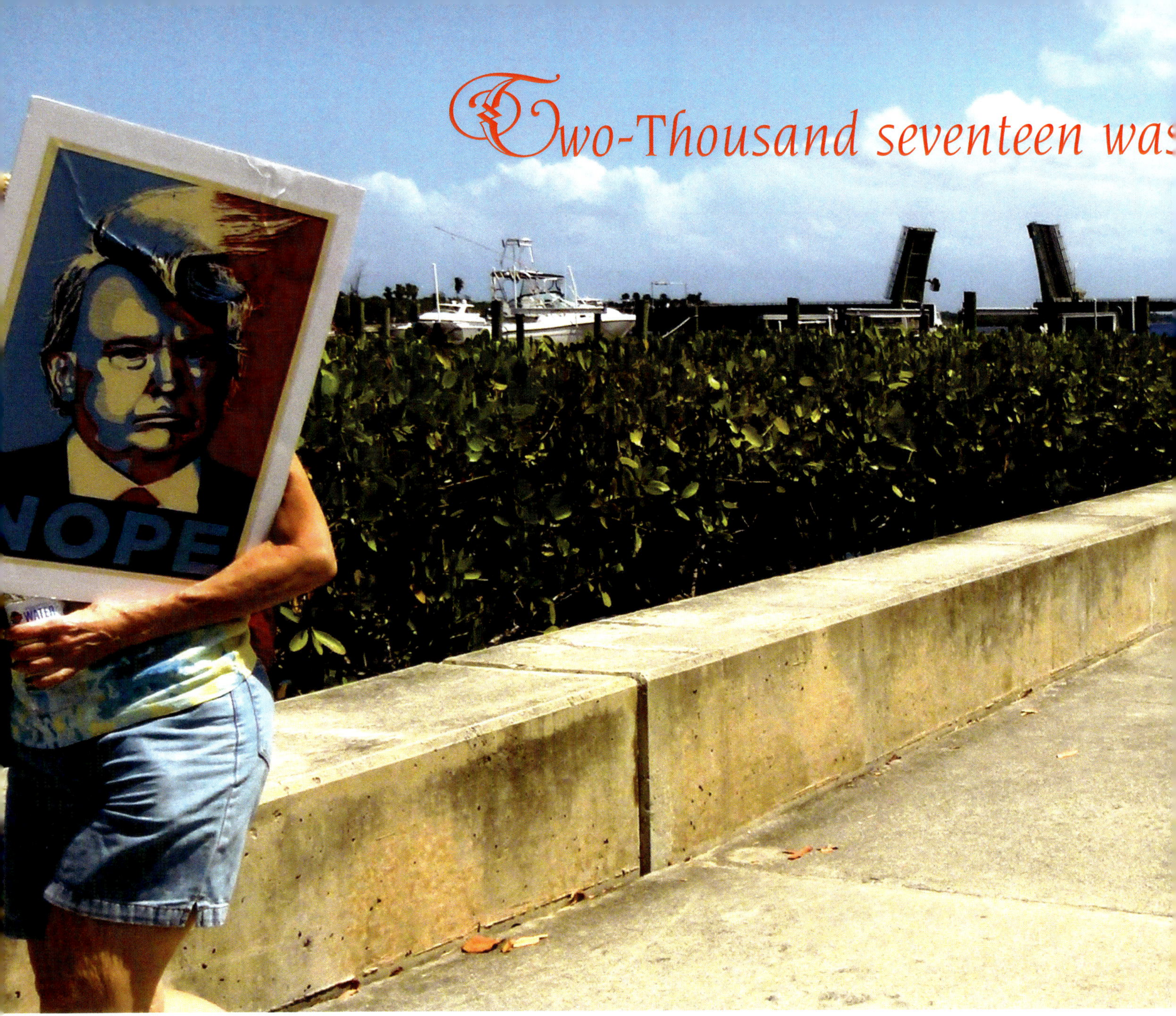

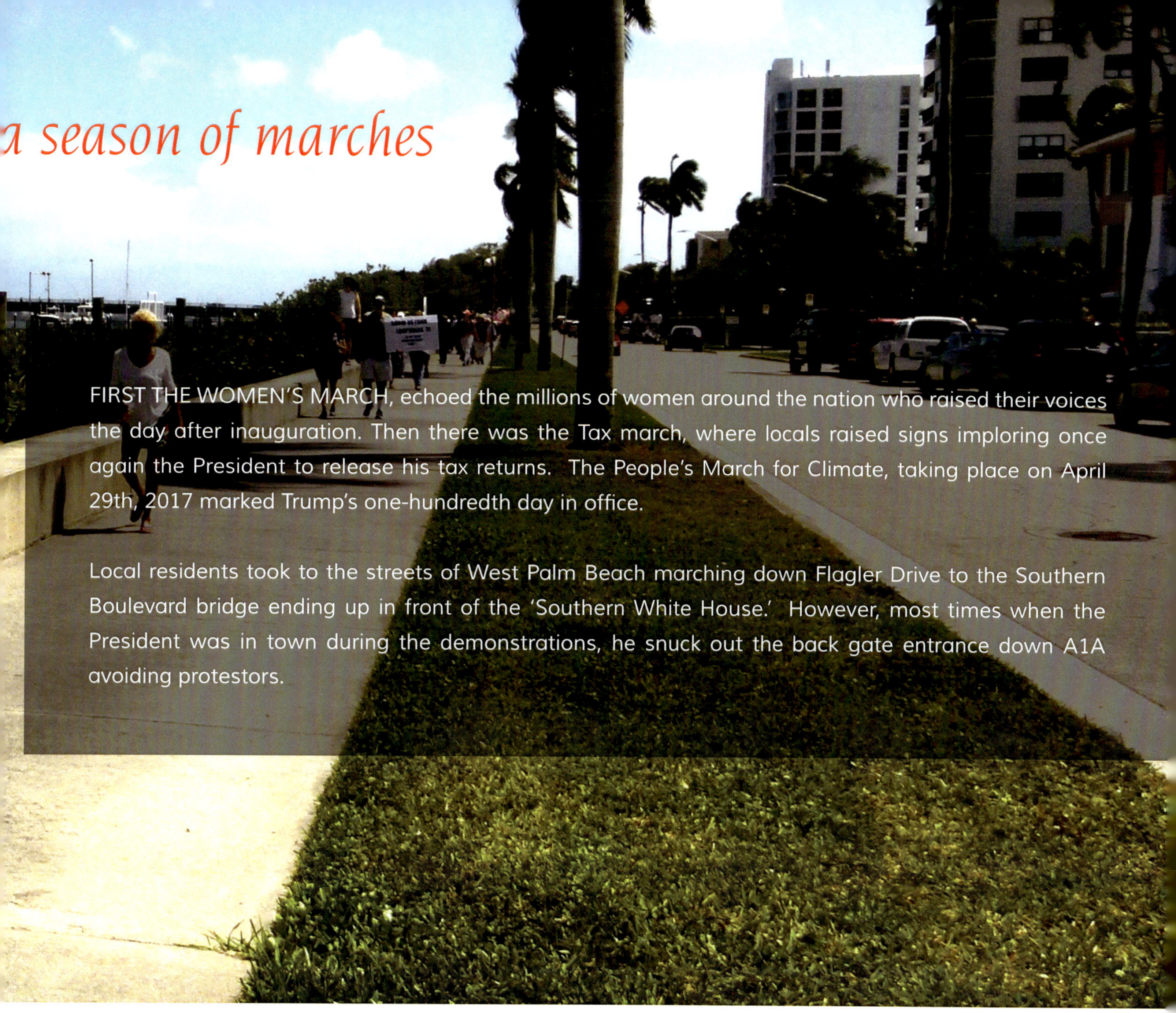

a season of marches

FIRST THE WOMEN'S MARCH, echoed the millions of women around the nation who raised their voices the day after inauguration. Then there was the Tax march, where locals raised signs imploring once again the President to release his tax returns. The People's March for Climate, taking place on April 29th, 2017 marked Trump's one-hundredth day in office.

Local residents took to the streets of West Palm Beach marching down Flagler Drive to the Southern Boulevard bridge ending up in front of the 'Southern White House.' However, most times when the President was in town during the demonstrations, he snuck out the back gate entrance down A1A avoiding protestors.

Signs of

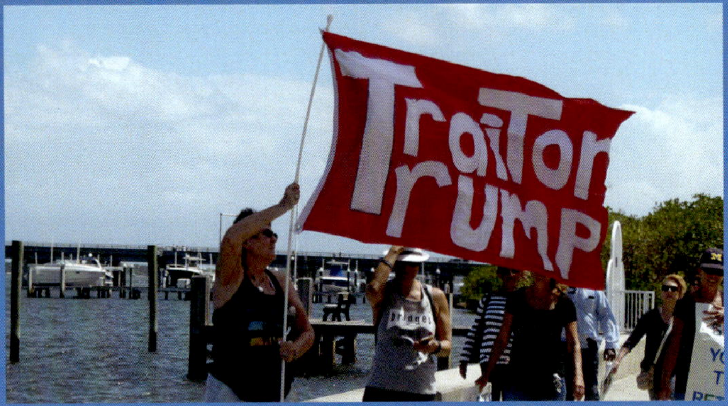

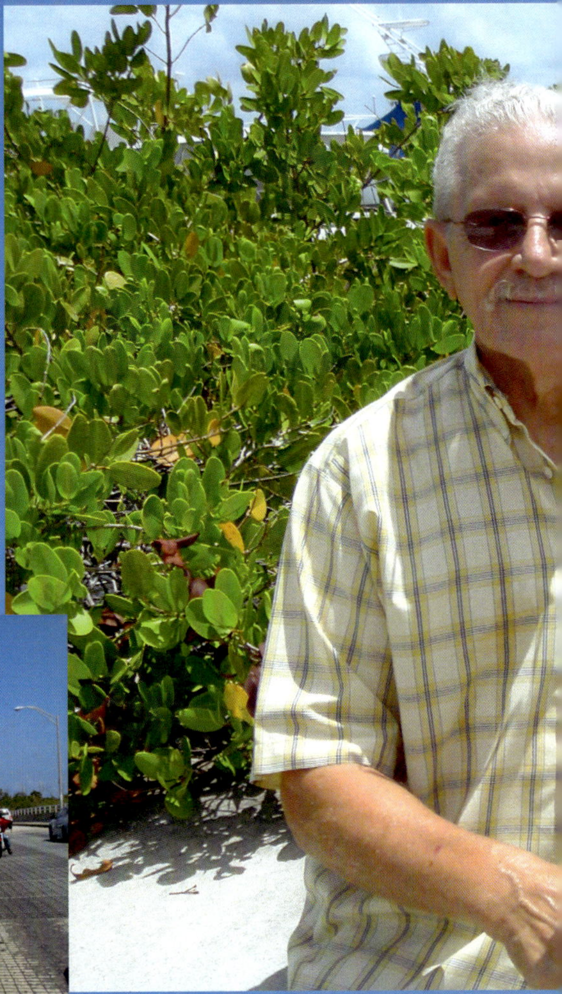

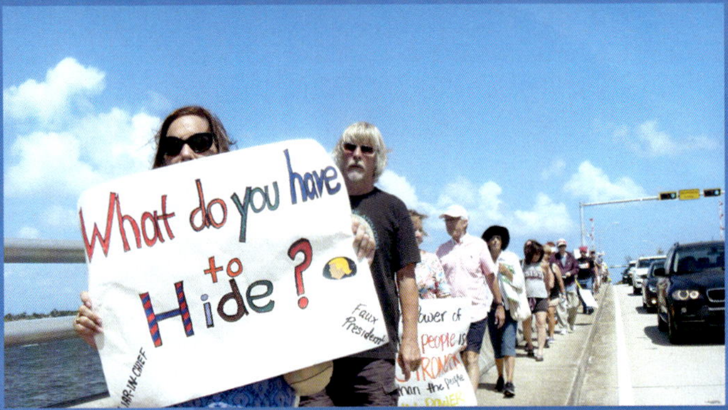

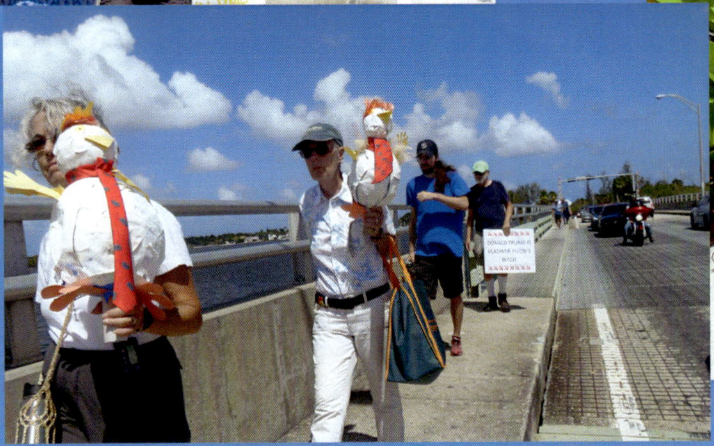

the Times

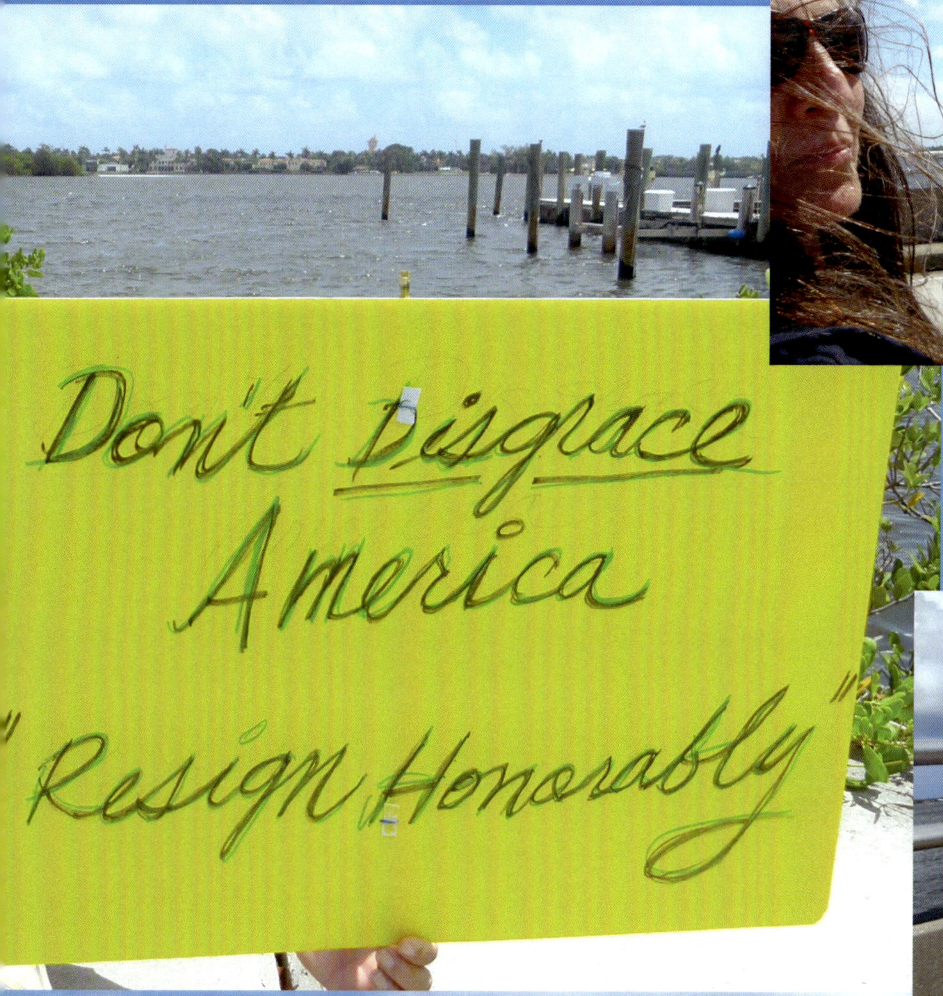
Don't Disgrace
America
"Resign Honorably"

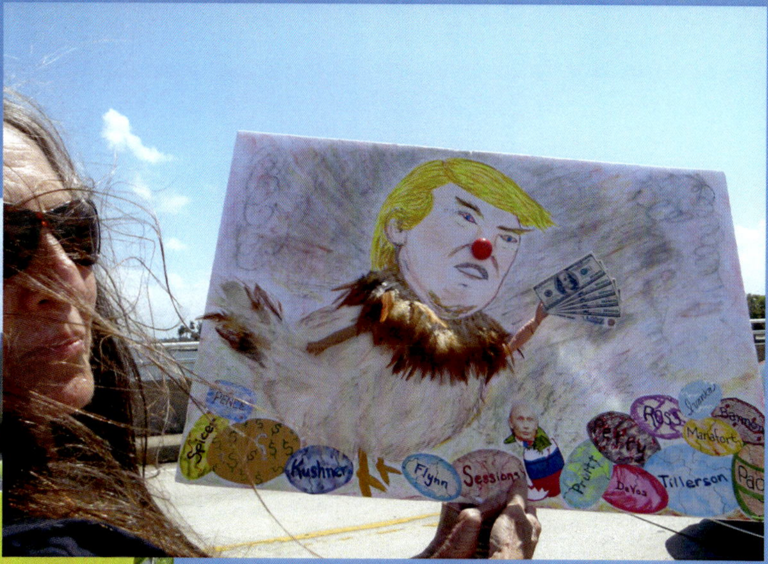
Spicer
Kushner
Flynn
Sessions
Pruitt
DeVos
Tillerson
Ross
Manafort

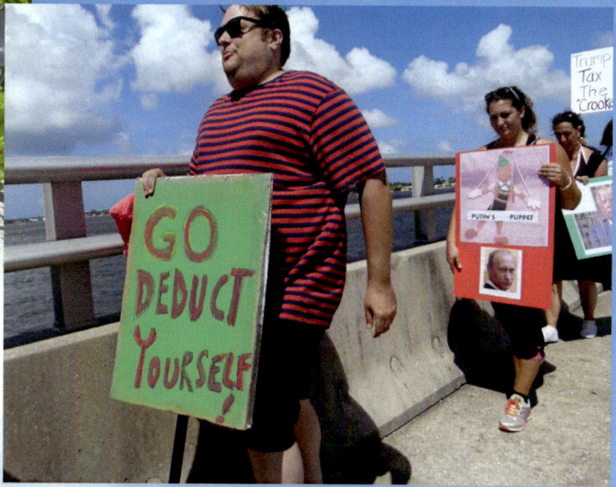
GO
DEDUCT
YOURSELF
!
PUTIN'S PUPPET
Trump
Tax
The
Crook

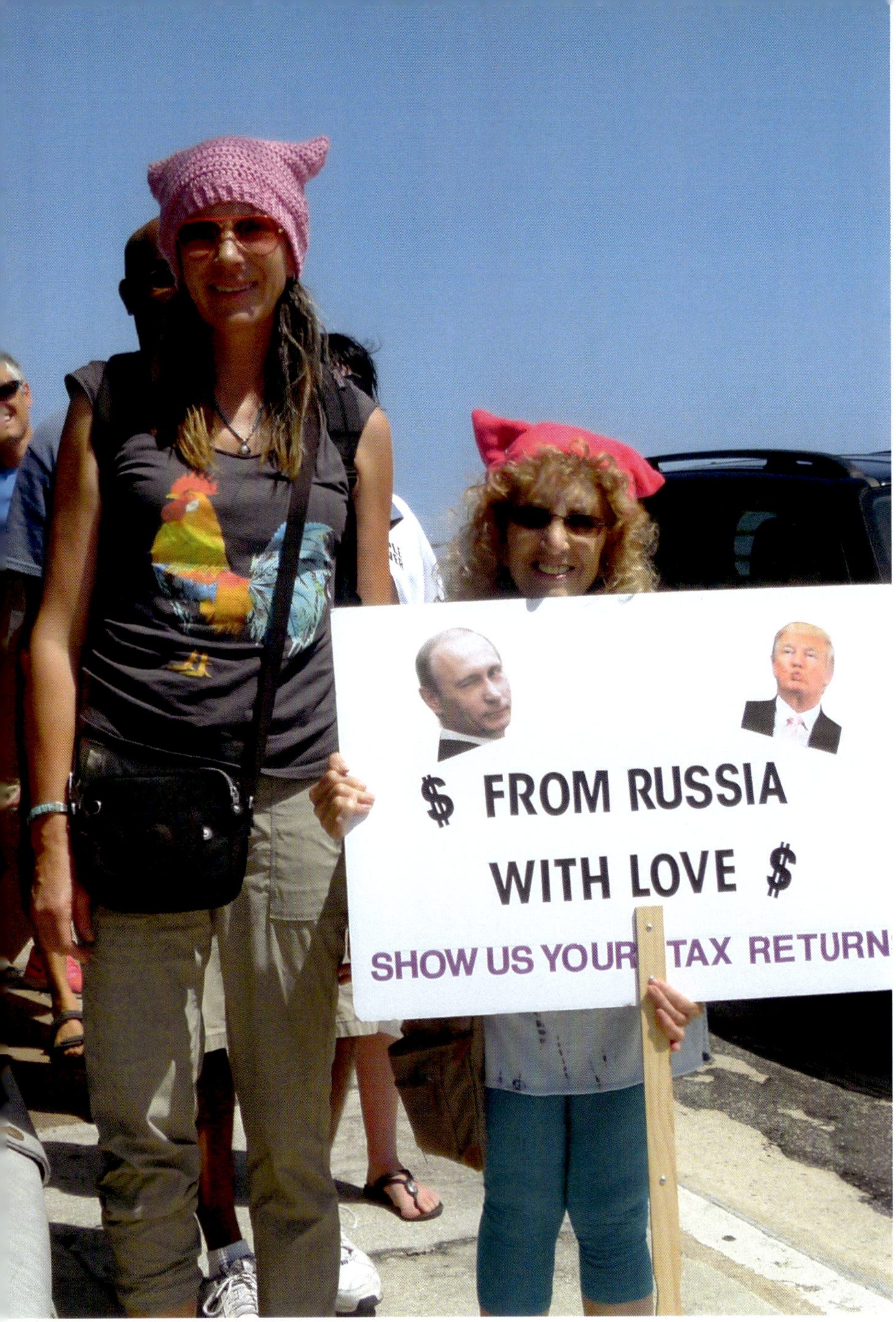
$ FROM RUSSIA
WITH LOVE $
SHOW US YOUR TAX RETURN

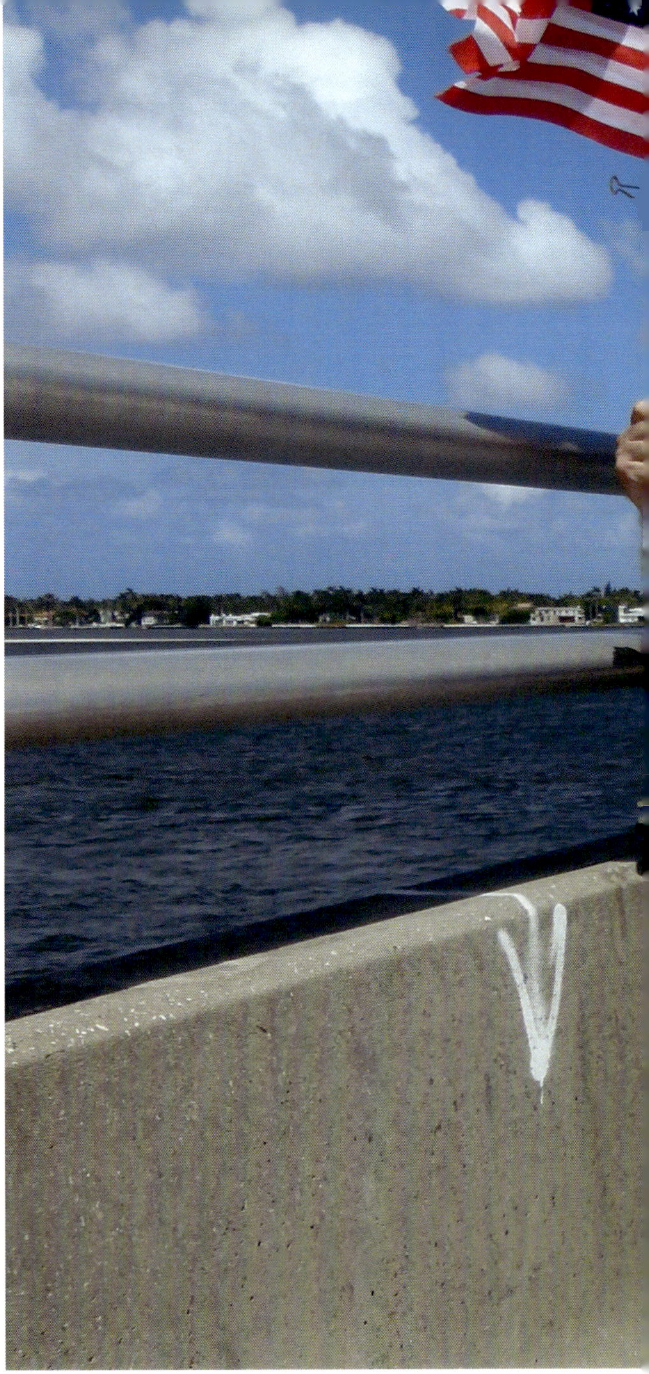

Tax March

April 15, 2017

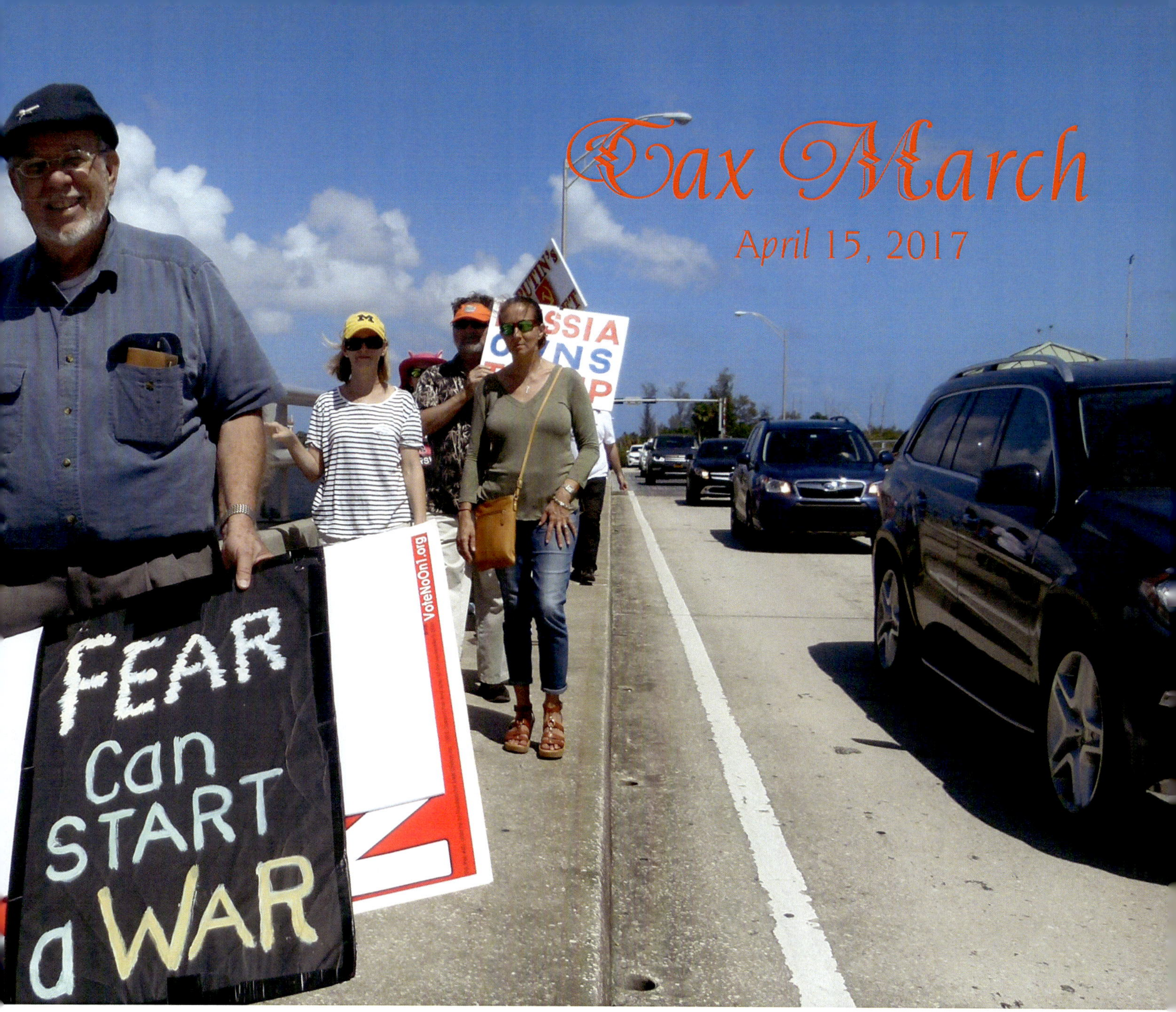

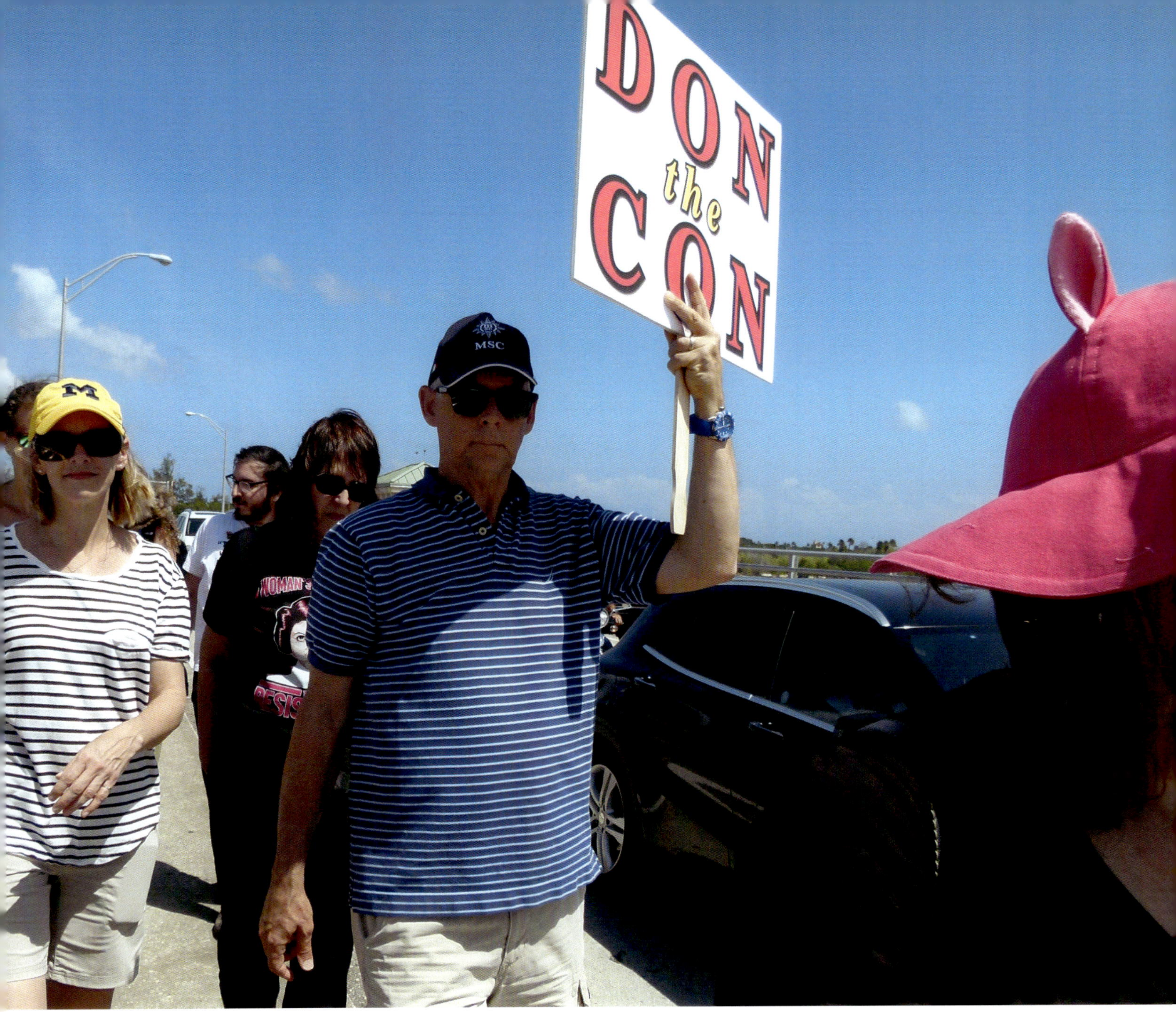
DON
the
CON

Climate March

April 29, 2017

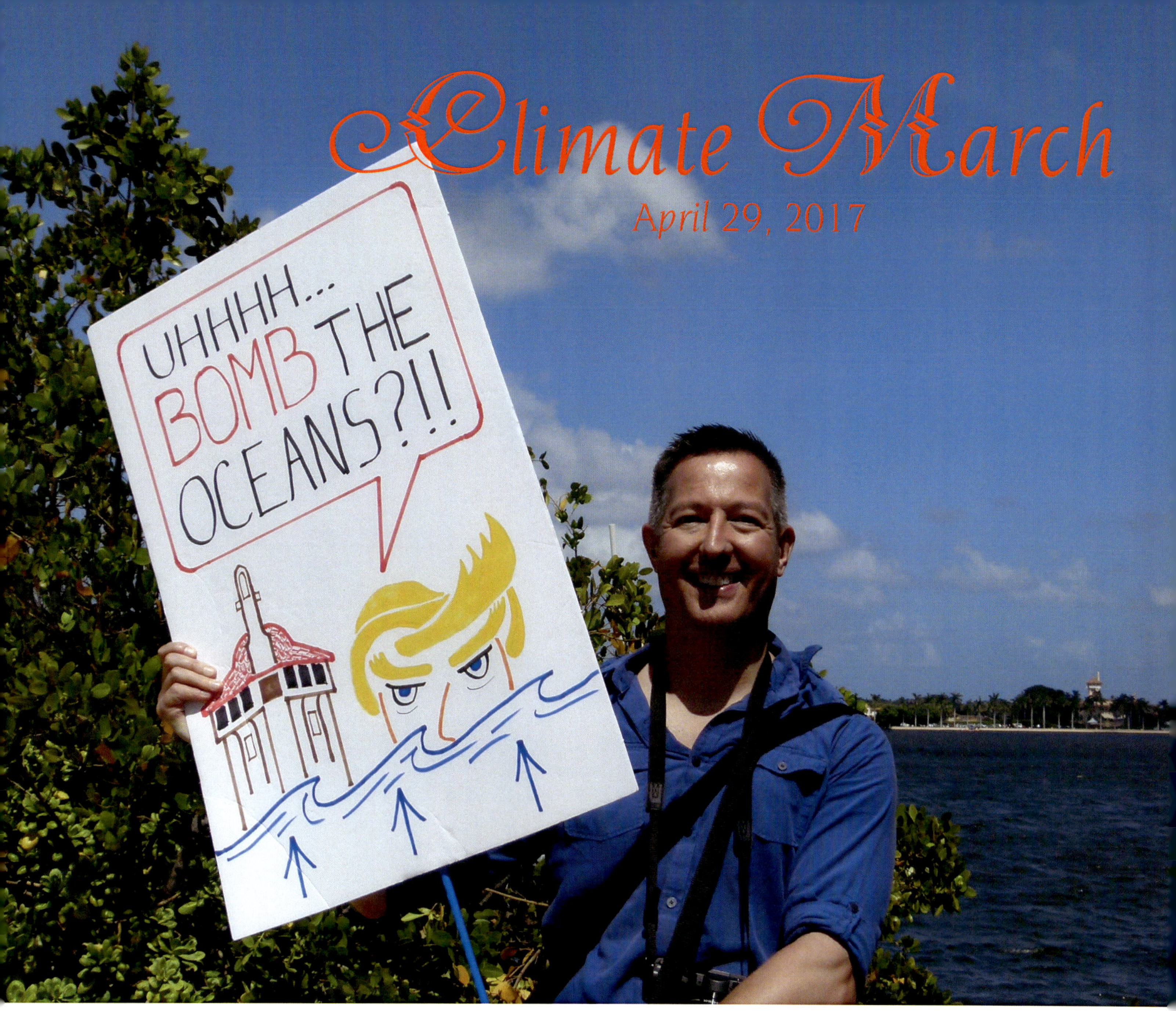

Women's March

February 4, 2017

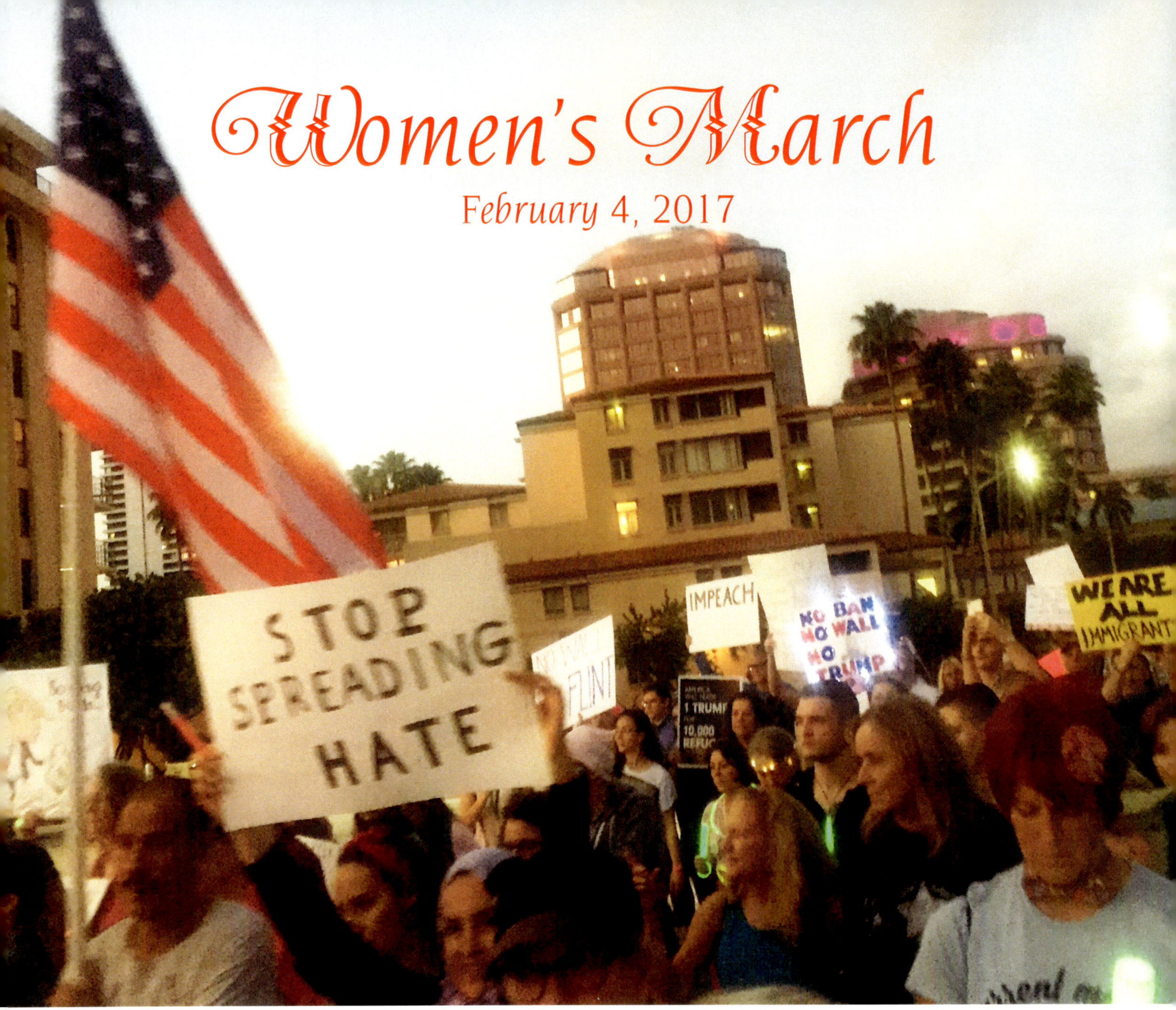

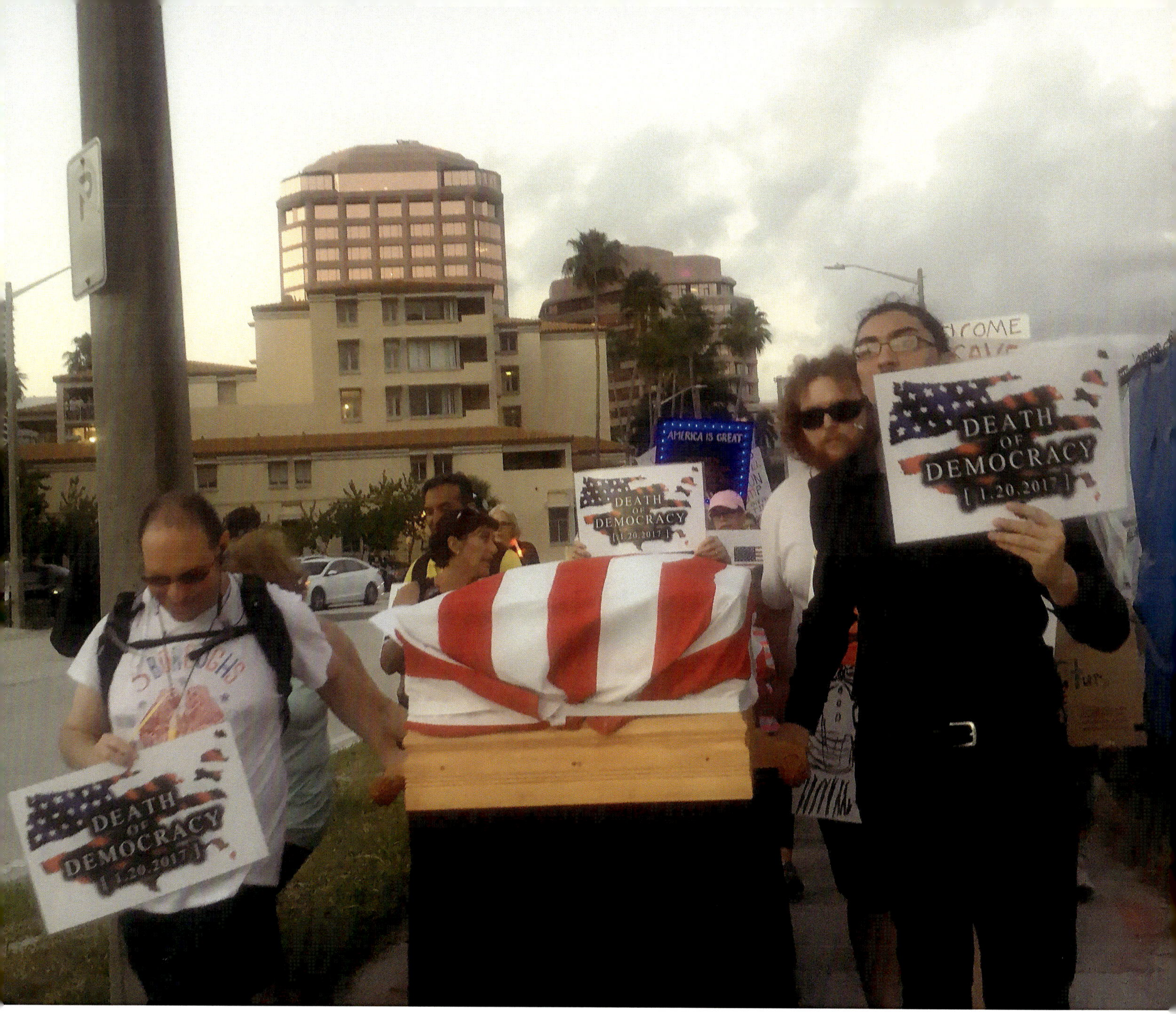
AMERICA IS GREAT
DEATH OF DEMOCRACY
[1.20.2017]
DEATH OF DEMOCRACY
[1.20.2017]
DEATH OF DEMOCRACY
[1.20.2017]

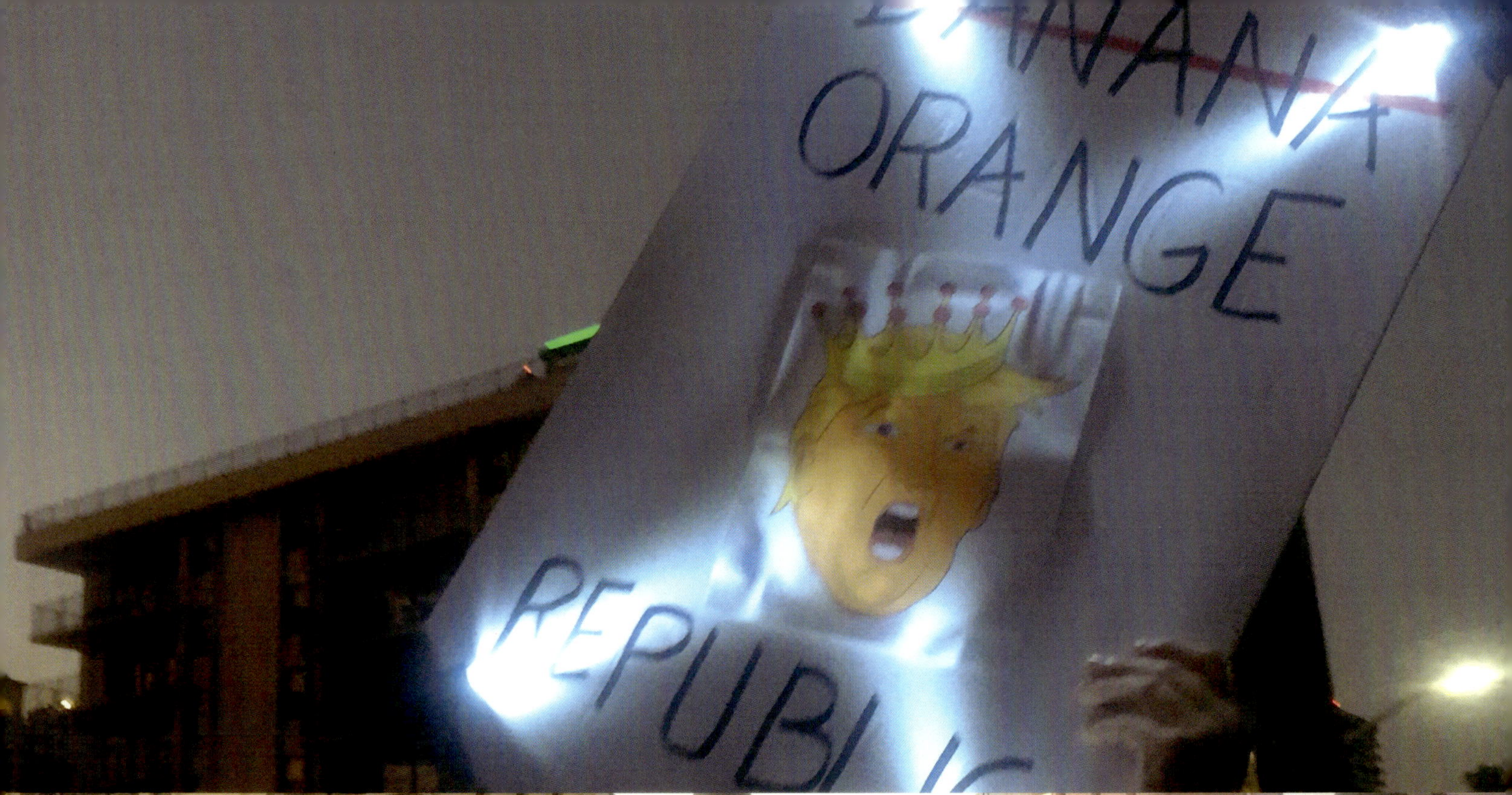
ORANGE

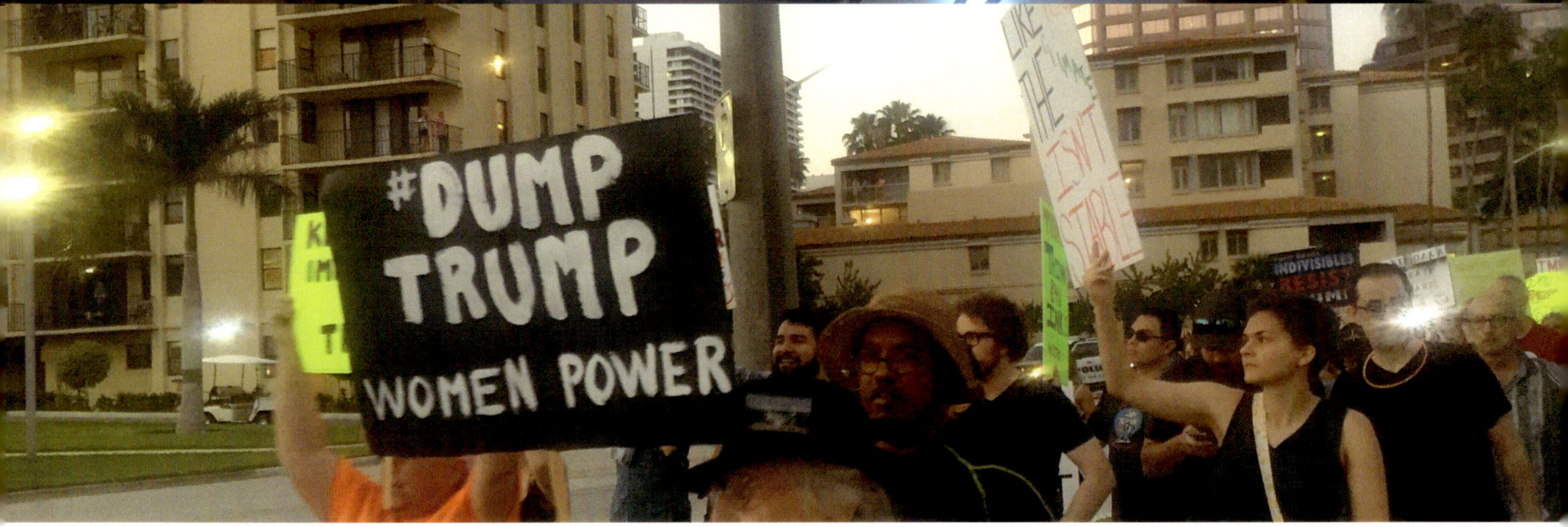
#DUMP
TRUMP
WOMEN POWER

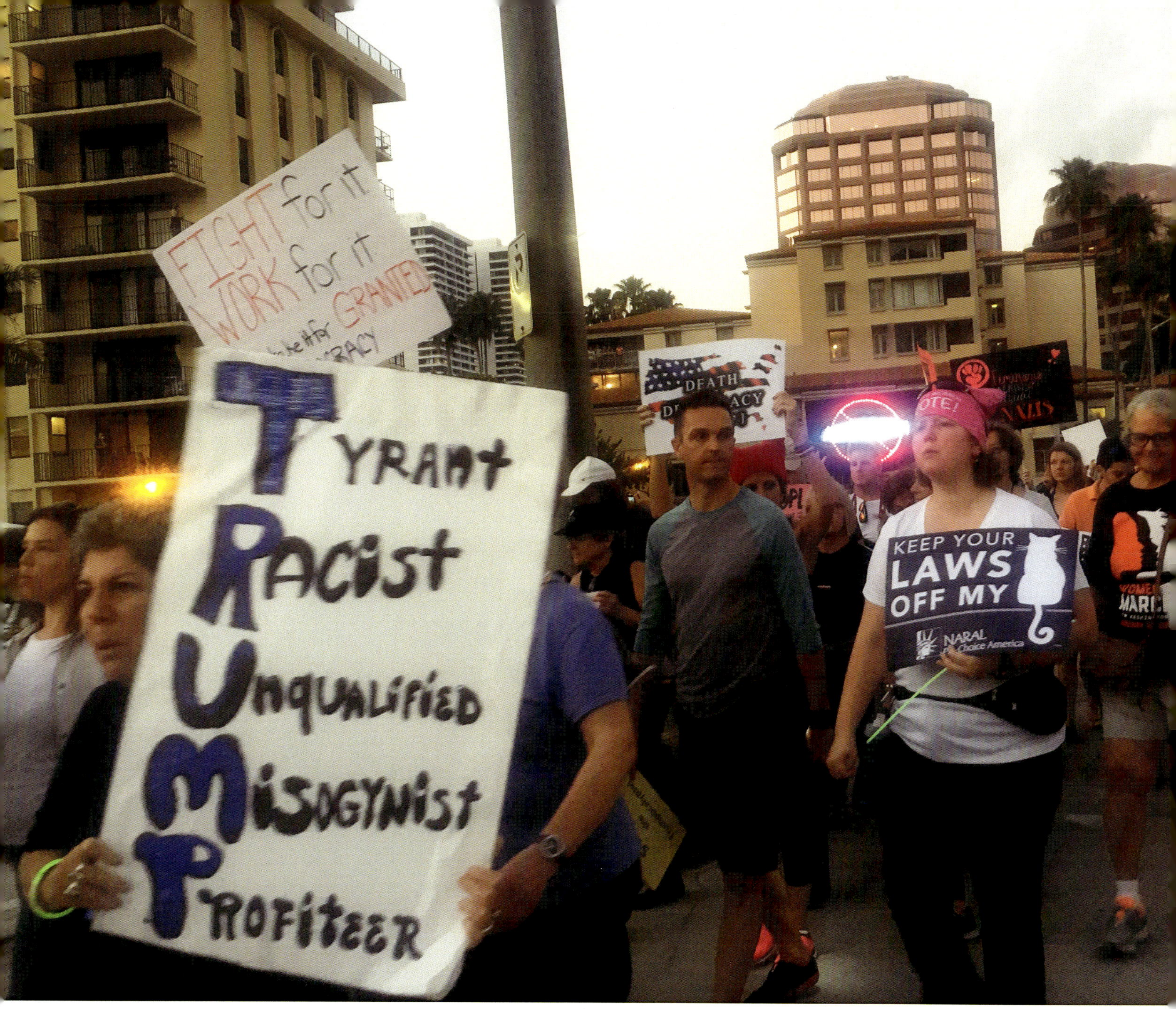
FIGHT for it
WORK for it
GRANTED
Tyrant
Racist
Unqualified
Misogynist
Profiteer
DEATH
NAZIS
KEEP YOUR
LAWS
OFF MY
NARAL
Choice America

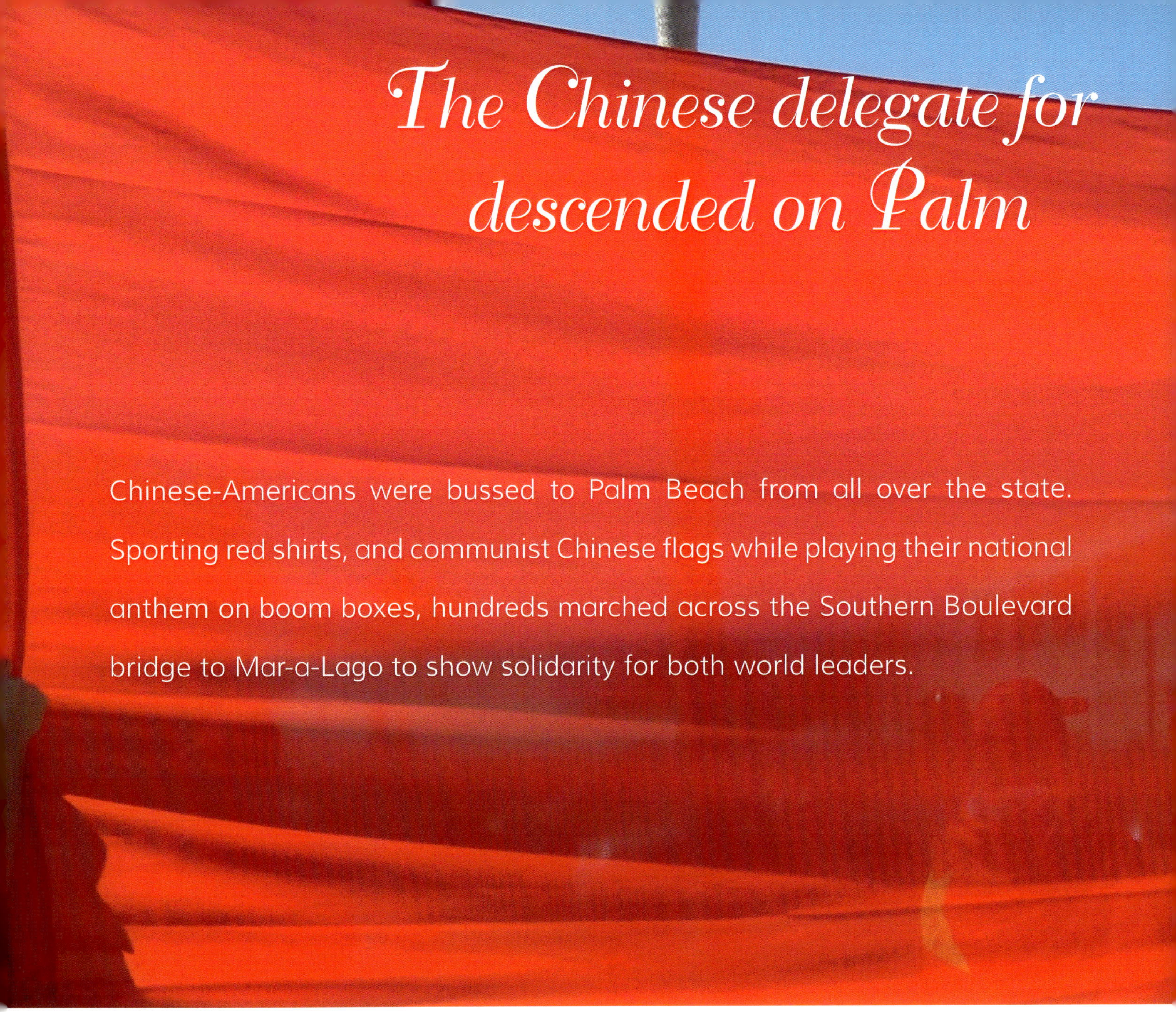

The Chinese delegate for descended on Palm

Chinese-Americans were bussed to Palm Beach from all over the state. Sporting red shirts, and communist Chinese flags while playing their national anthem on boom boxes, hundreds marched across the Southern Boulevard bridge to Mar-a-Lago to show solidarity for both world leaders.

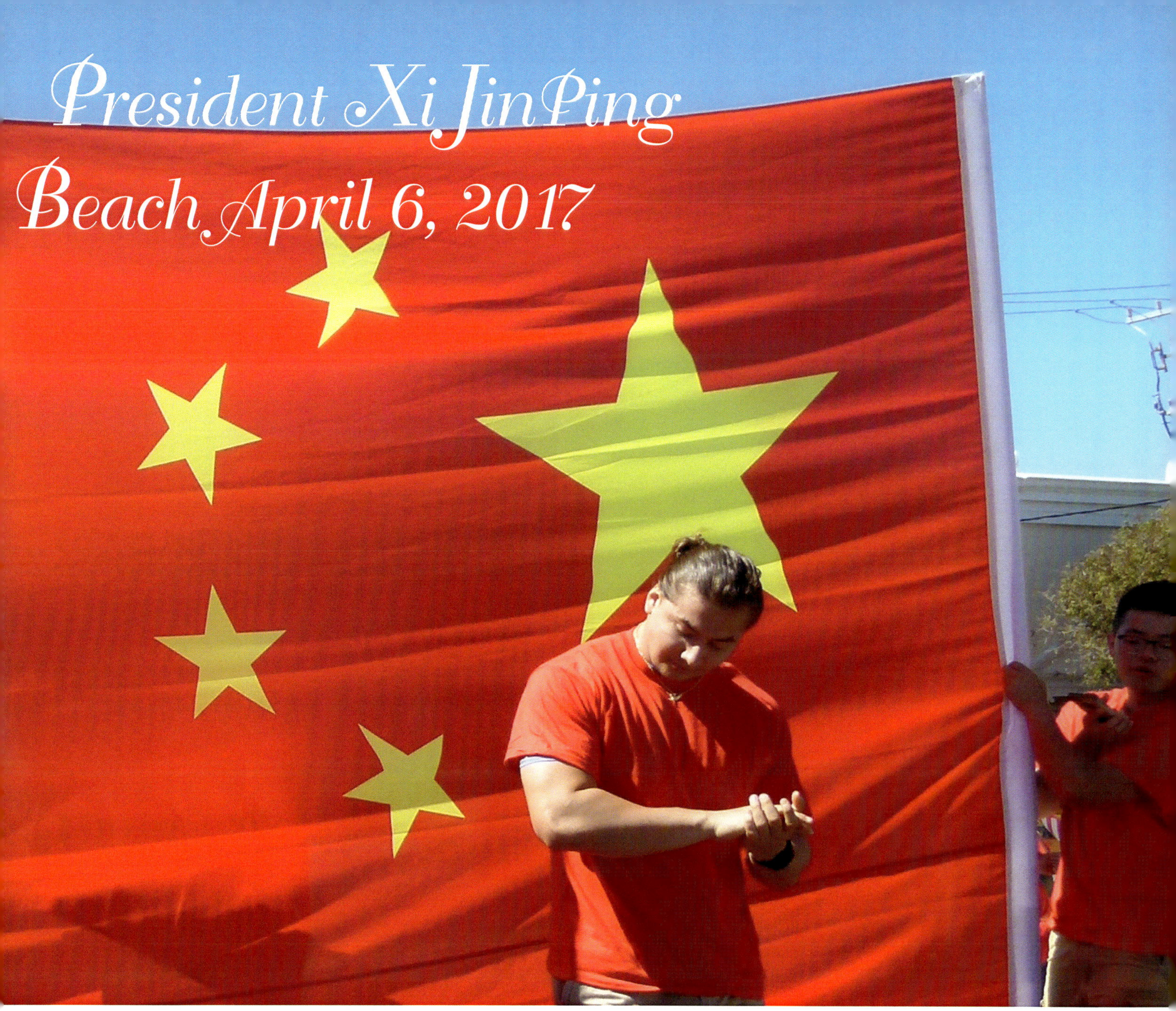
President Xi JinPing
Beach April 6, 2017

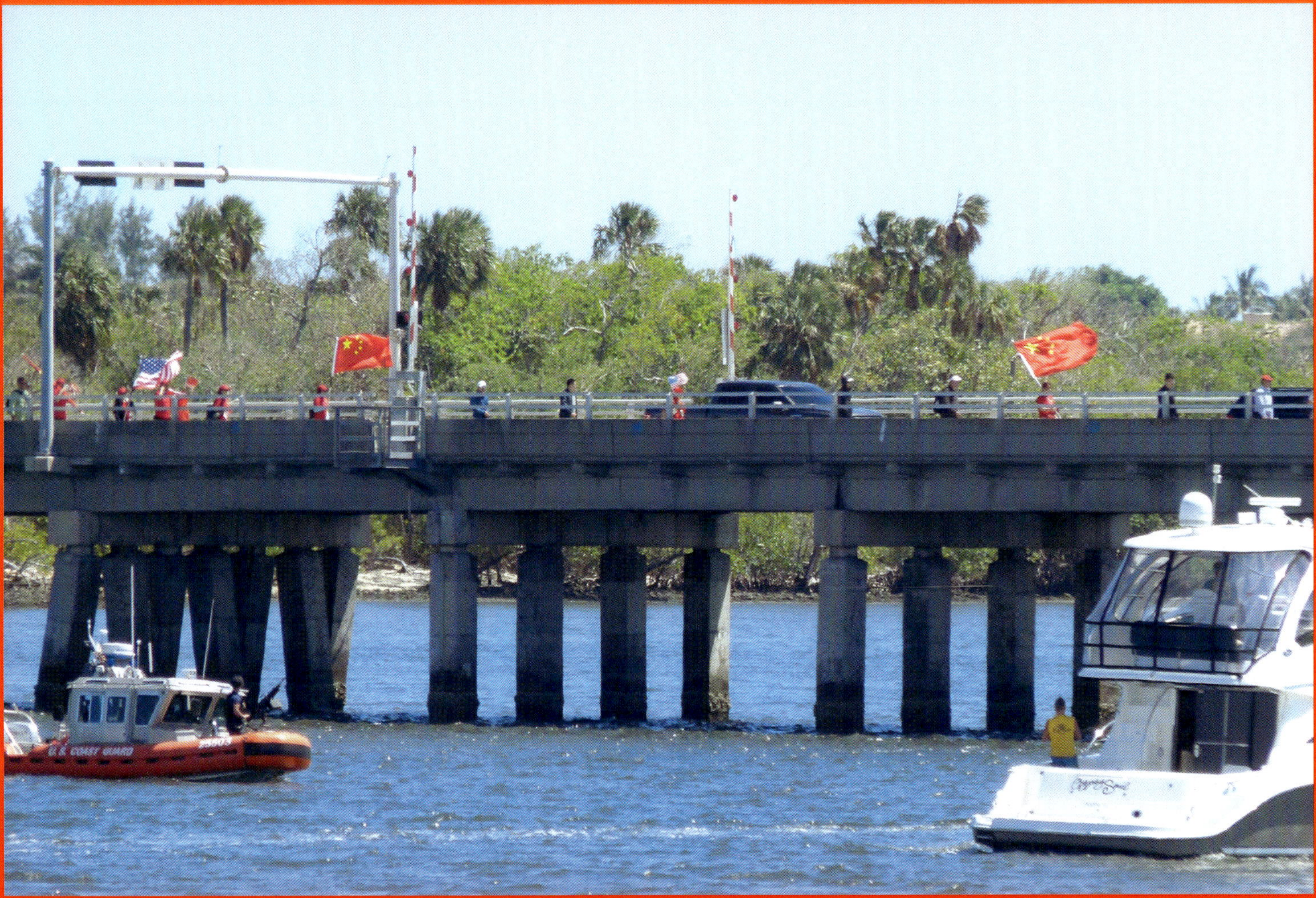
U.S. COAST GUARD

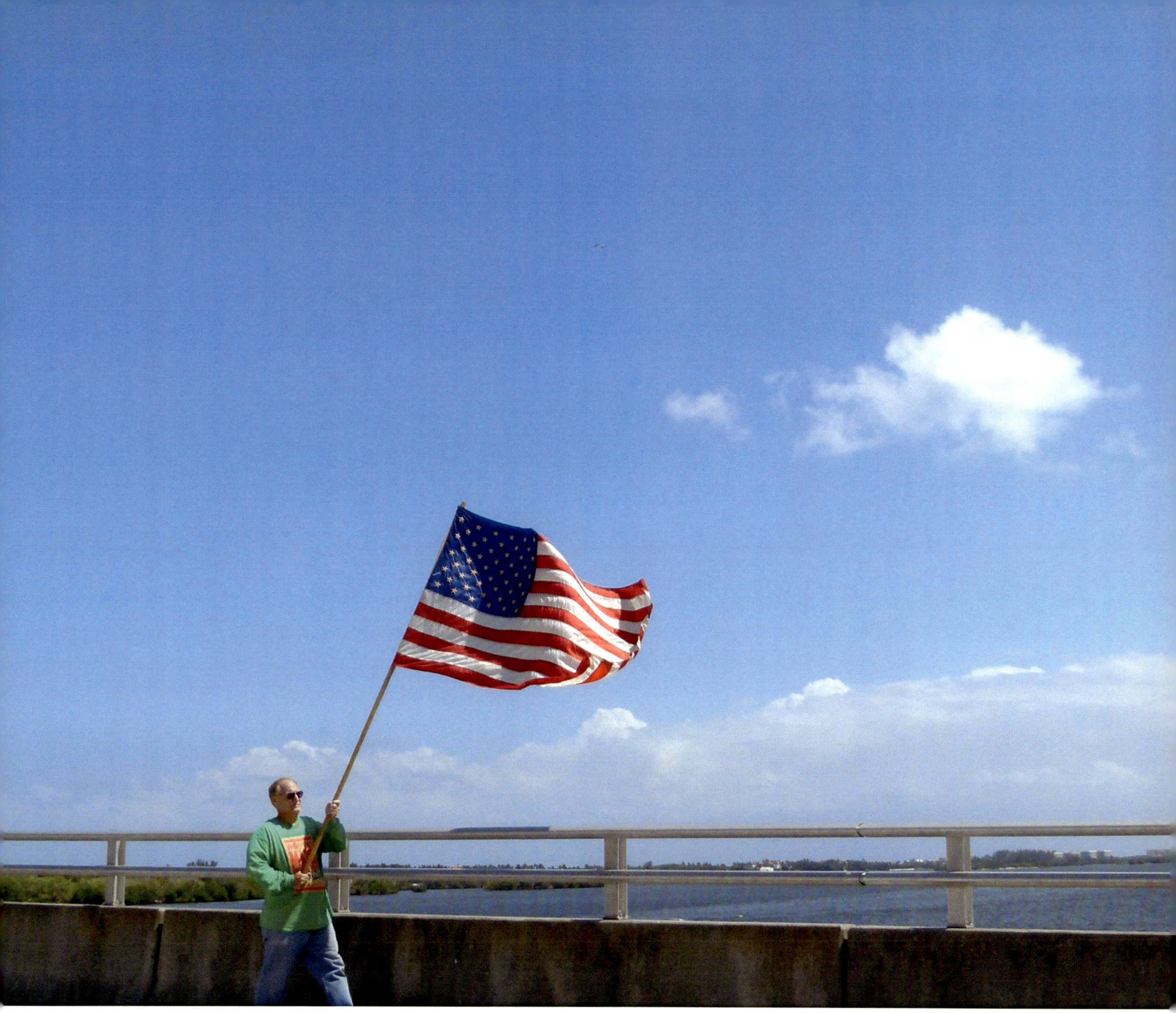

Media Circus

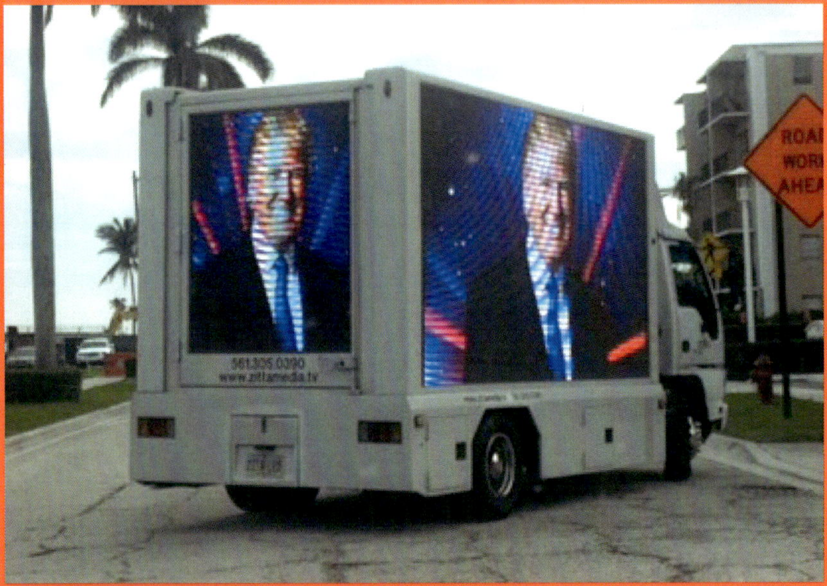

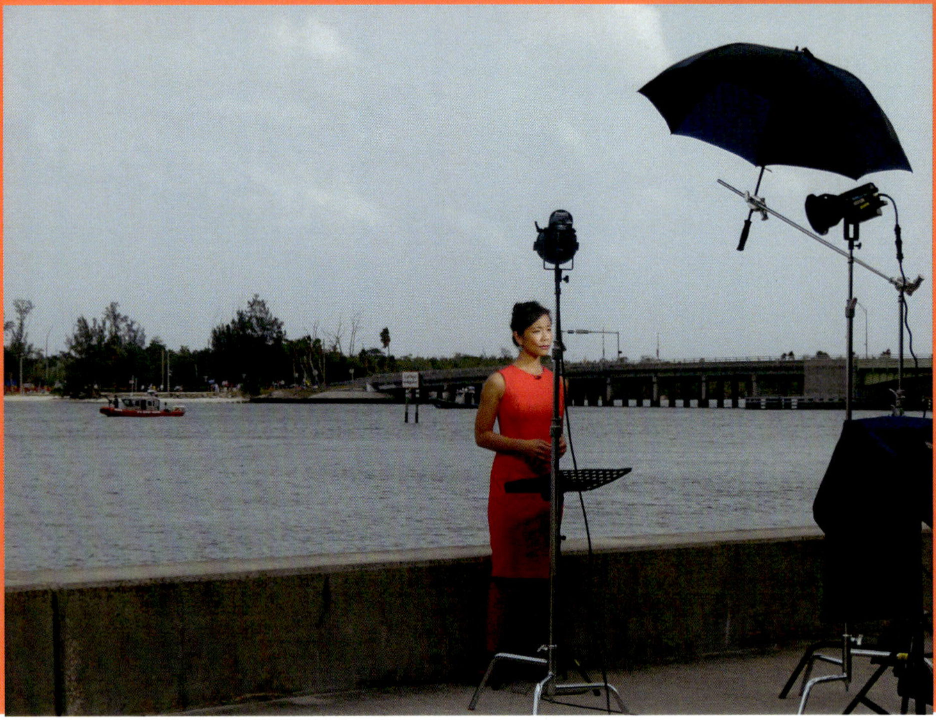

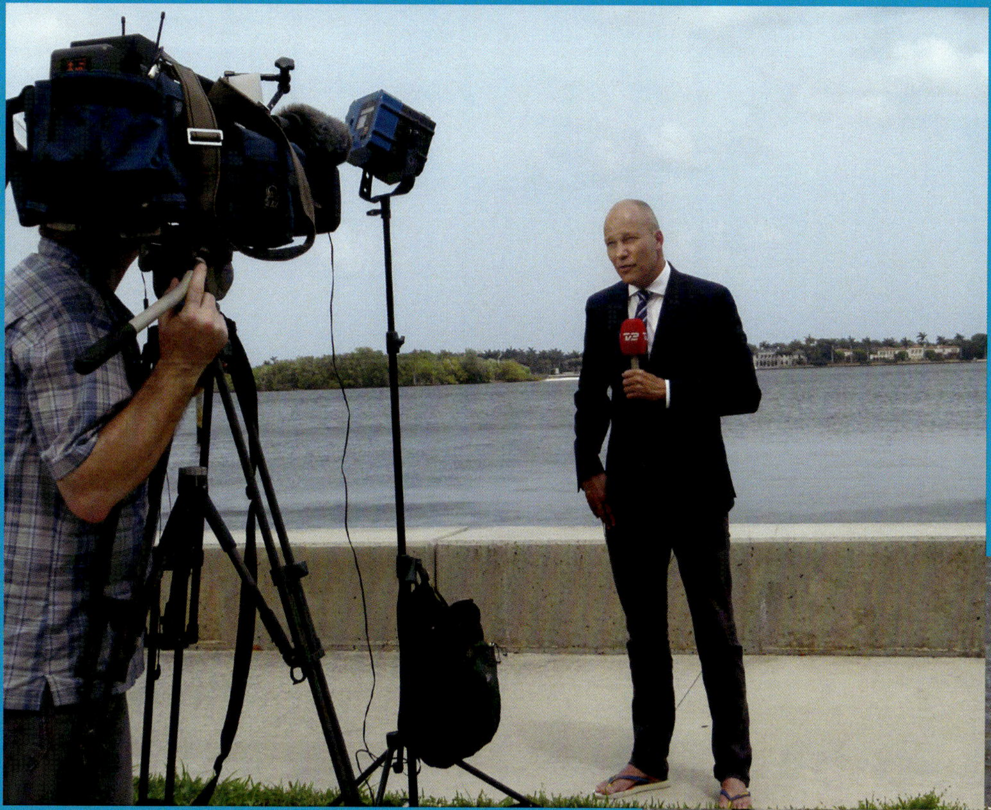

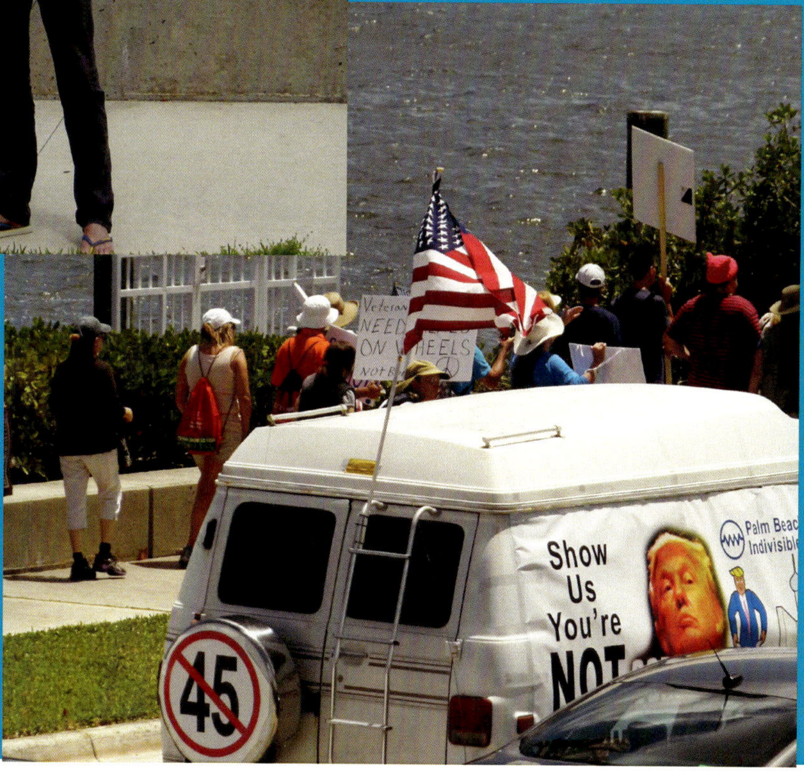
Show
Us
You're
45

Patriots and Protesters

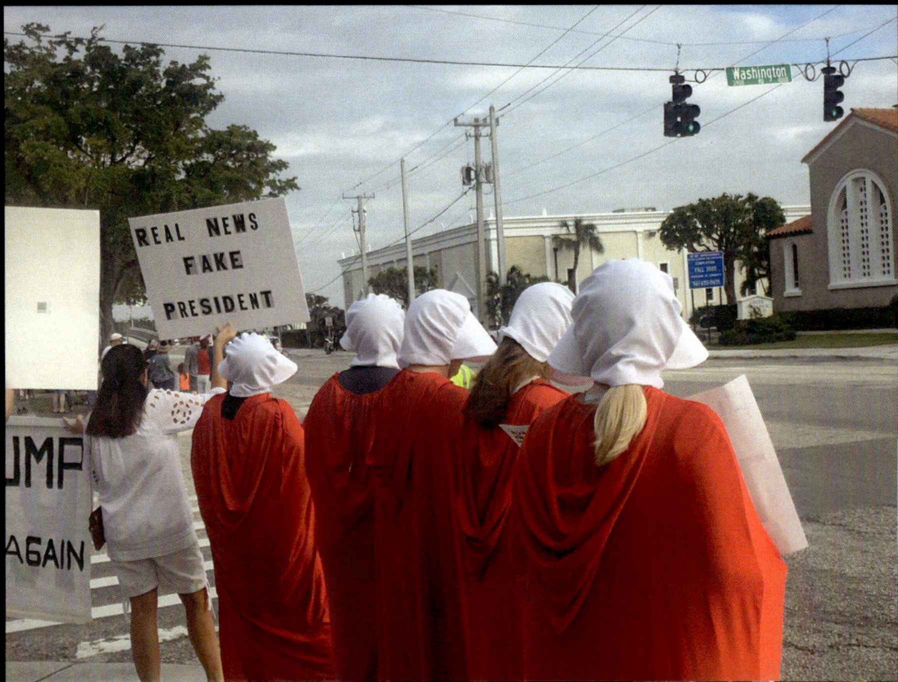

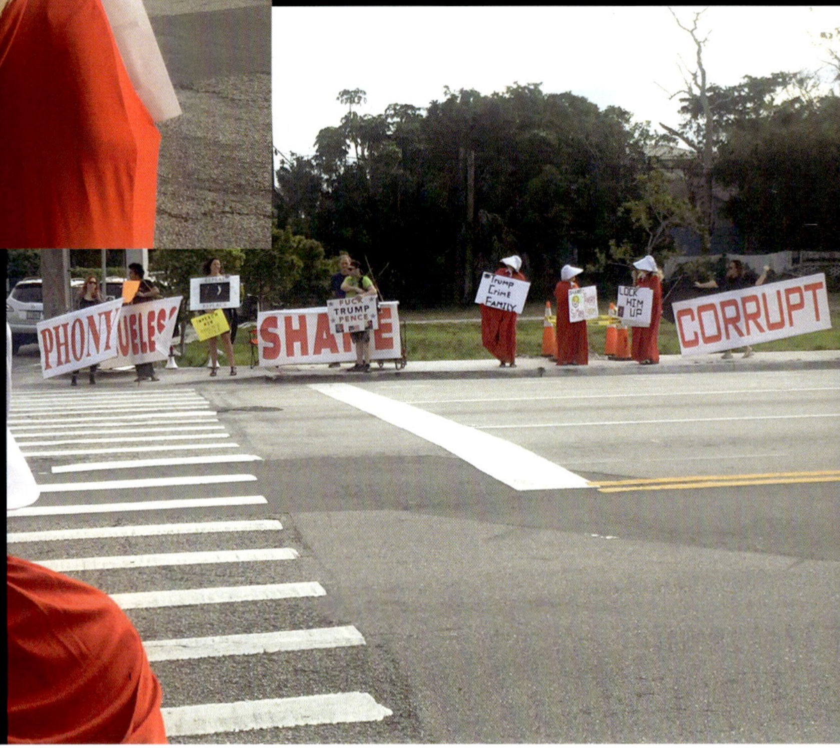

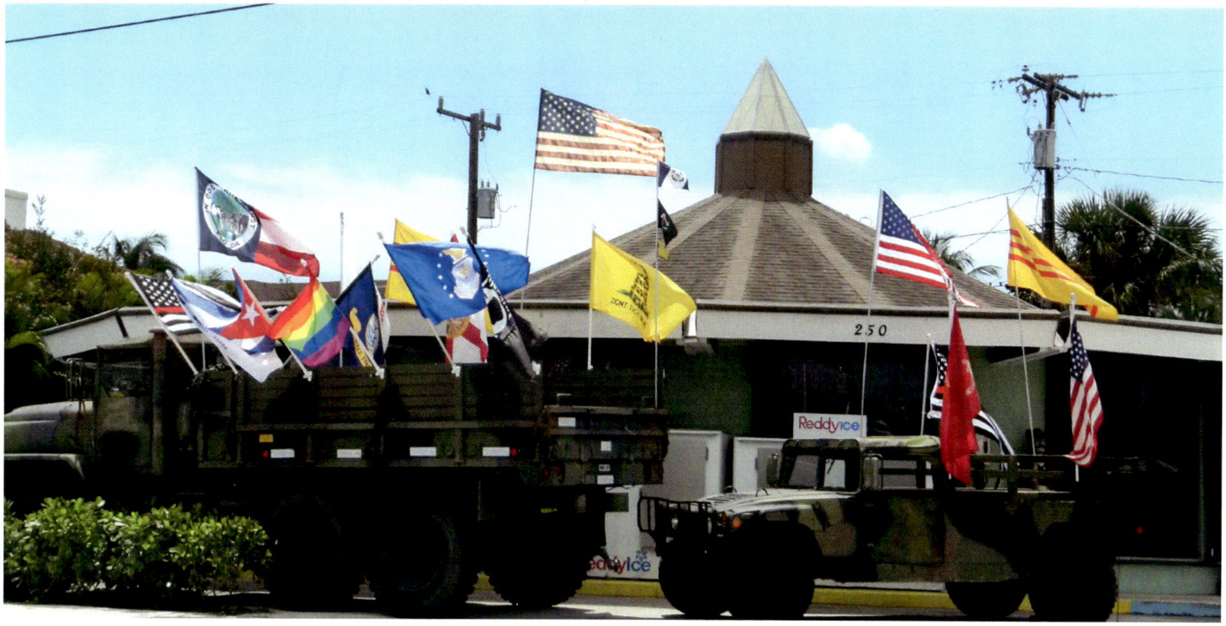
250
ReddyIce

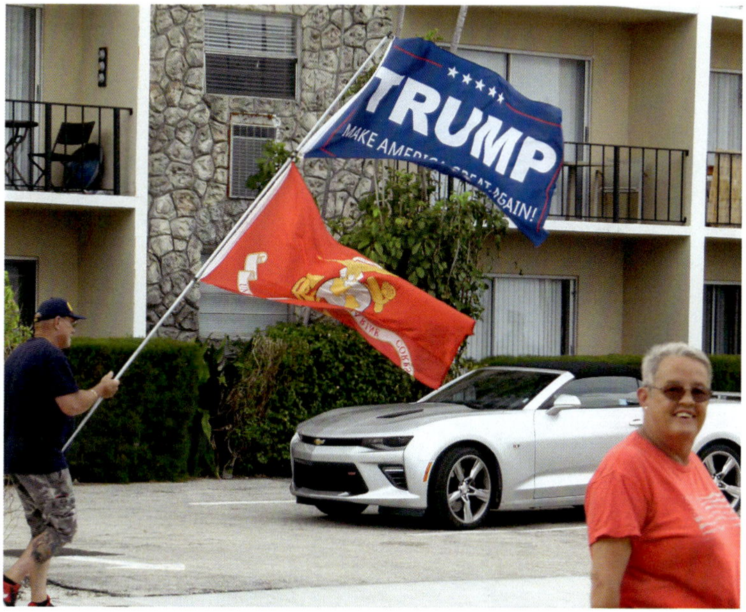
TRUMP
MAKE AMERICA GREAT AGAIN!

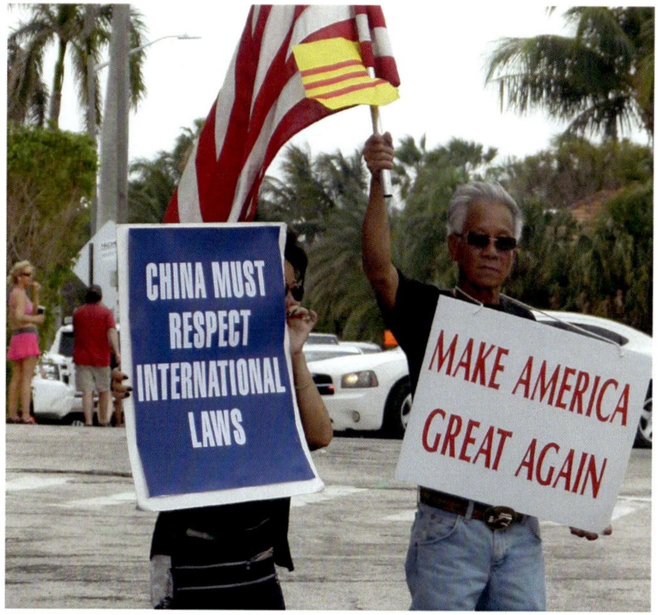
CHINA MUST RESPECT INTERNATIONAL LAWS
MAKE AMERICA GREAT AGAIN

Protecting the President

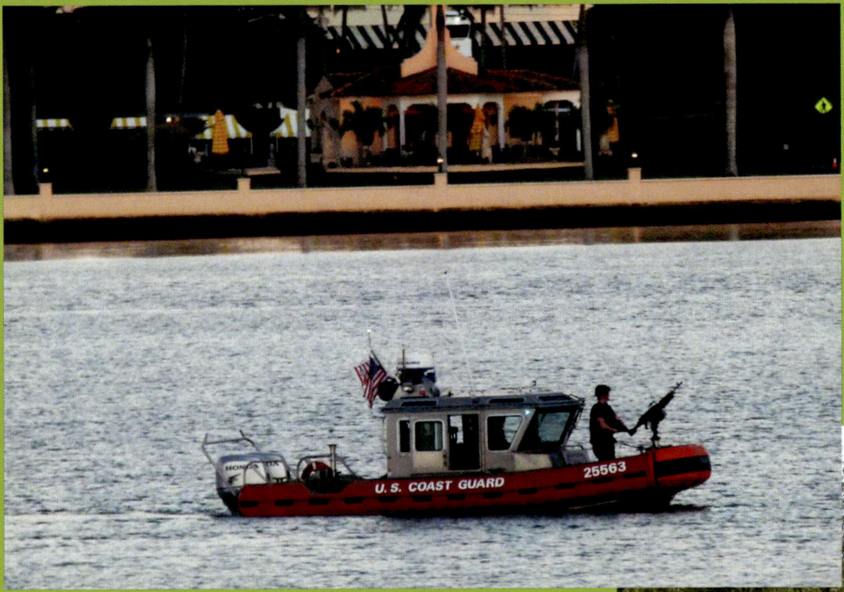

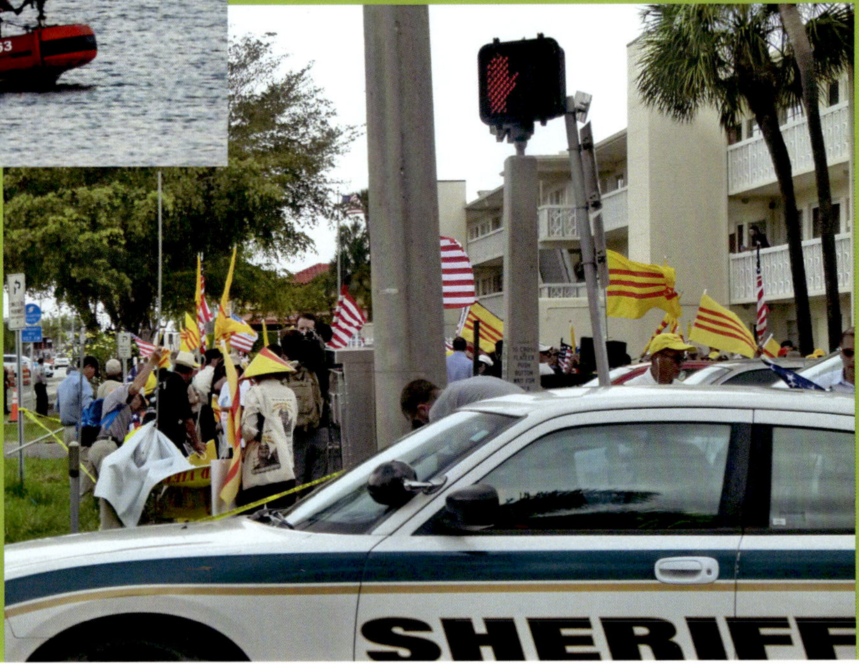

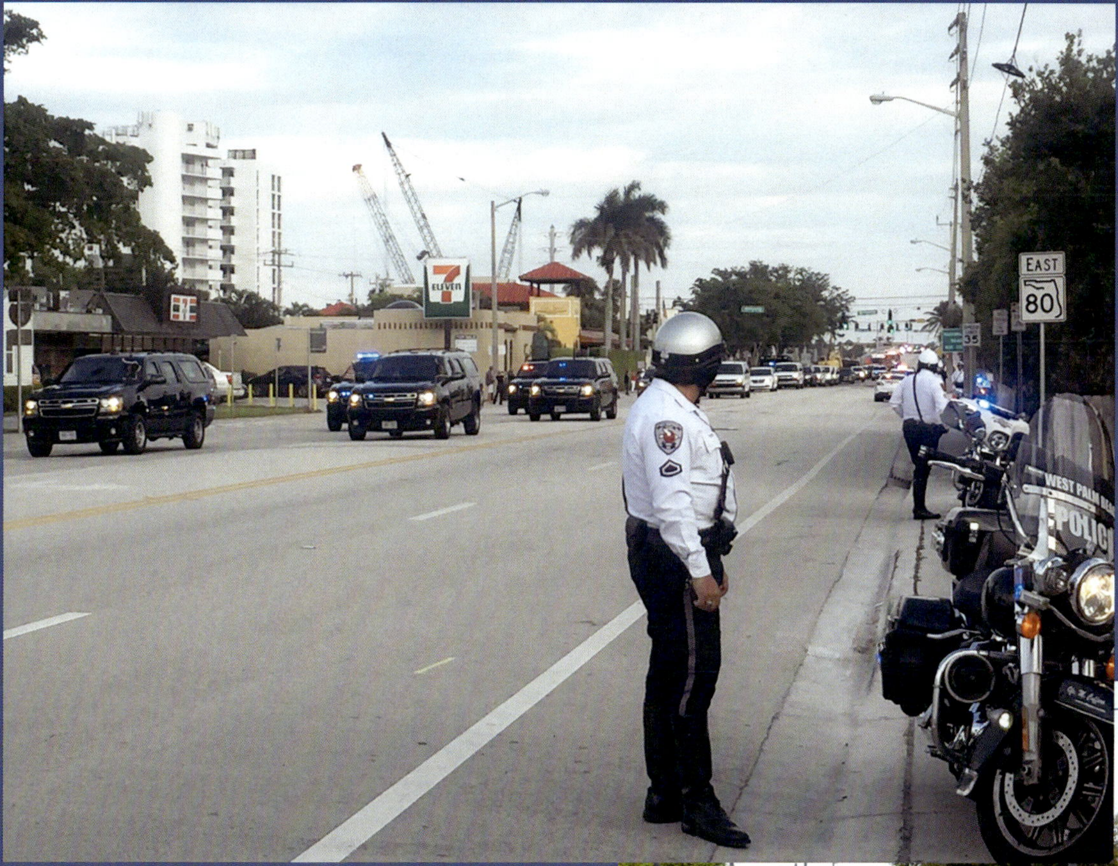
ELEVEN
EAST
80

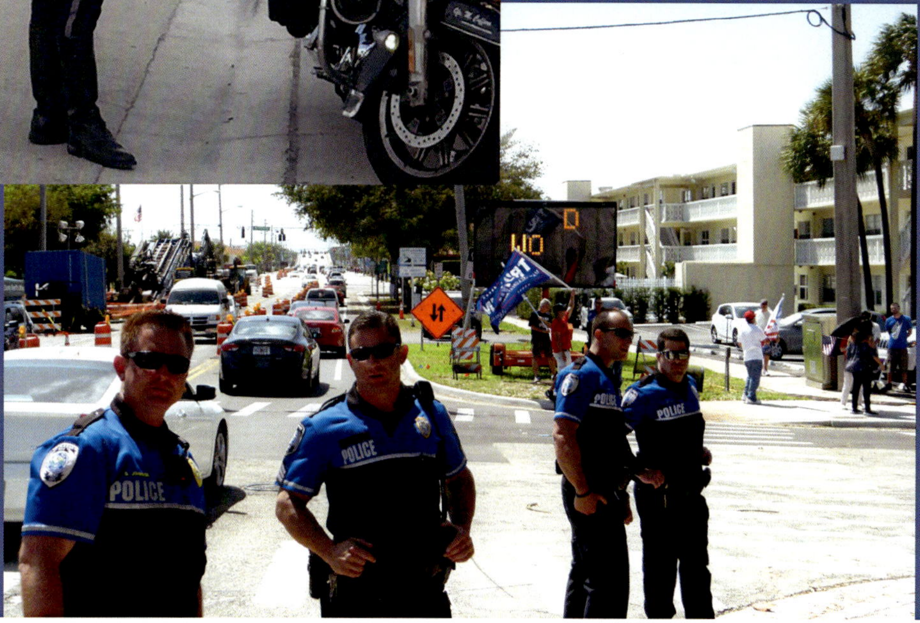
POLICE
POLICE
POLICE

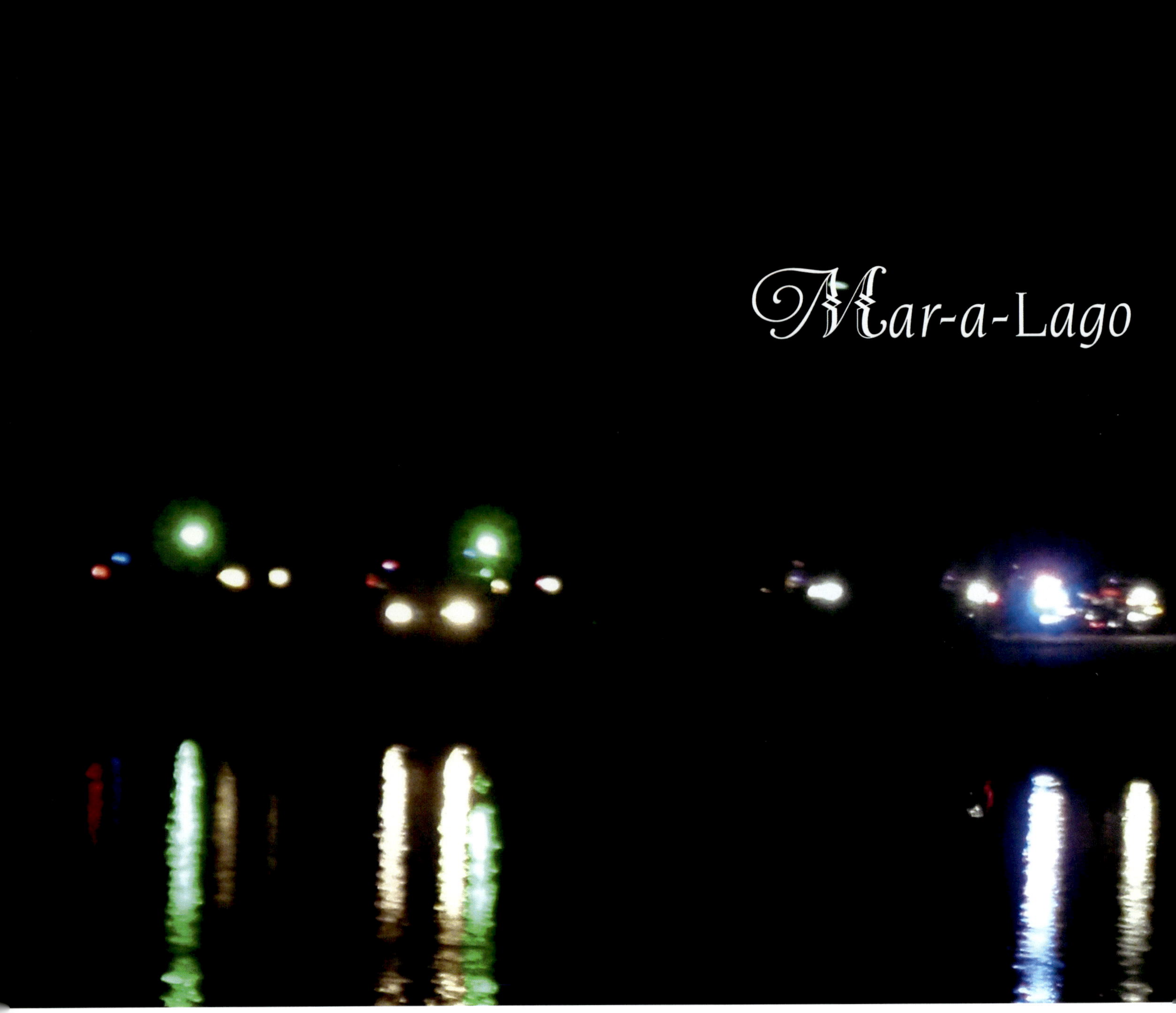

Mar-a-Lago

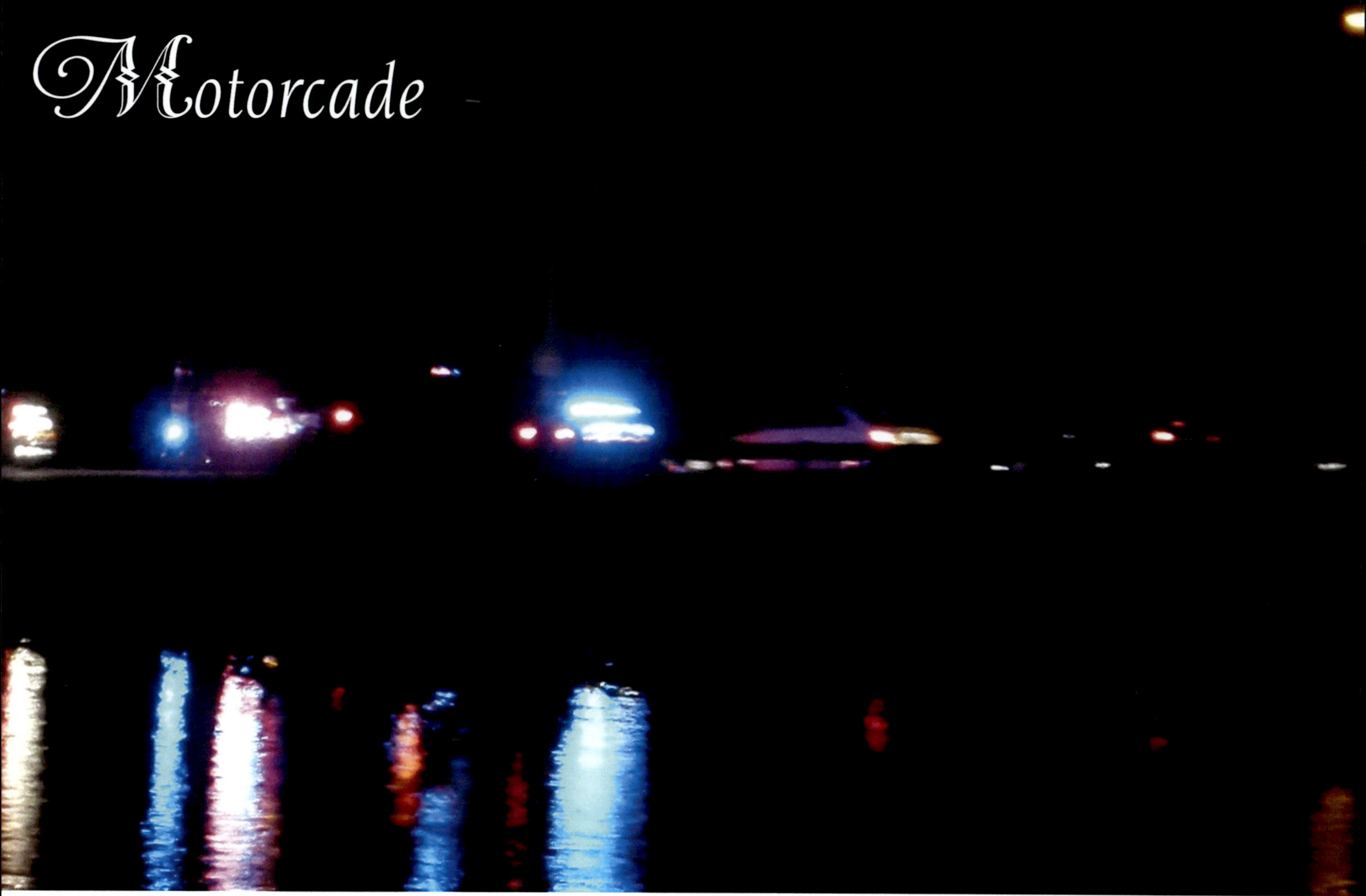
Motorcade

Stylist and Socialite

Inside the 2017 Red Cross

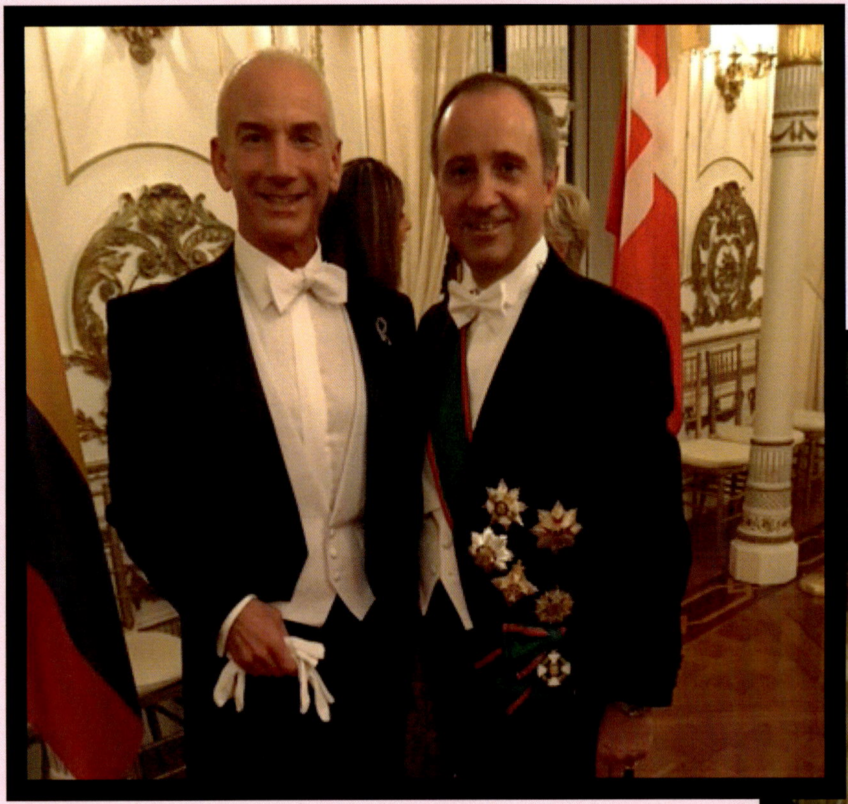

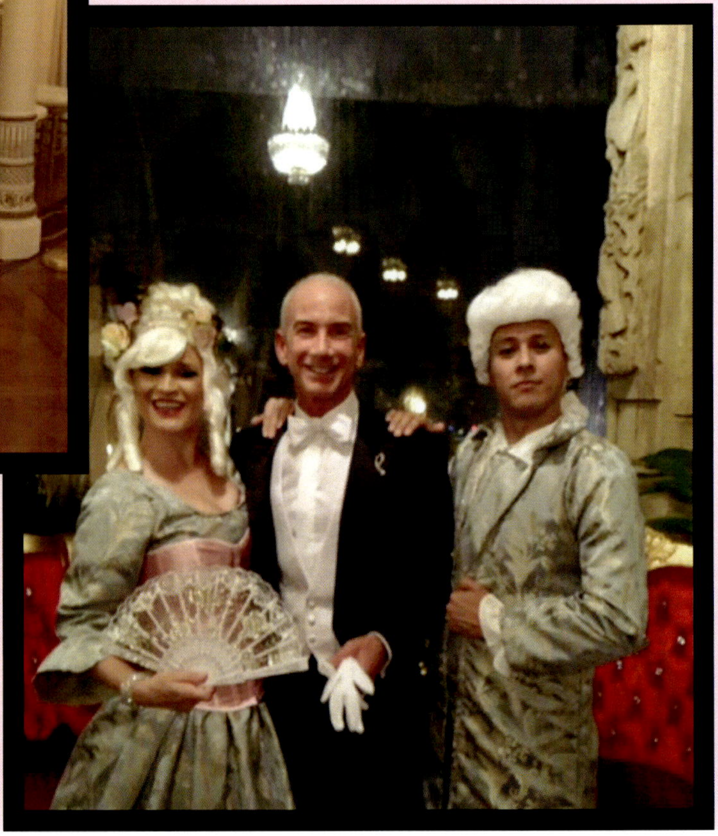

Chase Thomas escorts us…

Venetian Ball at Mar-a-Lago

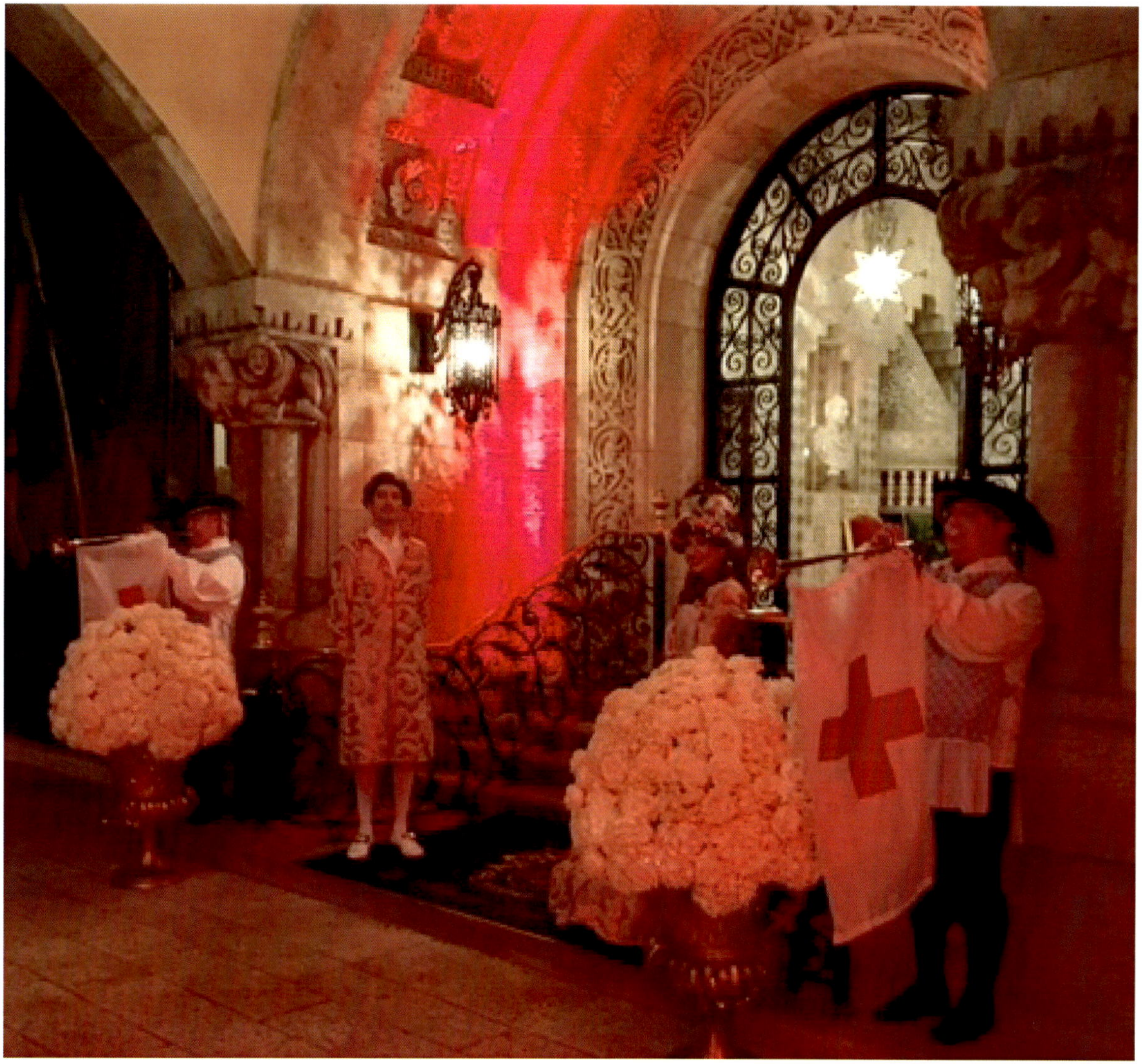

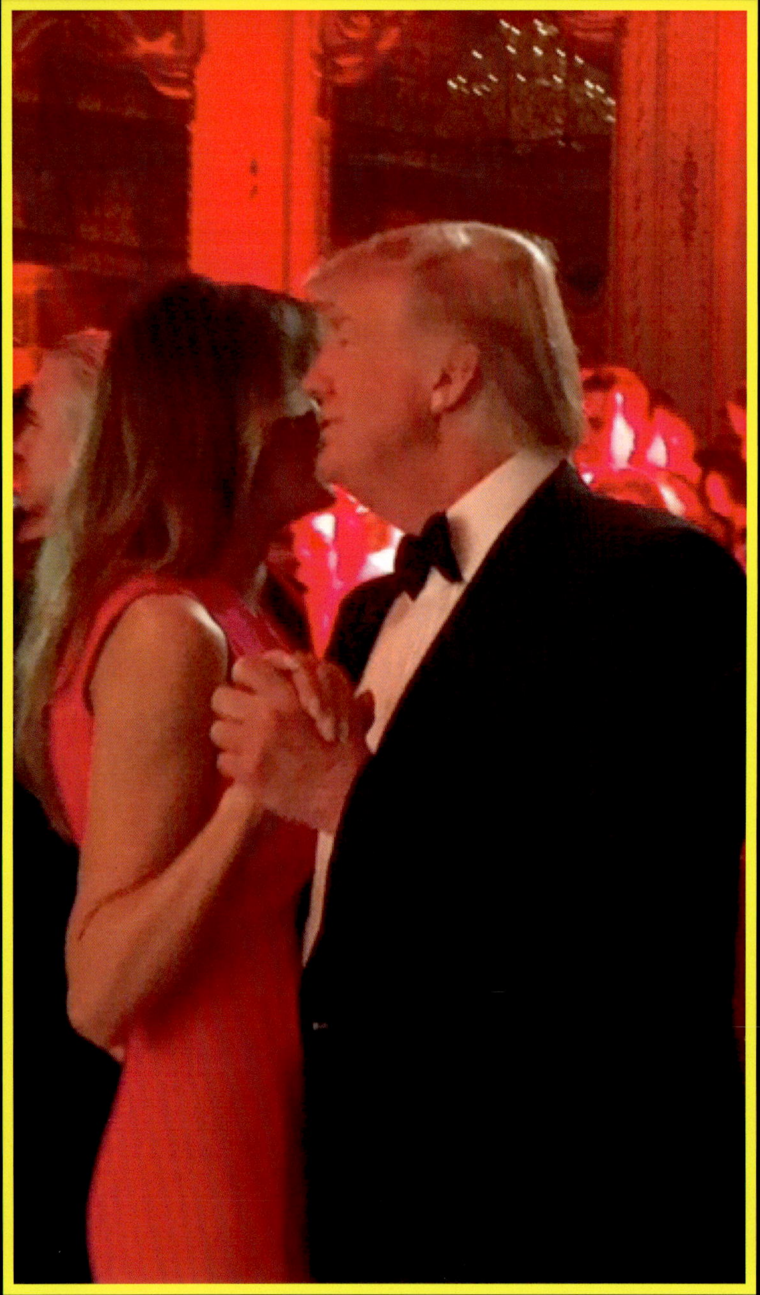

Life is grand…
One month into the presidency

Melania caught smiling

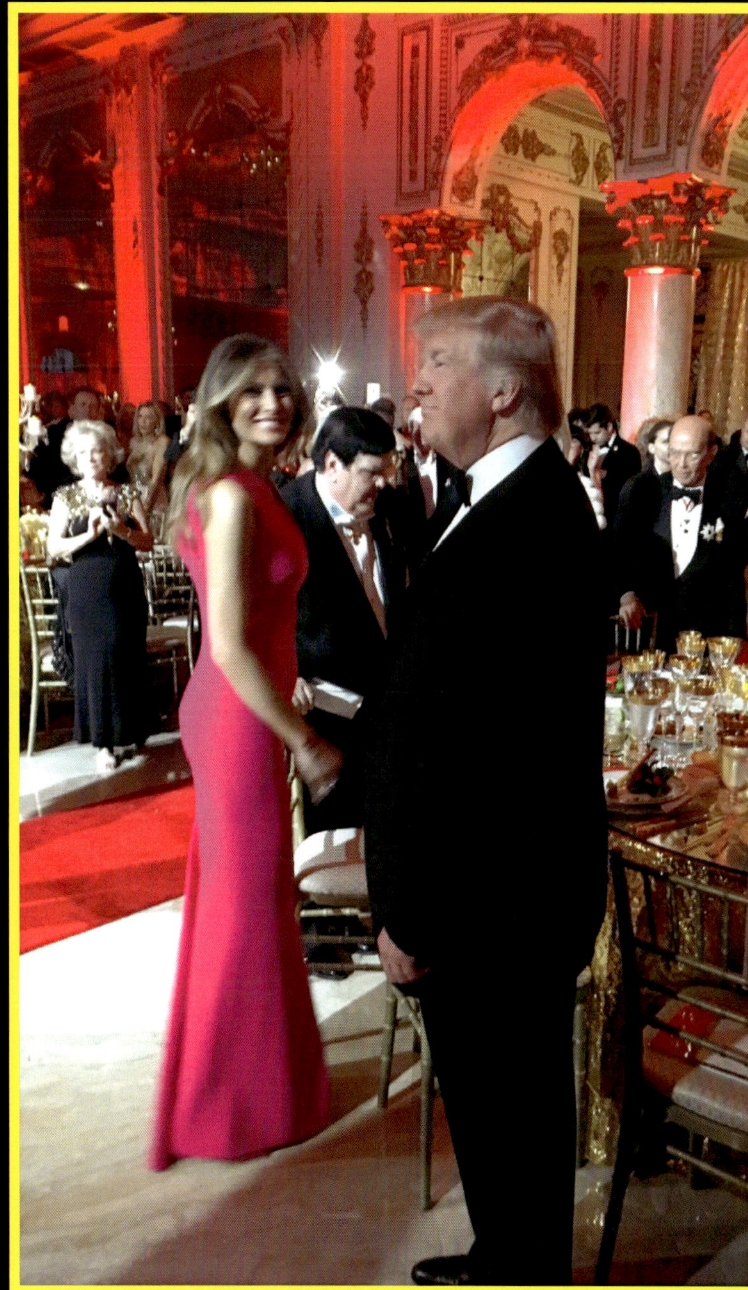

It was a magical evening

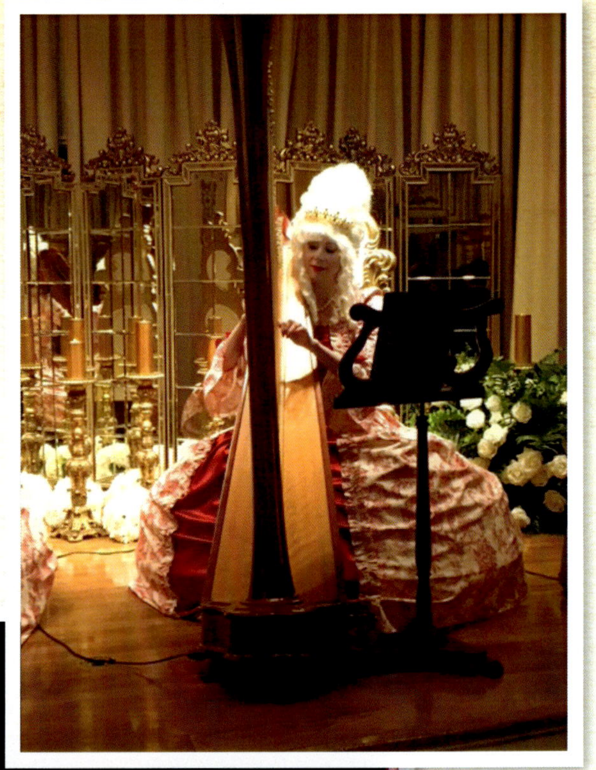

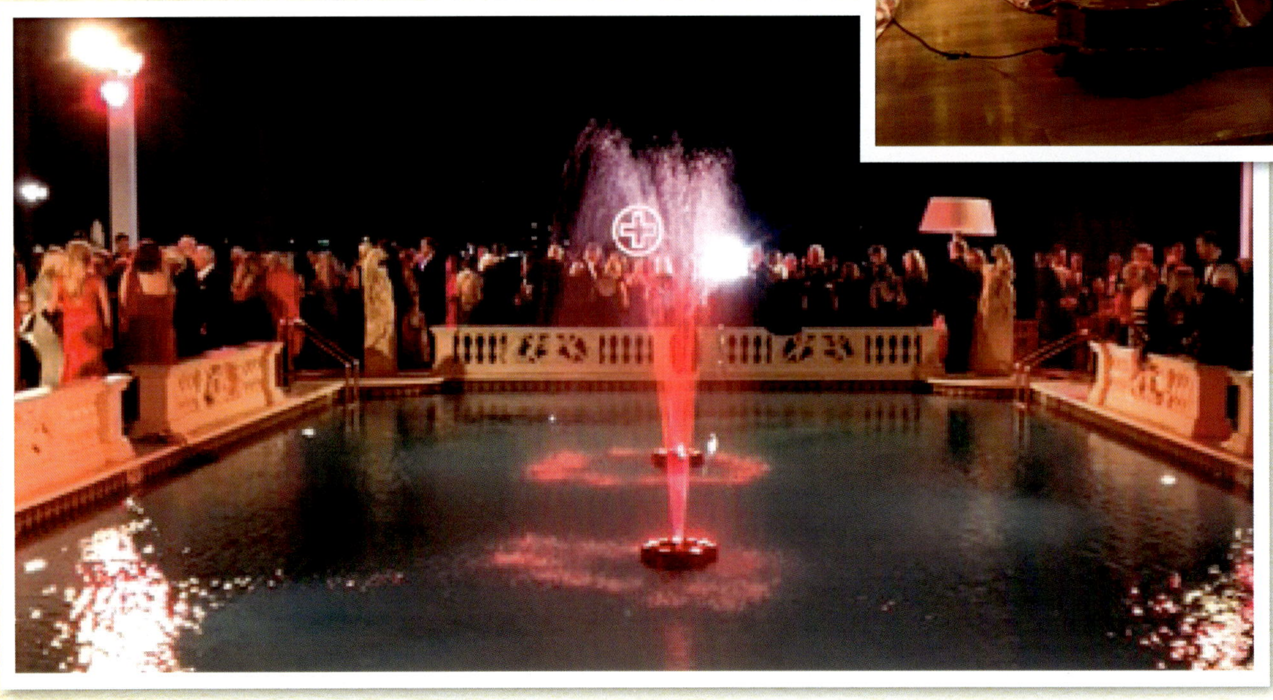

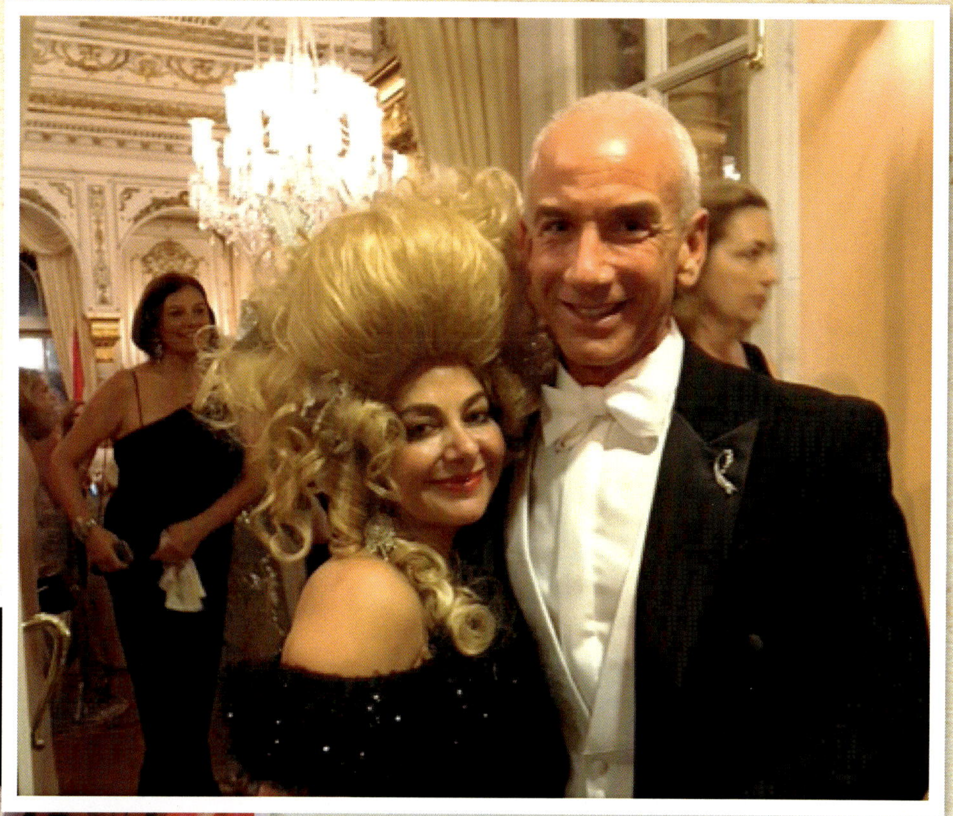

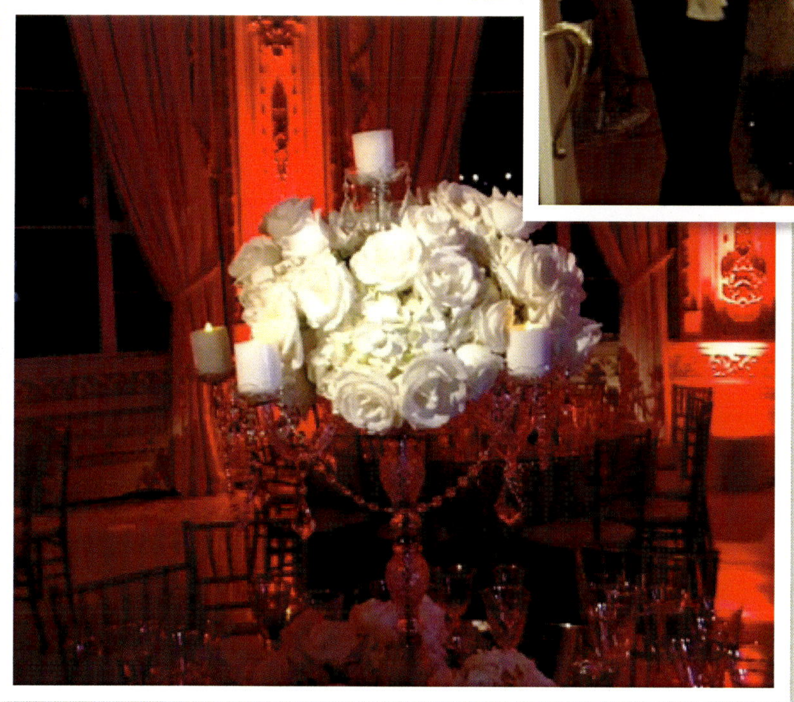

Thanks Chase!

XO

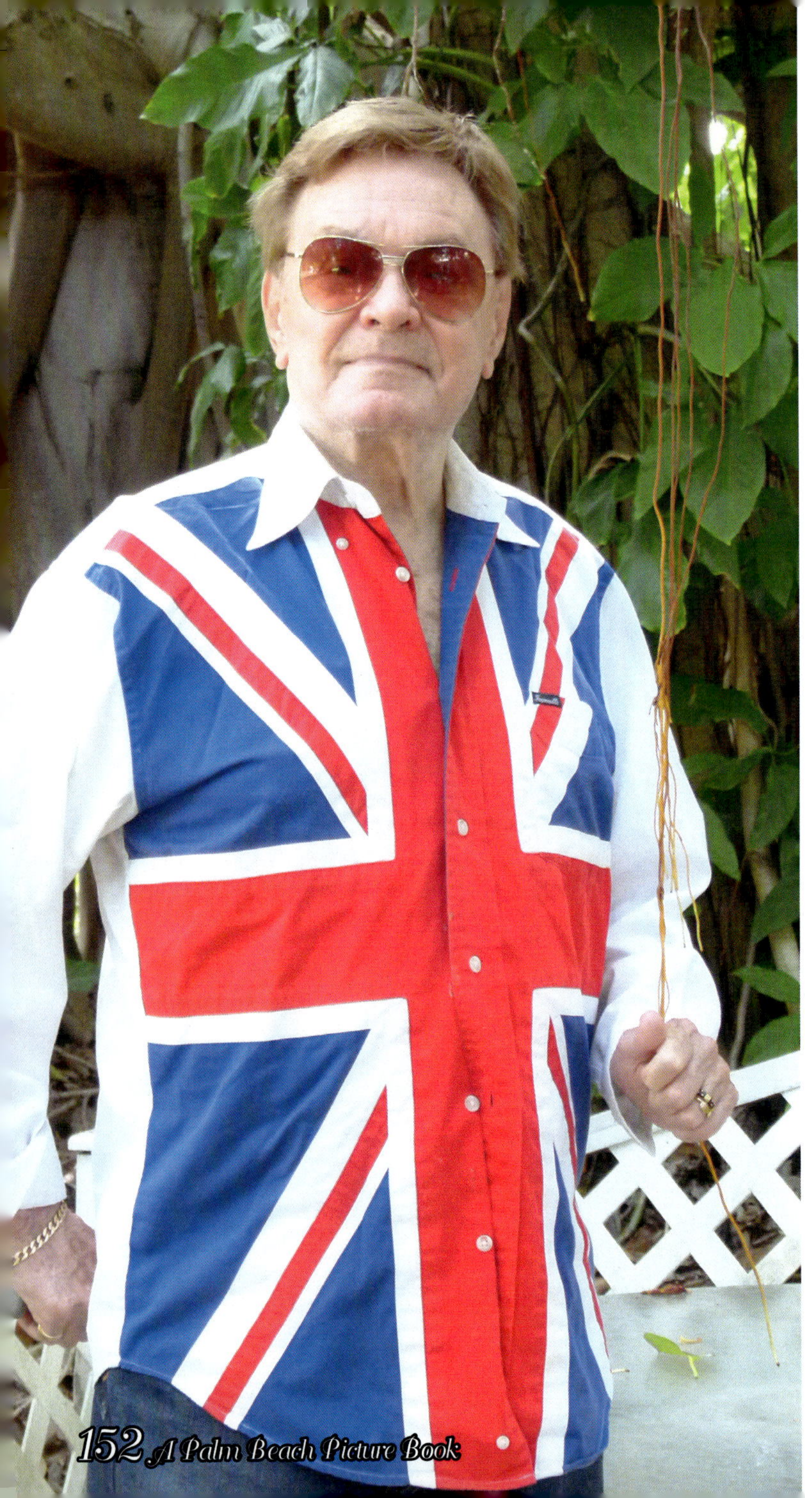

Artist Ralph Cowan first met Donald Trump in 1985. When driving by Mar-a-Lago one day, he saw some activity there and decided to stop in unannounced. Trump was there surveying his newest purchase. Since Cowan had been a regular there when Mrs. Post had owned it, he felt right at home and offered the new owner some free art consulting advice. Trump admired his social grace and tenacity, and invited Cowan to frequent his new club.

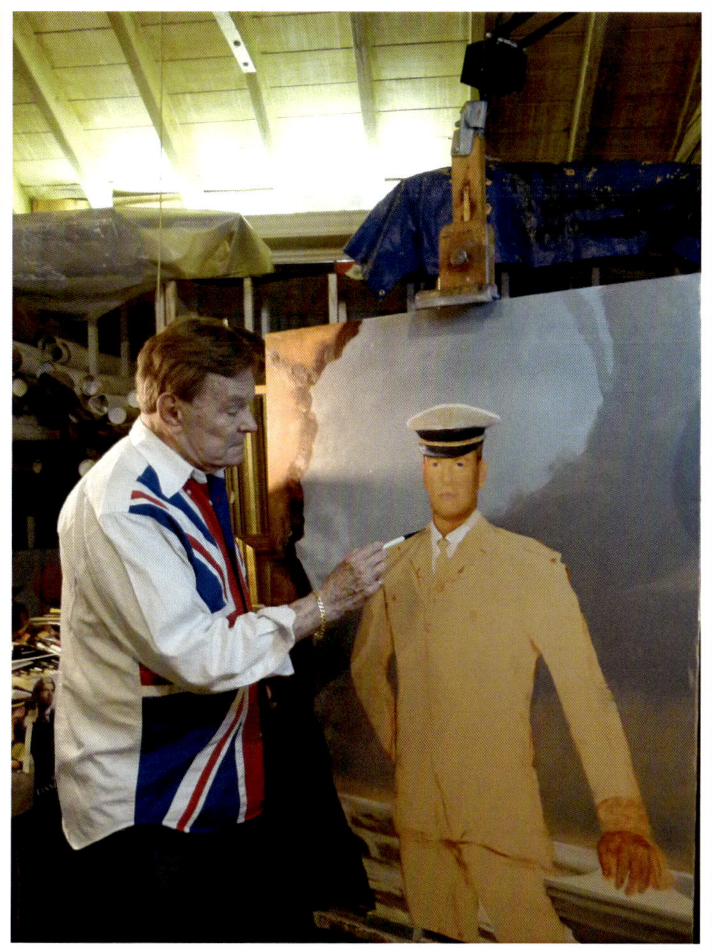

At left, working on his portrait of Prince Albert II of Monaco, Cowan is known for his royal portraits, such as Princess Grace of Monaco, and Princess Diana of Wales. His portraits hang in palaces throughout Europe.

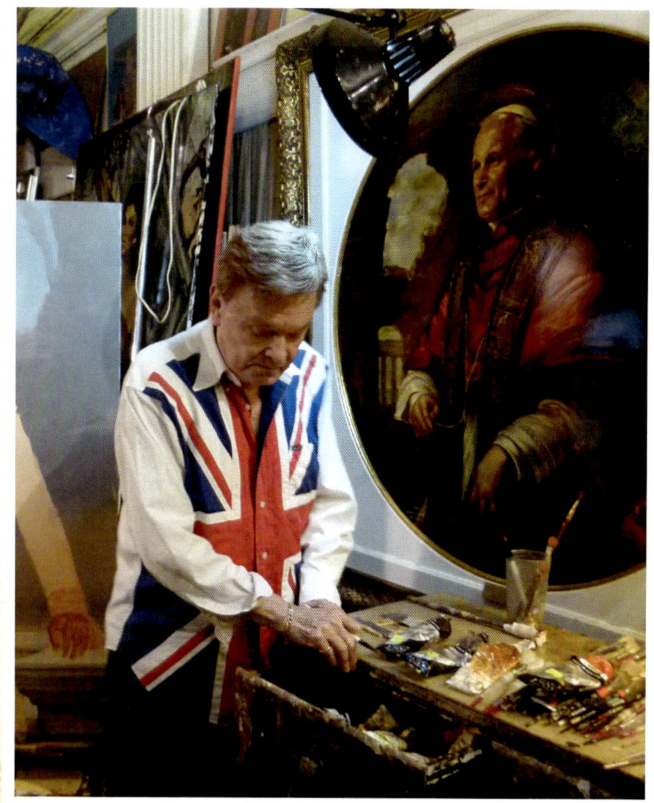

At right, a papal portrait gazes benevolently over the artist's studio.

Cowan, who has done portraits of everyone from Queen Elizabeth to Michael Jackson, was finally asked to do a portrait of 'The Donald.' He first did an oil sketch, to which Donald later had him add more detail and transform into the oil portrait, currently hanging in the lounge of the Mar-a-Lago club. The uncharacteristic casual tennis sweater, worn in the portrait, was invented by Cowan as an idealized version of Trump. Ralph told him, "I'm not painting you in that blue suit with the red tie. That's your New York look. I'm going to give you a Palm Beach look like all the men I paint, tan, healthy and standing erect."

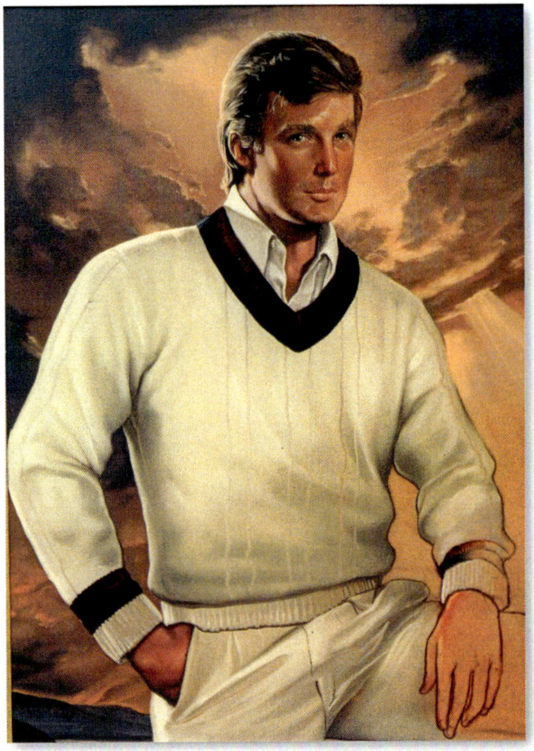

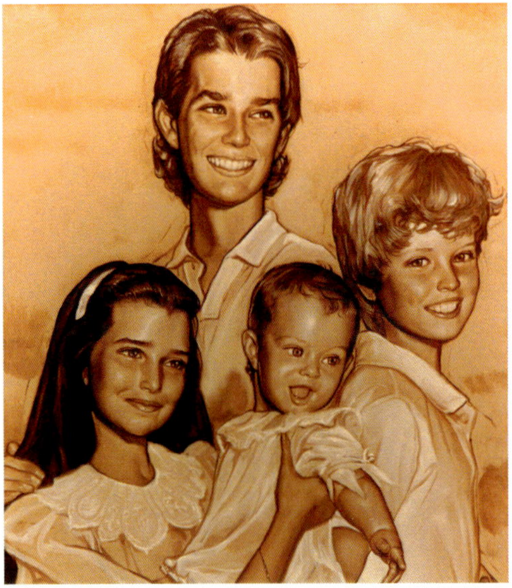

Ivanka, holding baby Tiffany, Eric, and little Donny Trump posed secretly after school for this portrait done as a surprise for Donald for Father's Day, 1995.

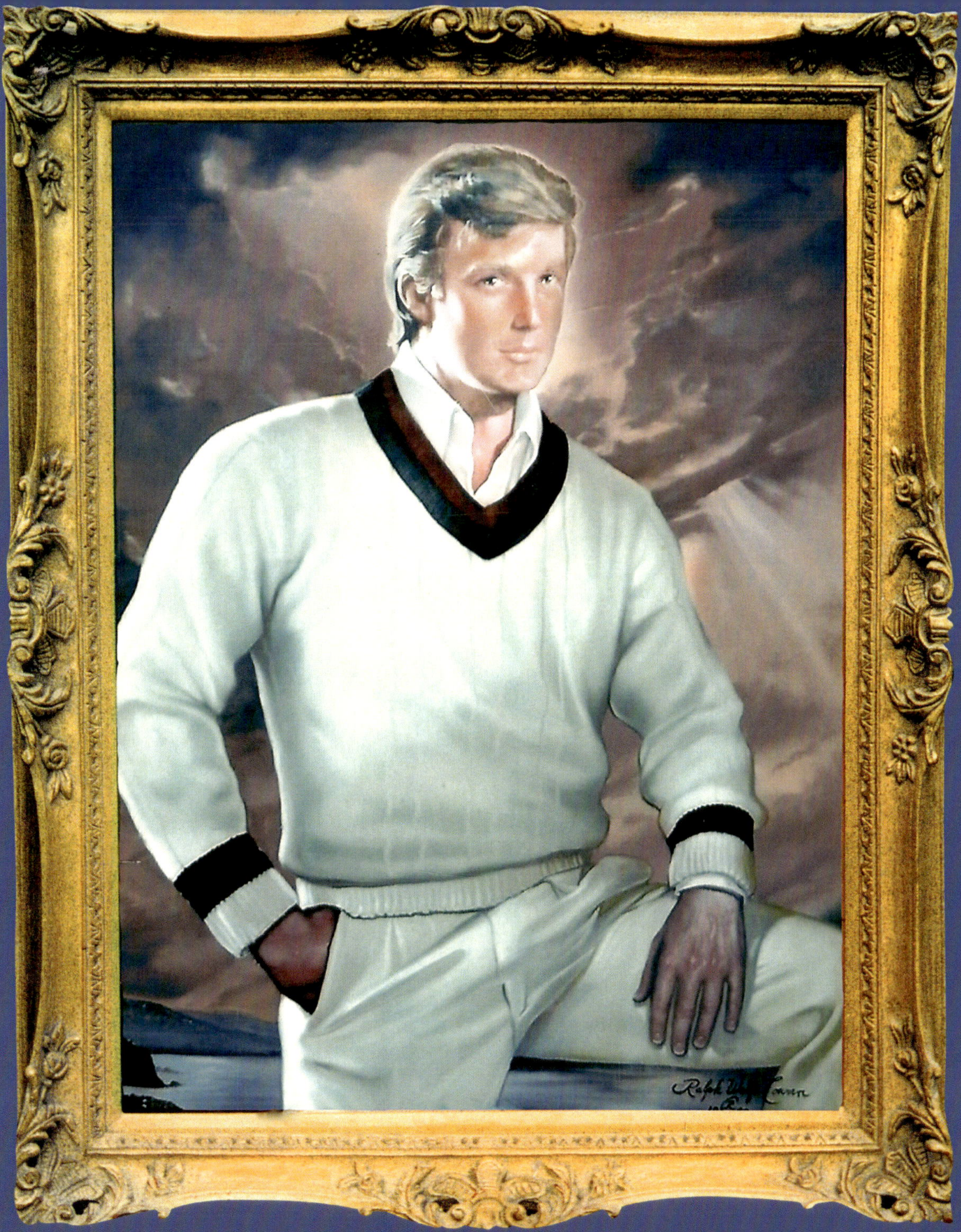

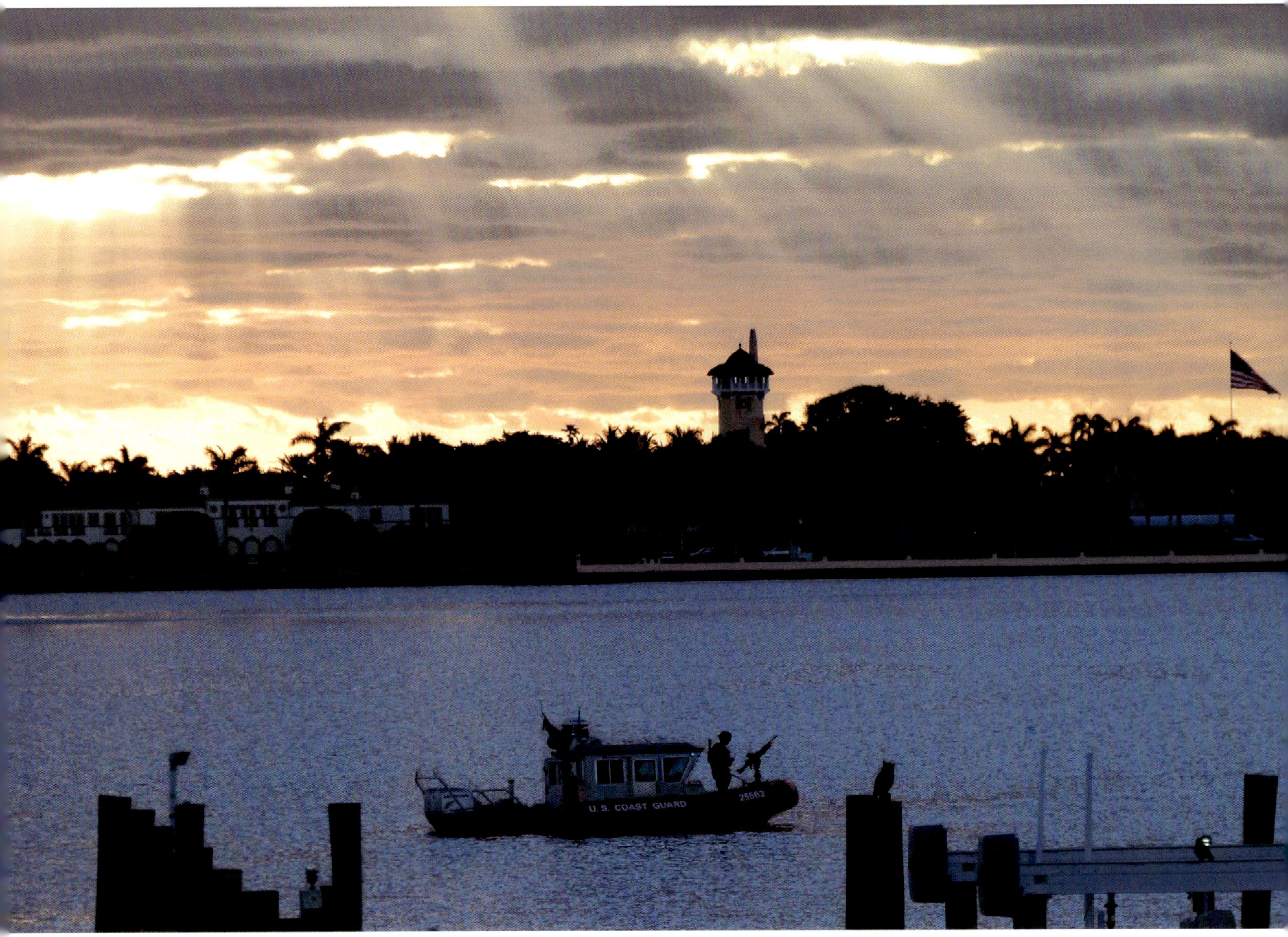
U.S. COAST GUARD
25563

Index of Photographs

Photo identification begins with upper left corner, proceeding clockwise, ending with center image.

Index of Photographs

Index of Photographs

Index of Photographs

Acknowledgements

I would like to thank all those who have played a part in my journey of making this book.

Thanks to Barry Zaid, the whimsical graphic designer whose playful and elegant sensibilities found wonderful ways to blend my pictures together.

Special thanks to new contributor Chase Thomas. Artistic appreciation goes to seasoned portraitist Ralph Cowan, who shared with us his stories and artwork of the Trump family. He will be greatly missed in Palm Beach.

Thanks to Robin Sweet and Steve Mohler for their assistance and support.

Thanks to my loyal friend Kirby Kooluris who always sees me in the best light.

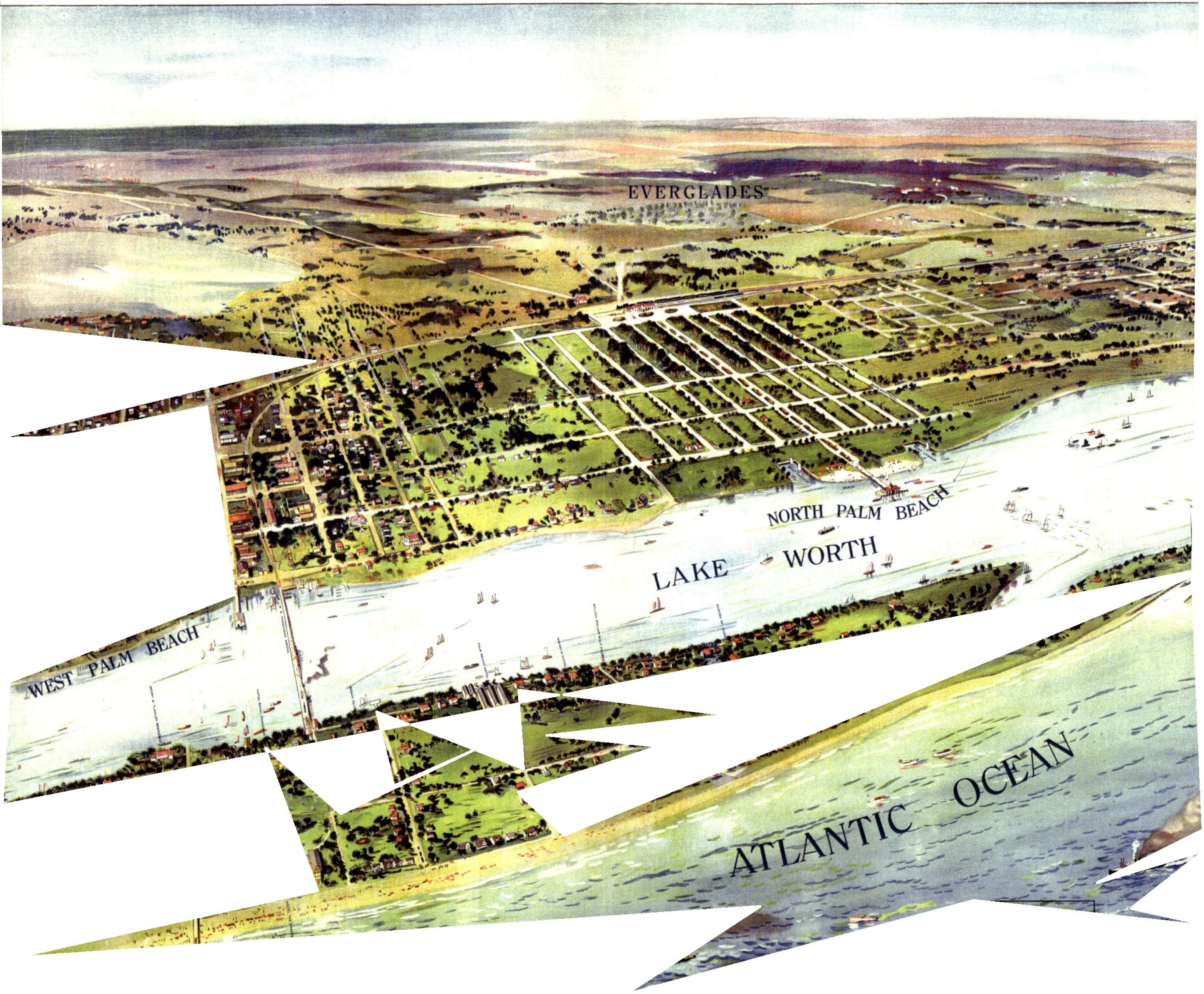
EVERGLADES
NORTH PALM BEACH
LAKE WORTH
WEST PALM BEACH
ATLANTIC OCEAN